The PRINCIPALSHIP

The

PRINCIPALSHIP

SECOND EDITION

William H. Roe
The University of Connecticut

Thelbert L. Drake
Ball State University

Macmillan Publishing Co., Inc.
New York

Collier Macmillan Publishers
London

Macmillan Publishing Co., Inc.
866 Third Avenue, New York, New York 10022

Collier Macmillan Canada, Ltd.

Library of Congress Cataloging in Publication Data

Roe, William Henry
  The principalship.

  Bibliography: p.
  Includes index.
  1. School superintendents and principals,
Training of. I. Drake, Thelbert L., joint
author. II. Title.
LB1715.R62   1980   371.2'012   79–12749
ISBN O–02–402680–8

Printing: 1 2 3 4 5 6 7 8   *Year:* 0 1 2 3 4 5 6

Preface

The world of the principal today is drastically different from the world of the principal when we went to elementary or secondary school. The principal of this decade deals with tension and conflict. The social revolution which has overtaken all of our communities to varying degrees has affected curriculum, school organization, discipline, student behavior, community relations, and the very nature of the teaching-learning process itself. Thus the old ground rules which fashioned our American schools into such similar and unquestioned molds are now largely obsolete—an obsolescence which has left the principal in too many cases without an acceptable mode of administrative behavior.

This books attempts to fill the void. It must be filled because the principal is a key factor in the survival of any school's effectiveness. He/she is the administrator of direct-line action, having first contact with the parent and the local community, with the teachers needing resources and direction, with the students in the learning environment, with the staff in the central administration, and with outside agencies and institutions wishing to make some impact upon each individual school unit.

The authors contend that there are common understandings and competencies essential to administering an elementary school, a large comprehensive high school, or a transitional junior high or middle school. These provide the principal with perspectives about our changing society and about teaming up with individuals and groups within the framework of formal and informal school organizations. As an educational executive, the principal must be capable of implementing an administrative process which utilizes and stimulates inputs from all people within the community and at the same time provides leadership for the future. This book makes available patterns for this process which are workable, responsible, and yet not so rigid or brittle that they shatter under stress. Examples of proven theories, principles and practices which are presented are not intended to be formulae for success, but rather intended to stimulate the reader to make practical applications appropriate to his/her organization and social setting.

The overriding philosophy of this book is the simple but often neglected principle that instruction of the students and learning by the students is the supreme reason for the school's existence. Organization and administration must then be considered as means and not ends. In developing this point of view, the teacher becomes the most important agent in carrying out the educational process. Therefore, a principal's most important function is to help establish, develop and maintain a teaching staff that will provide the best possible opportunities for teaching and learning. He/she then works with the teachers and students so that the teaching/learning climate is of the highest order.

It is from this viewpoint that this book is directed to principals and their superintendents, to prospective principals, and those who prepare people for the principalship.

The book assumes that the reader is well grounded in educational foundations and has an introductory knowledge of school administration. It spends little time, therefore, with the history and background of educational administration. It is concerned primarily with the effective functioning of the principal in providing the best possible learning environment for children and adults in a society which is continuously assuming radical new dimensions.

The authors wish to recognize the many obligations they have to the investigators and authors whose works are cited throughout this book and to many colleagues at the University of Connecticut, Ball State University, and in local schools who helped shape the preparation of this text.[1] Specific mention is due to Dr. Robert Seitz of Ball State University and Drs. Patrick B. Mullarney, Gerard Rowe, and Joan Seliger Sidney of the University of Connecticut. In addition, we want to express our gratitude to Ms. Louise Patros for invaluable assistance in typing and providing resources necessary to put together the various drafts of this book.

We also give special thanks to our wives, Vi and Suzanne, who understood.

W. H. R.

T. L. D.

[1] An honest attempt has been made throughout the text to avoid the use of masculine pronouns when referring to people in general, however, on rare occasions a masculine pronoun has been used in reference to humanity at large for purposes of succinctness.

Contents

Part I
Bases for Operation

The principal of today and tomorrow faces a continuously changing environment. The political, social, economic and environmental forces which are influencing our society so dramatically are in turn having dramatic impact on all aspects of the school itself—the curriculum, the school organization, the faculty, student behavior, community relations, and the very nature of the teaching–learning process. An important ingredient for the success of both elementary and secondary school principals operating in this dynamic setting is that they bring to the position a solid foundational base that will give them perspective about our changing society. In addition he/she must have expertise in teaming up with individuals and groups within the formal and informal school organization to make our schools responsive to the changing needs of society. The next seven chapters attempt to provide the potential educational leader with the elements of this important foundational base.

Chapter 1 A Social Base for School Operation: Coping with a Myth

Although the American school can by no means be considered a major agent of change in our society, it has had thrust upon it more and more responsibility for maintaining our society. In a matter of a relatively few years the school has changed from an institution serving only a part of our youth through a limited curriculum to an institution attempting to serve all youth for all of society.

The public is nearly unanimous in its endorsement of an educational system that will serve all children and youth. One notes, however, a great reluctance to give it *carte blanche* in its role as an agent of change for our society. Herein lies a great debate that is causing confusion both within the profession and society at large.

The School and a Changing Society

In 1932 George S. Counts asserted that "only in the rarest of instances does it [the school] wage war on behalf of principle or ideal." [1] His thesis was that schools should not exist just to preserve and maintain the status quo or merely to pass on accumulated knowledge of the past. Rather, he proposed that teachers should lead the way to the utopian, better life.

> We should, however, give to our children a vision of the possibilities which lie ahead and endeavor to enlist their loyalties and enthusiasms in the realization of the vision. Also, our social institutions and our practices, all of them, should be critically examined in the light of such a vision. [2]

[1] George S. Counts, *Dare the Schools Build a New Social Order* (New York: The John Day Company, 1932), p. 5. This publication was based on three papers presented by George Counts at major educational meetings in February of 1932. The titles of these papers were "Dare Progressive Education be Progressive?" "Education Through Indoctrination," and "Freedom, Culture, Social Planning and Leadership."

[2] Ibid., p. 37.

Counts' controversial and dramatic statements in his papers entitled *Dare the Schools Build a New Social Order* touched off a series of lively debates and discussions in professional societies and graduate schools of education throughout the country. The more daring were the "changers" and the more conservative were the "maintainers," and for approximately fifty years this lively discussion has ebbed and flowed to the point that there probably is not a thinking educator in this country who has not participated in some if not many such debates. Unfortunately, these discussions generated much heat but little action. The schools of today still follow a course which has tied them inexorably to the establishment, forcing them into a difficult and almost untenable position; for while the mainstream of the profession has maintained and supported the present system, the world has been changing, values have been questioned, and society is in the midst of a major social and economic upheaval.

Alvin Toffler in his book *Future Shock* describes this phenomenon most succinctly:

> This storm, far from abating, now appears to be gathering force. Change sweeps through the highly industrialized countries in waves of ever accelerating speed and unprecedented impact. It spawns in its wake all sorts of curious social flora—from psychedelic churches and "free universities" to science cities in the Arctic and wife-swap clubs in California.
>
> It breeds odd personalities, too: children who at twelve are no longer childlike; adults who at fifty are children of twelve. There are rich men who playact poverty, computer programmers who turn on with LSD. There are anarchists who, beneath their dirty denim shirts, are outrageous conformists, and conformists who, beneath their button-down collars, are outrageous anarchists. There are married priests and atheist ministers and Jewish Zen Buddhists. We have pop . . . and op . . . and *art cinetique* . . . There are Playboy Clubs and homosexual movie theaters . . . amphetamines and tranquilizers . . . anger, affluence, and oblivion. Much oblivion.
>
> Is there some way to explain so strange a scene without recourse to the jargon of psychoanalysis or the murky cliches of existentialism? A strange new society is apparently erupting in our midst. Is there a way to understand it, to shape its development? How can we come to terms with it? Much that now strikes us as incomprehensible would be far less so if we took a fresh look at the racing rate of change that makes reality seem, sometimes, like a kaleidoscope run wild. For the acceleration of change does not merely buffet industries or nations. It is a concrete force that reaches deep into our personal lives, compels us to act out new roles, and confronts us with the danger of a new and powerfully upsetting psychological disease. This new disease can be called "future shock". . . .[3]

The Faith of People in Education

The people of our country have immense faith in education—and rightly so for the success of our birth and development as a vibrant democracy

[3] Alvin Toffler, *Future Shock* (New York: Bantam Books, 1970), pp. 9–10.

could be attributed to an educated, enlightened citizenry. Schools were always a part of the American way and American dream.

In early America, as today, education was the central unifying force of a civilization, the common denominator of life. There was something in it that stirred the popular pulse. More than three hundred years ago the colonists on the bleak shore of Massachusetts, in the presence of their privations, found the willpower and the means to create the Boston Latin School and Harvard College. Over the years, as Americans moved toward the setting sun, the education of their children was a foremost common concern. From the little they laboriously took from forest and soil they built their schoolhouses and paid their schoolmasters, and plowed back their savings into coming generations. This process still continues.

It was in America that there first was heard the voice of authority that said to all that they must provide for the education of all. America was the cradle of the free public school. It was in America that universal education first established itself upon the largest scale. Here citizens of all sorts were the first to be forbidden to grow up unlettered and uninstructed. Here secondary education, as well as elementary education, was made available to everyone. It was in America that free public education was first used as the instrument for creating a constantly broadening middle class, so that all people might eventually be equal participants in the free, competitive, yet cooperative, and productive life of the nation. It was in America that an educational ladder was first erected so that all people might ascend, from bottom to top, according to their impulses and talents: ascend, if they might, to positions of the highest leadership in arts and letters, in science, business, industry, and agriculture, in technology, in the professions, and in public affairs. It was in America that education found a new serviceability to man by dealing with the realities of everyday life as well as with the more distant gleanings of the scholars of the past. A German, Goethe, once said that children are so brilliant that, if they fulfilled their early promise, the world would be peopled with geniuses. But it was the unresting American spirit that contrived, and is still patiently contriving, a system of schools, colleges, and universities designed upon the dream of making Goethe's observation come true.[4]

The schools served our country well in this regard for they gave man the fundamental tools—reading, writing, and arithmetic—necessary for an enlightened citizenry. This was no myth. The public schools did spread literacy and general knowledge throughout the country, encouraging each American to be confident of his/her ability to rise to his/her highest level.

---

[4] For a more extensive development of this concept the reader is referred to Ch. I, "Education and the American Way of Life," in the book *State School Administration* by Lee M. Thurston and William H. Roe (New York: Harper Bros., 1957). The authors are indebted to Thurston and Roe for many of the ideas developed in this chapter.

Is It a Myth?

The role of the common school was no myth in regard to helping build America through creating a literate citizenry; however, as our population grew and society became more complicated, and as public and private education became more extensive, it became obvious that a myth had developed. We are discovering that some of our fundamental beliefs are fallacious. Because the schools were so important in the building of our country, as society became more complicated—fraught with a Gordian knot of tangled problems of urban migration, breakdown of the family, crime, race relations, poverty, unemployment—people turned confidently to the schools and said, "They'll fix it!" Educators with a naive faith that learning solves all problems responded with, "All we need are more resources and to get all the children for longer periods and society's problems will be solved." But, just more of the same was too simple an answer for the complicated problems. We deluded ourselves by assuming that there was a basic value system that could be a foundation for our teaching; that just sitting together in a classroom and working together in schools—the rich and the poor, the black and the white, the washed and the unwashed— would impart to everybody an understanding and respect for each other and give each the ability and the desire to become citizens capable of making their unique contributions to this great country.

Henry Steele Commager points out that it was most unreasonable to expect the schools to either fashion a new society or solve the problems of national and world affairs. This, says Commager, is society's responsibility.

> Rarely, we may say, have so many been exposed to so much with results so meager. To judge by the experience of the past forty years, reliance on the schools to reform society and usher in the millenium by teaching social problems, or world history, has been an almost unmitigated failure. After half a century of exposure to world culture, world history, and world politics—most of it contemporary, of course—Americans turned out to be culturally more alienated and politically more isolationist and chauvinistic than at any time in our history.
>
> It is of course folly to blame this on the schools. The responsibility is on society itself for requiring the schools to do far more than they could do and deflecting them from doing those things they had done well in the past and were prepared to do well in the present.[5]

The myth was that schools could do anything and anything they did would be right. This is just not true! Many people have been disillusioned because they believed so strongly in this myth. It may be more accurate

---

[5] Henry Steele Commager, *The People and Their Schools* (Bloomington, Ind.: Phi Delta Kappa, 1976), p. 31 (Fastback).

to say that more responsibility has been thrust upon our schools than they should accept; more results have been expected than they could possibly produce; and in too many cases, schools have assumed more than they should. An approach to dispelling this myth is to admit that the schools have been essentially maintainers and reinforcers of existing systems and they really were not established and have not been supported to build a new social order and we are asking for "what never was" if we assume they can do so.

In truth then, education finds itself in a real bind—if it acquiesces to the myth that schools can do anything and that anything they do is right; right away schools become tabbed as failures because of urban crises, pollution of the environment, civil disobedience, increases in drug abuse, crime, ghetto living, family breakdowns, prejudice, hate, racial devisiveness, and inadequate social welfare.

Many well-meaning and some opportunistic intellectuals and educators have made reputations and much money by writings and speeches attacking the institution of education as a failure. They have blithely accepted and perpetuated the myth and used this as the basis for criticizing schools in such vigorous terms that the public, both liberal and conservative, is fast losing faith in them. Schools are accused by some people of being repressive, authoritarian, inflexible, dull, unequal, unfair, oppressive, and essentially middle-class. The more conservative ones see the drugs, sexual freedom, violence, and lack of discipline as symbols of hotbeds for free living and revolution.

The school principal as administrator of the local school unit faces the brunt of these attacks. Unfortunately, in response and reaction he or she stands alone without defense because the old ground rules that structured our American schools into such similar and unquestioned molds are now largely obsolete—an obsolescence that has left the principal in too many cases without an acceptable mode of administrative behavior.[6]

It's a New World

In addition to the myth about the infallability of the school as a corrector of social ills, changes in society and education itself have stimulated new pressures, new approaches, and new value systems that create a brand new administrative world for the school principal. For example:

1. Racial balance, busing, compensatory education.
2. Teacher militancy, negotiations, teacher power through unions and professional associations.

[6] R. Freeman Butts, Donald H. Peckenpaugh, and Howard Kirschenbaum, *The School's Role as Moral Authority* (Washington, D.C.: Association for Supervision and Curriculum Development, 1977).

3. Community components in an adversary role.
4. Drug abuse.
5. Child abuse legislation mandating reporting by professionals.
6. Student unrest.
7. Emphases upon the civil and individual rights of students.
8. Socially oriented teachers.
9. Staffing patterns such as teaming, differentiated roles, utilization of paraprofessionals.
10. Economic and programmatic accountability demands, mandated evaluations of programs and personnel.
11. Educational technology boom.
12. Early childhood education.
13. Contract education, alternative schools, alternative curricula.
14. Changes in social attitude toward women's roles.
15. Experiments in "family" living.
16. Open education, independent learning.
17. Marriage and divorce patterns.
18. Competency testing.

The emergence of the foregoing makes us realize that the simple community power concepts of the past can no longer be accepted in an unquestioning mode. More and more people are recognizing that many of the values and traditions that schools have transmitted are not the values and traditions of all the people. Schools essentially have been responsive to the community power system, the dominant power groups, but not to all segments of the community.

Charles V. Willie [7] makes the point most clearly in a number of his papers. Willie contends that school—community relations are in difficulty and often even at loggerheads because school administrators have been responsive only to the dominants in the power structure. It should be recognized there are subdominants too and today these subdominants are shaking the very foundations of the social order and the "safe" ground on which schools have usually tried to stand. According to Willie, the school administrator of today must do more than join the Rotary Club and play golf with those who are influential in the community, business, and government.

> He must also come to know the sub-dominants. This may require eating chitterlings and corn pone with the poor as well as recreating with the rich, if he is to synthesize the disparate interest groups in the community into a phalanx of support for a creative public policy designed to achieve quality education for all.[8]

[7] Charles V. Willie, "New Prospectives in School Community Relations," *Journal of Negro Education*, 37 (Summer 1968), pp. 220–226.

[8] Charles V. Willie, "A Success Story of Community Action," *Nursing Outlook*, 9 (January 1961).

There is no question but dominants and subdominants are people of power. The school must learn to do business with both. One thing is certain—it is the principal who comes in closest contact with the subdominants because they are localized within smaller community segments. In most cases he/she may have to take the most heat and may receive the brunt of direct action from this group. At the same time he/she is in a key position to show that the school wishes to, and can, be responsive to the subdominants particularly if the decision-making apparatus is such that key decisions may be made in the local area or if the school principal is brought into the central administration's efforts to involve subdominants. Dan W. Dodson emphasizes this latter process as a creative approach to decision making.

> New forces are emerging that are going to require our boards of education and superintendents of schools to move into new approaches to the issue of decision making . . . . people must honestly come to face each other and honestly say that we have differences and ask how we can reconcile and compromise and how do we work them out to some sort of viable solution. From this process will come a new sense of education. . . . All the community will feel involved in the dynamics of the decision-making process and a new sense of worth will emerge.[9]

It is a new, exciting world for the principal. It is a world in which the only constant is an increasing rate of change. Dare the principal identify him- or herself with such a world and make it real in the school? Can he-she even avoid it? Is it not time to take the offensive? [10]

There is no need for educators, particularly the school principal, to believe he/she alone should lead the way to the good life for all society. This viewed objectively is a most arrogant point of view. On the other hand, in the face of the great problems facing our society there is a necessity for the educator to say to the people, "The schools are one of the great and important institutions of our nation. Let's work in partnership to identify important goals of our society and then let's work hand in hand in meeting them."

For Further Thought

1. Do parents really want the schools to change?
2. If we accept the point of view that education should get its sense of direction from the kind of social order we desire to build, what core values should we seek to build into our civilization?

[9] Dan W. Dodson, "New Forces Operating in Educational Decision Making," in Meyer Weinberg, Ed., *Integrated Education: A Reader* (Beverly Hills, Calif.: The Glencoe Press, 1968), p. 21.

[10] For an interesting discussion of the role of the public school as a socializing authority, read R. Freeman Butts *American Public Education: From Revolution to Reform* (New York: Holt, Rinehart, and Winston, 1978).

3. As a principal, what do you think is the proper function of a school—
   (a) To accept the existing social order but appraise it critically with
   a view to shaping its future; (b) to accept the social order as it exists
   and hope it will shape itself; (c) to plan a new social order and encourage children to accept it?
4. Who should control the power to cause or inhibit change?
5. Do you agree that leisure is taking on a new meaning in our society
   and that education for leisure poses a real problem? Discuss the issues
   involved.
6. Are the changing conditions of our time such as to make it desirable
   and even necessary that we reconsider the function and purposes of
   education? Specify.
7. Review the most recent sociological studies dealing with the status of
   the family in American life. What is the prognosis regarding the future
   of the family? How will this affect schools?
8. List the seven cardinal principles of education. Are these appropriate
   today? How would you modernize them?
9. List five to ten areas of conflict in the national and world scene. How do
   these relate to the task of the school?
10. In 1960 the President's Commission on National Goals issued their
    report, *Goals for Americans* (The American Assembly, Columbia Uni-
    versity, 1960). Are these goals appropriate today? Who must take lead-
    ership in achieving national goals?

Chapter 2 The Principal—The Person and the Profession

Both the duties and the career role of the principal, whether elementary, junior, middle, or secondary, become a riddle of considerable proportion if one allows oneself to be analytical in assessing the position.

By reading the literature, attending state and national meetings, and discussing the position with present incumbents, one gets a mental picture of a professional person being torn apart on the one hand by intense interest and desire to lead in instruction and learning, and on the other hand by the responsibility to "keep school" through the proper administration and management of people and things as expected by the central administration. In this little drama the eternal struggle takes place and in the end the strong instructional leadership role is set aside because of the immediacy and press of everyday administrative duties.

This story is so common—and it is so uncommon to discover any principal who believes that he is really satisfying his instructional leadership role—that it becomes very obvious that the whole area warrants a serious review. It isn't enough to make a functional study of the principal's present activities as has been done so many times. It is already well known that principals spend most of their time on management details. Even in those studies that show instructional activities being performed, the depth and effectiveness of these efforts are not assessed. What is needed now is an honest national appraisal of the principal's role and an honest answer by parents, board members, teachers, superintendents, and principals themselves to the question, "Do we really want the principal to be primarily an instructional leader or do we expect him/her to be primarily a manager of people and things?" Under present circumstances it is expected that the principal be primarily an administrator and manager. The instructional leadership talk is often lip service paid to create a greater self-respect within the professional group itself.

Factors Preventing Instructional Leadership

While such an assertion may appear overly critical, to be fair it must be understood. There are an overwhelming number of factors that prevent the principal from spending time on instructional leadership.

1. The great majority of schools are so organized that the principal is the chief building administrator and held responsible for all management details.
2. The central administration places priority on a "well-run" school with major considerations on smooth operation; i.e., getting reports in on time; maintaining a well-kept building and grounds; good management of supplies and equipment; lack of personnel problems, community controversy and discipline problems; and so on.
3. If the community does not observe a well-run building they lose confidence in other operations of the school.
4. There is greater prestige in the business community associated with being considered an executive who is "administratively in charge."
5. It is easier to evaluate and account for job activities when dealing with people and things than with instructional leadership and ideas.
6. "Safe," well-understood operational procedures, teaching methods, and instructional processes create less controversy and conflict.
7. Professional preparation programs for principals invariably are swallowed up by the overall administration program that has as its major emphasis the school superintendency.
8. Preparation programs for principals emphasize more management and administration than they do instruction, curriculum, program evaluation, supervision, and human relations.
9. The principalship is considered by the majority of professors in educational administration as a stepping-stone to a central office position or the superintendency rather than an important professional career position in its own right.
10. Many school principals themselves consider their position a stepping-stone to the superintendency.
11. Rather than relating to the teachers as a colleague, master teacher, head teacher, or principal teacher, the principal creates the image of administrator or chief executive.
12. Recent movements by school boards and school superintendents to encourage principals to side with them as part of their "administrative team" or "management team" have tended to swing the principalship away from the idea of "principal teacher" to "principal administrator."
13. Both the National Association of Elementary School Principals and the National Association of Secondary School Principals have endorsed

and joined the Educational Leaders Consortium, which is a consortium of educational administration professional organizations dedicated to "participative management through the administrative team."

14. The unprecedented growth in the school-age population following World War II created so many logistical problems that communities had great difficulty in establishing sufficient schools. The principal became caught in this situation and as a result his primary efforts during the fifties, sixties, and early seventies by necessity were managerial. In a sense this has served to structure duties toward management in the eighties.

Thomas B. Stone's provocative article on the principalship chides the principal and superintendent because the administrative–managerial syndrome seems to dominate their thinking. He states, "It is safe to conclude . . . that principals as a group are relatively unimportant as a vital force in making American education the kind of dynamic, creative vehicle for maximizing human potential it is capable of becoming."[1] He then points out that in the present conventional managerial climate that surrounds the superintendency a person entering the principalship usually has three choices.

> *First,* he can play the togetherness game (with the superintendent] and be reasonably comfortable as an administrative manager. *Second,* he can seek employment among that relatively small number of superintendencies whose collective behavior and values are the antithesis of the climate described. *Third,* the principal can attempt by his own behavior to change the climate and direction of the superintendency. The desired and necessary behavior required in such a setting may be termed constructive abrasiveness.[2]

Of course this behavior, which Stone calls constructive abrasiveness also would create a role conflict and on the basis of past experience the principal would be more likely to lose his/her job than change the attitude of the superintendent and the climate of the school.

Tridimensional Concept in Analyzing the Principalship

Daniel Davies is given credit for developing the tridimensional concept of school administration.[3] He analyzed the role of the administrator in relation to *the job,* the *social setting* for the job, and *the person* as he/she re-

---

[1] Thomas B. Stone, "The Elementary School Principalship—Toward the Twenty-First Century," in *Selected Articles for Elementary School Principals* (Washington, D.C.: Department of Elementary School Principals, N.E.A., 1968), p. 21.

[2] Ibid., p. 21.

[3] Davies was coordinator of the Cooperative Program in Educational Administration in the Middle Atlantic Region, a nationwide effort to improve school administration, established under a grant from the W. K. Kellogg Foundation in the 1950s. Davies used "the man" instead of "the person" as used here.

lates to both. It is appropriate to utilize this tridimensional approach in attempting to understand the principalship as it exists today.

The Job

In analyzing *the job* of the principal it is possible to divide it into two broad categories: the administrative–managerial emphasis and the educational leadership emphasis with all sorts of gradations in between.

The Administrative–Managerial Emphasis is characterized by placing primary responsibility upon those tasks that have to do with the smooth operation of the schools. It deals with instruction as well as the resources to back up instruction. However, it limits itself to overseeing and supervising the programs and teaching processes required by the central office. Major duties involved with this emphasis are:

1. Maintaining adequate school records of all types.
2. Preparing reports for the central office and other agencies.
3. Budget development and budget control.
4. Personnel administration.
5. Student discipline.
6. Scheduling and maintaining a schedule.
7. Building administration.
8. Administrating supplies and equipment.
9. Pupil accounting.
10. Monitoring programs and instructional processes prescribed by the central office.
11. Communicating to the students, staff, and the school's community as spokesman for the central office.

In reviewing the many surveys conducted to analyze the principal's job, this is the emphasis that predominates nationally. It will be noted that the tasks are essentially routine, managerial, and supervisory—operating by prescription from the central administration.

The Educational and Instructional Leadership emphasis is concerned with (1) changing the behavior of those involved in teaching–learning acts aimed toward achieving the goals of the school, and (2) building a cohesive social system within a school that "pulls together" to achieve the school's goals. In such a system, all staff and students work in harmonious relationship in defining, interpreting, and establishing school goals, developing a dynamic curriculum, and implementing educational processes that will create a stimulating and productive learning environment for every child enrolled.

This is the emphasis that most principals profess they dream about but can't achieve. It will be noted that this "job" as defined is not prescriptive in the sense that the principal is administering functions as identified by the central administration. It is a position that concerns itself with purposes as well as processes, with development as well as implementation, with initiating new ideas and approaches as well as monitoring the effectiveness of existing systems. It also means that students, teachers, parents, and community people are heavily involved in the processes and feel an important part of the system that is committed to learning.

Functions or duties of the principal with this emphasis are to:

1. Stimulate and motivate staff to maximum performance.
2. Develop with the staff a realistic and objective system of accountability for learning (as contrasted to merely monitoring programs and instructional processes in input terms as prescribed by the central office).
3. Develop cooperatively operable assessment procedures for ongoing programs to identify and suggest alternatives for improving weak areas.
4. Work with staff in developing and implementing the evaluation of the staff.
5. Work with staff in formulating plans for evaluating and reporting student progress.
6. Provide channels for involvement of the community in the operation of the school.
7. Encourage continuous study of curricular and instructional innovations, and provide help and resources for the establishment of those that are most promising.
8. Provide leadership to students in helping them to develop a meaningful but responsible student government.
9. Establish a professional learning resources center and expedite its use.
10. Develop cooperatively with the staff a dynamic professional development and inservice education program.

Without question the administrative–managerial duties need to be performed and performed well. Schools must operate smoothly and efficiently with proper resources provided when needed. However, on the basis of observing scores of school systems and talking to hundreds of principals, it is the opinion of the authors that it is virtually impossible to assume that the principal can be a real instructional leader and at the same time be held strictly accountable under number one priority for the general operational and management detail required by the central office. It is time for a reassessment of the principal's role. When this reassessment is achieved, organizational changes can be made so that both proper management and instructional leadership function in harmony, but the central office will need to establish priorities and procedures so that management is servant to instruction, not vice versa.

Job Description

Reviewing job descriptions for principals throughout the country, the instructional leadership functions of the principal descriptively are in balance with general administrative duties. Figure 2.1 presents a job description for a typical principalship in a city school.[4] The fact remains, however, the reward system of the Board of Education and the Central Office gives top priority to handling of management detail, discipline, and evaluation. Robert J. Krajewski made a study to determine if the roles principals play are the roles they prefer.[5] The principals were asked to rank order items on two different levels: (1) The real level—how they actually see the routine duties of school principals, and (2) the ideal level—how they would like to see the principal's duties. The results, rank ordered in ascending scales on the ideal dimension, are as follows:

Duties	Principal Ideal Rank	Principal Real Rank
Instructional supervisor	1	5
Curriculum supervisor	2	8
Staff selector/"orientor"	3	9
School program administration/ (materials and facilities)	4	1
Teacher evaluator	5	3
Morale builder	6	7
Public relations facilitator	7	6
Pupil services coordinator	8	4
Disciplinarian	9	2
Self evaluator	10	10

A National Study of the senior high school principalship yielded a similar result. Secondary school principals were asked to indicate the amount of time they spend on various activities for a typical work week and then to indicate the areas of responsibility on which they should spend time.[6]

[4] National Association of Secondary School Principals, *Job Descriptions for Principals and Assistant Principals* (Reston, Va.: The Association, 1976), pp. 20–21.
[5] Robert J. Krajewski, "Secondary Principals Want to be Instructional Leaders," *Phi Delta Kappan,* (Sept. 1978), p. 65.
[6] National Association of Secondary School Principals, *The Senior High School Principalship* The National Survey (Reston, Va.: The Association, 1978), p. 20.

FIGURE 2.1. Louisiana: New Orleans Public Schools.*

JOB TITLE: SCHOOL PRINCIPAL

JOB GOAL: *To administer and supervise all the activities and personnel within an assigned school, toward the fullest possible development of the skills and motivations of each pupil for fulfillment as a responsible and significant human being.*

REPORTS TO: District Superintendent

DIVISION: Division of School Administration

SUPERVISES: All professional and nonprofessional staff assigned.

JOB RESPONSIBILITIES:

1. Supervises the school's instructional and extracurricular programs and all activities within the school.
2. Works toward the improvement of the instructional program within the school through faculty study groups and other evaluation processes.
3. Implements all board policies and administrative rules and regulations.
4. Develops and encourages programs of orientation and self-improvement of teachers and others within the school.
5. Determines the work assignment of all professional personnel assigned to the school.
6. Plans and conducts faculty meetings.
7. Observes and reviews the performance of all personnel to provide a basis for effective counseling and for encouraging optimum performance.
8. Assists in the selection of teaching personnel, and recommends to the assistant superintendent for personnel candidates for positions.
9. Provides for the health, safety, and welfare of students and staff within the school.
10. Maintains standards of student discipline designed to command the respect of students and parents and to minimize school and classroom interruptions.
11. Coordinates the use of student transportation services provided for the school.
12. Develops working relationships among school staff and school system resource personnel available to the school.
13. Makes regular and thorough inspections of the school plant and school properties.
14. Supervises the preparation of all school reports, student records, and the school's internal accounts, and maintains a record-keeping system.
15. Approves or initiates requisitions for supplies, equipment, and materials necessary for the operation of the school.
16. Interprets activities and policies of the school to the community and encourages community participation in school life.
17. Makes recommendations to the district superintendent and the superintendent concerning policy, practice, or personnel for the purposes of improving the quality of the school system.

QUALIFICATIONS:
- *Master's degree, including 12 semester hours of professional education at the graduate level.*
- *A valid Type B state teaching certificate (or the equivalent).*
- *At least three years successful teaching experience during the five-year period immediately preceding appointment to principalship.*

EMPLOYMENT FACTORS: *Forty- or forty-two-week year for elementary and secondary principals respectively. Salary and work year to be established by the board.*

EVALUATION: *Nontenured principals shall be evaluated twice annually for a three-year period.*

* See footnote 4, p. 16.

Allocation of Time for a Typical Work Week

Area of Responsibility	Do Spend Time	Should Spend Time
School management	1	3
Personnel	2	2
Student activities	3	4
Student behavior	4	7
Program development	5	1
District office	6	9
Planning	7	5
Community	8	8
Professional development	9	6

These principals saw program development as their most important area of responsibility while they were spending most of their time on school management. The tone of the entire survey was that in order to assist schools in realizing an effective educational program they must be given more freedom from administrative detail and trivia.[7]

The situation facing the elementary principal is essentially the same. The elementary principal operating in a smaller, more compact school setting has greater possibilities for developing a faculty team devoted to improving instruction. On the other hand, he or she has fewer if any assistants, and therefore becomes totally responsible for management detail and discipline. William Pharis, Executive Secretary of the National Association of Elementary School Principals, expressed his feelings at the National School Board Association's annual meeting concerning the elementary principals' deteriorating leadership position, especially as the result of collective bargaining. Because of school board negotiations, said Pharis, "Right now you have the highest paid staff member in the school building—the principal—supervising lunchrooms, loading buses, and taking care of the playground."[8]

The Social Setting

The social system or community in which the principal works has a major influence upon his role behavior. Figure 2.2 depicts some of the forces that have an impact on the principal and in a sense shape his/her role in the school. By the same token, these forces shape the various positions within

---

[7] See also, National Association of Secondary School Principals, *Summary Report of The Senior High School Principalship*, Vol. III (Reston, Va.: The Association, 1979).

[8] National School Public Relations Association, *Education U.S.A. Report* (Washington, D.C.: The Association), April 10, 1978, Vol. 20 No. 32, p. 244.

FIGURE 2.2.   Influences shaping a principal's role performance.

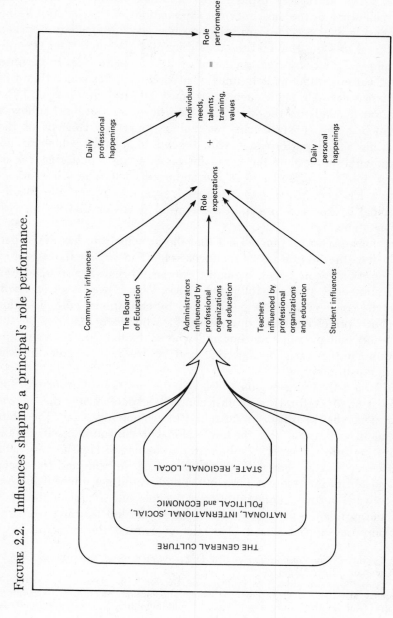

Role
performance

=

Individual
needs,
talents,
training,
values

Daily
professional
happenings

+

Daily
personal
happenings

Community influences

Role
expectations

The Board
of Education

Administrators
influenced by
professional
organizations
and education

Teachers
influenced by
professional
organizations
and education

Student influences

STATE, REGIONAL, LOCAL

NATIONAL, INTERNATIONAL, SOCIAL,
POLITICAL and ECONOMIC

THE GENERAL CULTURE

Adapted from Donald J. Leu and Herbert C. Rudman (Eds.), *Preparation Programs for School Administrators* (Michigan State University, 1963), p. 113.

the school. They can best be explained by resorting to role theory. Erving Goffman makes one of the most succinct explanations of this theory.[9] Using a lead from a famous Shakespeare soliloquy he makes an analogy between a person's "real life" position and the unfolding of a play on a stage. People holding different positions in an organization have definite roles to perform and a great variety of factors determine what kind of performance they will give in these roles. Although each actor must interpret his role and the interpretation depends on the kind of person he is, yet he must follow a script (which is the constituencies' written or unwritten concept of the role) and his actual performance will depend to a large extent on his interaction with the rest of the cast, the director, past performances of actors in a similar role, and indeed the audience itself. The school as an organization has certain role structures and expectations and the incumbent principal is expected to exhibit the type of behavior that fits in with these expectations.[10,11,12]

Our previous discussion pointed out that the principalship has developed essentially into the administrator–manager role. The principal was thrust into this position by necessity in many instances because just managing the sheer number of students following World War II was a job in itself. However, the concept has been perpetuated by educational administration experts (both professors and administrators) who were believers in the strict line and staff pyramid concept and who evaluated the success of the organization on the basis of reporting and controlling all units for the central administration.

It would be folly for a person to accept the position of principal and say, "Now I shall perform as an instructional leader," when the central administration, the board of education, the community, and the state department of education, and the professional organization itself, expect him/her to perform primarily as administrator–manager. He/she very soon would discover that his/her individual concept of the role and the social systems concept of the role were in conflict and would get into difficulty.

Some forward-looking communities and schools have made a thorough study of the problem and resolved that instruction and learning were the primary purposes of the school. They have charged the principal with

---

[9] Erving Goffman, *The Presentation of Self in Everyday Life* (Garden City: Doubleday and Company, Inc., 1959).

[10] How people perform their job in organizations, or "role theory," has attracted much scholarly attention over the last few years. The authors recommend a thorough study of this field by the aspiring principal. It will help him/her to understand the operation of a complex organization such as a school.

[11] William G. Monahan, *Theoretical Dimensions of Educational Administration* (New York: Macmillan, 1975), pp. 348–360.

[12] Luvern Cunningham, Walter G. Hack, and Raphael O. Nystrand, *Educational Administration, The Developing Decades* (Berkeley, Calif.: McCutchan Publishing Company), 1977.

instructional leadership responsibilities and encouraged performance of this role by giving the school greater instructional autonomy and providing back-up resources from the central administration with a minimum of red tape. However, these instances are rare and in a sense are contrary to trends. If a turnabout in the primary role of a principal is to take place it must be a national movement possibly spearheaded by the principals themselves but endorsed by school superintendents, school boards, teachers, and citizens at large. Perhaps only a turnabout of this magnitude can help us develop the type of schools we need in the twenty-first century.

While the authors have stated repeatedly that administrative efficiency in management is a necessary ingredient in any school, it is merely one of the means to the end that every boy and girl attend a school that can provide a learning environment that will motivate him or her to reach full potential. Administrators must be considered the servants of organizational purpose. How can schools like this develop unless the school has a leader who sees the development of an environment conducive to learning as a major responsibility and is held accountable for outstanding instruction rather than for management detail?

Systems Analysis

Systems analysis has become a very useful way for the administrator to understand how the school operates within a particular social setting. It is both analytic and holistic. Systems analysis is a way of viewing an existing whole by breaking it down into its constituent parts or elements for the purpose of depicting the interactions and relationships of the parts to the whole and to each other in various combinations. In systems analysis, it is essential to view each "whole" as being a subpart of an even larger system. Therefore, one must consider how the outside environment (matter, energy, and information) has an impact on the system as a whole and its parts singly and in various combinations.

For the principal the process would begin by considering the school as the specific system with which he or she is concerned. In analyzing the situation he/she would begin by first considering the environment or supra system in which the school operates, breaking that down into meaningful parts (note Figs. 3.1 and 3.2, Ch. 3) and then identifying the various component parts of the school itself (various formal administrative structures, teachers and their various formal and informal organizations, students and their various formal and informal organizations, and so on). This then provides the framework within which any particular problem is examined. The principal who has developed a concept of each element, its role, and its various parts can proceed to analyze the relationship between the school and its environment and the way the various parts of each relate both to each other and to the whole, within and without the system. In this relationship both long- and short-term effects must be considered.

Approaching situations according to systems analysis directs one to think both in conceptual as well as concrete terms. It helps the principal to recognize the dynamic interrelationships of the school and understand that specific behavior problems that may create a crisis are not generally solved alone by a specific isolated solution but rather by the intelligent application of some general overall principles.

One of the most understandable approaches to studying organization as systems is provided by James G. Miller.[13] He considered organizations as dynamic living systems and divided them into their smallest identifiable parts. Then, to speculate on how different actions would affect these parts separately, in different combinations, and as a whole, he set up a series of hypotheses, applied these to the systems in various combinations, and theorized their effect on the system and its parts. This process of using cross-level hypotheses can be very useful to the principal practitioner who wishes to become more of a student of the school and its social setting.

The Person

While the person in a particular position in an organization occupies a certain specified role and is shaped through interaction with the various elements of the social system, at the same time, as an individual, he/she shapes that role too by his/her needs, drives, talents, and training or the various capacities he/she has as an individual.

We will discuss the individual and his/her impact on the organization in the chapter dealing with leadership. Now a major question arises as to how we educate this individual so that he/she can perform effectively with a minimum of role conflict.

One of the reasons that the principalship overemphasizes administration and management is that the training program for principals is oriented in that direction.

Bernard C. Watson, in reviewing problems of principals, makes this point in dramatic fashion:

> Thus, the principalship, overwhelmed by and immersed in maintenance duties is often perceived by superintendents and principals as a middle management position in the educational hierarchy. The emphasis is on administration, but the problems that the principal faces demand effective educational leadership. The skills demanded are highly varied, but many

[13] James G. Miller, *Living Systems* (New York: McGraw Hill, 1978).

administrators find that the tools with which they are equipped are valuable only in maintaining the status quo . . ." [14]
A major problem, however, is how to recruit and train individuals so that they become educational leaders rather than administrators. Procedures concerning recruitment and training have been affected by the changes in the last twenty years, but the sad fact is that the training of administrators is still in the stage of the Model T." [15]

A survey of colleges and universities having graduate programs in educational administration revealed that the professor of educational administration believes principals should be spending the greatest proportion of their time in the improvement of instruction and that they should be trained accordingly.[16] However, the fact that the typical educational administration departments' courses deal mostly with management and administration influences the beginner's early program in that direction. Professors note the overemphasis on management and administration occurs during the Masters and Sixth Year (Certificate Program) programs rather than at the doctorate level. It is at this beginning stage candidates are encouraged to take more administration courses so professors of educational administration can become more familiar with them and their work. In addition they contend requirements for the administration certificate force the beginner to take management-type courses. While it is fortunate that the doctorate is becoming more flexible and oriented toward an individual's specific needs, it is unfortunate that the same cannot be said for the certificate program (masters and diploma program). This is just the period when a young man or woman enters the principalship and, in a sense, establishes his/her general style and mode of operation as an administrator. It is at this stage that special emphasis should be placed on instructional leadership.

Actually one can review the series of courses required for the principal and for the superintendent in the typical university and find little or no difference in the courses required of each. It is little wonder then that the administrative–management emphasis predominates.[17]

Scholars in the field, however, do recognize that there is a uniqueness about the principalship that should be considered in his/her preparation program, even though most of them place him/her primarily in the administrator category. The place where there is disagreement is determining the degree to which different administrative positions require special-

[14] Bernard C. Watson, "Issues Confronting Educational Administrators," in Luvern L. Cunningham, et al., ed., *Educational Administration. The Developing Decades* (Berkeley, Calif.: McCutchan Publishing Corporation, 1977), p. 85.
[15] Ibid., p. 88.
[16] Ibid., p. 90.
[17] Paula Silver, Dennis W. Spuck et al., *Preparation Programs in Educational Administration* (Columbus, Ohio: The University Council for Educational Administration, 1978).

ized types of training. Of course this brings one back to the old questions: Do we think the principal should be more closely allied with the teaching–learning process or with administration? Should the principal be more the instructional leader ·or the administrator–manager of the building? In a sense it is a matter of degree. The principal should have preparation in broad areas of both instruction and administration. He/she should serve as a colleague as well as a leader with teachers and still be part of the administrative structure. However, what should be his/her strongest affiliation and, in preparation programs, what should be his/her greatest emphasis?

In a survey of secondary school principals throughout the country an attempt was made to determine what preservice courses in schools of education should be considered most important for the beginning principal. From the viewpoint of these practitioners the eleven courses listed by 85 per cent or more as highly useful or essential represented a compromise between the extreme of becoming a "superspecialized technical manager" or "a broadly learned educational leader."

Highest Rated Courses [18]	
School management	(96%) *
Curriculum and program development	(96%)
School law	(95%)
Supervision of instruction	(95%)
Human relations	(93%)
Secondary school principalship	(92%)
School finance and budgeting	(92%)
Personnel administration	(91%)
Leadership	(90%)
Community relations	(87%)
Internship and field experience	(87%)

* The percentage number represents the percentage of principals responding to the questionnaire who rated these courses as highly useful or essential.

The National Association of Secondary School Principals suggested the model depicted in Figure 2.3 as a systematic approach to preparing principals. Within each process, diagnostic, prescriptive, implementative, and evaluative, the following behaviors are identified according to domains: [19]

1. Knowledge.
2. Comprehension.

[18] National Association of Secondary School Principals, *The Senior High School Principalship, the National Survey* (Reston, Va.: The Association, 1978), p. 9.
[19] Donald Brandewie, et al., "The Preparation and Development of Secondary School Administrators," *NASSP Bulletin* (March 1972), pp. 28–29.

FIGURE 2.3. A systematic approach to preparing principals.

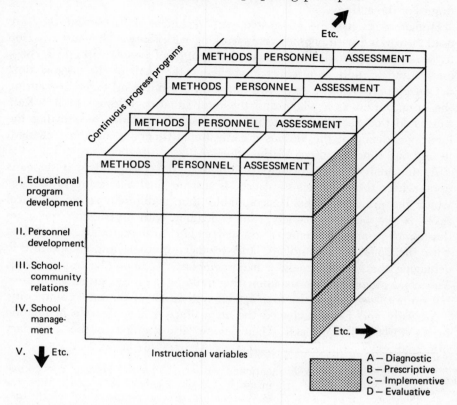

Source: See footnote 18.

3. Application.
4. Analysis.
5. Synthesis.
6. Evaluation.
7. Affective.
8. Skills.

The Three-Skill Approach to Administration

A number of experts have attempted to determine the proper preparation of principals on the basis of the Katz three-skill approach to administration.[20] Katz categorizes the skills needed by any administrator into three broad divisions—*technical skills, human skills, conceptual skills.*

Technical skills involve specialized knowledge and proficiency in a

[20] Robert L. Katz, "Skills of an Effective Administrator," *Harvard Business Review,* 33, No. 1 (January–February 1955), pp. 33–42.

specific kind of activity, along with facility in the use of tools and techniques of the activity.

Human skills may be contrasted with technical skills in that they are used in working with people versus working with things. They aid a person to work effectively with individuals and groups of people to build a cooperative and friendly team effort in achieving the goals of the organization.

Conceptual skills in a sense are the ability to put it all together—sensing the organization as a whole and the total situation relevant to it.[21] Katz suggested that seeing the enterprise as a whole includes recognizing the interdependency of the various organizational functions and how changes in any one function affect all the others.[22]

Again, analyzing the principal's job from this perspective, it depends upon where the emphasis is placed. If instructional leadership is that for which the principal is held accountable, then a different set of technical skills is emphasized, namely, those dealing with instruction, program development and evaluation, and curriculum and materials. In dealing with the community, students, and teachers in their mutual interest in achieving the school's goals, a major emphasis is upon the human skills. The conceptual skills focus upon the building and the attendance area, but do not lose sight of the total school system nor of the total community.

McNally and Dean reviewed the elementary principal's role in relation to the three-skill approach. Their review also applied to the secondary principal: [23]

> All three types of skills mentioned earlier (technical, human, conceptual) are important at all administrative levels. Rather, it appears that the differences arise mostly from the nature of the problems to which they may be applied. For example, conceptual skill is probably most important at the level of chief school officer, for here decisions must be made with the welfare of the entire system constantly in mind. Nevertheless, the elementary school principal also has to exercise conceptual skill in seeing local community and school problems in relation to the system-wide picture, in maintaining balance and integrity in the overall program of his local unit, and in conceiving creative innovations for improvement in relation to local situations and needs.
>
> Likewise, human relations skills are of critical importance at all levels of administrative responsibility. Differences among the administrative levels with respect to human relations skills lie primarily in the kinds of situations in which they are exercised. The superintendent, for example, has more formal kinds of relationships. He is at the lonesome pinnacle of the organizational hierarchy, with no status peers in the system.
>
> The elementary school principal on the other hand, is daily immersed in less

[21] Chester I. Barnard, *Functions of the Executive* (Cambridge, Mass.: Harvard University Press, 1938) has an excellent discussion on this. See particularly p. 235.
[22] Katz, op. cit., p. 36.
[23] Harold J. McNally and Stuart E. Dean, "The Elementary School Principal," in Donald J. Leu and Herbert C. Rudman, Editors, *Preparation Programs for School Administrators* (East Lansing: Michigan State University, 1963), pp. 119–120.

formal, intensely personal contacts. He confers and counsels individually with staff members, parents and pupils. He works with small parent groups, with faculty groups and with community groups in much less formal ways than does the chief school officer. In common with the secondary school principal, he works with both subordinates and superiors in the organization. With respect to technical skills, also, those important to an elementary school principal's functioning are similar in nature and principle to, but different in their specific application from those important in other administrative positions. The principal needs greater command of the skills of close personal supervision of professional and non-professional staff, of pupil personnel administration, of selection, utilization, and control of elementary school instructional supplies, and of the administration of internal activity funds.

All that has been said in the foregoing could also be applied to the secondary school principal. Differences in the specialized emphasis of his preparation from those of his elementary school colleagues should stem from the special nature of the enterprise he administers; its unique social and educational organization, its objectives, its program, the nature of its staff, and its place in and relation to the rest of the school system, and to the community.

Downey has this to say regarding the unique aspects of task of the secondary school principal, and again the same could be said for the elementary school principal: [24]

Most formulations of the task areas of educational administration include: finance and business management, physical facilities, community relations, organization and structure, staff personnel, student personnel, and program development or instructional leadership.

All of these task areas are of concern to the secondary school principal, as they are to every other administrative official in the educational system. Comparisons among the tasks performed by various administrators reveal, however, that the tasks assume different priorities and call for different degrees and levels of involvement from one position to another. For example, the superintendent's tasks with respect to finance and business management are crucial and require involvement in the procurement, the distribution, and the utilization of resources. The principal's tasks in this area are less crucial, involving mainly the utilization, and not the distribution or procurement of resources. So it is with each of the task areas. For one administrator, the task is crucial and requires specialization involvement; for another it is less crucial and requires limited involvement.

It is suggested that, in the case of the secondary school principalship, the order of priority that should be assigned to the various task areas is *exactly the reverse of the order in which they are listed above*. That is to say, finance and business management is the least crucial and calls for the lowest level of involvement; program development and instructional leadership is the most crucial and calls for the highest level of specialized involvement. In fact, I would contend that *it is primarily the unique aspects of the secondary school principal's tasks in program development and instructional leadership that make his position a specialized one in educational administration.*

[24] Ibid., Ch. VII, Lawrence W. Downey, "The Secondary School Principal," pp. 129–130.

Specialized Learnings–Competencies Necessary
  for the Principal

These authors, in their analyses of the specialized learnings necessary for the elementary principal and the secondary principal, considered the principalship a distinctly different subspecies of the species "educational administrator." They were startlingly similar in that they placed strong emphasis on the need for special training in the instructional leadership area. The following summarizes some of the specialized learnings and competencies important for the effective principal of today.

1. The principal should be thoroughly conversant with findings of psychology concerning the nature, growth, and learning that underlie teaching methods and curriculum organization.
2. The principal should have a strong sociological background in order to understand the school and the school community as social systems. In particular, sociology of organizations and of juvenile cultures can contribute to his/her understanding of the problems that he/she faces.
3. He/she needs to know school programs as intimately as a physician knows anatomy, as an integral pulsing system with its complex detail.
4. He/she should be knowledgeable of the strengths and weaknesses of various programs and methods and be skilled in effective ways to bring about improvement in them.
5. He/she should understand how to best utilize auxiliary services such as those provided by curriculum workers, librarians, audiovisual specialists, health and guidance personnel, and remedial specialists.
6. In addition to the principal's intimate knowledge of programs he/she needs to learn well the knowledges and techniques necessary for effective classroom supervision and the broader tasks of instructional improvement.
7. All principals ought to know the general element of good teacher selection policies and procedures and above all the process of inducting and orienting new staff on the job.
8. Having a closer relationship with teachers and staff than any other administrator the principal's problem of maintaining and improving morale is more personal, more immediate, and more intense.
9. The principal must be concerned specifically and intimately with the school's attendance district—the socioeconomic level; problems and needs of individual community members and families; objectives, role, and functions of community and parent organizations. Along with this the principal must understand the relationships with the entire community and the availability of community resources to the school.
10. In regard to pupil personnel he/she certainly needs to know the tech-

nical procedures of handling admission, attendance and transfer, and accounting.

11. He/she must be knowledgeable in techniques of working with students on a large group basis in developing realistic student government, social and recreational activities for the students, and civic contributions by the students.

12. He/she must be thoroughly grounded in organizational process and social systems so that variations of organizations for learning can be tried and evaluated.

13. He/she must help to institute and administer ways of assessing pupil progress and establish methods of reporting to parents and accounting to the community at large.

14. He/she should have the ability to serve as coordinator, mediator, and arbitrator among the various forces that attempt to influence the direction and purpose of education in the school.

15. He/she must have a broad educational foundation providing a strong intellectual base on which to develop a well-conceived personal philosophy of education to give his/her leadership respect and direction.

16. His/her educational base must be broad enough so that the faculty and staff do not attack for meddling in specific subject or technical areas but rather respect his/her sensitivity and insight into the world and its togetherness and his/her ability to reveal imbalances, undue emphases, and inconsistencies whenever they occur.

17. He/she must have ability to work with teachers in the selection and evaluation of educational procedures from the multitude of these procedures presently advanced.

Table 2.1 provides a consolidated review of the various tasks of the school principal. It becomes obvious in this review that one would find little disagreement over the responsibilities that the principal has and the tasks that he/she must perform or oversee. Most everyone will agree, too, that the principal must be an educational leader, an administrator, and an efficient manager of his/her school building. However, the priority of the role emerges when certain activities are rewarded, reinforced, and praised and others are disregarded or discouraged. *The reality of the situation is that central administrations and boards of education reward and reinforce the well-managed, efficiently operated school.* Although they will not deny that instructional leadership is important, they become concerned and fearful when individual schools deviate from normal routine instructional procedures. The give and take of opinion and the dynamic interchange of ideas among faculty and with the community too often spells controversy to the central administration. Experimentation and innovation are risk-taking ventures that may rock the boat too vigorously. Therefore, when one does see real instructional leadership performed in a school it is the result of one or more of the following ingredients: (1) a

TABLE 2.1 *Task Priorities* [25]

Administrative and Leadership Tasks of Principal	Priority		
	Low	Medium	High
Finance and management	X *		/ †
Budget—regular program	X	X	/
Physical facilities	X		/
Supplies and equipment	X		/
Staff personnel administration	X		/
Professional personnel administration		X	/
Student accounting		X	/
Professional staff development		/	X
Student growth and development		/	X
Student activities and government		/	X
Curriculum development		/	X
Instructional improvement		/	X
Utilization of materials of instruction		/	X
Community relations (attendance area)	/		X
Community relations (school district)	/	X	
Accountability in teaching and learning	/		X

* Represents priority necessary to exert strong instructional leadership.
† Represents actual priorities as revealed by studies of what the typical principal actually does.

courageous and creative principal, (2) a forward-looking superintendent, (3) a dynamic community.

A U.S. Office of Education Commission appointed to study teacher education reported on a study on the relationship between training as a principal and success as a principal. The study concluded: "The less extensive the formal preparation of principals, the greater was their staff leadership." In other words, more training resulted in less effective leadership![26] The report concluded a high percentage of principals are "followers" of central administration rather than leaders in their own right.[27] Without further analysis one can only hypothesize as to why the report came to the conclusion it did. One hypothesis would be the training program's emphasis on management creates detail persons more devoted to the maintenance of the organization than to improvement of instruction.

For Further Thought

1. Is administration properly considered an art, a science, or a process?
2. In general, which is the most important influence in bringing about

[25] Ibid., p. 131.
[26] Study Commission on Undergraduate Education and Education of Teachers, *Teacher Education in the United States: The Responsibility Gap* (Lincoln, Nebr.: University of Nebraska Press, 1976) pp. 52–53.
[27] See also Ch. 6, "Leadership."

educational changes—educational leaders and statesmen or changes in economic, social, and political conditions of the times?

3. To what extent should a school faculty be involved in the selection of a new principal? Develop a plan for the selection process and defend it.

4. Present arguments for and against specialized education for administrators in general versus specialized education for principals. Is it a matter of emphasis?

5. Identify and discuss the specific certification requirements for the position of principal in your state. Is the emphasis on instructional leadership or on administration? How different are the requirements from those for the position of superintendent?

6. Compare the traits of successful and unsuccessful administrators.

7. Are there some reliable tests for predicting administrative potential? Review and analyze them.

8. What are the personal qualities you believe a school principal should have? Can you defend this on the basis of objective evidence?

9. Study the succession patterns of administrators in your area. How many insiders are there compared to outsiders? Are there differences in the succession patterns of elementary school principals, middle school or junior high principals, senior high principals, and superintendents?

10. Interview a number of teachers, students, and parents, and ask them what they consider the important duties of a principal to be. What are the similarities and differences in response?

Chapter 3   The School and Its Communities

The old idea of the school as an academic island existing apart from the more turbulent mainland has never been real. Certainly it is not real today! The public school is only one of many activities and problems of concern in any community. Education is so complex that it is accomplished through a number of institutions, agencies, and activities of which the formally organized public school is only one important agency. Cooperation among all agencies of community life is essential to the realization of desirable educational outcomes.

The School as Part of Civil Government

From the standpoint of the community itself the school is a part of the civil government, which consists of public works, public health and safety, recreation, welfare, and education. In addition, making up the community in a less structured way we have churches, voluntary cultural, social, recreational and welfare agencies, and economic activities of various types. To the people in the community all these activities are important although some will appear in stronger focus at different times, depending upon the people involved and the problems that confront them. To complicate the community forces even more, none of these institutions or organizations are self-sufficient within the community itself; all are subject to strong regional, state and national influences. Thus public education is a part of an intricate complex. There must be cooperation with all because in most cases the activities of the school overlap considerably with the activities of these agencies; it must be sensitive to all because the school's wellbeing as a social institution is dependent upon their good will; finally, it must compete with all of these other agencies for the general support of the public.

The influence of the community on the school and the school on the

FIGURE 3.1. The character of the community.

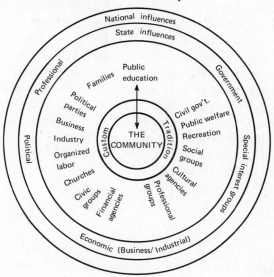

community is a continuous interaction process. The school's influence on the community is more subtle, long term, and indirect. The community's influence on the school, however, is far from subtle. Figures 3.1 and 3.2 illustrate these mutual influences and the various sources of influences upon the community and upon public education.

FIGURE 3.2. Influences upon public education.

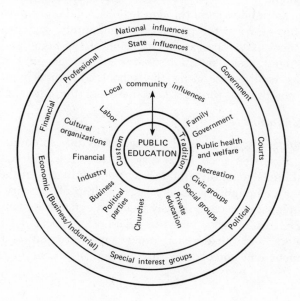

As an agency responsible for the education of the community's children and youth the school finds itself subject to the stresses and strains of every organized and unorganized activity within the community and under parental and general adult scrutiny at every point. This places the principal and his staff in a very sensitive position. While some are inclined to resent the community's intrusion upon the school, the enlightened principal accepts this as a natural state of being for an institution as important as the public school. Rather than resent, fight, or disregard it, the successful school administrator will involve the school as fully as practical in community affairs, and involve the community as fully as practical in school affairs so that the purpose, value, conditions, and needs of each will be fully understood and appreciated.

Principles

1. The process of education extends beyond the walls of the formally organized public school. The influences of outside forces are so important that close cooperation with other community agencies, institutions, and organizations is essential to the development of a sound educational program.
2. The American public school reflects the cultural milieu of which it is a part. It is responsible not only for conserving the useful past but also for preparing the way for progress and change. It must be attentive to the wishes of all the people. Because it must generally operate by consensus it will always be subject to criticisms by both reactionary and radical opinion.
3. The American public school through legal delegation of power represents a partnership between the people, the community, and the state; therefore the school, in a sense, is an extension of the home and necessitates the active and intelligent participation of parents in the educational program as well as requiring the school continuously to inform the people of conditions, purposes, and needs of the educational program.

What Is a Community?

In the foregoing discussion of the school and the community, the term "community" has been used in a very broad sense with city and town governmental limits generally establishing the boundaries of the community. The concept of community is as elusive as a drop of mercury on a marble tabletop. Sociologists are continuously trying to define it in numerous studies that have given us insights into the relationships between people, their group behaviors, and the decision process in communities. However, we hope the student will not become discouraged in attempting to pin down an exact definition. As far back as 1955 Hillary identified ninety-four different definitions of community.[1] As of this date the numbers would run into the hundreds. Probably almost as many different definitions could be found for social systems and institutions. The more one studies the research and writing the more obvious it becomes that it is almost impossible to precisely define what a community is as compared to a social system as compared to an institution. They all begin to converge as well as diverge. As Hope Hensen Leichter pointed out in her analysis of the structure of families, systems, institutions, and communities, the more one studies and looks into these, "the more it isn't there".[2] The possibility of such diversity of definitions is not meant to confuse but to show that a community is not the simplistic phenomenon that many would believe. The precise issue is to alert scholars of education to the complexity of clustering and labeling people, their activities, and their organizations. There is a vast variety of possibilities, depending upon one's perspective and purpose.

Communities have been studied from the viewpoints of space, population groupings, shared institutions and values, interactions between local people, power structure, ethnic structure, and social systems.[3] Campbell and co-authors cite the territorial system view of the community that serves as a framework in which the "game" of education can take place in a territory bounded by a district but not closed either socially or politically.[4] Much of the literature stresses the concept of the community as a social system. A system may be thought of as ". . . a set of *components* surrounded by a *boundary* which accepts *inputs* from some other system and discharges *outputs* into another system".[5] It is clear that a community can be made up of several systems, and in turn those social systems may be made up of subsystems.

A number of books on school administration follow this pattern. They will identify the community generally as the governmental unit known as the school district and then consider the interacting units within these boundaries as social systems. Invariably, when attempting to analyze the role of the individual within this system they present the Getzels and Guba model showing the organizational and personal dimensions of social behavior.

[1] G. A. Hillary, Jr., "Definitions of Community: Areas of Agreement" *Rural Sociology,* 20 (1955), pp. 111–123.

[2] Hope Jensen Leichter, "Families and Communities as Educators: Some Concepts of Relationship," *Teachers College Record,* May, 1978.

[3] For a review of these analyses of the community, see Roland F. Warren, *The Community in America,* 2nd ed., (Chicago: Rand McNally & Co., 1972), pp. 21–52.

[4] Roald F. Campbell, et al., *The Organization and Control of American Schools* (Columbus, Ohio: Charles E. Merrill Publishing Co., 1970), pp. 431–434.

[5] F. K. Berrien, "A General Systems Approach to Social Taxonomy," *People, Groups, and Organizations* (New York: Teachers College Press, 1968), p. 111.

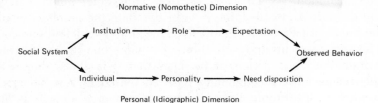

Normative (Nomothetic) Dimension

Personal (Idiographic) Dimension

A person within a social system such as the school makes a decision or performs an act (administrator, teacher, or student). Based on the Getzels Guba model, this act or action is conceived as deriving from both the normative and idiographic dimension. In other words, one may say that behavior in the school is a function of the role the school expects of the person and his/her personality as defined by a needs disposition.

While this model has provided a useful way of analyzing the particular behavior of an administrator, teacher, or student, unless carefully explained it is in itself too simplistic. The assumption is too often made when considering the normative or nomothetic dimension that only one institution, the school, influences the role. Thus, it becomes a static rather than dynamic situation. The fact is, for any given person many institutions of which he/she is a part of at that particular time, influences role—the church, political party, the social club, ethnic group, the communities, the professional organizations. Influence on behavior is dynamic and ever changing.

The same may be said for the idiographic dimension. This if often seen as a static condition of personality based upon past experiences and influences. These influences are of major importance. However, present-day influences (friends, accidents, unusual experiences, and so on) of the moment may change personality and behavior drastically at any given time.

Getzels recognized the need for more emphasis on the dynamics of behavior in a later discussion of communities.[6]

He added to his model the dimension of the ongoing influence of various communities (or systems) of which a person is a part.

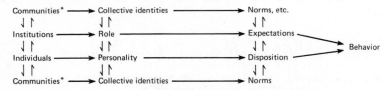

*Includes: (1) local communities, (2) administrative communities, (3) social communities, (4) institutional communities, (5) ethnic communities, (6) ideological communities

Although it is not the intent of this chapter to treat institutions, social systems, and communities in detail and in as disciplined a way as the

[6] J. W. Getzels, "The Communities of Education," *Teachers College Record*, (May, 1978), pp. 659–682.

foregoing studies, we recommend any and all of these as areas of careful study in the preparation program of every principal.

Because community implies people and is more personal than the terms "system" and "institution," we will use the term "community" as we deal with an analysis of the way people relate and cluster in the school. Our definition of community in this sense is simple: a group of people conscious of a collective identity through common physical, cognitive, and affective educational relationships. On the basis of this definition there can be several communities within a broader school community. Each individual within the school community may well represent a variety of different communities, all of which makes a complex network to consider in attempting to understand the values and expectations of each.

The School's Community

The school is part of a total school community known as the school district, which is the governing unit for all of the schools in the district. The school principal then is most immediately concerned with that portion of the community that is part of his/her school. Whereas within the broad community he/she shares limited leadership responsibility with the superintendent of schools, the central office staff, and other school principals, the principal of the neighborhood school becomes the most logical first contact about education for those parents and citizens who live in that neighborhood. The boundaries of this community are determined by the general attendance area of the school itself. All citizens living in this attendance area and all persons employed by the school are part of this community. They may be (a) citizens without children in school, (b) parents of children in school, (c) children in school, and (d) teachers and other employees of the school.

For the most part these school communities have fixed attendance area boundaries; however, with the advent of the voucher system, open school attendance, magnet schools, and busing to eliminate segregation, the community may be extended and dispersed.

This dispersion makes it difficult to delineate who makes up the school community and complicates communication; however, it does not eliminate the idea that this is or can be a community.

The rapid growth and complexity of communities with accompanying growth and complexity of school districts in the twentieth century make it impossible for schools to remain as close and responsive as they were in the eighteenth and nineteenth centuries. The feeling of actually belonging, participating, being a co-partner with the school is rapidly disappearing. The intimate community spirit is becoming lost with the rapid growth of schools in the megalopolis and in the organization of the sprawling rural–suburban consolidated district. These larger districts have tended to develop into mechanized professional organizations that are highly bureaucratic. Many people are inclined to resent the growth, centralization, and reorganization that has taken place in schools and propose that we go back to the "good old days" of the small neighborhood district. This is regressive thinking and can never really happen. The growth in population alone would prohibit this as a possibility. There is no doubt that educational opportunity and educational process has been improved by consolidating into larger educational units; however, in planning the educational unit there was not invented or established a realistic organized way to keep parents and citizens intimately associated with the schools. It can truly be said, the schools have kept pace with change technically but not organizationally and operationally as far as close relationships to their publics are concerned.

It Happened to Schools

With the complexities of government and the complexities of the schools there is a growing belief that there have been both unconscious and conscious moves to gain control of schools by professionals and distant governmental bodies. Reviewing both sides of the case, there is more than a little evidence to support these claims. Researchers from the Center for Educational Policy and Management of the University of Oregon developed a historical review of the phases by which school control is being "wrested from the people." [7] Their major thesis is that local control was first destroyed by the growth of educational professionalism and is under further assault by a "political reformer elite" who see the schools as agents of social and economic change to be manipulated by federal legislation. In the latter instance, to make their point they review the effect of the Elementary and Secondary Education Act in 1965 plus other federal legislation and court cases dealing with school finance, segregation, and other social issues.

Richard W. Saxe makes a more subtle reference to deteriorating citizens' participation by observing that attempts at better relations are neutralized by elements of the "bureaucratic professional model." [8] The teachers' fear of parents causes them to don an armor of expertise and professionalism to keep parents at arm's length. Another negative factor that drives citizens

[7] L. Harmon Zeigler, Harvey J. Tucker, and L. A. Wilson, "How School Control Was Wrested from the People," *Phi Delta Kappan* (March, 1977), pp. 534–539.
[8] Richard W. Saxe, *School Community Interaction* (Berkeley, Calif.: McCutchan Publishing Corporation, 1975), pp. 23–24.

away, according to Saxe, is the need to maintain a safe environment for students portrayed by a typical sign in Ohio schools:

ALL VISITORS
MUST REPORT TO THE PRINCIPAL'S OFFICE

Visitors—State Statute 2917.21.1 of the Ohio Code prohibits the trespassing on School Property. This regulation pertains to the Buildings and Grounds.

Rosabeth Kanter makes an even stronger statement regarding the loss of community influence on schools:

> Seeking discipline and wanting to legitimate their own authority claims, schools removed children from the family, set up a system of authority based upon state sanctions and expertise . . . . and instituted a "work discipline" strikingly similar to that of adult organizations. . . . Today the relations between school and parent and between teachers and parents, despite alleged community control of schools, are not unlike the uneasy relations of corporations and families, with the family often unable to intervene in or influence organizational policies even tho' these policies have great effect on their lives.[9]

Much the same allegation is made by the Carnegie Council on Children.[10] They assert that parents deal with schools from a position of helplessness, frustration, and inferiority. With their special credentials and jargon the professionals in the various institutions, including the school, have essentially taken over the control of the child.

Develop a Special School–Community Program

The principal as the official first-line contact of the school to the community can do much to dispel the feeling that the professionals are eroding the public's influence on schools. A special series developed by the National Community Education Association has excellent suggestions for improving community–school relations. They have developed ten "How To" pamphlets that provide step-by-step suggestions: *People Helping People, The Community Council, Public Relations, Community Surveys, Models of Community Education, Financing Community Education, Organizing Volunteer Programs, Involving Senior Citizens, Evaluating Community Programs,* and *Community Decision Making.*"[11]

[9] Rosabeth Kanter, *Work and Family in the U.S.: A Critical Review and Agenda for Research and Policy* (New York: Russell Sage Foundation, 1977), pp. 12–13.

[10] Kenneth Keniston and The Carnegie Council on Children, *All Our Children: The American Family Under Pressure* (New York: Harcourt Brace Jovanovich, 1977).

[11] Published by and available from the Pendell Publishing Company, Midland, Mich. 48640.

The Student Community

The Student and School Governance

As one reviews the textbooks in curriculum, supervision, and administration of elementary and secondary schools one observes a serious concern for teaching of citizenship and providing prototype adult experiences that show how our democracy works. This well-meaning approach to the education of children is an example of some of the artificiality that pervades our educational system. We do need to use make-believe situations, examples, and case studies to liven up and put more meaning in teaching but the student community is not a make-believe situation. It is a real live situation with all the ingredients to make it a bona fide democratic community. Students are not make-believe citizens; they are actual citizens who are not only part of the school community but the community at large. The child is often called the "invisible citizen" because between the parent and the school, both of whom supposedly are acting in the best interests of the child, the child's rights as a citizen are seldom considered.

Justice Jackson, who delivered the opinion of the court in the famous "flag-saluting" case, admonished school authorities for disregarding students' basic rights as citizens.[12]

> The Fourteenth Amendment as now applied to the states, protects the citizen against the state itself and all of its creatures—Boards of Education not excepted. These have, of course, important delicate and highly discretionary functions, but none that they may not perform within the limits of the Bill of Rights. That they are educating the young for citizenship is reason for scrupulous protection of constitutional freedoms of the individual, if we are not to strangle the free mind at its source and teach youth to discount important principles of our government as mere platitudes.

This brings us to a very sensitively balanced mode of operation for the school and raises issues in regard to administration–student, teacher–student, and adult–student relationships. Immediately, one can hear the usual questions raised, "Who's in control here, anyway—me or the students?" "Are you going to let the students run the school?" "What are principals and teachers for if they can't tell students how to behave, what to do, and what not to do?"

To allow children to participate fully in their own government threatens a very basic value system going back to the Middle Ages—a "divine right" that adults had over the young and the schoolmaster had over students: "Children should be seen and not heard." "Children shall obey the will of the master." "Teacher knows best." "The parent knows best." That

---

[12] West Virginia State Board of Education v. Barnette 319 U.S. 624, 63 S. Ct. 1178, 1943.

school administrators and teachers must have absolute control over students in order not to lose control altogether is a perpetuation of a long-standing myth.

An Institution Responsive to Students

Educators too often restrict their consideration of the school to the formal organization that they themselves set up. There is a growing body of research on the student in relation to school environment, the formal and informal student organization, the student community, the student social system, the social climate of the school and classroom, and the influence of in-school and out-of-school peer groups.[13] In any given student body the incidents of daily interaction between students can number in the tens of thousands; yet teachers and administrators are inclined to count these interactions as inconsequential unless they themselves are involved in the interaction. Actually, the social climate of the classroom, the school, and the general community has an important influence on student behavior and student achievement.

Jack R. Frymier expands the idea of educational institutions as social systems in his book *Fostering Educational Change*.[14] He makes the point that every social system is a human undertaking aimed at furthering or realizing human goals. Each person has his/her goals and each group has its goals, some of which are clear and some not so clear. With a student body, when problems come into focus and the students feel repressed, denied, or restrained because the institution is not moving happily toward desired goals or because they are not respected as an important part of the system—whatever the nature of the problem, the first logical move is to request a change. Employing the traditional concept of following the administrative hierarchy, students go through the various levels of authority to bring about the change. Then, if this fails and they have been unsuccessful in their efforts to persuade the powers that be to change, they have only three choices: give in, get out, or revolt. Each of these choices creates very special problem areas in schools. If the students give in—do as they are told—it is a submission that creates resentment and frustration and a developing antagonism. The students may choose to get out and do so psychologically either through apathy or by excessive absences, or physically by actually dropping out of school. Finally, comes the most extreme option of major protests, striking back and revolting because of the rigidity and inflexibility of the system. This became a popular mode of action beginning in the late sixties and early seventies and is an indication that youth will

[13] Campbell, et al., provide us with an excellent discussion of the student in the school setting in *The Organization and Control of American Schools*, 2nd. ed., pp. 301–326.

[14] Jack R. Frymier, *Fostering Educational Change* (Columbus, Ohio: Charles E. Merrill Publishing Co., 1969).

not be "knuckling under" so easily in the future.[15] If a system is unresponsive to change over the years it builds up a larger and larger body of
people who become antagonistic to the system. Not only are there the
students already in school but there is a growing number who have left
school either by graduation or drop out. So both from within and without
a developing antagonistic force is being created that can either destroy
the system or force change by sheer power. In either case, the inflexible
institution gradually loses the support it needs as a public institution,
responsive to the people.

An Intra-School Community

Much has been made of assessment and accountability of teachers, administrators, and institutions to the public in the past few years. Accountability
is being responsive to the public, which is made up of parents and citizens
at large. However, the most intimately affected public is the students
themselves. Very little has been written about assessing the school as a
viable, responsive social system for students. The student council has been
the *pro forma* establishment way of facing this problem but in far too
many cases this organization is operated with "tongue in cheek" by both
students and administration. They know that the principal can step in at
any time and veto any of the proposals, and there is no simple procedure
for appeal nor a method by which the decision of the principal may be
evaluated by an impartial group.

If children are to understand that they live in a democratic society that
is ruled by laws established by the people, they should become familiar
with the democratic process. This is not to suggest that students govern
themselves totally. It is to suggest that there be well-established policies
in every school system that provide guidelines for students to participate
in their school social system; that there be a student Bill of Rights that
clearly establishes basic right of all students; that there be established
system-wide a clear simple process for review and appeal of decisions
handed down by a teacher or a principal; and that each individual school
in the school system have some form of self-government that operates
within the limits of the district's policies and student Bill of Rights. This
government should provide for realistic student input on decisions relating
to the entire school. Some form of government in each individual school
should operate according to a constitution developed by and for the mem-

[15] Three out of five secondary school principals had experienced active student
protest of one kind or another in their schools. In large urban areas it is three out of
four, according to Gregory R. Arnig in "Those High School Protestors: Can Boards
Put Up with Much More?" *American School Board Journal*, 157, No. 4 (October
1969), pp. 20–24.

FIGURE 3.3. Model depicting an intraschool constitutional government.

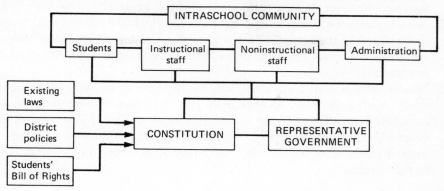

bers of that particular school's social system composed of students, faculty, administration, and nonteaching personnel (see Fig. 3.3). If schools are to remain responsive and close to the people, if citizens and students are to remain advocates instead of adversaries of the schools, then adversary situations must be eliminated. The rule by one person, whether teacher or administrator, must be replaced by a government of law, and those who are in the school social system must have a meaningful input into the development of that law.

Arnig, in his study of student protest, urged school board members to think more in terms of educational change than in terms of repression and control when considering student unrest.[16] He then makes six constructive suggestions:

1. All school districts should follow the lead of those urban districts that are encouraging increased involvement, and are sharing real power with teachers, students, and parents.
2. School boards must find alternatives to the "tight ship" syndrome that characterizes the regimented life a student faces, especially in our high schools, where even the need to go to the washroom requires a public declaration in class and a brightly colored plaque visible en route.
3. School boards must open up new and broader communications with their patrons and clients—the students in our schools. Our schools, our economy, and our homes seem to be prolonging childhood for a serious generation of young people who want to be a part of the action. We need to listen to youngsters in the fullest sense and to judge the merit of the views—not the age or appearance of the speaker.
4. School boards need to seek greater relevance in learning—relevance to the world of work, and relevance to the community with which the student identifies. Most school-sponsored work experiences, as we know,

[16] Ibid., pp. 23–24.

begin after the student is eligible to drop out of school—often too late for him to recognize that learning is relevant to earning a living.

5. School boards need to change the ways in which they select and train those who take the critical job of principal. Should seniority, certification requirements, and examination scores prevail over sensitivity and imagination?

6. Finally, school board members and all the rest of us who have some power in this business of education must be more willing to look at ourselves critically, to judge our own actions and reactions regarding those who confront and trouble us, and be willing to change our attitudes toward others who are claiming what they see—often quite accurately— as their rights.

The Student and Community Conflict

In considering the student it is important to realize that one of the major problems may be that he or she is embedded in a variety of communities, each of which may have expectations in regard to the student that compete and conflict with each other and those of the school.

It is difficult for the principal and teacher to comprehend how serious these conflicts are and how much they will influence the behavior of the students in school for their effects cannot be determined without serious study. Getzels, in his excellent article on the "Communities of Education" sees the need for a major research thrust in analyzing the continuities and discontinuities, values, and expectations that a student must resolve as he/she deals with the variety of communities of which he/she is a part.[17]

There is a growing body of research that utilizes the network process to arrive at an understanding of human behavior. Although very little has been done in relation to children and youth it could create new possibilities for understanding the complexities of their behavior.[18]

Unconsciously or consciously when a principal or teacher identifies with a boy or girl it is that boy or girl as part of the school community. So often the principal or teacher does not consider all the other forces impinging on the student that affect his/her actions in school. The network approach is so simple it is hard to understand. It focuses on the person! It looks at the boy or girl wherever he or she is and traces the effect of the network of relationship (including the school) on the person. Nicholas

[17] J. W. Getzels, "The Communities of Education," *Teachers College Record*, May, 1978.

[18] For further information on network research see R. A. Thompson, "A Theory of instrumental Social Networks," *Journal of Anthropological Research*, 29 (1973), pp. 244–254; Seymour B. Sarason et al., *Human Services and Resource Networks* (San Francisco, Calif.: Jossey-Bass Publications, 1977).

Hobbs follows a similar pattern by studying the child's "life space" in an effort to understand the child, not just the child in the school.[19]

The Faculty Community

Anyone who has ever been a teacher in a school knows that when considering a faculty of a school you are speaking of a social system, a formal–informal organization that has a definite personality, a great variety of parts making up the whole, interrelationships that run the gamut of closeness and distance, and wide variations of opinion bordering from either extreme to neutral. Nonetheless, the challenge of teaching, the complexity of relationships with students, the great goals of the profession tie the diverse personalities into some unbelievable whole that we call the faculty. Although the *typical* faculty defies description, it truly portrays the definition of an organic system in that it is an interacting entity whose healthy existence depends upon effective working relationships between the various parts. To disrupt one element in the system is to create stress in the system that may in turn result in noticeable effects on the entire system.

To a limited degree an administrator may deal with a teacher as an isolated individual; however, a serious mistake is made if he/she believes that this carries through in all cases. Each teacher represents him- or herself but also represents a total faculty that not only consists of individuals but also of many primary groups that are linked together by a whole series of bridges that may range from very strong to temporary and weak. Many forces shape the teacher's thinking and behavior as illustrated by Figure 3.4.

Numerous studies have been made of the extralegal powers of the informal group structures of the faculty, noting how these informal organi-

FIGURE 3.4.   Some forces that impinge upon the teacher.

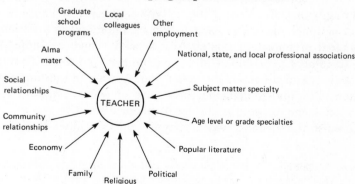

[19] Nicholas Hobbs, "Families, Schools and Communities: An Ecosystem for Children," *Teachers College Record*, (May, 1978).

zations have had an unusual influence on the operation of the formal
school organizations.[20] Teachers become members of these extralegal groups
for a variety of complex reasons but for the most part because such groups
provide for the satisfaction of professional needs that they are unable to
obtain through the regular structure and normal work flow. Organizational
factors that influence the formation of these primary groups include proximity of teaching stations, scheduling of free periods, teaching assignment,
age, sex, marital status, committee and work assignments, race, and college
background training.

When these primary group relationships develop, they play an important
role in the complex group structure. These primary groups become the
major source of communications. They also solidify opinions and stances
on common problems. In a sense these groups establish a united front on
common issues and may become a source of major opposition to the
school administration or be solicited as a major means of cooperation.

The Professional Organizations

Many of the earlier studies of the organizations of school faculties were
inclined to depict the formal organization only as that sanctioned and
controlled by the school administration. This approach usually neglected the
professional associations that form a growing area of faculty influence.
The number and strength of these associations no longer allow one to
consider these as either informal or extralegal organizations. Well over
five hundred national and regional associations are identified in the *Education Directory* published by the U.S. Office of Education, and the number
of state, intrastate, and local associations is legion. All of these professional
groups are conscious that there is power in numbers, and faculty members
facing the facts of contemporary life realize that teachers will not get the
attention and resources they want at the local, state, and national levels
nor even a decent hearing about possibilities and needs, unless they can
speak through organizations. Thus, a typical teacher belongs to a local,
state, and national educational association or union and in addition usually
a professional organization related to a specialty such as Industrial Arts,
English, Reading, Curriculum, Child Development, and so on. Through these
professional organizations the teacher has a way of getting into communication with, and influencing the course of events on the larger state
and national scene as well as the local school district.

An administrator dealing with a given faculty member then deals with

[20] Richard A. Gorton, *Conflict, Controversy and Crisis in School Administration and
Supervision* (Dubuque, Iowa: Wm. C. Brown Company, 1972); Olive Banks, *The
Sociology of Education* (New York: Schocken Books, 1968), Chapter 9; Laurence
Iannaconne, "An Approach to the Informal Organization of the School," in *Behavorial
Science & Educational Administration*, Samuel E. Griffiths, Ed. (Chicago: University
of Chicago Press, 1964), pp. 233–242.

a many-sided individual professionally. Disregarding the nonprofessional influence of the community, each teacher is a person influenced by the general educational organization, a specialty educational organization, a primary education group locally, and by individual professional concerns in the classroom.

The strong development of professional organizations has led to the national movement of legalizing a professional association to negotiate for teachers. As teachers have gained strength and obtained a larger share in decision making, school administrators have found that they must accommodate themselves accordingly and alter their pattern of decision making. This is creating a re-examination of administrative and managerial rights and a re-evaluation of faculty participation in the decision making process. It is possible that the increasing power of teachers through collective negotiations could alter the entire concept of school administration. Certainly the process has violated numerous time-honored administrative principles and eroded away some normally accepted prerogatives of administrators.

Education and Resource Networks

In viewing the school and its communities a theory that holds strong promise for schools in their relation to communities is the resource network theory.[21] This concept follows procedures recommended by typical school community relations experts whereby a network of various publics is identified to further support communications and relationships. Sarason and his colleagues place emphasis on the relations between the community and its resources, including the school, but they add a very important ingredient. They add the planned exchange and bartering of resources as the key to establishing a productive network for action. Their study and reflections led to the conclusion that agencies must accept the fact of limited resources. To achieve goals under this limited resources concept would require the exchange of resources with others who had needed resources; this in turn would create a more satisfying sense of community. Agencies and institutions need each other and their resources in order to achieve their goals. Accepting this, they then establish a network of agencies that would mutually contribute to each other's resource needs through ideas and resource exchange. This sounds simple and it's difficult to disagree with the idea but it isn't that simple, mainly because each agency is thinking essentially of itself and the resources for it to achieve its goals. They don't really comprehend that they can multiply their

[21] See Seymour B. Sarason, et al., *Human Services and Resource Networks* (San Francisco, Calif.: Jossey-Bass Publishers, 1977).

resources countless times by establishing a network with other agencies rather than getting money to do their own thing. To quote Sarason: [22]

> The stance of the school is typical of all agencies: Additional resources are needed, but it requires money to obtain them or to be the basis of an exchange of resources. As a consequence, agencies spend a good deal of time trying to get more money, in effect competing with each other for these additional financial resources. And that stance makes it inordinately difficult, and in practice almost impossible, to do three related things: to confront (if only as a possibility) that resources are and will be limited; to examine critically the accepted relationship between problems and solutions; and *to figure out possible ways in which agencies can learn to exchange resources in mutually beneficial ways and without finances* being a prerequisite for discussion or the basis of exchange.

Sarason in his study raises an issue that has bothered the authors for many years. Both have been administrators in a variety of educational levels. It seems any time something different or something extra needs to be done it can't be done without more staff, more supplies and equipment, and therefore more money. It is the unusual situation when educators can say, "Look, we can't have any more money—let's figure out how we can solve this problem or accomplish a solution with the resources we have plus utilizing other resources within the community."

Most agencies as they see the need for more resources and attempt to get them cannot help but feel the sense of competition for funds. They feel alone and beleaguered rather than a part of a mutually supportive community family. The key, according to Sarason, is to forget new money and work as hard on working with fellow human agencies, to establish a network where resources can be bartered. "Let's work together! How can we help you? How can you help us? Let's exchange in a meaningful, efficient way."

One of the movements utilizing much of this theory is the community school movement. The building principal is a key to the leadership in developing a community school.

The Community School [23]

A community school is a school with a much broader vision than most schools in that it attempts to involve itself fully with the entire community as well as with children of school age. With this expanded viewpoint it accepts two major functions:

---

[22] Ibid., p. 21.

[23] The authors are indebted to Patrick B. Mullarney, Associate Professor of Education at the University of Connecticut, for providing valuable assistance in writing this section. Dr. Mullarney is also Director of the New England Center for Community Education.

First, it is responsible for the formal education of children and youth assigned to it but in performing this function it:

1. recognizes the educational process extends beyond the walls of the formally organized public school and works in close cooperation with other community agencies, institutions, and organizations in the development of its educational program;
2. makes a special effort to develop and use the resources of the community as a part of the educational facilities of the school;
3. encourages parents and citizens to be partners in the education of children and establishes organized ways to involve them.

Second, it accepts responsibility for serving as catalytic agent to provide the structure for the continuing education of adults and to rally the resources (people and institutions) of the community in an organized attempt to improve the welfare of people in the community. In performing this function it:

1. believes the power of the educational process can be used to solve problems related to the needs and interest of that community by the appropriate use of available resources and through the encouragement of proper organizing and planning.
2. accepts the philosophy that the schools belong to all the people and that as a nonpartisan, nonsectarian, classless agency it can serve as a common meeting place for the resolution of problems, many of which may be highly controversial.
3. accepts the idea that there is a growing need for life-long education in our society and the formally organized public school is the logical agency to provide the leadership in meeting this need.
4. attempts to develop a faculty who has empathy and understanding for community participation and expertise in working with adults as well as children.

Defined and described in this way, community education becomes almost an operational model of the resource network theory in that it provides a process for people in a community to assess their needs and existing resources, and meet those needs by sharing those resources in an efficient and effective manner to build a better school and a better community.[24]

The heart of this model becomes the citizens who play a significant role in the decision-making process. The school is usually centrally located in a community and is often the largest tax-supported institution. The community school can serve as a focal point for many community resource and human service agencies in providing client-centered programs. Com-

[24] For a more thorough discussion on the community school read Maurice F. Seay et al., *Community Education: A Developing Concept* (Midland, Mich.: Pendall Publishing, 1974).

munity school programs should be identified by some sort of needs assessment, planned with citizen advisory council input, and implemented in the school that has the space as well as the human and physical resources. Remember that the school facilities belong to all of the people in the community. With this concept, people form a partnership with the educational leaders in determining how their school as a community resource will be used.

The community school principal is an important person in the management of this broadened educational process and program. The principal is not only responsible for the instructional program for the usual school-age students in the attendance area, but also must encourage and facilitate educational growth and service opportunities for all residents in the community. To provide these programs without the cooperation and direct participation of other agencies and experts in the community would not be reasonable nor cost effective. The principal must be a skillful manager in this operation. He or she must orchestrate the community and the school resources so that proper expertise and products are made available to clients/consumers in the community. There must be cooperative planning that includes the administration, teachers, students, industrial and business persons, human service agencies, local government personnel, and citizens in general. The community school, as an open system with shared decision making, encourages the multi-agency or network approach.

Through cooperation community-wide duplication of facilities, personnel, finances, equipment, supplies, and other goods and services can be avoided. In addition, community schools and the multi-agency approach enhance the total instructional program and provide additional opportunities for the school staff to know the whole child. With a better understanding of the child's home and community environments, the teachers and administrators will have additional information to provide an appropriate instructional program for that child.

To effectively manage a community school and facilitate resource exchange, the principal must have a leadership orientation toward group action and participative decision making and promote a climate in the school that is open and receptive to community input. He/she must be the type of person who can serve as a catalyst who can stimulate citizens to plan and organize activities based upon the needs of the community. The principal must work with all facets of the community to provide an atmosphere where the community feels welcome in its facility and a communication vehicle for a free flow of information. The role of the community school principal is a very special one and demands broad conceptual, technical, and human skills. Traditional principals may not embrace this role opportunity. To maintain a lighted schoolhouse is almost a twenty-four-hour job. But, perhaps this is the only way we can give schools back to the people.

The principal cannot be expected to administer and manage the community school program alone. The principal should have an assistant to administer some of the daily functions in the school and a community education coordinator to assume responsibility for programming community activities in the school during the afternoons, evenings, and weekends —beyond what would be considered the "normal" school hours. This person normally may be a school employee; however, he or she may be paid by a variety of financial sources (agencies) in the community. This is part of the sharing effort.

We stressed in Chapter 1 how educators had often unconsciously created the myth that the school can lead the way to the good life for all society. The true community school does not fall into this trap. It does assume a pro active role in the improvement of society and the community but it realizes it can't "go it alone." The community school is based on cooperation and colleagueship. It attempts to serve as a catalyst. It attempts to identify, improve, and utilize leadership wherever it may be—in school or out. As an important public institution it says to the people, "This is your school. Use it as your community center. As educators let us work with you to identify important goals of our society, then let us work with you hand in hand to meet those goals."

Summary

The school is a social system within several larger systems and in turn is composed of several social systems such as students, teachers, noninstructional staff. The concept of community involvement within and between the school and its community is rapidly becoming lost. The principal is in a key position to help to turn this trend around. The development of a working school government of, by, and for the people of the local school community is a realistic approach to teaching citizenship in a participatory society. The local school can be more responsive to community and individual needs resulting from real input mechanisms if a degree of budget and program freedom is provided. The local school must become a more open social system if it is to realize its goal of serving the community that supports it.

For Further Thought

1. Discuss the relationship, if any, between these statements: "Citizenship can be taught effectively without providing participatory 'citizenship' to immature learners" and "We learn best by doing."

2. How may the principal maintain anticipatory awareness of changes in key subsystems that will affect the total system?
3. What advantages and disadvantages may be realized when administrators use opinion polls to find out what students and adults think of their schools? Give specific examples.
4. If a school is a good school, is a public relations program needed? Is the PR problem of a school comparable to the PR problem of a local business? Are the terms "school publicity," "public relations program," and "school communications" synonymous?
5. Should youth and their parents be encouraged to think of educational opportunity as a right, a privilege, or an obligation?
6. Do the schools with which you are familiar give adequate attention to the major problems in our society about which the citizen should be informed? Discuss.
7. Review the extent of utilization of community resources in the teaching–learning process of a typical school. Can you propose a plan for increasing school–community interaction in instructional activities?
8. Is it really possible for modern-day schools to be an interactive, responsive part of the community? Some educational experts claim we should move even more rapidly away from the provincial influence of the local community and strengthen the influence of the professional educator. Discuss.
9. In a school with which you are familiar review the amount of active student participation in making curricular and co-curricular decisions. Is student involvement meaningful? Is there a relationship between the amount of involvement and the students' "feeling" for the school?

Chapter 4 Theory, Research, Principles—
A Basis for Action

The "how-to-do-it" approach to the study of educational administration has been a popular mode of training, for the principal as well as the superintendent. It is a simple formula: Ask the "old hand" (the outwardly successful principal) how does he/she do it or how did he/she do it.

This approach to the study of school administration, called by some descriptive, has always been popular but it was the essential method of study and training for educational administrators through the thirties.

Then, in the late thirties and early forties, as the teaching of educational administration became popular in major colleges and universities of the country, a few of the professors in the field began to realize there were few pat answers that could apply to all situations. Our society was ever changing. Each school organization was a dynamically different system consisting of different personalities and combinations of different people who were living in different communities with schools administered and operated by different executives with different styles.

Confounding variables were nullifying the pat "how-to-do-it" answer. In the ensuing search for some universal verities that could give direction to administrative action, several professors of educational administration—notably Arthur B. Moehlman of the University of Michigan [1] and Paul Mort of Teachers College, Columbia University [2]—advanced the idea that although there are few pat answers there is a body of knowledge about our culture essentially derived from the literature of behavioral sciences. Properly distilled, this knowledge could be combined with logically developed purposes of education to form principles to test the wisdom of administrative action. Both expressed the point of view that principles and the technical aspects of the administrative job are two mutually supporting approaches

[1] Arthur B. Moehlman, *School Administration, Its Development, Principles and Function* (Boston: Houghton Mifflin Company, 1951).
[2] Paul R. Mort and Donald H. Ross, *Principles of School Administration*, 2nd Ed. (New York: McGraw-Hill, 1957).

to studying administration and they presented their textual material in that mode.

Moehlman's and Mort's books were used by the great majority of graduate schools throughout the country. Their principles approach was essentially functional in that they did gather into logical continuity many concepts of administrative action that had wide popular professional acceptance and others that were imperfectly organized. However, the roots of the principles were based in the culture and well grounded in the political, social, and economic disciplines.

As the study of educational administration began to thrive and advanced training of principals and superintendents became more important, both the practitioner and the professor realized an even more scientific, analytic basis was needed to give direction to administrative action. In the face of a rapidly changing growing society the principles appeared to be too value laden and general. However, they *were* developed from a theoretical base that did point the direction to a new movement in the study of educational administration.

Enter the Theory Movement

The theory movement in educational administration started in the fifties. The ground was prepared by professors such as Moehlman and Mort. The seeds were planted by the Cooperative Program in Educational Administration.[3] It was brought to flower by the National Conference of Professors of Educational Administration.[4] It bore fruit under the leadership of the University Council of Educational Administration.[5] The study of the contribution of various people representing and working through these organizations is interesting but too long to be told here. The important point as far as school administration is concerned is that through emphasis on research, interdisciplinary study (particularly the behavioral sciences) and hard comparative analysis the study of educational administration began to move from the folklore and testimonial stage toward a more scientific and disciplined base.

This does not mean educational administration developed its own researchers and theoreticians. Despite the concentration on theory and the amount of talk and writing about it, one has difficulty singling out professors

[3] Hollis A. Moore, Jr., *Studies in School Administration: A Report on the CPEA* (Washington, D.C.: American Association of School Administrators, 1957).

[4] National Conference of Professors of Educational Administration, *Administrative Behavior in Education* (The Conference, 1957).

[5] University Council of Educational Administration, A Consortium of Universities Having Educational Administration Programs, The Ohio State University, Columbus, Ohio.

of educational administration who can be considered researchers and theoreticians in their own right. However, a major contribution of these professors has been applying the knowledge, research, and theory from sociology, psychology, political science, business, and the military to the practice of educational administration.

Administrative Theory

Administrative theory may be defined in many ways. Much of the literature on theory in educational administration is devoted to arguments about its definition. We don't want to join these arguments. We define theory as systematically organized information and knowledge with a series of assumptions or hypotheses devised to help analyze, predict, or otherwise explain the specific nature and/or behavior of people and their organization.

Figure 4.1 presents a brief historical review of organization and management theory as contributed generally by behavioral scientists and thinkers over the years. As with many movements it is dangerous to divide it into specific thrusts and name particular contributors because so many people were involved and there is so much overlapping. Generally, however, through the years at least four major thrusts seem to emerge relative to the theory of management of people and their organizations: managerial efficiency, organizations as social systems, human relations, problem solving and decision theory.

Managerial Efficiency

The organization efficiency movement has been classified by a prominent labor leader as the movement that attempted to attain organizational goals without concern for means being used or people involved. If we were to accept that statement at its true value, Machiavelli could be considered the true "father" of the movement. As it is Frederick W. Taylor is considered the "Father of Scientific Management." [6] Best known for his "time and motion studies," he pioneered in the application of the scientific method to the problems of management.[7] His recurring theme was that management was a true science based on clearly defined principles and laws. Even today Taylor's ideas as revised and adopted by other students in the field form the basis for much of business and industries efficiency control procedures.

[6] William H. Roe, *School Business Management* (New York: McGraw-Hill, 1961), pp. 62–63.
[7] Frederick W. Taylor, *Scientific Management* (New York: Harper, 1911).

FIGURE 4.1. Development of organization and management theory.

Date line	Management efficiency	Human relations	Organization and social systems	Problem solving decision theory
1900	Marshall	Mather	Weber	
1910	Taylor Fayol Gilbreths			
1920	Gantt	Meyer		
1930	Mooney Gulick	Mayo Whitehead	Lynd and Lynd Barnard	
	Urwick	Roethlisberger		
1940	Armed Forces Dean	Follett Lewin Lippett	Parsons Warner	Barnard Simon Armed Forces
1950	Van Neumann Dale	Maslow Nat'l Training Laboratory Rogers	Hunter Homans Maslow Argyris	Tannenbaum Bross RAND Experiments Simon
1960	Koontz Hitch	Bradford Likert	Merton Simon Getzels Guba Likert	March Cyert

1970 — 1980 — 2000 A.D.

Shared decision making · Organizational development · PERT · Systems analysis · PPBS · Conflict management · MBO · Resource networks · Accountability · Computerized decision making · Teaming · Administration by consensus · Organizational change · Futurism

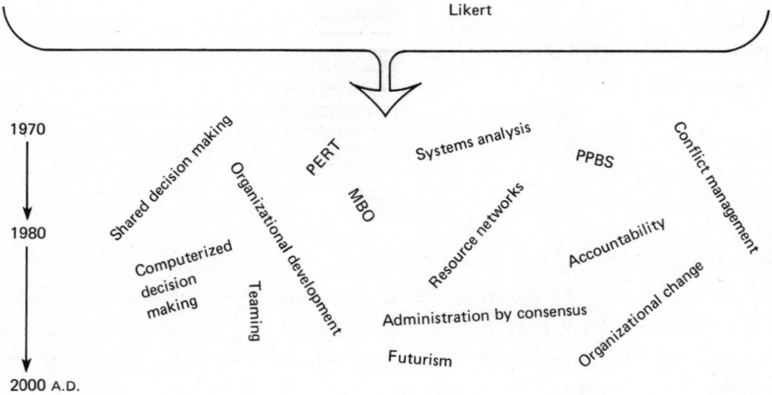

Fayol, Gulick, and Urwick analyzed management as a process.[8, 9] Their work eventually resulted in the refinement of such well-known concepts as unity of command, span of control, line and staff, scaler chain, delegation of responsibility, authority, power, and morale. Of course, one should not overlook the identification of the logical functions of the executive under

[8] Henri Fayol, Administration Industrielle et Generale, Translated by Constance Storrs, *General and Industrial Management* (London: Pitman, 1949).

[9] Luther H. Gulick and Lyndall F. Urwick (Eds.), *Papers on the Science of Administration* (New York: Institute of Public Administration, 1937).

the familiar acronym PODSCORB, (Planning, Organizing, Directing, Staffing, Coordinating, Reporting, and Budgeting). The Armed Forces and the United States Government furthered the rationalization of the formal organization process during and immediately following World War II. During this period, many who later became executives in business, industry, government, and education went through Armed Forces and government-sponsored management training programs based on these concepts.

Many authors are inclined to imply the scientific movement died out in the thirties and forties. The movement is still with us—alive and healthy but with the addition of the computer as its basic tool. Its approach has been somewhat diluted by the human relations movement but traces of Taylor, Fayol, Gulick, and Urwick can be found in research and theory of business, industry, and government. Practically every school of business administration requires the theory of scientific management as a basic core of knowledge. Even in the field of education [10] it is not too difficult to trace the influence of these early pioneers to Management by Objectives (MBO), Program Planning and Budgeting Systems (PPBS), Program Evaluation and Review Techniques (PERT), Operations Research, Critical Path Planning, Systems Analysis along with many of our evaluation and accountability procedures.[11]

Organization and Social Systems

Max Weber, a German sociologist, was one of the early students of organizations.[12] He was concerned with the general unreliability of human judgment and therefore advocated the depersonalized organization. He created a theory of bureaucracy that encouraged large-scale organizations to formalize and systematize their activities to the point of minimizing human error. Talcott Parsons studied Weber's work and early in his career even translated some of his writings.[13] However, Talcott Parsons went well beyond Weber by putting people in systems. He developed a theory of social objects that covered a wide range of options. He contended action is a process occurring between two components of the system, the actor and the situation. He then established five sets of pattern variables as a

[10] For an interesting account of how the business and industrial efficiency model influenced educational administration, read Raymond E. Callahan, *Education and the Cult of Efficiency* (Chicago: University of Chicago Press, 1962).

[11] Many are inclined to class this as a separate movement often called the Systems Process Movement. There is some logic to this interpretation. Our approach is to consider computer systems as a continuation of the overall efficiency movement but to recognize that Social Systems theory and Human Relations theory had an impact on these developments.

[12] Julien Freund, *The Sociology of Max Weber* (New York: Random House, 1968).

[13] Max Weber, *The Theory of Social and Economic Organizations,* translated by Talcott Parsons (New York: Free Press, 1974).

basis for classifying the action. Although Parson's work has often been controversial because it lacked a research base, he can be credited with stimulating more intellectual discourse on the nature of social systems than any other contemporary writer or theoretician.[14]

In a generalized way, one should not overlook the contributions early community studies made to the developing theories on organizations and social systems. These studies provided fascinating descriptions of formal and informal relationships of people in the community in addition to how power structures developed and how public schools and other public agencies were influenced by community leaders.[15]

Chester Barnard is an example of a businessman (Chief Executive of New Jersey Bell Telephone) who made a strong contribution to the theory of organization and administration. His classic book, *The Functions of the Executive,* set forth a number of theories on cooperation and incentives in organization. Barnard believed the formal and informal organization were intertwined. His central theme was that the vitality of an organization lies in the willingness of individuals to contribute to the cooperative system.[16]

As the human relations movement was coming into its own it had a decided influence on psychologists and sociologists and many began to investigate the person in the organization. Bakke and Argyris proposed the "fusion theory." This theory was essentially that it was the responsibility of leadership to "fuse" the individual and organization to the point where they both obtain optimum self-actualization.[17, 18]

A. H. Maslow [19] suggests that the force that causes people to stay and work within an organization is a hierarchy of needs that move in order of satisfaction from physiological requirements to security to social needs to esteem to autonomy to self-actualization. As needs are met at lower levels, higher-level needs emerge, thus supporting the idea that man is a continuously wanting being. A study of Maslow's theory indicates that if behavior is to be motivated, it must be done so at the level of a need that is currently unsatisfied. Stated differently, a need that is satisfied is no longer a need, therefore, is not effective as a motivator in settings with which educational leaders are ordinarily concerned.

[14] Talcott Parsons, *The Structure of Social Action* (New York: McGraw-Hill, 1973); Talcott Parsons and Edward A. Shils, *Towards a General Theory of Action* (Cambridge, Mass.: Harvard University Press, 1951).

[15] For example see Robert S. and Helen M. Lynd, *Middletown in Transition* (New York: Harcourt, 1937); William L. Warner et al., *Democracy in Jonesville* (New York: Harper, 1949); Floyd Hunter, *Community Power Structure* (Chapel Hill: University of North Carolina, 1953).

[16] Chester I. Barnard, *The Functions of the Executive* (Cambridge: Harvard University Press, 1938).

[17] E. W. Bakke, *The Fusion Process* (New Haven: Labor and Management Center Yale University, 1955).

[18] Chris Argyris, *Personality and Organization* (New York: Harper, 1957).

[19] A. H. Maslow, *Motivation and Personality* (New York: Harper and Row, 1954).

Figure 4.2. Hierarchy of motivational needs.

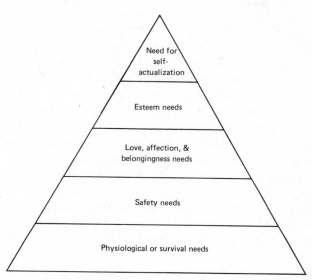

HIERARCHY OF MOTIVATIONAL NEEDS

A.H. Maslow

Need for self-actualization

Esteem needs

Love, affection, & belongingness needs

Safety needs

Physiological or survival needs

Adapted from: *Maslow's Hierarchy of Needs,* presented by Salenger Educational Media, 1635 Twelfth St., Santa Monica, CA 90404.

McGregor's Theory X and Theory Y attempted to explain certain motivational factors that are important to the operation of an organization.[20] While one is the antithesis of the other, the acceptance of one or the other will certainly affect the way the administrator behaves in an organization.

Theory X postulates that the average human being dislikes work and will avoid it if possible; thus, he must be controlled, directed, and implicitly or explicitly threatened so he will work to achieve the organization's goals.

Theory Y postulates the opposite in that work is satisfying; therefore, a person will direct and control himself if he is committed to an organization's goals. The best rewards toward achieving commitment are self-actualization and ego satisfaction.

J. W. Getzels and E. C. Guba are two social scientists who applied social systems research and theory development to the field of educational administration.[21] Their studies of role and personality as key factors in social behavior, power, and leadership are quoted widely in textbooks and made

[20] Douglas M. McGregor, *The Human Side of Enterprise* (New York: McGraw-Hill Book Company, 1960), pp. 35–57.
[21] J. W. Getzels and Egon C. Guba, "Social Behavior and the Administrative Process," *School Review,* 65 (1957).

an important contribution to understanding the behavior of the school administrator.[22]

The study and theorizing of organizations as social systems continues at an even accelerated pace today.[23] But in the early sixties a new term "Organization development" began to appear with increasing frequency in the administrative theory literature.[24] Organizational development is a planned organization-wide effort by the central administration to increase the *esprit de corps* and effectiveness of the organization through particular inservice and development programs that utilize behavioral science knowledge. Beckhard identified important elements in operational development that seem to match much of the rationale established by the Educational Leaders Consortium for emphasizing administrative teams: (1) The basic unit for improvement emphasis is the team; (2) encourage trust and confidence by more communications and collaboration between and across levels of the organizations; (3) locate decision making at the new information source; (4) organization goals must be continually revised and adapted to units and subunits of the organizations and activities and controls flexibly adapted to these goals; (5) people affected by change must be allowed to plan and participate through the change process.[25]

Human Relations

The human relations movement ushered in a consideration for people and their welfare as an important ingredient in the study of management and organization. Strangely enough, prior to the time this movement gained real strength (and unfortunately even today) an employee was too often considered only on the basis of his/her contribution to the organization. The person's personal welfare along with external and internal motivations were largely overlooked.

One of the early pioneers in the United States in helping to improve the lot of the worker was Lemuel Shattuck, who was instrumental in establishing the American Statistical Society in 1839. Much later, William Mather and C. S. Meyers in England made strong contributions in researching working conditions and their relationship to productivity. Mather experimented with reducing the work week and Meyers directed a number of

[22] For further discussion on the school and community as social systems see Ch. 3.
[23] See Ch. 3 for some recent developments.
[24] Ralph B. Kimbrough and Michael Y. Nunnery, *Educational Administration* (New York: MacMillan, 1976), p. 129.
[25] See Richard Beckhard, *Organization Development: Strategies and Models* (Reading, Mass.: Addison-Wesley, 1969); Freemont E. Kast and James Rosenzweig, *Organization and Management: A Systems Approach* (New York: McGraw-Hill, 1974); Wendell L. French and Cecil H. Bell, Jr., *Organization Development* (Englewood Cliffs, N.J.: Prentice-Hall, 1973); Robert R. Blake and Jane S. Moulton, *The Managerial Grid* (Houston, Texas: Gulf, 1964).

research studies on worker fatigue and general welfare through the National Institute of Industrial Psychology established in 1921.[26, 27, 28]

Mary Parker Follett was one of the first to theorize human relations as a key ingredient in administration and management. She believed developing and maintaining dynamic and harmonious relationships within an organization were fundamental to the success of that organization. Further, she considered conflict and controversy normal and properly directed should be accepted as a "process by which socially valuable differences register themselves for all concerned." [29] Actually, Ms. Follett's early writings had little impact on the times. Today they are considered classics by many students in the field.[30]

It was not until the late thirties that the studies by Mayo, Whitehead, Roethlisberger, and others helped conceptualize human relations as an important theory to be considered. As a result of these studies *people* became really important in management. Known as the Hawthorne Studies, or as the Western Electric Experiment, the studies showed the necessity for the development of a new and more disciplined approach to work motivation and dealing with people in the organization.

The major report of the results came out in 1939 in Roethlisberger's and Dickson's *Management and the Worker*.[31] Other books based on the Hawthorne studies are *Human Problems of an Industrial Civilization*,[32] *The Industrial Worker*,[33] and *Management and Morale*.[34]

The implications drawn from the Hawthorne studies were enlarged and promoted by a great variety of researchers and scholars. A number of the studies on human motivation had strong human relations ties even though they were conducted by social scientists focusing on organizations in social systems.

In the thirties the main thrust of the human relations movement was centered at the University of Iowa, where Kurt Lewin was experimenting

[26] William G. Monahan, *Theoretical Dimensions of Educational Administration* (New York: MacMillan Publishing Company, Inc., 1975).

[27] Bertram Gross, *The Managing of Organizations*, (New York: MacMillan Publishing Company, Inc., 1964).

[28] Roe, op. cit., pp. 42–43.

[29] Mary Parker Follett, *Creative Experience* (London: Longmans and Green, 1924), p. 300.

[30] Mary Parker Follett, *Dynamic Administration: The Collected Papers of Mary Parker Follett*, Henry C. Metcalf and Lyndall F. Urwick, Eds. (New York: Harper, 1941).

[31] Fritz J. Roethlisberger and William Dickson, *Management and the Worker* (Cambridge, Mass.: Harvard University Press, 1939).

[32] Elton Mayo, *Human Problems of an Industrial Civilization* (New York: The MacMillan Company, 1933).

[33] Thomas N. Whitehead, *The Industrial Worker* (Cambridge, Mass.: Harvard University Press, 1938).

[34] Fritz J. Roethlisberger, *Management and Morale* (Cambridge, Mass.: Harvard University Press, 1939).

with and developing interesting psychological theories on leadership and human behavior. These theories attracted an almost fanatical following of both theorists and practitioners devoted to group dynamics and human relations. One major focus of the movement was through the National Training Laboratories at Bethel, Maine, established in 1947. This laboratory's major role was experimentation with human interaction individually and in groups along with the development of technique that could be used in the training of individuals in group dynamics. The laboratory soon became very popular as a source of training for leaders in business, industry, and education through T-groups, encounter groups, and similar sensitivity-training sessions. Contributors to this movement are too numerous to mention here.[35] It suffices to say that the movement ushered in an important alternative to the traditional notion of authority from the top to the bottom. Its unabashed emphasis was on the importance of people within organizations and their relationships individually and collectively. This was expressed both theoretically and operationally through such terms as (1) shared decision making, (2) group authority, (3) collegiality, (4) democratic leadership, (5) participating leadership, (6) morale, (7) shared authority, (8) group dynamics, (9) group interaction.

Problem Solving and Decision Theory

Because much of the job of the principal is involved with problem solving and decision making, theory relative to the area is extremely important.[36] The generally recognized steps of problem solving are:

1. Awareness of and identification of the problem.
2. Definition and limitation of the problem in terms of the goals of the enterprise.
3. Determination of who should be involved in the problem-solving process and how.
4. Collection of appropriate data specific to the problem.
5. Formulation and selection of possible solutions.
6. Prediction of consequences of possible solutions.
7. Identification of preferred solution with rationale for selection. (Also identify alternative solutions in priority order.)
8. Putting the preferred solution into effect.
9. Establishing evaluative process for determining success.[37]

[35] Leland Bradford, Jack R. Gibb and Kenneth Benne (Eds.), *T-Group Theory and Laboratory Method* (New York: Wiley, 1964).

[36] A problem may be simply defined as a state of affairs that creates dissatisfaction in an organization. A decision is that action that is taken to resolve that dissatisfaction.

[37] The steps in problem solving have been discussed so widely in the general literature that it is impossible to credit specific authors to these steps. Although not clearly identified as such, Fredrick Taylor and Henry L. Gantt used these steps as the basis

Chester Barnard was one of the first to theorize relative to the decision-making process.[38] He is most perceptive in his observation that often the executive will create unnecessary problems by attempting to solve a problem or make a decision inappropriately. He proposed that there is a fine art in decision making that consists of (1) not deciding questions not now pertinent, (2) not deciding prematurely, (3) not making decisions that can't be effectuated, (4) not making decisions others should make.

S. J. Bross's contribution to decision-making theory within social systems was to observe that people within organizations and subsystems of organizations are affected by varying degrees (positively and negatively) by a particular decision. One of the administrator's responsibilities in relation to decision making is to identify the various individuals and groups affected by a decision and to analyze the intensity of their feelings on the basis of whether the decision is favorable or unfavorable to them. Appropriately the effective administrator will stand ready to make necessary adjustments based on group feelings when a decision is put into effect.[39]

Herbert A. Simon theorized that decision making is the heart of administration.[40] The task of deciding is truly as important as the task of doing; therefore, principles of organization must be established that insure correct decision-making processes.[41]

All people in the organization make decisions of one type or another; thus, there should be horizontal specialization in decision making as well as vertical specialization. Simon advocated that regular routinized channels be identified for arriving at decisions no matter their source in the organizational hierarchy. These would be called programmed decisions and he attempted to develop these as part of a management science.

March and Simon identified problems or breakdowns in the standard decision-making process as creating "conflict." [42] This breakdown causes an individual or group to experience difficulty in selecting action alternatives. Conflict management is an important area of inquiry in the management field. It is definitely related to decision making and how different goals and purposes will affect the type of decision of an organization—indeed, how the decision of an organization can affect the outside environment.[43]

---

for the development of scientific management techniques. Several in educational administration have advanced theoretical knowledge in this area, including Daniel E. Griffiths's "Administration Is Decision Making" and John K. Hemphill's "Administration as Problem Solving," both chapters in Andrew W. Halpin (Ed.), *Administrative Theory in Education* (New York: Macmillan, 1967) and Daniel L. Stuffelbeam et al., *Educational Evaluation and Decision Making* (Itasca, Ill.: Peacock, 1971).

[38] Barnard, op. cit., p. 194.
[39] Irwin D. J. Bross, *Design For Decision* (New York: Macmillan, 1953).
[40] Herbert A. Simon, *Administrative Behavior* (New York: Macmillan, 1950).
[41] Herbert A. Simon, *The New Science of Management Decisions* (New York: Harper, 1960).
[42] James G. March and Herbert A. Simon, *Organizations* (New York: Wiley, 1958).
[43] Chris Argyris, *Personality and Organizations* (New York: Harper, 1957).

The use of quantitative techniques in the field of decision making has become a productive area of theoretical inquiry. As scientists are becoming more sophisticated in the use of the computer, with the possibility for storage, mix, comparison, and retrieval of data almost unlimited, the possibility of its use in organization, management, and administration are just beginning to be realized.[44]

Research and Theory

In the development and testing of these theories a large body of research has accumulated. This research can often be as good or better a source of direction for the principal as the theory itself. However, variables relating to the study will often be much different when applied to a school situation or an educational problem. It is important for the student of educational administration to recognize this.

Unfortunately, very little solid long-term research has been conducted that applies specifically to organization and administration of schools. Reviewing research activity in educational administration one is elated to find excellent elementary research (theoretical, experimental, quantitative) represented by doctoral dissertations over the past ten years. At the same time one is deflated when further investigation reveals very little continuation of this research by the doctoral recipients and almost no follow-up and/or long-term research by the educational administration professor.[45] When considering the application of industrial- and business-focused theory and research to the school one must be very conscious of the difference between the school as an organization and the business, industrial, or military organization. In attempting to fit schools into the organizational framework of business and industry one fails to account for what is special about educational organizations. Actually there is no organization like the public school.[46] Although the school has certain aspects in common with many other bureaucratic organizations, it should be observed that in the school the bureaucracy exists essentially in central administration. A school district does have a definition of staff roles, a hierarchial ordering of offices. It

[44] Time Share Corporation, *The Computer in Educational Decision Making: A Guide for School Administrators* (The Corporation, P.O. Box 974, Hanover, N.H., 1978).

[45] Roald F. Campbell and L. Jackson Newell, *A Study of Professors of Educational Administration* (Columbus, Ohio: University Council for Educational Administration, 1973).

[46] Many would say the public school corresponds with hospital organization. Actually there is a great difference. The hospital does have a large professional staff but there is a very recognizable hierarchy in the staff relating to business administration, medical doctors, nurses, technicians, practical nurses, and so on that is much different than the school. In particular they do not have a social system similar to the teacher and the classroom, which represents the largest number of people and is the place where the major purposes of the school take place.

operates by specific rules, procedures, and schedules but the main bureaucracy and hierarchy are in the central office whereas the controlled schedules and procedures in the local schools themselves are really mechanisms for coordinating large groups of people and directing them in classrooms. They are *not* really in control of the classroom itself where the primary action of the school, teaching, and learning take place. Viewed in this way the school is a coordinated system of diverse forms of organization.[47] The true activity of the school is to teach and to learn. These activities take place in the classroom. Here the teacher is the decision maker and all forms of subcultures, including the student subculture, has almost as much effect on the operation as the central administration.

In the nonprofessionally staffed organization it is accepted that the administrative hierarchy dominates the direction of operation. Constant supervision is exercised to assure precise implementation of operational procedures. In the school situation the teacher is the key executive in the classroom. Direct supervision seldom takes place or at most, two or three times a year. Therefore, control at the most important level of operation is almost impossible to realize.

Theory—A Guide to Action?

The preceding brief review of the development of organization and management theory should not give the impression there is a solid body of theory that can be applied by the school principal in the operation of his/her school. Such is not the case. Rather, what have been described are developing theories that warrant study and consideration by the practitioner.

The theory movement has done much to make the study of educational administration more scientific and disciplined but contrary to expectations a theory or set of theories did not emerge that could provide overall direction to administrative action. Professors were expecting too much of theory. It became an "in" concept associated with everything studied for over fifteen years. Gradually, however, the educational administration professor is becoming disappointed and is at a loss when an advocated theory does not stand up in replication studies and when clear relationships to educational practice cannot be shown. They had made a mistake by their failure to differentiate between the use of theory as a guide to action and use of theory as a tool of research. In the latter use, theory is imperative; in the former, it is an adjunct.

But what has this got to do with the school principal? If there is not a theory to provide a basis for action what is its use? Although theory admittedly has been oversold it still can be very useful for the administrator.

[47] Rodney Riffel, "The Paradoxical Nature of Educational Organization," *Research Bulletin,* Horace-Mann Lincoln Institute, Vol. 17, No. 1 (May, 1977).

The principal can compare himself/herself with the teacher as he/she faces twenty-five to thirty children in class and is faced with developing a teaching strategy that will permit the best conditions for learning. There are hundreds of learning theories that have been developed over the years by outstanding theoreticians and researchers, but few teachers will say, I accept completely this theory or that theory, and teach accordingly. Instead, the outstanding teacher tries any and all theories under a great variety of circumstances depending upon the students, personal style, experience, and the situation at that particular time. The same pattern can be followed by the school principal as he/she operates within the school. As a problem arises he/she will diagnose the situation, and then prescribe a course of action based upon knowledge of theory, research, values, and experience and then operate accordingly.

Should a Principal Have Principles?

As professors of educational administration became more immersed in the search for theories very little consideration was given to furthering the identification of principles (as developed by Moehlman and Mort) as guides to administrative action. In some cases they were merely forgotten because of preoccupation with theory. Others discarded them with the thought they were outmoded and too value laden.

We think this was a mistake. We think there is a place for principles for principals. Like practically everything else in our world principles can become outdated and they do have a cultural bias, but if one recognizes this and adjusts accordingly they will provide a consistent framework for action. We agree with Moehlman and Mort, there are value concepts generally agreed upon in our society that can be recognized as principles; there are logical purposes and procedures based upon educational philosophy and legal precedent that can be recognized as principles; and that there are practices that have been so thoroughly tested that they can be recognized as principles.

In addition, we believe each principal who becomes a student of his/her "art and craft" can develop his/her own personal administrative principles that are based upon personal experience, values, style, and knowledge of the field. These principles accepted by the principal provide him/her and the school with a consistency of action that in a sense makes up his/her administrative style.

The outstanding principal, then, is one who is a student of people, of organization, and of management. Through his/her knowledge of research and theory in these fields; through his/her understanding of himself or herself, values, skills, and experience, and through the acceptance of certain principles he/she develops a mode of action and guide on which to operate.

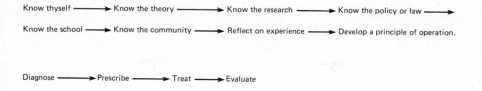

Know thyself ⟶ Know the theory ⟶ Know the research ⟶ Know the policy or law ⟶

Know the school ⟶ Know the community ⟶ Reflect on experience ⟶ Develop a principle of operation.

Diagnose ⟶ Prescribe ⟶ Treat ⟶ Evaluate

Principles—For Example

The following are examples of principles we believe can be accepted logically as a guide to administrative action. As one analyzes each principle one can see in varying degrees the influence of culture, political and educational philosophy, educational practice, and legal opinion. We believe there is enough universality in these principles at this time in our culture that they can have specific application to practice. We agree they can be outdated as our society changes; however, this does not decrease their value for here and now.[48]

1. There can be no invisible citizens. A child of four is just as much a citizen as a man or woman of thirty or ninety-three. Certainly the student in school is of an age where we should be particularly scrupulous in protection of constitutional freedoms. Care must be taken that we do not unconsciously teach youth to discount important principles of our government as mere platitudes.
2. The process of education extends beyond the walls of the formally organized classroom. Important learning takes place within the school community as within the classroom itself and every effort must be made to make this learning positive, effective, and productive.
3. The influences of forces outside of the school are so important that close cooperation with other agencies, institutions, and organizations is essential to the development of a sound educational program.
4. The American public school reflects the cultural milieu of which it is a part. It is responsible not only for conserving the useful past but also preparing the way for progress and change. A public institution especially must be attentive to the wishes of all people. However, because it cannot hope to please all people it will always be subject to criticisms.
5. The goals, objectives, and roles of the school must be effectively communicated to the various social systems of which it is a part. Those in responsibility must stand ready to work with these social systems to revise and adapt these goals, roles, and objectives to changing times.
6. Those affected by administrative action should be involved in the development of policy relative to action taken. Involvement will depend on the sophistication of the staff and upon varying circumstances.

[48] Other principles may be found listed throughout the book.

7. Policy should be in a state of continuous development and revision. Instead of operating on a visceral base from conflict to conflict, the administrative leader must be sensitive to changes in our social system that might require new policy or revision of policy.
8. The chief administrator and staff are responsible (in varying degrees) to and for all social systems and power elements that are a part of the institution.

For Further Thought

1. Utilizing human relations theory and the theory of social systems, make a case both for and against the principals' associations joining the educational leaders consortium.
2. In recent years some of the luster of the Hawthorne studies has been tarnished by the so-called "Hawthorne Effect." What is this? Could this be developed into a theory that might be important to the administrator? Discuss.
3. Chester Barnard in his book *The Functions of the Executive* asserts that many administrators create unnecessary problems through the decision-making process. Identify what he calls the fine art of decision making. Can this be developed into a theory or principle of administration?
4. What is the difference between theory of administration and principles of administration? Is it possible the failure to operationally define these terms creates confusion in our study of administration?
5. Through the process of systems analysis prove or disprove there is no organization quite like the public school. What implication does this have for the theory propounded by the educational administration professor that is essentially derived from business, industry, and government?
6. Review the principles propounded by Arthur B. Moehlman or Paul Mort. How many are appropriate today? What causes some of them to appear outdated?

Chapter 5   Organization

Our system of public schools is different from those developed in other countries of the world. In the United States education is a state function, not a national function. This philosophy, accepted by the men who shaped our Constitution, embedded in the constitutions of the states, and reinforced by court decision, has resulted in a nation with fifty different state school systems. Still further differences arise because the legislatures of practically all states have delegated the operation of schools to the local communities.[1] Thus, while all systems are not exactly alike, all have much in common. All twelve-grade school districts have a top administrative officer, usually known as the superintendent; all have some type of board of education or local administrative board; all schools have principals or head teachers; all school systems have some federal funding as well as state and local funds. Besides, all states have recognizable patterns of local school organization and school curricula; all work under certain minimum standards; and all attempt to provide a minimum of twelve years of schooling. These similarities exist because the educator–statesman has observed the developments and inventions of the systems around him/her and has adapted or used in his/her own system the good ideas of his/her neighbor.[2]

Even though this exchange of ideas has produced similarities in school patterns, little objective study has been undertaken to determine the best way to organize a school district within a given situation. Very little indeed has been done as far as the administration and management functions of a school are concerned. What services, controls, and powers should be provided? How should they be related to the instructional program, and how should each be organized to carry out its particular function? Opinions and practices vary widely. Among other phenomena; e.g., sensitivity to

---

[1] Few of our states have state systems in the strict sense; an exception would be Hawaii, and to some degree, Alaska, Delaware, and Nevada.

[2] Ch. 9, "Organizing to Improve Learning" expands on some of the universal similarities in school systems of the United States.

race, poverty, humanism, the phenomenal growth of cities and suburban fringe areas has revealed the inconsistencies and focused attention on an area of school administration that deserves serious study.

What Is an Organization?

Theodore Caplow defines an organization as follows: ". . . an organization is a social system that has an unequivocal collective identity, an exact roster of members, a program of activity, and procedures for replacing members." [3]

Caplow further clarifies this definition by giving certain illustrations:

> By the definition given at the outset, a family, a political party, a work crew, a criminal gang, a platoon or regiment or army, a bank, a board of commissioners, a government department, a neighborhood church, a labor management council would all be specimens of organization, as would a baseball team, an order of knighthood, a steel company, a bridge club, a government, a symphony orchestra, a college sorority, and a band of terrorists. If our assumptions about social organizations are valid, these very diverse entities will resemble each other in certain significant ways—for example, they will initially respond to an outside threat by increased solidarity and they will overestimate their own prestige compared to that of nearby organizations of the same type.
>
> It is also necessary for the purposes of this discussion to identify social systems that are *not* organizations. Many of these are enormously important, but they lack an organization's capacity for unified purposive activity. Among the more conspicuous non-organizations are races and ethnic groups (they have no programs), social classes (their collective identities are not unequivocal and their rosters not exact), cliques and play groups (they lack a collective identity), interest groups such as "liberals" or "old-fashioned conservatives" (they have no rosters). Solitary individuals and pairs are not considered to be organizations, since they do not display a network of interaction.
>
> The modern *nation* is not an organization, but the *state* is. The professions and the skilled trades differ from other occupations in being organized. A clique or a crowd may transform itself into an organization by adopting a collective identity and setting up a program. It also happens, although rarely, that an organization dissolves but leaves an informal group as its successor. [4]

Organization is the process of systematically establishing proper relationships within an administrative structure. [5] When a school administrative unit has been properly organized there are means at hand for getting things done; routines have been established for doing them; responsibility for

---

[3] Theodore Caplow, *Principles of Organization* (New York: Harcourt Brace Jovanovich, 1964), p. 1.

[4] Ibid., pp. 2–3.

[5] See also William M. Evan, *Organization Theory: Structures, Systems and Environment* (New York: Wiley-Interscience, 1976).

seeing that they are done has been fixed upon competent shoulders; and decisions are made by the most qualified members of the staff. In an effective organization things get done speedily and well. In an ineffective organization the unimportant things tend to get done and important ones tend to be slurred over and neglected; the decision-making process is carried out in a halting and often irresolute fashion; and eventually the constituted authorities may be bypassed and decisions made in obscurity by a power system that has taken over without a lawful assignment of responsibility.[6]

William H. Newman in his excellent book on administrative action uses an architectural analogy when he likens the haphazardly organized unit to the old New England farmhouse that grew without any general plan.[7] The first two or three rooms were constructed when the family was small and money was scarce. Then, as the family grew, a room was added here and a wing there until the house became a sprawling ill-matched structure, with foundations, floors, and walls bearing little relationship to one another except for their physical proximity. Too often the organizational structure of today's school system follows this same pattern of topsy-turvy-like growth.

Designing an Organizational Structure

Organizational structure deals with the overall organizational arrangements in an enterprise. It establishes human and material relationships consistent with the objectives and resources of the organization and harmonizes activities through strategically placed executive officers who can facilitate administrative details. The organizational setup should take into account the benefits of specialization, the limitations of functional status authority, the problems of communications, and the need for stimulation and leadership. Above all, it should provide proper balance so that personal relations are harmonious and satisfying.[8]

A pattern of organization sets the bounds of action of particular individuals and groups; it outlines the way they work and provides them with a base or framework within which to work. We must emphasize, however, that organizational structure is a pencil-and-paper affair but its actual operation is a matter of human relationships. A pattern of operation is in reality but a basic theory of personal relationships within an organization. Thus, because they deal with people, both organization and operation must

[6] Some claim that teachers' associations and unions have tended to foster ineffective school organization by usurping some of the normal decision-making prerogatives of the school administrator. The authors would contend that poor organization and ineffective operation often cause unions and educational associations to force decisions on school systems.

[7] William H. Newman, *Administrative Action* (Englewood Cliffs, N.J.: Prentice-Hall, Inc., 1953), pp. 278–279.

[8] Jay Galbraith, *Organization Design* (Reading, Mass.: Addison-Wesley, 1977).

be flexible and adaptable and not absolutes. This is most important in a school system. Any school organization that institutionalizes its working relationships, rigidly stratifies its personnel, and develops a stolid hierarchical form of control without allowing the full reservoir of abilities of the staff to be utilized will fail to reach its full potential. By the same token, because public school systems belong to the citizenry at large they must be sensitive and responsive to the public need.

Begin with the Objectives [9]

In designing an organizational structure, one logically starts with the goals and objectives of the enterprise. These must be planned and with minor modifications accepted as constants at any given moment. How should people and responsibilities be grouped to function best? What organization and structure will best utilize personnel to focus upon the objectives? It is not possible to prescribe a precise formula appropriate for all school districts. Many conditions within a state or local community affect the character of the organizational structure. These conditions may be (1) custom, tradition, and local cultural patterns; (2) constitutional provisions; (3) the degree to which statutes define the authority and responsibility of school districts or schools within the districts; (4) the way courts have interpreted the constitution and the statutes; (5) the number, competencies, and abilities of personnel; (6) finances available for operation; (7) educational needs in the state and community; and (8) the importance of education to the people of the community.

Some of these conditions may be altered, but American education, because of its closeness to the people, demands an organization flexible and adaptable enough to fit local conditions.[10] Therefore, although structures and patterns of organization and the way they operate will be different, basic principles that guide their adoption should be followed. As Mooney[11] so aptly put it, "Organization is an art and as such, it must have its technique, based on principles. That the great organizers of history applied the principles unconsciously proves only that their technique was inherent in their genius."

The following principles are suggested as guides to the development of proper organizational structure for schools:

Principles of Organization

1. The value of all organizational forms, agents, agencies, and practices should be based upon their contribution to the achievement and objectives of education.

[9] Jay Galbraith, op. cit.
[10] H. Peter Drachler and Bernard Welpert, "Conceptual Dimensions and Boundaries of Participation in Organizations," *Administrative Science Quarterly*, March, 1978.
[11] James D. Mooney, *The Principles of Organization* (New York: Harper and Brothers, 1939), pp. 2–4.

2. The plan of organization should help obtain and hold the most able leadership and stimulate leadership activities.
3. The organization should provide for the division of the total work into related parts that will ensure the most effective utilization of the services of available personnel.
4. The organization should attract and retain the most competent personnel by providing, insofar as is possible, conditions under which they can do their best work.
5. The school should be so organized, that unity and teamwork are emphasized through the effective coordination of the efforts of all educational agencies toward fulfillment of the objectives of education.
6. The organizational structure should be as simple as possible, consistent with the need to coordinate the work of the school.
7. Each unit in the structure should have a clear definition of its functions and of the authority and responsibilities of the individuals comprising the unit. Everyone should participate in the exercise of authority, commensurate with his/her responsibilities and without confusion or duplication.
8. An individual should clearly understand to whom he or she is responsible for the performance of particular functions.[12] Moreover, final authority should be clearly vested. Whenever authority is vested in a group, the group should have a single executive officer who is responsible for the execution of group decisions.
9. The number of persons directly responsible to an individual should not be greater than can be coordinated effectively. Activities should be grouped into the smallest feasible number of units without creating an inflexible administrative hierarchy.
10. The organization of the school should reflect the complete service offering in education. It should be possible to identify easily the various activities both individually and in relation to broader areas.
11. All personnel within the school should feel that they belong to an identifiable group and have a definite home base. Administrative units within the school should have similar and compatible groupings so that subgroups within the units have real group identity.
12. While the organization must have a basic stability it should have a built-in flexibility with sensitivity for the need to change so that it can adjust easily and adapt itself to the future.

---

[12] An oft-repeated administrative principle is that a person should be responsible to only one administrative officer. It has usually been compared to the Biblical quotation, "A man cannot serve two masters." There is no reason why a person cannot serve several administrators so long as it is clear to whom one is responsible for a particular function, and there are clearly specified, open lines of communication between those to whom he/she is responsible. See Ch. 8 for further discussion of this principle.

Principles of Operation of a School Organization

An organization itself is sterile and lifeless until it is in operation. Thus, operational principles are as important to success as is the organizational structure itself.

1. A school cannot exceed effectively the restrictions placed upon it by the popular understanding of its function. A low degree of public confidence and understanding will limit the effectiveness of the school.
2. The importance of education demands that it be protected from interruption by vagaries of partisan politics.[13]
3. The educational process is so complex that it can only be carried out through a number of institutions, agencies, and activities. Cooperation, coordination, and unification of educational and social agencies are essential activities of any school.
4. An effective organization will emphasize and constantly utilize in proper balance the constituent elements of administrative activities: (a) planning, (b) organizing, (c) staffing, (d) leadership, (e) communication/interpretation, (f) evaluation and appraisal.
5. Persons affected by policies, both within and outside the organizational structure, should have a part in shaping those policies. The level of democratic action at any time depends upon the competence and conscience of the individual involved.
6. The aim of administration is to facilitate learning and the instructional process. Administrative personnel should provide leadership in improving instruction and should see that the members of the staff have the necessary time, sufficient materials, and proper working conditions for the performance of their functions.
7. To achieve excellence, staff members must be allowed to avail themselves of opportunities to make significant contributions locally, nationally, and internationally. The prominence of a school will be measured by the kind of job it does and by the achievements of its personnel as they work individually and cooperatively.
8. A school organization should have enough flexibility and adaptability to handle newly developing needs. Its structure, policies, and programs should be subject to continuous evaluation. However, there should be sufficient continuity of organization and program to provide the necessary feeling of security for both the staff and the public at large.
9. A major purpose of the school is to help preserve the benefits of our present culture and pass on the accumulated knowledge of the past. At the same time it has a basic responsibility to exert leadership in

[13] Much has been written in recent years on the politics *in* education and the politics *of* education. While politics is a part of daily life and one of the realities of our national life, schools specifically and education generally should be protected from the polarization and party-line action that characterizes so much of partisan politics.

the overall improvement of our society. This requires a certain amount of risk-taking and courage in propounding causes that may not always be the most popular.

10. Goals and objectives of the school organization should be jointly developed by the constituent elements of that organization and processes established for their periodic review and revision. Administrative and supervisory personnel are responsible for keeping all members of that organization continuously aware of these goals and objectives.

11. The school organization should have easy access channels for communications and feedback so that each subunit of the organization may formally react to its relationships with other subunits and the central administration.

Major Administrative Divisions of School Systems

The organization of a school system is actually a translation of its purposes, principles, and activities into a structural administrative plan; thus, it is realistically developed by listing all the work that is and should be accomplished and then grouping these activities into related areas. How definitive the grouping is or how many categories are accepted as major areas of work makes the difference in the pattern.

Probably the classical model of school organization today is that school district that divides itself administratively into three major functions: (1) instruction, (2) educational services, (3) business management. Instruction deals with the teaching process itself in each local school and includes the certified personnel who teach, and the consultants and specialists who help with the specific teaching function. Educational services are provided by people trained in the field of education who assist the teachers directly through specialized professional services. These include media utilization, guidance and counseling, physical and psychological services, child accounting and attendance, visiting teacher services, and research. Business management is that phase of the organization that serves the other two functions in a facilitating and supporting role. It may be simply defined as that part of school administration dealing with the management of finances, facilities, and similar noneducational services necessary for the operation of a school system.

In the past there has been no universally accepted pattern of organization for these functions. One may study schools throughout the nation and find almost every conceivable type of organization, including those with multiple and dual executives; top-heavy, highly departmentalized structures; or the simplest unit type of organization that deemphasizes the administrative hierarchy.

Present studies show, however, that there is a growing national accep-

FIGURE 5.1. A typical line-and-staff organization adapted along functional lines to emphasize that the administration staff and all personnel must work as a team to improve the instructional process.

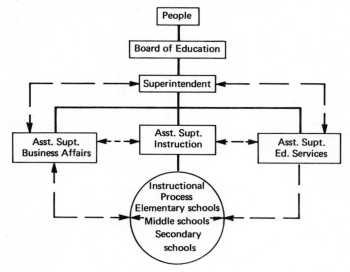

tance of the administrative philosophy that organization should be so arranged that instruction is highlighted as the key activity of the school system, with all other activities placed in an auxiliary or facilitating role. This has led most administrative theorists to advocate a unit type of control with centralization of all administrative activities under the leadership of one administrator who is a professional educator and who serves as the chief executive to the board of education. Figure 5.1 illustrates an organizational pattern of this type in its simplest functional sense.

Studying the historical development of this type of organization in our schools and observing that the unit type of executive with its perfect pyramid is a rather recent development in today's schools, one would assume that this type of organization is a modern device.[14] Actually it is not. Theodore Caplow shows that the concept it represents is very ancient by citing examples from the Old Testament (Exodus XVIII: 14–22), the ancient Chinese empire under the Ts'in and Han dynasties, following through the Roman republic, the Venetian State, the Prussian Civil Service under Frederick William I, The U.S. military structure and finally up to the present industrial and business organizational patterns.[15] Although

[14] See William H. Roe, *School Business Management*, op. cit., p. 29. In 1926 it was reported that the majority of public schools of 25,000 or more had a dual or multiple-type executive. While in 1958 Roe reported that 79 per cent of these schools had a single executive with all administrative officers reporting directly to the superintendent, today it is estimated that 90 per cent of the schools have a single executive.

[15] Theodore Caplow, *Principles of Organization*, op. cit., pp. 50–56.

generally popularized by Max Weber and Talcott Parsons [16] in the early 1940s neither the pyramid type of organization nor the complicated flat line and staff organization is a modern invention.

The Impersonal and Unresponsive Organization

While the various organizational structures of our schools today may have some inherent and sacred values because of long and established use, they certainly cannot be retained on the basis that they are a modern adaptation to present-day society.

There is no national or state requirement that school organizations be the same, although a study of school districts throughout the country will reveal more similarities than differences. Each emphasizes the pyramid type of approach and as one studies the typical line and staff chart it may be observed each places its greatest administrative emphasis at the top of the pyramid structure with the local elementary, middle, and secondary school unit essentially lost in the maze of administrative and organizational lines.

Big cities are beginning to realize that this organization is becoming too impersonal and unresponsive as far as local schools are concerned. The bureaucracy that has developed too often leaves the local parent with the feeling that they can have little or no impact on the school that their child attends. Rather than being advocates of the schools as in the past, when they were so much a part of them, the parents become adversaries who criticize and take a negative approach to the school practices that are being tried because they know so little about them.

The rapid growth and complexity of communities with accompanying growth and complexity of school districts in the twentieth century make it impossible for schools to remain as close and responsive as they were in the eighteenth and nineteenth centuries. The feeling of actually belonging, participating, being a co-partner with the school is rapidly disappearing. The intimate community spirit is becoming lost with the rapid growth of schools in the megalopolis and in the organization of the sprawling rural–suburban consolidated district. These larger districts have tended to develop into mechanized professional organizations that are highly bureaucratic. Many people are inclined to resent the growth, centralization, and re-organization that has taken place in schools and propose that we go back to the "good old days" of the small neighborhood district. There is no doubt that educational opportunity and educational process has been improved by consolidating into larger educational units; however, in plan-

[16] Max Weber, *The Theory of Social and Economic Organization,* Translated by Talcott Parsons (New York: Free Press, 1947).

ning the educational unit there was not invented or established a realistic organized way to keep parents and citizens intimately associated with the schools. It can truly be said, the schools have kept pace with change technically but not organizationally as far as close relationships to their publics are concerned.

The Cult of Efficiency

Democratic competence is not an inheritance that is simply passed on *in toto* from one generation to another. There are adaptations and adjustments that must be made by each succeeding generation, for a democracy by its very nature is dynamic, changing day by day, week by week, month by month. Thus, the procedures and processes of democracy to be effective must be adapted to the future. To teach democratic competence to each succeeding generation and to help them to adapt to change is one of the major objectives of American education. The public schools and the community itself form the real laboratories where lessons appropriate to the present and future can be developed. Local participation of people in the government has been eroding away year after year as the powerful sweep toward "efficiency" through centralization has taken place. We are reaching a stage where efficiency of representative government at state and national levels is prospering at the expense of local participation. As local communities have faced massive problems of growth, the state and national government stepped in with proposed solutions. In most cases this was necessary because many of the problems resulted from conditions that were beyond the scope of the local communities to solve. However, when state and national action helped to solve the immediate problems, nothing was done to modernize the inefficient and outdated local government unit. Rather, the state and national governments actually centralized and strengthened themselves and by the process created an atrophy in the local government that is closest to the people. As a result we have growing criticism of the bureaucracy of state and national government and its affiliation with the military–industrial complex and no one seems to know what to do about it. What has happened in government has also happened with schools as a part of this government.

The Person in the Middle

The principal of the local elementary, middle, or secondary school is in the middle of this developing administrative bureaucracy. As titular head of the school building unit he/she is the person who, with the teachers, is the closest communications link with parents and citizens in the school's

FIGURE 5.2.   Illustration of bypassing the principal.

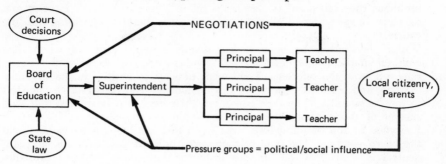

attendance area. At the same time the principal's office is represented as the switchboard or closest local communicating link to the central administration. Despite this, in too many cases organizational structure and operational procedures make the principal a school building manager who is responsible for maintaining the day-by-day routine but little else (see Fig. 5.2). He/she is bypassed by local pressure groups when they attempt to influence school activities or policy. He/she is not included by teachers when they decide on issues for negotiations.[17] He/she is not significantly involved by the central administration in the development of major policy decisions and operational procedures that significantly affect the operation of the school.[18]

As school districts have become larger, teachers more independent through negotiation processes, the social life more dispersed, and the value systems more cosmopolitan, it becomes more difficult for the local school principal to be an influential leader or change agent in the school because there are so few opportunities for the principal and the teachers and students in the building to make important independent decisions that affect their own welfare either instructionally or otherwise.

Contracts have been negotiated that specify how many meetings can be called by the principal and how long they are to last. In addition, stipulations have been made regarding classroom visitations by the principal or other supervisory staff requiring written notice, maximum length of visit, and maximum number of visits per year. Under present conditions it is very easy for an adversary situation to supplant the more desirable colleague relationship.

An example of bypassing the principal is illustrated in the following case:

> One of the many presentations at an evening open house at the high school was centered on the benefits of the family life discussion course. A film was

---

[17] For a discussion of this problem, see David C. Smith, "Should Administrators Negotiate?" *National Elementary Principal*, 52, No. 5 (February 1973), pp. 109–112.
[18] The National School Public Relations Association, *Education U.S.A., Report* (Washington, D.C.: The Association, April 10, 1978), p. 244.

presented and students outlined some of the discussions held concerning problems they felt were important to them. The course is an elective and students present signed parent-approval cards before registering for the course.

Within days after the open house, several parents, none of whom had children in the course, had formed a pressure group to have the course removed from the offerings. They went directly to written media available to them, and personally contacted board members and conservative ministers in the community. They then presented their case at a board meeting with several of those whom they had contacted in attendance.

Everyone at the building level was by-passed until the issue came up at the board meeting. The only role open to the principal, teachers, and students was a reactive role. In this instance, they made excellent presentations at a subsequent board meeting.

Adapt the Organization to Society—Not Vice Versa

Of course local schools have attempted to overcome some locked-in organizational and operational structures through special devices such as parent–teacher associations, local parent and attendance-area advisory committees, parent task forces, and teachers' committees. As the years have worn on it has become obvious that such groups have less and less influence on significant matters. As their recommendations have been lost in the inactivity of the central bureaucracy, they have become less enthusiastic and less effective—in many cases dying a slow and agonizing death.

Rather than trying to adapt students, teachers, and parents to the organization that exists, perhaps more significantly the organizational structure of the schools needs to be radically changed in order to adapt to society. The schools belong to the people. They require public support if they are to continue. To maintain the supportive parent–citizen's advocate role (as contrasted to the adversary role) organizational structures must be developed that keep the parent–citizen in close communication with the school and allow the individual school to be responsive to student as well as to parent–citizen concerns and desires.

A report by the New York State Fleischmann Committee highlights in rather dramatic fashion how traditional organizational structure and operational procedures have been unable to cope with our new and developing society. This report was reviewed as follows in a newsletter by the American Association of Colleges for Teacher Education.[19]

Tracking Down the Grim, Joyless Classrooms

The American high school, plagued by strikes, arson, vandalism, rioting, physical attacks, and other violence is on the psychiatrist's couch under-

[19] AACTE *Newsletter for Teacher Educators, Concern,* American Association of Colleges for Teacher Education, Vol. II, No. 3, (November, 1971).

going extensive analysis these days. One new study warns bluntly that *the traditional teacher–student relationship is breaking down and that a major crisis of morale is seriously threatening teaching itself.* The 195-page report, "High Schools in Crisis," was ordered by the New York State Fleischmann Committee, which is looking into the quality and financing of education. *At the heart of these crises the report says, are the high school's massive size, monolithic structure, and authoritarian lines.*

While such findings are hardly news, the report is valuable in underlining student dissatisfaction and also in pinpointing deep teacher tensions as it examines the student–teacher and other relationships.

According to the report, whose chief author was Dr. Alan E. Guskin of Community Resources Limited, "the more potent issues in high schools are the crises in the organizational structure of the school."

The report calls for *a drastic altering of the organizational and educational structures of our high schools* so that "students will learn, within such settings, how to cope with their future in order that they may gain a sense of the potential of a democratic society, that they may understand their own equality as humans and thereby gain a sense of determining their own lives, and that they may understand their own role as potential change agents of society."

Three major changes in the high school structure are proposed: (1)creating small school units and schools without walls; (2) increasing the hiring of minority teachers and administrators; and (3) establishing joint decision-making bodies composed of students, teachers, administrators, and even community members. Such changes, the report frankly states, when implemented, will be *resisted* by school managers and other professional educators. But they will work if "a concerted and clear mandate by a state legislature is reinforced by a state education department and if there is wise phasing of these innovations into school districts."

A. Harry Passow analyzed the reports of eight different national commissions and panels that had studied education in detail from 1972 to 1976. These reports examined the nature and causes of the problems of educating youth and detailed shortcomings of the school. The common theme running through these reports was for a significant restructuring of education.

> Viewing the present-day high school as an overburdened, beleaguered institution, sometimes on the verge of collapse, the various panels and commissions have recommended that secondary educators, with community participation, assert leadership in the building of a system of youth education that uses more of the community's educative resources—including those of the high school.
>
> There are many educating and socializing agencies, some or many of which may be more influential than formal schooling in their developmental effects on youth. The reports propose reforming the schools by integrating the learning resources of school and community, by making available a wide variety of educational options and program alternatives to attain educational objectives, by involving the school in providing valid and meaningful work experiences for all, and by the school's shedding some of its primary and ancillary functions.[20]

[20] A. Harry Passow, "The Future of High Schools," *Teachers College Record,* Sept., 1977. pp. 28–29.

A Test of Organizational Effectiveness

American children and adults are in a mood today where they question rather sharply some of our most accepted institutions. The schools have experienced at least their share of these questions. Nonetheless, the schools are public institutions and as such must expect sharp reactions if they do not adapt to the perceived changing needs of the public.

The Fleischman Report along with the more recent reports reviewed by Passow, were straightforward in their viewpoints that present school organization is ineffective for they did call for "a drastic altering of the organizational and educational structures." To test the validity of these recommendations one could go back to the expert theoretician on organization, Theodore Caplow. Caplow has devised what he calls the SIVA Variables as a means of measuring organizational effectiveness.[21]

> *Stability*—an organization's ability to conserve or increase the status of its position in relation to its total environment.
> *Integration*—the organization's ability to control internal conflict. It implies better mutual adjustment, less factionalism, more communication, greater concensus.
> *Voluntarism* (or Valences)—roughly equivalent to morale. It implies gratification, colleagueship, satisfaction—the desire of the members to continue to participate as part of the organization.
> *Achievement*—the net result of an organization's activity. It implies success or failure in attaining the general and specific goals of the organization.

Caplow points out that a dynamic organization is a network of relationships between people who occupy various positions in the pursuance of the real or perceived goals of the organization. The above-mentioned points then are descriptive measurable variables that allow one to determine the degree of success or failure of relationships internally as well as those with the environment.

Using Caplow's SIVA Variables to measure public education both internally and externally, one concludes that the reports are essentially correct. Public education is due for some significant organizational changes if it is to be responsive to our changing society. The following is a generalized analysis of public education using the SIVA Variables:

1. *Stability*—the voice of the public through practically every communication medium—TV, radio, newspaper, periodical, public meeting—will reveal that the public at large is most uncertain of the actual effectiveness of the schools. There is confusion, contradiction, and much controversy.

---

[21] Caplow, op. cit., p. 121.

All segments of the school are under attack. There is no question but what the stability factor has decreased.

2. *Integration*—even the most solid supporter of public education must agree that there is greater factionalism and more internal conflict in our schools today than ever before, particularly in secondary education. Teacher strikes, student rebellion, taxpayer's revolts, and community-school controversies bear testimony to this condition.

3. *Voluntarism*—to arrive at a true measurement of the degree of voluntarism in our schools today one needs to utilize some rather sophisticated evaluation devices. However, it is safe to say that the problems of the inner city, rapidly changing value systems, and the move away from acquiescence to traditional school operation modes have created confusion, frustration, and despair in many of our students, teachers, and administrators. This is the warning in the previously mentioned study entitled "High Schools in Crisis." Many students are finding their school experience painful and unenjoyable. Furthermore, the study found that teachers are torn between progressive educational ideals and the everyday demands made on them to maintain order. Blame for the breakdown in teacher–pupil relations is traced to large, impersonal, bureaucratic schools. In such an environment, the report charges, teachers and students are almost bound to feel and behave the way they do. The study recommends that schools be broken up into units of no more than 150 to 200 students that can operate within present school buildings.

4. *Achievement*—as implied in Chapter 1 most Americans believe in the dream that education can correct all the ills of society. This American dream created some goals for education that were and are impossible to achieve through the schools alone. Add to this the fact that for a large number of children and youth today, represented by functional illiterates, dropouts, and the disenchanted, the schools do not appear to work. These represent large enough numbers so that the public at large concludes that schools have not achieved their goals.

This is illustrated by the results of the Gallup Poll, which each year measures the public's attitudes toward the public schools. Figures show that there has been a slight but steady drop in the public's ratings of schools since 1974.

Thus, along with the other variables, achievement falls short in organizational effectiveness.

Based upon these variables, which Caplow proposes as measures or criteria of organizational effectiveness, it becomes apparent that school districts of today must consider some innovative approaches to school organization that will allow sensitive adaptiveness to a changing and dynamic society.

Gallup Poll—Rating of the Public Schools [22]

Ratings Given The Public Schools	National Totals				
	1978 %	1977 %	1976 %	1975 %	1974 %
A Rating	9	11	13	13	18
B	27	26	29	30	30
C	30	28	28	28	21
D	11	11	10	9	6
Fail	8	5	6	7	5
Don't know	–	–	–	–	–
No answer	15	19	14	13	20

Trends in School Organization

The authors wished to determine if some national movement could be detected that would counteract the growing concern over "bigness," "impersonal learning environments," and "lack of responsiveness to the people." Therefore, in early 1972 they conducted a representative survey of the organizational structure of school districts divided according to the following sizes: 1,000,000+; 300,000–999,999; 100,000–299,999, and under 100,000 population.

It is interesting to note, the returns from this stratified random sample of some five hundred districts show only one or two school districts had developed organizational patterns in which individual schools were highlighted or emphasized. As noted in Figure 5.3, the organization chart of the typical school district, the local schools (the actual teaching unit) are lost in the superstructure of the central administrative hierarchy. Unfortunately, this is also too often true in the way the district actually operates. The survey did turn up a small number of sporadic attempts to down-play bigness through group house plans, school within schools, alternative schools, and big city regionalization, but the movement was so small at that time it could not be called a trend.

Two bright lights on the horizon as far as responsiveness to the people is concerned seemed to be the regionalization of the big city central administration and the pattern of governance of the alternative school in some districts. Unfortunately, under close investigation the lights dim and even flicker out on both of these as a trend. In the large cities, though supposedly the regions were smaller and more responsive, they were still too large for realistic involvement. Furthermore, the overall board seemed

[22] 10th Annual Gallup Education Poll, *Phi Delta Kappan* Vol. 61 No. 1 (Sept., 1978), p. 35.

incapable of developing enabling policy that would allow local school units to operate independently in directions appropriate to their particular attendance-area social system.

The governing of alternative schools did take a different direction in some school districts. They were first considered "wild offshoots" that had to be tolerated. When a board of education finally succumbed to certain public pressures to have an alternative school, they gave tacit approval for great latitude in its operation through citizens' committees, etc. However, the trend has been for the pressure to lessen within a year or two and the alternative school that once was so responsive to a particular group was soon assimilated into the hierarchial organization.

A follow-up of the 1972 organizational survey was made in 1978. The returns in '78 revealed a definite trend was taking place. A growing number of school districts had developed magnet schools, open enrollment schools, alternative schools, multi-unit schools, schools within schools, educational parks featuring house plans, and multi-phased programs of great variety with flexibility in schedules to allow independent study and community experiences. In the six years between these two surveys significant attempts had been made to combine new instructional strategy with organizational structure to provide educational models designed to personalize instruction and provide greater flexibility in what and how students learn. Central administration was making observable moves to humanize, individualize, and personalize instruction and communicating widely about their efforts through press releases and brochures. Unhappily, at the same time, no discernible move is being made to bring the governance of the school closer to the people. On the contrary, there is considerable evidence that just the opposite trend is taking place.[23]

Regardless of the degree of efficiency of the central administration, a dynamic democratic organization cannot be maintained without active and intelligent participation at levels where results can be observed. A dynamic participating democracy requires that each citizen see that his/her ideas, wishes, and efforts have an impact on public agencies and institutions at their unit level. At the same time these units should have strength enough to have an impact on larger units and so on up to the central government.

The nucleus of people at this basic participating unit naturally should be determined by some type of community relatedness. A community whose boundaries are determined by the legal units of a megalopolis, or a sprawling school district, is just too large to maintain an intimate participating spirit. The complicated organizational structure of a typical school district and its relationship with regional state, and federal educational agencies tend to create a bureaucracy that is difficult for the layman and sometimes even the average educator to understand.

[23] See Ch. 3, "The School and Its Communities," for further discussion on this topic.

FIGURE 5.3. Typical organization of a larger city district.

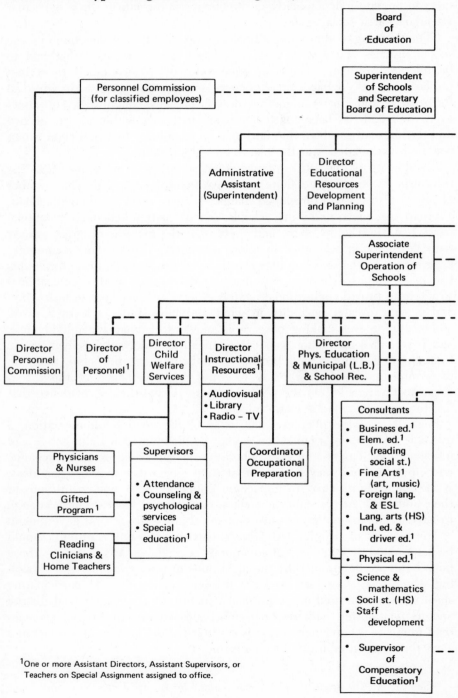

[1]One or more Assistant Directors, Assistant Supervisors, or
Teachers on Special Assignment assigned to office.

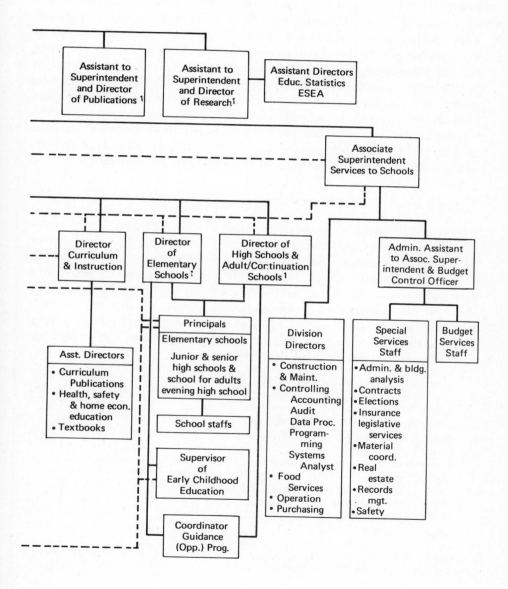

An organizational change needs to be made in school government so that each school within a school district may establish a closer liaison with parents and citizen groups in the local attendance area. This liaison must go beyond the usual know-your-school week, citizens committee, P.T.A., or advisory group process. While these school–community efforts are laudatory and for the most part have been serious attempts to involve the citizenry in the school, it has been made clear to the adults that the institution is master and important decision making is still the prerogative of the district. School districts should be reorganized internally so that each school within the district has a maximum of self-determination, and parents and citizens within the attendance area have a reasonable impact upon the decision-making process. Only through such radical legal change in school district structure can true local citizen advocacy and partnership be maintained. Although some of the large communities, e.g., Philadelphia, Detroit, and Memphis have been experimenting with such approaches, they haven't really succeeded because the city boards have been reluctant to give up any real authority and as a result the attempts have been "patch-ups"—attaching something new to an already outmoded structure.[24]

Is Decentralization the Answer?

Freeman H. Vaughn in an excellent article in the *American School Board Journal* made the point that the local community school is the bulwark of a democratic society. Schools can be brought closer to the people by decentralizing them but such efforts will not succeed unless governance is actually passed down and principals are ready and capable of handling the move. He asserts that if principals aren't ready, all that the board is likely to create is another thick layer of bureaucracy for the local schools to break through in order to function. Vaughn then quotes several authorities to further his points about decentralization.

> Decentralization, according to Harold Howe, U.S. Commissioner of Education, "involves more than simply shifting bureaucrats around to different offices. It requires that the local administrator be given more leeway in tailoring his school to the character of the community, welcoming the contributions of parents and helping parents understand what kinds of contributions they can make. It calls not only for letting parents see how the school is run and explaining to them its policies and programs, but also converting the school into a community resource that offers adults instruction in a range of subjects, whether the activity be a benefit cake sale or a voter-registration drive. It means a school whose doors are open nights, weekends, and summers. It means alliances between the school and community agencies of all kinds."

[24] Freeman H. Vaughn, "Forget About Decentralizing if Your Principals Aren't Ready", *American School Board Journal*, Vol. 156, No. 5, (December, 1968), pp. 24–26.

Achieving all of that requires a special kind of principal. Don't think for a moment, however, that just breaking up a large system into smaller units is going to solve all problems. It's hard to escape the conclusion that there is a strong feeling of alienation of the neighborhood school from the community that has grown up around it.

The authors are convinced that decentralization is an answer. The move to humanize and personalize instruction for students is an important educational adaptation for our changing society. With this move must go stronger parent and citizen involvement in schools both for the education of children and as a resource for any adult's own personal growth. Involvement, support, and advocacy, cannot be created by impersonal bureaucracies. They are created by responsive understandable organizational structures that provide opportunities for citizens to have a reasonable impact upon the decision making process.

The organizational model in Figure 5.4 depicts an attempt to restructure an overall organization to break the usual pattern of centralization that has been viewed as universally sacred. This model proposes that each local school within a given school district be provided with a maximum amount of self-determination for its own direction. The school district board would still be responsible for overall legislation of the school district and retain basic authority and responsibility through minimum standards, broad basic policy, and leadership. However, it would consciously create *enabling* policy whereby each school unit operating through an elected board of representatives within its attendance area has authority with responsibility to determine specific policy and direction appropriate to its local needs. This means each school would have a central budget that, once approved by the district board, would allow them to operate within it for the year. It means long-range program planning would be encouraged and the central board would make reasonable long-range commitments to each individual school. It would mean the principal, faculty, students, and parents of each school could develop their own operational procedures and programs and establish their own codes as long as they complied with minimum standards of the district. It means a faculty would be required to make a stronger commitment to a particular school as an overall personnel policy of the district. Hopefully, through careful deployment of central administrator staff to the existing schools, it would mean the elimination of excessive superstructures that are developing in the central offices of our school districts throughout the nation.

One of our management-oriented big-city superintendents recently reacted to this proposal with the exclamation, "But you're involving so many people!" That's exactly the point! Involvement and participation are the key to this model. We think they are the key to a responsive school and a dynamic democracy.

FIGURE 5.4.   An adaptive, responsive organizational structure with a local board of representatives for each attendance unit.

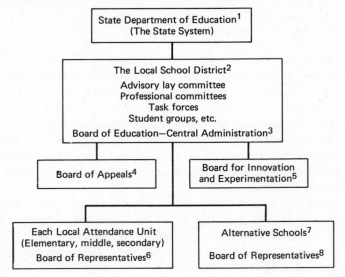

[1]The State Department of Education exerts direction and leadership according to the State Constitution, legislation, and recommendations from state lay-professional advisory groups.

[2]The local school district is enlarged to include complete metropolitan areas (urban and suburban) and strong larger rural town areas.

[3]The Board of Education responsible for overall legislation of the school district retains basic authority and responsibility through minimum standards, broad basic policy, and leadership; however, it consciously creates ENABLING policy whereby each school unit has authority with responsibility to determine specific policy and direction appropriate to the local needs.

[4]Proposed is a six-member board appointed by the Board of Education and composed of students, teachers, and Board members. This board reviews and rules on cases of conflict and overlap. (A new professional position may emerge in connection with the activities of this board and recent court actions. This would be an appeals administrator to handle procedural duties in connection with problems arising out of due process situations,etc.)

[5]This board approves, reviews, and evaluates radical deviations from basic patterns. It too would have six members appointed by the Board, representing students, teachers, and Board members.

[6]There would be a Board of Representatives for each local school attendance unit. It is recommended that this board be a nine-member board consisting of two students, two teachers, four lay citizens (each elected by their constituency), and the school principal who acts as executive officer by virtue of his office. This board's responsibility is to develop and endorse school policy and advise on operational procedures in the school.

[7]Alternative schools are open for attendance by any appropriate student in the school district. Such schools are characterized by being innovative and experimental, deviating rather radically from the conventional school by concentrating on open and self-directive approaches to learning.

[8]Same as item 6.

For Further Thought

1. Discuss the problem of people versus functions in organizing.
2. What effect might the composition of boards of education have upon growth and development of schools? Should the principal be involved in influencing who should serve on the board of education?

3. What aspects of education do you think should be under the control of (a) the local community; (b) the state; (c) the federal government?
4. Is there a point where an elementary school, middle school, or high school can become too large? Present arguments, research evidence, and authoritative opinion to support your position.
5. Why is it not uncommon to find the principal bypassed when groups wish to influence the schools? What implications does this have for the role of the principal?
6. Should the principal ever be found as an advocate for parents and pupils versus the board? Discuss.
7. Develop some enabling policies that a district board of education could develop to give a local school greater autonomy and the school community greater self-determination.

Chapter 6 Leadership

It is time for a new generation of leadership to cope with new problems
and new opportunities. For there is a new world to be won.

John F. Kennedy

The principal of a school is viewed from almost every quarter as being
the leader of that school. The board of education hired him/her to lead.
Research indicates that the teachers want him/her to lead. The community
holds him/her responsible if he/she does not lead. Of 2,410 elementary
principals surveyed, ninety-five per cent expected to lead.[1] The latest survey
of secondary school principals indicated they want to lead.[2] It is apparent
that the question facing the principal is not whether he/she must behave
as a leader; rather, it is a question of how shall he/she behave to be an
effective leader.

Opportunities to exert leadership are abundant. New approaches to
teaching and learning assessment programs, new budgeting systems, increasing demands of the community for meaningful evaluation, accountability to the various communities served by any one school—all these are
part of the new world to be won, as are the needs of the child who has
multiple disabilities, or the needs of a child whose ragged, ill-kept clothes
and different speech patterns contribute to his/her devaluation by others.

The increasing activity of professional–union organizations acting on
behalf of teachers can be viewed by some as a negative and by others as
a positive leadership factor. Such activity can be viewed as discomforting
for the principal who sees his/her role as one of maintaining a well-oiled
organizational machine. On the other hand, the possibility of concentrating
the efforts of a professional group of well-educated persons toward solving

[1] *The Elementary School Principalship—A Research Study, Thirty-Seventh Yearbook
of the Department of Elementary School Principals* (Washington, D.C.: National Education Association, 1958), p. 39.

[2] The National Association of Secondary School Principals, *The Senior High School
Principalship* (Reston, Va.: The Association, 1978).

many of the complex problems facing education today cannot be ignored as an opportunity.

The old patterns of principal behavior will not be sufficient to meet the new opportunities for leadership. No longer can the principal pass on the image of the benevolent "father/mother figure" spending time on efficiently organized "administrivia" as evidence of his/her role being competently fulfilled. In fact, an attempt to do so may provide evidence to the contrary. This is not to say that the details are unimportant. To ignore them would be to undermine many of the other gains hoped for by the leader. The administrative details must be ordered in a hierarchy of importance and alternatives must be sought to get them done well, but not so that the doing replaces the higher priority items facing the principal.

Panush and Kelley remind us that the principal's concentration on modes of behavior that may have been successful yesterday can leave the principal in the position of being reactive.[3]

The Principal of now and of the future must be increasingly willing to prepare for wise and critical participation in a society characterized by conflict and chronic change. This is his/her pro-active role.[4]

The principal of today and tomorrow finds him- or herself in a continuously changing environment. To accept the idea of administering a school solely based upon the directives in the board policy, the memoranda from the superintendent, and the behaviors of principals of the past is to cast oneself into a reactive role. The person in such a role finds adversary relationships developing or reinforced, finds him- or herself defending behavior to those who expect leadership, and finds the role seriously questioned.

Views of Leadership

Leadership as Traits

The concept of leadership has been examined over centuries. Volumes have been written analyzing the qualities of recognized leaders. The focus upon persons such as Charlemagne, Churchill, Ghandi, Napoleon, and even Hitler traditionally has been to find traits that made them the leaders they were. Hundreds of studies tried to identify specific qualities or characteristics that distinguished leaders from nonleaders. Many of the qualities studied seemed to be inborn attributes, such as physical characteristics or intelligence, and some were acquired skills such as impeccable social behavior or dynamic public speaking. However, for the most part these studies have failed to yield any truly discriminating traits or sets of traits.

[3] L. Panush and E. A. Kelley, "The High School Principal: Pro-Active or Reactive Roles," *Phi Delta Kappan*, 52, No. 2 (October 1970), p. 90.
[4] Ibid., p. 91.

Stodgill, in leadership studies that have spanned over a quarter of a century, asserts that leadership characteristics by themselves hold little significance for purposes of either prediction or diagnosis of leadership. However, he does not discount traits entirely as do many researchers. It is his belief that collectively these characteristics appear to interact, to generate "personality dynamics advantageous to the person seeking the responsibilities of leadership." [5] He classified these traits in three categories: (1) *Self-oriented traits* that include intelligence, physical, social, and personality characteristics; (2) *task-related characteristics* such as achievement, enterprise, and drive for responsibility; (3) *social characteristics* such as cooperativeness, prestige, diplomacy, sociability.

Analysis of Leadership Behavior

An early study on leadership that attracted a great deal of attention was conducted by Lewin and others in 1939. In one study, three groups of nine to twelve-year-old boys were to complete a carpentry assignment. Each group was "led" by adults who acted in leadership styles labeled democratic (gets commitment from group members to do specific tasks and helps with suggestions as needed); autocratic (arbitrarily assigns tasks on a continuing basis); laissez-faire (brought in instructions and drawings and remained completely passive).[6] The results are illustrated in Table 6.1.

Leadership behavior can vary greatly along an autocratic–democratic continuum. As simple as they were, studies of this nature did encourage a great deal of further research and contributed to the understanding of group and individual reactions to certain styles of leadership.

In a follow-up of many of these research studies Owens identified five main leadership styles: (1) authoritarism, (2) democratic, (3) laissez-faire, (4) bureaucratic, and (5) charismatic.[7]

TABLE 6.1   *Illustration of Results of Leadership Styles*

Leadership Style	Leader Leaves	Leader Returns	Task Completion
Laissez-faire	Boys leave	Empty room	Incomplete
Autocratic	Pandemonium	Order restored Work continues	Completed
Democratic	Work continues	Work continues	Completed

[5] Stodgill, R. M., *Handbook of Leadership*. (New York: The Free Press, 1974), p. 82.

[6] A complete discussion of these studies may be found in Ralph White and Ronald Lippitt, "Leader Behavior and Member Reaction in Three 'Social Settings,'" in Dorwin Cartwright and Alvin Zander (Eds.) *Group Dynamics: Research and Theory* (Evanston, Ill.: Row, Peterson, 1953), pp. 585–611.

[7] Robert G. Owens, *Organizational Behavior in Schools*. (Englewood Cliffs, N.J.: Prentice-Hall, 1970) p. 134.

More Recent Studies

Within the past thirty years leadership research has concentrated on analyzing leader behavior and attitudes, relating these with production and performance and with the motivation orientations of people. The literature is replete with reports of research studies in these areas; therefore, this chapter can use but a few main examples of the work being done. Many of the studies can be categorized into people-focused or performance-focused or a combination of these. Bowers and Seashore provided an excellent summary of the correspondence of leadership concepts of different investigators from 1950 to 1964.[8] They concluded that the research up to that point identified four dimensions of leadership: (1) support, (2) interaction facilitation, (3) goal emphasis, and (4) work facilitation. Brown identified systems- and persons-orientations as leader behavior factors.[9] Thus an impressive array of word salad greets the reader of several studies. If one merges the illustrations of leadership theories it becomes clear that there is a congruence of opinion about the two dimensions with which the leader must concern him- or herself. These are centered about the needs, goals and performance of *people* and the needs, goals, and performance of *organizations*.

One of the most useful series of studies for the school administrator were those known as the Ohio State Leadership Studies commencing in 1945.[10] A major contribution of these studies was the development of the Leadership Behavior Description Questionnaire (LBDQ.). This questionnaire generally abandoned the notion of leadership as a trait and attempted to concentrate instead on an analysis of the behavior of leaders.[11] The LBDQ has been used in numerous studies to analyze the leadership behavior of school administrators. Two major dimensions of leadership behavior that have consistently emerged through use of the LBDQ have been identified as *initiating structure* and *consideration*. These were first identified by Halpin and Winer through factor analysis.[12] Other investigators have consistently substantiated their findings.[13]

Initiating structure is a type of behavior by the leader which clarifies the relationship of the staff within the organization and what is expected of

[8] David G. Bowers and Stanley E. Seashore, "Predicting Organizational Effectiveness with a Four-Factor Theory of Leadership," *Administrative Science Quarterly* 2 (September 1966), p. 248.

[9] Alan Brown, "Reactions to Leadership," *Education Administration Quarterly*, 3 (Winter 1967).

[10] Initiated and directed by Dr. Carroll L. Shartle and reported in Andrew W. Halpin, *Theory and Research in Administration* (New York: Macmillan, 1966.)

[11] This questionnaire was originally developed by John K. Hemphill and Alvin E. Coons in 1949 but has since gone through many revisions by several different authors.

[12] Halpin, op. cit., p. 88.

[13] Donald A. Erickson (Ed.), *Educational Organizations and Administration* (Berkeley, Calif.: McCutchans Publishing Co., 1977), p. 456.

them. It implies a well-planned coordinated operation which has clearly identified goals and standards of performance with procedures established to encourage maximum achievement.

Consideration refers to a relationship with the staff which implies friendship, cooperation, team work, rapport and approachability. The leader is thoughtfully considerate of the staff, essentially treating them as equals.

Effective principals consistently score high on both of these dimensions. They may score high on one or the other but it doesn't seem to matter as long as one is not completely canceled out.

Luthans points out that these studies were the first to emphasize the importance of both *task direction* and *consideration of individual needs* in assessing leadership behavior.[14]

At approximately the time of the Ohio State Studies the University of Michigan conducted research on leadership styles. In the Prudential Study, Likert identified high-producing supervisors as: (1) employee oriented, (2) spending more time on the job with a major portion of their time devoted to general and specific supervision of employees, (3) receiving general supervision from their supervisors, and (4) liking the authority and responsibility of their job.[15] In continuing his research on leadership and on the basis of reviewing hundreds of other research studies Likert found that it is likely production will improve and/or remain high if a system is associated with leadership processes based on teamwork, trust, and participation in decision making.[16]

Sergiovanni, Metzcus, and Burden studied the relationship between teachers' needs orientations (based on Herzberg's hygiene-motivation theory [17]) and their perceptions of the ideal principal. They concluded that ". . . teachers, regardless of needs orientations, see the ideal principal as being both systems- and persons-oriented." [18] They further identified two "qualities" of leadership style that they called "optimizing" and "controlling." [19] Again they found that teachers, regardless of orientation, generally responded favorably to the optimizing style rather than to the controlling style of leadership.

Current research indicates that the effective leader will optimize or facilitate the meeting of the needs and the achievement of the goals of

---

[14] F. Luthans, *Organizational Behavior* (New York: McGraw-Hill, 1977).

[15] R. Likert in D. Katz, N. Macoby, and N. Morse, *Productivity, Supervision and Morale in an Office Situation* (Ann Arbor: University of Michigan Survey Research Center, 1950).

[16] Rensis Likert, "Management Styles and the Human Component," *Management Review*, Oct., 1977, p. 23.

[17] See Ch. 3, p. 48, for a brief description of this theory.

[18] Thomas J. Sergiovanni, Richard Metzcus, and Larry Burden, "Toward a Particularistic Approach to Leadership Style: Some Findings," *American Education Research Journal*, 6, No. 1 (January 1969), p. 77.

[19] Ibid., p. 73.

both the organization (school) and of the people who make up the organization.[20]

The Situational Approach to the Study of Leadership.

The situational approach to leadership conceives leadership as basically a group situation in which the characteristics of the group and the style of leadership are important. In other words, leadership depends on the situation. Various types of situations determine the type or style of leadership that should be exerted. Situational variables that became special areas of study in situational research were *organizational climate*,[21] the *task* or *type of assignment* performed by the group,[22] *degree of formal authority or power*.[23] A large amount of research was conducted in these areas during the sixties and early seventies. Fred Fiedler and his associates utilized much of this research in the development of the contingency model of leadership.

The contingency theory is that the group's effectiveness is contingent on the interaction between two variables: (1) the motivational system of the leader—his style in relating to his group, and (2) the favorableness of the group situation—the degree to which the situation allows the leader to control his group. The theory is that leaders with given styles will perform better in situations favorable to their style. The leadership situation included three components listed in order of importance: (1) leader–member relations—degree to which group members support, respect, and like the group leader, (2) task structure—the degree to which groups tasks are spelled out, (3) position power—power vested by the organization in the leader's position or the degree to which the position enables the leader to get the group to accept his/her leadership.

Fiedler classified leaders as either task oriented or human relations oriented as determined by the leader's score on a personality measure, The Least Preferred Co-Worker Scale (LPC). He then tested his theory on the findings of over eight hundred studies completed between 1951 and 1963. Analyses of the studies indicated: (1) low LPC or task-motivated leaders were most effective in high-control or low-control situations, and (2) high LPC or human-relations-motivated leaders were most effective in situations of moderate control.[24]

While Fiedler's work is controversial and he implied the leader's style

[20] Erickson, op. cit.

[21] Campbell, J. P., et al, *Managerial Behavior, Performance and Effectiveness* (New York: McGraw-Hill, 1970).

[22] Shaw, M. E., *Group Dynamics, The Psychology of Group Behavior* (New York: McGraw-Hill, 1971).

[23] Cartwright, D., *Studies in Social Power* (Ann Arbor: University of Michigan Institute of Social Research, 1959).

[24] Fiedler, F. E., and Chemers, M. M., *Leadership and Effective Management* (Glenview, Ill.: Scott Foresman and Co., 1974).

of management is incapable of being changed, others following up on his research have critically examined leadership methods and maintained leaders can and should alter their style of leadership in concrete situations to better fit their style to the demands of the situation.

Principal Power

Much of the literature on leadership centers on power or control. Without control little progress is made but hierarchical control can evolve into rigid authoritarianism and decentralized diffused control can degenerate into chaos. Thus a dilemma! One has further concern when analyzing the legitimate power base of the principal for it will be discovered that it is really quite small when compared to the usual concept of an administrator's power.

Our analysis of the power base of the typical principal shows that much of the old-fashioned legitimate power of the principal is more imagined than real. Looking at the dwindling of his power from this viewpoint a typical principal might be very jealous of the power he has left and guard it with fervor.

The Upward Look

The reader is familiar with this type of administrator who relies entirely upon the legal resources or status of position for power and control. Various behaviors are typical of this orientation. They are exemplified by a very careful checking for compliance with written regulations and "how to" directives; attention to the letter of the law rather than the spirit thereof; and putting off decisions on any unusual situation. The principal can easily find him- or herself in such a situation and, indeed, it may be "comfortable" for him/her to behave that way. Briner and Sroufe may have pointed out why.

> we discover that the principal is usually a man who is delegated all responsibility, but no power to fulfill it. The principal's position is quite hollow and, like a priest, he is only the defender of higher authority. Being thus dependent, his eyes are ever cast upward and are little concerned with those around him.[25]

The classic bureaucratic model immediately comes to mind in which administrators can act solely upon written rules and regulations from above. If a unique situation occurs outside his/her specified authority, the administrator forwards it upward for decision. He/she tries to understand the way those above him/her think so that his/her own actions will conform

---

[25] C. Briner and G. E. Sroufe, "Organizations for Education in 1985," *Educational Futurism 1985* (Berkeley: McCutchan Publishing Corp., 1971), p. 80.

to their norms. Those around the teachers and students are not the major concern in this model.

Though we may make light of this type of principal, there are many more than we would like to admit. Thomas Wiggins writes that the role of the principal as "administrator leader" and instructional leader is questionable under the scrutiny of the test of research.[26] He states we need to reexamine the presumption that the power, authority, and influence of school principals provide the major source of leadership thrust to the school. Much of the research shows that the principal has had little or no effect on school climate in the typical urban district. The explanation of these research findings is that the principals are selected in the "image of the school district." Many had been reared as teachers, vice principals, and in other service positions in the same district. They were selected and prepared to behave in a rational, predictable, and uniform manner acceptable to the district, and the longer they were in the system the more they perpetuated existing tradition and acted like the central administration expected them to act. (In other words, they were good apprentices.) Thus, rather than a leader the principal becomes a supporter of the central system and thus the school approaches a state of homeostasis.

The Principal as Leader

One can become very pessimistic when reading the statements and findings of Briner, Sroufe, Wiggins, and others. We do not believe the situation is as gloomy as implied. The principal can be and is in many instances a positive leadership force. It must be realized, however, that leadership does not come from the power base of old. We face a new world in educational administration, our processes must be geared to a changing society and a changed educational organization. We need a new definition of leadership and updated administrative processes that are appropriate to education in its present and future context.

We would like to comment briefly on the implications of the research to the principal's leadership role, provide what we believe is a realistic definition of leadership, and then reanalyze power in light of our leadership definition. How does the principal who wants to be a leader use the research findings on leadership? Certainly he/she would become frustrated in trying to apply the findings directly to his or her job situation. However, the studies do give cues and possible direction that can be helpful in sharpening one's knowledge of leadership and in assessing and improving it. It must be realized that leadership is a complex dynamic interactive

[26] Thomas Wiggens, "The Influence of Role and Organizational Climate Upon Principal Behavior" in William G. Monahan, *Theoretical Dimensions of Educational Administration* (New York: Macmillan, 1975), pp. 348–360.

process. The studies reveal that "leadership effectiveness" depends upon how we define leadership, the criteria we use to evaluate it, the type of organization within which the leader operates, the type of staff, their proficiency, the tasks they have, and the situations they face. One hears an increasing number of speeches and reads increasing amounts of professional literature lamenting the declining power of the principalship. The authors have faced a growing number of principals at professional meetings or coming back for further graduate training who are bitter about the lack of leadership opportunities provided by central administration or the lack of teacher receptiveness of their leadership efforts.

It is our contention that leadership opportunities are still as great and exciting as ever if one could just forget the heroic image of the old-fashioned leader. What is needed is a new definition of leadership appropriate to a new context of school organization and operation. A review of the textbooks in educational administration today still implies the leader operates from an influential power base and will be surrendering leadership if he/she is not the initiator of action. "The leader is viewed as a potent force for good in the organization; his task is to use the influence of his office to bind the wills of his subordinates in accomplishing the purposes beyond their own self-serving ends." [27]

We do not believe that this is a realistic viewpoint for today's schools. To be realistic the findings of research must be applied to the context of *today's* school organization, and the definition of educational leadership should be comprehensive enough to recognize the growing professional influence and growing competency of teachers.

Leadership Defined

With this as our rationale we define leadership as a *planned process* that results in the following:

1. The challenging of people to work toward an ever-expanding vision of excellence in the achievement of organizational goals and objectives.
2. The creation of a threat-free environment for growth so that the creative talents and skills of each person are used to best advantage.
3. The encouragement and building of working relationships that are individually and organizationally satisfying, unifying, and strengthening in the realization of mutually determined goals and objectives.
4. The optimization of available material resources.

With this definition, leadership is where you find it. We believe a major leadership role of the principal is to identify and nourish any ideas, acts, and efforts that will further the goals and objectives of the institution.

[27] Edwin M. Bridges, "The Nature of Leadership" in Lavern Cunningham, et al., *Educational Administration: The Developing Decades* (Berkeley, Calif.: McCutchans, 1977), p. 204.

Power Base

Considering our definition of leadership let's relook at the whole question of principal power and analyze it on the basis of today's schools.

French and Raven list five bases of legitimate power: (1) *reward power*—ability to reward; (2) *coercive power*—ability to threaten or punish; (3) *legitimate power*—power or authority the organization assigns to the leadership position along with internalized values of staff members that gives leader authority to influence them; (4) *referent power*—person's feelings or desire to identify with person possessing power; and (5) *expert power*—the extent that subordinates attribute expertise and knowledge to the leader.[28]

Considering today's school and the professional staff, none of these sources provide a full measure of power. *Reward power* is blunted by collective bargaining. Few schools have merit increases. The salary scale agreed upon at the bargaining table applies to all (good, bad, or medium) of like experience and education. Reward by praise and special recognition becomes the main source of this power in today's schools. *Coercive power* is blunted by tenure and grievance committees. True, the principal has responsibility for rating teachers but this affects only the very poor and the very good. Few teachers are concerned with threats of punishment although they do respond favorably to positive professional overtures to help them improve their teaching. *Legitimate power* is blunted by the general professional role of the teacher. We pointed out in Chapter 5 that the school organization is different from any other organization in that the main function of the school is carried out in the classroom by the teacher who is the chief executive of that classroom. Few teachers stand in awe of the legitimate power of the principal. The teacher is a professional equal who probably knows more about his/her subject and how to teach it than the principal. The teacher is "monarch in the classroom castle," and is backed completely by the professional organization. *Referent power,* with the adversary relationships established in collective bargaining procedures, often operates in just the opposite direction. Many teachers do not wish to identify with the administrator possessing legitimate power, particularly the autocratic or bureaucratic administrator. In the area of *expert power,* the typical principal may be no more expert in subject matter, curriculum, or teaching than the typical teacher. If he/she is considered competent and knowledgeable in these areas this is a leadership plus. The areas of expertise that the principal must exhibit in his/her school and which are

[28] French, J. R. P., and Raven, B. H., "The Basis of Social Power" in D. Cartwright (Ed.), *Studies in Social Power* (Ann Arbor: University of Michigan, Institute of Social Research, 1959). See also Amitai Etzioni, *A Comparative Analysis of Complex Organizations* (New York: Free Press, 1961) for his concept of power sources.

more impressive to the teacher and are certainly backed up by the research are: (1) Skill in dealing with people individually and in groups and identifying leadership whenever it exists; (2) a keen intellect and curiosity along with conceptual skills in relating education to the present and future of our society; (3) a broad general knowledge of teaching and learning theory along with a keen understanding of growth and development of children and youth; (4) skill in establishing a well-planned coordinated operation with clearly identified goals along with procedures for encouraging maximum achievement; (5) skill in dealing with central administration so that desired plans and programs can be approved and appropriate resources are forthcoming for their implementation; (6) a thorough knowledge of the operational details of the local, state, and national educational structure.

This is the type of expert power that will help the principal in his/her leadership role. It is the type of power that will work best in schools of today. A review of research shows that schools that rate the principal as having and using expert power received high scores for teacher morale, teacher satisfaction, and teacher high performance. At the same time schools with coercive principals showed the lowest scores.[29]

Sharing Power

The typical point of view is that power exists in a fixed quantity, that it is limited to the point that if one person gains power then someone else in the organization has to lose it. Research indicates that this is not true. The evidence points to the viewpoint that power is both expansible and reciprocal, that it has synergistic qualities.[30]

It would appear that the best way to exercise power and authority and at the same time to acquire the same is to share it. Dimock's discussion [31] states that the creative growth of individuals is dependent upon individual motivation throughout the organization. He further associates creative growth with the exercise of power. The implication is that power is really dead apart from growing individuals. The acceptance of responsibility is important to the growth of individuals. John Dewey suggested that:

> Absence of participation tends to produce lack of interest and concern on the part of those shut out. The result is a corresponding lack of effective responsibility.[32]

[29] ERIC Clearinghouse on Educational Management, *Research Action Brief* (Eugene, Oregon: University of Oregon, Number 2, June 1978), p. 4.

[30] Ibid., p. 4.

[31] Marshall E. Dimock, A *Philosophy of Administration toward Creative Growth* (New York: Harper, 1958), pp. 166–171.

[32] Morris Mendelson et al., "Social Power and Commitment: A Theoretical Statement," in Netzer et al., *Interdisciplinary Foundations of Supervision* (Boston: Allyn and Bacon, 1970), p. 219.

The principal can foster the acceptance of responsibility by sharing the authority.

Look at this reciprocal theory of power in another way. With collective bargaining and the growing strength of the professional teacher organizations the teacher members of the staff collectively may have more real power than the principal. If the principal fully shares his/her power with the teachers and has the expertise to develop a true team spirit within the school the teacher support and power will increase the principal's power with teachers, the central administration, and the community. The combined forces can provide a strong base for the achievement of the school's goals.

The Eric Clearinghouse on Educational Management reinforces this viewpoint in an interesting issue devoted to a discussion on power and managerial control.[33]

> An impressive array of research challenges the traditional assumption that power in an organization exists in limited quantities. In doing so, the research challenges as well some of the traditional practices that have grown out of this "all-or-none" law of power. For principals in particular, the research points in some interesting managerial directions.
>
> Principals should take careful stock of the level and distribution of power in their schools. Their evaluation should consider the answers to such questions as, Is the principal comfortable with the amount of his own control over the school? Is the control used effectively? Does the principal have influence with teachers? Do teachers feel influential, and do they evidence high satisfaction with their work? Does the school function at a high level of efficiency and productivity?
>
> If the answers to these questions point to low levels of influence and employee morale in the school, the principal might well consider whether he has been overly cautious about parceling out power to the school's staff and even to students. Knowing that the power in an organization is not limited but is capable of expansion, the principal will look for ways to increase the total amount of power for the benefit of the school.
>
> Because power is reciprocal, an increase in the power of teachers should lead to a corresponding increase in the power of the principal. Conversely, the principal who is stingy with power also circumscribes his own power.

Participating Leadership

When one speaks of participating leadership and shared power it often conjures in one's mind a lumbering slow-moving organization with nothing ever really getting done because everyone has to have a say on everything. This should not be the case. Remember, in time after time research has shown that what has been called *initiating structure* is a major dimension of leadership. Teachers have identified it as a requirement for leadership in almost every major research study in which they have been involved.

[33] Ibid., p. 4.

To define it again, initiating structure is a type of behavior by the leader that clarifies the relationship of the staff within the organization and what is expected of them. It implies a well-planned coordinated operation that has clearly identified goals and standards of performance with procedures established to encourage maximum achievement.

There is nothing here contrary to shared power or participating leadership. One of the first things a principal should do when assuming the principal role is to work with the faculty and the central administration to clarify structure and operation. He/she should research legislation, board policies, and central administration directives that may be basic requirements for structure and then involve the faculty as fully as possible in filling in the gaps. The following four cautions should be observed when working with faculty in this process:

1. Do not neglect to clearly identify basic requirements from higher echelons—good or bad, they are requirements! They must be included! If they need to be changed let that be a separate battle. Don't disrupt process by allowing too much arguing over them.
2. Do let your "druthers" be known about how you believe things should be structured to fit in with your administrative style and be willing to debate the issues. Identify to the faculty processes and actions that are so important to you that you do not want a vote on them, explain to them why, and provide an opportunity for them to react.
3. Identify and establish a plan of procedure and process for establishing your initiating structure so that there is sufficient time for participation of faculty but also an understood system of closure on the issue. It is a leader's responsibility to see that discussion and involvement are brought to a logical conclusion in a reasonable time so that the work of the school can go forward.
4. Identify ahead of time those issues it is appropriate for faculty to vote upon and those that are nonvotable administrative prerogatives.

Planning an Important Factor in Leadership

Part of the initiating structure for participating leadership is proper planning and the providing of background information so as to make participation productive and enlightened. There is nothing more frustrating than to attend a meeting on an important problem and have the first few sessions no more than a pooling of ignorance with the more vocal members of the staff shooting "from the hip" in their thinking. The leader is responsible for seeing that the faculty is prepared to participate on an important problem. This requires providing necessary background information. For the most part this is a proper staff responsibility. Some of the following questions can be helpful to the principal and his/her planning staff as they prepare for planning.

1. *What already available background data are important in making decisions about the problem at hand?* If it is a program change, some pertinent data might include analyses of student achievement in the area to be studied; descriptions of, or actual samples of, current materials; expert evaluations of the materials; experiences of other schools using new, promising curricula; their instructional objectives, etc.
2. *What new data will be needed? From what sources will it be available?*
3. *Who, individuals and groups, within the system will be affected? Who outside the system?* As as example, if a new routing of buses is to be planned, there are several possible answers to the question above. Inside the system there would be at least drivers, children, principals, teachers, and the business offices. Outside the system parents, traffic control or street department, property owners, and insurance company, would be included.
4. *Is the real problem clearly defined? What are the subparts of the problem?* New dimensions will be identified as the process evolves. The leader is cautioned to avoid concentrating on only a symptom of a larger problem.

Implementing the Process

Step Sequencing. The first step in implementing a planning process is the identification of the steps necessary to complete the plan and the sequencing of these steps. A simple listing of steps with probable times to complete each step may be sufficient. If the plan involves several components interdependent upon each other over a long period of time, a more sophisticated approach may be in order.

The principal can use one of the network analysis techniques. The two most commonly referred to are the Critical Path Method (CPM) and the Program Evaluation and Review Techniques (PERT). The use of these and similar tools is increasing rapidly. Handy and Hussain indicate that pressures from outside the school are going to force the use of network analysis techniques. Governmental agencies, educational organizations, and private agencies such as architects or contractors bidding for work will influence the school into becoming conversant with network analysis.[34] They list some advantages of these techniques:

1. Network analysis establishes sequence and interrelationships of the activities needed to complete a project within predetermined time estimates.
2. Network analysis forces realistic planning.
3. Network analysis provides management by objectives.

[34] H. W. Handy and K. M. Hussain, *Network Analysis for Educational Management* (Englewood Cliffs, N.J.: Prentice-Hall, 1969), p. 15.

4. Network analysis provides up-to-date project status information.
5. Network analysis enables the project manager to quickly discover potential work slippages and shows the impact of slippage on other activities.
6. Network analysis identifies particular areas where the additional use of funds may accelerate the program.
7. Network analysis establishes a disciplined planning, communications, and systems operation.

A well-organized network system provides for monitoring the program progress and opening up communications throughout the planning. In addition, it should provide for a continuous qualitative evaluation of the programs and their parts. Evaluation is essential to the planning process in that it completes the feedback loop so that alternatives can be weighed and choices made to progress toward the desired objectives.

Research has noted that one of the dissatisfiers in education is the inadequacy of technical supervision. It is clear that this area is a "must" for the principal. A carefully planned evaluation program formed as an integral part of any planning process is a step toward eliminating this dissatisfier. Further discussion of evaluation can be found in Chapters 10 and 11.

Participation in Decision Making [35]

Participation and sharing of power does not mean a faculty needs to get together every time a decision is made. This in itself would be poor leadership! It means that procedures are established that provide the opportunity for the faculty to have appropriate input on decisions that may be important to them. The following may serve as a guide to the principal on faculty participation in decision making.

1. On various types of decisions, policies can be agreed upon by the faculty that will give the principal all the direction necessary to make a decision on his/her own.
2. Some decisions affect only certain members of the faculty or certain departments. Only faculty affected should ordinarily be involved.
3. Some decisions may be more appropriately handled by having a department head, chairman, or spokesman for a group provide feedback to principal to help him/her with the decision.
4. Some decisions may be handled by memoranda to faculty asking anyone with strong feeling about the decision to contact the principal. (Establish a time limit for contact.)
5. Some decisions may require only the involvement of recognized experts on the faculty.

[35] See The National Association of Secondary Principals NASSP Bulletin Vol 63 N 425 (March, 1979). A large portion of this issue is devoted to leadership.

6. There may be some decisions in which faculty aren't interested in being involved. These can be identified and classified.
7. There are some projects particularly related to curriculum changes or teaching procedures that will require deep involvement by faculty if the project is to be properly implemented and supported. Principals should make participation a planned educational process on decisions of this type.
8. There are some decisions that must be made exclusively by the administrator. This must be understood.
9. There are some decisions that everyone must realize must be made immediately. The administrator must have enough courage to do so and the faculty enough faith not to worry.
10. On some decisions the faculty may stall and procrastinate. The principal must have enough courage to make a final decision when closure is necessary.
11. Some faculty members don't want to be involved—they don't want to be bothered; yet, involvement develops interest and the sharing and caring necessary for teamwork. Principals can use decision making as a way of getting some faculty members involved.

Summary

Leadership is complex. It has been defined as traits, attitudes, behaviors, position, and several combinations of these. It is clear that leadership is a hollow term without people and without purpose—it cannot exist apart from a social setting. Furthermore, leadership does not result from a formula applied or from decrees from on high. It is a planned process of interaction in a social setting whereby goals that are mutually satisfying to the school organization and to the individuals in the school are established and means developed to achieve them. The following summarizes points made above regarding the exercise of leadership, but is not intended as a formula for the same:

1. Develop and maintain an environment of growth for each individual in the school—pupils, staff, and yes, the principal too.
2. Optimize the environment to satisfy the needs of both the organization and the people.
3. Develop leadership among the staff and pupils.
4. Look in more than one direction for a leadership base.
5. Share authority and responsibility with those whom one proposes to lead.
6. Accept the limitations of those with whom one shares responsibility.
7. Realize that one of the most effective leadership bases is that of professional competence. The principal must be able to "produce" in the

area accepted by those who are led as a proper source of authority for leadership.

To be effective, the principal will need to lead from a stronger base than just his/her status position or the controlling of, and accounting for, resources. He/she should be able to make significant programmatic contributions to the achievement of the school's purposes. He/she will need to share, not abdicate, his/her authority.

The opportunities for exerting leadership in a school are almost innumerable and are, in a sense, the measure of the principal's responsibility to lead.

For Further Thought

1. In your own words, define "educational leadership"; then give some examples of leadership acts.
2. What criteria are appropriate in determining what authority shall be shared regarding instructional decisions?
3. What characteristics distinguish formal organization from informal organization? Do all informal leaders make effective formal leaders? Explain.
4. Have you ever observed a sharp rise or fall in the morale of a faculty? If so, what factors do you think caused such a marked change?
5. Is conflict necessarily bad and harmony always good? If the administration were so organized that the final decision making was delegated to the appropriate qualified expert, would all conflict be eliminated?
6. If you were the principal of a school where a faculty was content to let you run the school as you wished, would you try to involve them or be happy to run the school without interference?
7. Is a climate where mistakes are allowable compatible with evaluation and accountability?
8. Using the LBDQ-Form XII or any other well-known leadership measure analyze your own leadership style and potential.
9. Develop a flow chart or PERT/CPM network for solving an administrative problem. How would the network be different in different types of schools?

Chapter 7 Legislation and the Courts—
A Sound Base of Authority

In so many ways the principal is the person in the middle—having responsibility as leader and administrator of an institution operating in a society whose values are changing constantly, whose constituents represent extremes of conservatism and radicalism, and which is faced with rapid advancement in knowledge that often explodes old ideas and principles.

The principal soon discovers that nothing is really constant and the search for firm ground upon which to stand in order to make decisions is difficult. One major source of strength to the principal is the legal basis of educational operation. Even here problems can occur if one assumes that the law is inflexible and not influenced by social pressures; nonetheless, the law as we know it here and now should guide our mode of operation. At the same time, by observing some of the changing interpretations the courts have given these laws, one is able to make some reasonable observation of the directions society is going. We often think of the courts as being conservative; however, to observe the changes in the interpretation of our laws as they relate to the Constitution of the United States is to observe most startling social progress.

Stranger yet, schools generally lag behind in their administration of justice and upholding the rights of the individual. It can be easily documented that schools in many instances have been inclined to suppress individual rights and to be quite arbitrary in the suppression of unpopular and minority viewpoints. Reviewing cases regarding dress, pregnancy, married students, graduation restrictions, student newspapers, expulsion, saluting the flag, and even discrimination is to review numerous examples of oppression. It becomes even more a matter of concern when one recognizes that most students never litigate and are simply silenced by the plenary power that school authorities exercise over their lives. However, during the last decade in particular, the courts have begun to challenge the decisions of administrators who failed to recognize the constitutional rights of students and teachers.

A Knowledge of School Law Is Important

Courses in school law are often dismissed with the statement, "Let's not try to make an attorney out of the school administrator or teacher." Certainly that should not be the intent of such courses. Rather, the purpose should be to acquaint teachers and administrators with some of the legal fundamentals affecting their positions and the education profession. A hunter must know the hunting laws; the fisherman, the fishing laws. The car driver is responsible for knowing traffic laws. We all must know right from wrong, not only morally but also legally. Ignorance may be bliss, but not so far as the law is concerned. As John Selden stated: "Ignorance of the law excuses no man: not that all men know the law, but because 'tis an excuse every man will plead, and no man can tell how to confute him."

It follows that a school administrator must know the law concerning the professional field of education and the schools. One would not expect the school principal to consult a lawyer every time a professional decision needs to be made; yet, to carry a point to the extreme, to be on the safe side one would need to do so unless he/she had a working knowledge of school law.

This point has been reinforced by the United States Supreme Court in Wood v. Strickland. The court held that an administrator or school board member is not immune from liability for damages if he/she knew or reasonably should have known that the action officially taken would violate the constitutional rights of the students affected, or if the action was taken with malicious intention to cause a deprivation of constitutional rights.[1]

School districts are governmental agencies of the state through which the legislatures carry out their constitutional mandate to provide a system of public education. The courts have ruled that school officers are state and not local officers. As servants of the state they have only the powers that statutes grant them. We have heard many principals make the statement: "If there is nothing in the law saying we can't do it, we'll go ahead and do it." In the strict sense this is wrong. Schools have no inherent powers and the authority to operate them must be found in either expressed or implied terms of statute and the rules and regulations of both state and local boards of education. The legal viewpoint in relation to a school district and school officer is "Unless the law gives you power and authority to do it, you can't do it." Of course the laws cannot specify the what, where, and why of every possible condition; therefore, it is recognized that there must be a wide range of implied powers in order to permit the exercises of expressed powers.[2] Implied powers, because of their lack of specificity,

[1] 420 U.S. 308 321 (1975).
[2] Expressed powers are those specifically listed in legislation authorizing activity. Implied powers are not specifically enumerated but are activities that one might reasonably expect to be necessary to carry out the spirit and the letter of the law.

are a source of much litigation. On the other hand, they allow progress, growth, and experimentation by providing a frontier where imaginative and dynamic administration can take place. The good administrator searches for the delicate balance between what is necessary for the entire state and school district as illustrated by expressed powers, and what is best for the school as allowed by implied powers.

Implied powers may also serve to establish proving grounds to test administrative practices that may eventually become law or policy. A procedure designed by a school administrator to meet a particular educational problem in a particular school may spread through an entire school district as a logical way for all officials in the districts to operate. The procedure may stand unquestioned for several years and then, because of some question or controversy, the school board or legislature may feel obligated to pass permissive or mandatory policy or legislation to allow it to continue. In this way it becomes a definite part of the school code.

State Law a Framework for Administrative Action [3]

The concept that education is a state function can be easily proved. The roots of the American philosophy of education were firmly embedded in colonial law that foreshadowed existing state laws. The pattern of our educational system has developed through ordinances governing the territories that were to become states. When the United States became a reality the structural pattern of education as a state function was established: by the general reservation of power in the Federal Constitution, by positive expression in state constitutions, and by enactment of state school legislation. Today, each state constitution charges its legislature either directly or indirectly with the responsibility of establishing and maintaining a system of schools. All states delegate certain of these responsibilities to state educational agencies and local boards of education. Thus the springboard for any administrative action is derived broadly from the state constitution and more specifically from state legislation, administrative directives of state educational agencies, and policies of the local boards of education. The courts resolve questions of meaning or intent through judicial review of specific education questions or situations outside of education that have implications for educational policies, programs, and practices.

Every administrative action, then, fits into a legal framework that guides and directs the school administrator. One naturally expects a professional educator who acts for a school district to know these things. By the same token, administrators of a school that is part of a school district, which is

[3] For a more thorough discussion of this topic read William H. Roe, *School Business Management* (New York: McGraw-Hill, 1961), pp. 284–87.

a creature of the state, cannot be ignorant of the state school code or directives of the state educational agencies, or even national legal trends in regard to education.

A good school administrator understands state regulations and directives as well as local school policy. Logically, the professional educator might even be more expert in school law than the average lawyer. This does not mean that the school principal should serve as a pseudo lawyer. Rather, it suggests that school law is particularized and that the school administrator must have a professional knowledge of school laws in order to make decisions that affect education normally. It should not be necessary to use an attorney on school law itself unless there is some question of technical interpretation, unless a legal document has to be prepared, or unless legal action has to be initiated. On the other hand, although there is much law that relates specifically to education, a much greater body of law relates to the operation of government generally and affects education because education is a part of government. It is here where the services of an attorney are necessary.

Religion and the Public Schools

While any subject as nationally controversial as religion and the schools should be dealt with quite specifically by state legislation and districtwide school policy, the topic warrants at least a brief discussion. It is indeed an unusual year when the school principal is not accosted by some well-meaning parent and citizen because the school is or is not doing something in regard to religion.

The need for a "wall of separation" between the church and the state was expressed by our forefathers so emphatically because of the cruelty of religious persecutions in Europe and the American Colonies. Thus the first amendment to our Constitution guarantees religious and political freedoms. It has a double aspect in that it "forestalls compulsion by law of the acceptance of any creed or practice of any form of worship" and at the same time safeguards the "free exercise" of the chosen form of religion. In this double aspect of the First Amendment it places on the school as an arm of the state the responsibility of maintaining a "wholesome neutrality."

The question of furnishing free textbooks, transportation, school lunch, and other such "child benefits" have been tested hundreds of times in the courts and are matters that are determined by state constitutions and state statutes as they relate to the First Amendment to the U.S. Constitution. Other questions may arise that are more specific to the school.

The question of released time or dismissed time during regular school hours for religious ceremony or instruction comes up with some frequency in every school. State regulation and local school board policy should be clear in their handling of all aspects of this issue. The U.S. Supreme Court has acted on two cases involving released or dismissed time. In the first, known as the McCollom Case,[4] parents objected because the children were instructed in the classroom of their building and those students who did not want to participate were required to leave their classroom and go to another part of their building. The courts declared this unconstitutional. In the second case, a New York statute provided for released time permitting pupils to leave the building and grounds to attend religious centers for religious instruction.[5] The Supreme Court declared this constitutional. From these cases it is clear the Constitution does not require schools to be hostile to religion nor does it prohibit cooperation between schools and churches, but the nature and degree of cooperation is important; and if it exceeds certain reasonable limitations the relationship will violate the Constitution.

Much the same philosophy prevails regarding prayer and Bible-reading in the schools. In the Engle v. Vitale case the New York State Board of Regents had composed the following "nonsectarian" prayer that they recommended be read daily: "Almighty God, we acknowledge our dependence on Thee and we beg Thy blessings upon us, our parents, our teachers and our country." The Supreme Court ruled that it violated the establishment clause of the First Amendment, and therefore must be excluded from use by the schools.[6] There followed other numerous attempts to circumvent the ruling and develop truly nonsectarian prayers. In an Illinois school district the following simple verse was rejected by the courts even though it had no specific reference to God: "We thank you for the flowers so sweet; we thank you for the food we eat; we thank you for the birds that sing; we thank you for everything." [7]

Thus, the courts have interpreted the "school prayer" decision in such a way as to prohibit essentially any attempts to bring a spiritual message in the classroom.[8] While in some cases the courts have held that Bible-reading is a sectarian exercise the general result of many cases is that laws and regulations requiring almost any type of religious exercise is unconstitutional. However, the study of the Bible and religion, as a part of a secular program of education, for their literary and historic values is not unconstitutional.[9]

[4] People of the State of Illinois ex rel. McCollom v. Board of Education, 333 U.S. 203 (1948).

[5] Zorach v. Clauson, 343 U.S. 306 (1952).

[6] Engle v. Vitale, 370 U.S. 421 (1962).

[7] DeSpain v. DeKalb County Community School District, 428, 384 F 2nd 836, 837 (7th Cir. 1967).

[8] E. Gordon Gee and David J. Sperry, Education Law and the Public Schools: A Compendium (Boston: Allyn and Bacon Inc., 1978).

[9] School District of Abington Twp. v. Schempp and Murray v. Curlett, 374 U.S. 203 (1963).

Common Liability Situations

The law grants to each individual certain personal rights in regard to the way he/she may be treated by others. These personal rights are not automatically eliminated because he/she is a child or because he/she is in school. Defamation of character, (libel and slander) and assault and battery are common sources of trouble as far as schools are concerned because there are so many incidents of disciplinary problems where punishment is administered and statements must be made orally or in writing in the line of duty regarding a student's wrongdoing; teachers and principals make value judgments about a student's behavior based on their own standards, or tempers become high and statements are made in the heat of the moment.

To prove defamation of character (libel and slander) the following elements must be shown: (1) publish or communicate a false statement concerning another, (2) the statement brings hatred, disgrace, ridicule, or contempt upon another person, (3) damages resulted from the statement.[10]

Of course the professional person is protected if he/she indeed acts like a professional person. The courts are most understanding of the teacher and administrator who is responsible for many children and who must relate with all the parents and adults in a community; therefore, courts will not assess liability if communication was made in good faith, without malice, in answer to an official inquiry and done in performance of a duty to society.[11] Nonetheless, as one reviews the court cases, particularly in the last few years, one realizes that society is becoming more conscious of the rights of a student whether a six-year-old or a seventeen-year-old. The teacher is finding it more difficult to hide behind the cloak of *in loco parentis*. Accusations regarding copying, lying, stealing, questionable sexual behavior, intelligence, judgment, and so on, cannot be made carelessly or callously—nor should they be!

Adequate Supervision

The situation often arises in a school where some unfortunate incident takes place or unintentional injury occurs. The question then comes up whether the children were properly supervised or if adequate safety precautions were taken by the school. Historically school districts were protected from liability by the old common-law doctrine that the state is

---

[10] Oral communications of a defamatory nature are slander. Written communications of defamatory nature are called libel.

[11] Beckett v. Crossfield, 190 Ky. 751,(1921); Kenory v. Gurley 208 Ala. 623 (1923). Wood v. Strickland 420 U.S. 308 (1975); Monell v. New York City, 46 USLW 4569 (U.S. 1978).

sovereign and cannot be sued without its consent.[12] Educators riding on the tail of this old common-law cloak seldom were held liable for carelessness or questionable supervisory practices. However, again we see a change taking place. More and more governmental immunity is being considered a leftover from the Middle Ages. States are passing legislation overturning this concept and while recent court decisions often upheld the immunity rule, split decisions and dissenting opinions suggest the common-law doctrine may be of questionable validity in the future. As stated by the Illinois Supreme Court in the Molitor case: "We conclude the rule of school district toward immunity is unjust, unsupported by any valid reason and has no rightful place in modern day society."[13] In considering the teachers' and administrators' increased susceptibility to court action for lack of supervision or for improper safety precautions, the statement of the dissenting judge in Ohman v. Board of Education of City of New York is of interest:

> When a large number of children are gathered in a single classroom, without any effective control or supervision, it may be reasonably anticipated that certain of them may so act as to inflict unintentional injury upon themselves or their classmates. Children have known proclivity to act impulsively without thought of the possibilities of danger. It is precisely this lack of mature judgment which makes supervision so vital. It may be reasonably anticipated that the prolonged absence of authority at a time when children's activities are usually supervised will result in such a situation as is demonstrated in the instant case.[14]

While in general courts have been most sympathetic to the difficult role of teacher and administrator, the courts have held them generally responsible for the following: adequate supervision, proper instruction, and keeping all equipment in safe, reasonable repair.[15] The principal is not ordinarily liable for the negligence of teachers or employees if they are properly appointed and qualified. On the other hand, if duties are assigned for which the teacher or aide is not qualified and these duties do not fall within the scope of employment the principal may be held liable.[16]

The principal should also accept the responsibility for alerting teachers to ways of avoiding unfortunate incidents or injury to students during school activities. For example:

1. Teachers should be asked to analyze their courses and teaching procedures for possible hazardous situations and then take appropriate

---

[12] Derived from English law—"The King can do no wrong."

[13] Molitor v. Kaneland Community Unit District No. 302, Supreme Court of Illinois 18 Ill. 2nd 11 (1959).

[14] 300 N.Y. 306 (1949).

[15] Kern Alexander, Ray Corns, and Walter McCann, *Public School Law* (St. Paul, Minn.: West Publishing Company, 1969), pp. 363–364.

[16] Gray v. Wood, 75 R. E. 123, (1949); Garber v. Central School Districts 295 N.Y.S. 850 (1937).

steps to eliminate all dangers that can reasonably be avoided and/or provide special supervision and safeguards when they can't be avoided.

2. Written instructions, adequate warning of danger points, and close supervision should be provided when the student engages in activities that are dangerous and that require special skills and knowledge.

3. When engaging in field trips special instructions should be developed for all possible situations; parents should be informed of the trip; and additional parent or adult help should be solicited if the situation is such that the teacher cannot properly supervise all students participating. The school office should have a record of such arrangements.

4. A student should not be asked to help or assist with any task that is beyond the student's physical or mental capacity.

5. Arrangements should be made so that students are not mismatched or overmatched in recreational activities and intramural functions.

6. If a student must be sent home during school hours, parents or guardians should be notified and proper arrangements made for safe passage home. The school office should have on file emergency procedures in the event parents or guardians cannot be reached.

7. If a student is seriously injured, competent medical help should be summoned (if possible, with the approval of the parent). Nonmedically trained staff should not attempt to administer first aid directly unless it appears necessary to save a life.[17]

Corporal Punishment

Corporal punishment has become a major controversial issue within the last few years. More and more school districts are prohibiting or are placing restrictive controls on corporal punishment through written school policy. A number of states have adopted legislation prohibiting its use in schools.[18] The principal and teacher should understand that they must abide by the regulations of their school district and the laws of their state. Failure to do so constitutes insubordination. Just as serious, a teacher acting without authority opens the door for civil and criminal charges for assault and battery.

The question of the right of a teacher to punish a pupil has been a matter of contention since schools have existed. In State v. Lutz the Court presented a summary of some fifty to sixty court cases in regard to corporal punishment by listing six fundamental propositions of law.[19]

[17] See Gee v. Sperry, op. cit., p. T-28 to T-44, for a more thorough discussion of negligence in supervision.
[18] New Jersey was the first state to adopt such legislation.
[19] 113 N.E. 2nd 757 Ohio (1953).

(1) The teacher stands in loco parentis (i.e. in the place of a parent) and acts in a quasi-judicial capacity, (2) the teacher's responsibility attaches home to home (i.e. while the pupil is on the way to and from school), (3) there is a presumption of correctness of the teacher's action, (4) there is a presumption that the teacher acted in good faith, (5) severe punishment on the part of the teacher does not constitute a crime unless it is of such a nature as to produce or threaten lasting or permanent injury or unless the state has shown that it was administered with either express malice (i.e. spite, hatred or revenge), or implied malice (i.e., a wrongful act wantonly done without just cause or excuse), and beyond a reasonable doubt. (6) The defendant teacher is entitled to all the benefits and safeguards of the well-known presumption of innocence.

Although these propositions generally would pertain today, greater discretion must be used in punishment because of (1) the present-day tendency to limit the in loco parentis concept, (2) the greater emphasis on individual rights of students, (3)state legislation and local school policies that restrict the right of teachers in regard to corporal punishment.

It is interesting to note that two federal district courts refused to rule corporal punishment in the public schools unconstitutional on the basis of either the Eighth or Fourteenth Amendments. In both cases it was noted that no other federal courts have held corporal punishment to be a denial of due process. Both courts were reluctant to interfere with the discretion of school authorities in disciplinary matters unless their action was clearly arbitrary, unlawful, or excessive.[20]

The U.S. Supreme Court generally reinforced these decisions in 1976 and 1977. Because they are the first two court cases involving corporal punishment to come before it they are considered most authoritative.

In the first, the Baker v. Owen Case, the Court ruled that under the Fourteenth Amendment parents did have the right to determine and choose among the means of disciplining their children. Beyond that, however, it asserted the state has a countervailing interest in the maintenance of order in their schools. "It should be clear beyond peradventure, indeed, self-evident, that to fulfill its assumed duty of providing an education to all who want it a state must maintain order in its schools." [21]

In the second case the U.S. Supreme Court asserted that public schools are open to the scrutiny and supervision of the public and thus there are sufficient safeguards against abuses prevented by the Eighth Amendment to our Constitution. The Court stated:

> Public school teachers and administrators are privileged at common law to inflict only such corporal punishment as is reasonably necessary for the proper education and discipline of the child; and punishment going beyond the privilege may result in both civil and criminal liability. As long as the

[20] Ware v. Estes, 328 F. Supp 657 (ND Tx 1971); Sims v. Board of Education, Independent School District No. 22, 329 F. Supp. 678 (D. N. Max 1971).
[21] 423 U.S. 907 (1976).

schools are open to public scrutiny there is no reason to believe that the common law constraints will not effectively remedy and deter excesses such as those alleged in this case.[22]

Legal Representation of Students and Parents

In serious disciplinary cases, e.g., cases of suspension and expulsion, the request is frequently made by parents that the child and parents be represented by an attorney. Although an attorney can always represent someone where due process of law is not followed, it is not necessary nor required at a conference for the purpose of providing an opportunity for parents, teachers, counselors, and administrators to plan educationally for the benefit of the child. This was well stated by the court in Madera v. Board of Education of the City of New York.[23]

> The conference is not a judicial or even quasi-judicial hearing . . . . the trial court misconceives the function of the conference and the role which participants therein play with respect to the education and welfare of the child. Law and order in the classroom should be the responsibility of our respective educational systems. The courts should not usurp this function and turn disciplinary problems, involving suspension, into criminal adversary proceedings—which they definitely are not. The rules, regulations, procedures and practices disclosed on this record evince a high regard for the best interests and welfare of the child. The courts will do well to recognize this.

Confidentiality of School Records

Considering the school's concern for the welfare and best interest of the child and the counseling activities in relation to this child leads to the whole question of the student's school records, their character, and how private and public they actually are. With the advancement of the computer and capacity to gather, store, and immediately retrieve massive amounts of personal data, the potential conflict between concerns for the individual's privacy and the school's need for information was becoming a difficult issue particularly as to data protection, confidentiality, and accessibility. Congress's enactment of the Family Educational Rights and Privacy Act (FERPA), commonly known as the Buckley Amendment, generally established legal principles applicable to access and disclosure of student records.[24] Actually, the Buckley Amendment established control by withholding federal dollars if schools failed to adhere to its provisions; however,

[22] Ingraham v. Wright 97 S. Ct. 1401 (1977).
[23] U.S. Court of Appeals, 386 F. 2nd 778 (1967).
[24] FERPA was enacted as Public Law 93-380, August 21, 1974. It was generally clarified by H.E.W. Rules and Regulations, 41 Fed. Reg. 24662 et seq. (June 17, 1976).

because of the power of the federal purse most state legislatures required their agencies to enact regulations consistent with FERPA; thus, it now stands as the controlling law dealing with the maintenance of school records. The Act states that education records mean: "those records, files, documents, and other materials which—(i) contain information directly related to a student; and (ii) are maintained by an education agency or institution or by a person acting for such agency or institution.[25] Generally, FERPA (1) allows parents or students to examine and review their children's or their own school records maintained on students; (2) provides opportunity for parents or students to challenge those records that are "inaccurate, misleading, or otherwise inappropriate"; (3) prohibits, except under special circumstances, the release of student record information to a third party without consent from parents and/or students; (4) requires the school to provide parents and students information concerning record-keeping procedures and their rights under FERPA. [26, 27]

The Student as a Responsible Citizen with Certain Inalienable Rights

There is no question but what our society is moving toward the recognition that children have certain inalienable rights as citizens, protected by our constitution. These rights cannot be abrogated even though the child is a minor or is a student in a public or private school. The unquestioned authority of the school is being questioned and the doctrine of the school standing *in loco parentis* continues to be more restricted and narrowed in its applicability.

Any consideration of the rights and responsibilities of students must start with the historic Supreme Court opinion in Tinker v. Des Moines Independent Community School District:

> in our system, state-operated schools may not be enclaves of totalitarianism. School officials do not possess absolute authority over their students. Students in school as well as out of school are "persons under our Constitution . . . in the absence of a specific showing of constitutionally valid reasons to regulate their speech students are entitled to freedom of expression of their views." [28]

A problem of concern is whether school authorities can censor student material prior to its publication and distribution. The courts have ruled

[25] 20 U.S.C.A. 1232g (a) (4) (A) (Supp. 1976).

[26] 20 U.S.C.A. 1232 g (e) (Supp. 1976). In addition to being knowledgeable about FERPA, school administrators should also have some understanding of the Freedom of Information Act, Pub. L. 93–502, 88 Stat. 1561 (U.S. Code) Cong. and Ad News, 93 Congress, 2nd Session 5758 (Dec. 15, 1974) and the Privacy Act, 1974.

[27] See "The Buckley Amendment: Opening School Files for Student and Parental Review," *Catholic University Law Review* 588 (1975).

[28] 393 U.S. 503 (1969). See also Goss v. Lopez, 419 U.S. 565 (1975) and Wood v. Strickland, 420 U.S. 308 (1975).

there is nothing basically unconstitutional in requiring students to submit
materials to the school administration prior to publication and distribution.
However, they must exercise restraint of distribution with great caution.[29]
Enough recent cases have been determined in favor of students' freedom
of speech and expression that it can be said that schools must be armed
with strong burden of proof that censorship was absolutely necessary for
the effective operation of the school.[30] A principal could very well apply
the standards used by the U.S. Supreme Court as reasons considered sufficient cause to curtail freedom of expression: [31] (1) prevention of incite-
ment of others to commit unlawful acts, (2) prevention of the utterance
of words so inflammatory that they provide for physical retaliation, (3)
protection of the sensibility of others, and (4) assurance of proper respect
for the national emblem.

Of course, when these standards are applied it is done on the basis of
someone's judgment and value and as such they are subject to scrutiny
and review. Courts are frequently using the lack of acceptable review and
appeal procedures as evidence of unreasonable restraint.[32] Even distribution
of literature on school property cannot be considered under the absolute
control of the school administration. Several court cases in this regard are
somewhat contradictory; nonetheless, in the two best-known cases the
courts were clear in asserting that unreasonable restrictions can be infringe-
ments on the rights of free speech.[33]

The National Association of Secondary School Principals recommends
the establishment of policy or guidelines to help the principal in the administration of his/her duties: [34]

> Guidelines of at least a general nature should be established clearly cate-
> gorizing material which is libelous, obscene, scandalous, or clearly provoca-
> tive as unacceptable. It may well be necessary for principals to insist upon
> the right of distribution, or prior review, to ensure that they have an
> opportunity to make this judgment. To avoid unnecessary legal confronta-
> tion, suspension, and/or disruption, school regulations should provide for
> the appeal of the principal's decision leading to final determination by the
> board. This would afford the board more participation in case-by-case
> process. It would also avoid throwing an impasse immediately over to the
> courts and assist in achieving uniformity within a particular school district.
> Generally, the restrictions and regulations governing responsible journalism,

[29] Shanley v. Northeast Ind. School District 462 F. 2nd 960, 969 (5th Cir. 1972).
[30] Scoville v. Board of Education of Joliet Township High School District 204 (Ill.)
286 F. Supp. 988 (1968); 425 F2nd 10 (1970).
[31] Korn v. Elking, 317 F. Supp. 138, Maryland (1970).
[32] Tinker v. Des Moines Independent Community School District, 393 U.S. 503
(1969).
[33] Eisner et al. v. Stanford Board of Education et al., Civ. No. 35345 (Ct., 1971);
Riseman v. School Committee of the City of Quincy, No. 7715 (1st Circ., March 11,
1971).
[34] National Association of Secondary School Principals, "Student Publications", A
Legal Memorandum, Oct. 1, 1971, pp. 4–5.

as defined by the American Society of Newspaper Editors, should be applied with the clear understanding that school officials have the authority, indeed the duty, to provide for an ordered educational atmosphere free from constant turmoil and distraction.

Regulation of Dress and Personal Appearance

The controversy over the regulation of dress and personal appearance of pupils has been long and somewhat tiresome. Unfortunately, in many of these cases the school administration is made to look arbitrary and reactionary.

This area provides an unfortunate example of how the schools seem to lag behind society. Cursory examination of any newspaper morgue will show that this appears to be a primary problem of schools beginning in the first quarter of the twentieth century with the concern being transparent hosiery and cosmetics up to the seventies where long hair, dungarees, shorts, miniskirts, and no bras become major issues. Until recently the courts have been inclined to agree with school authorities that unusual styles can be a disruptive classroom influence, ruling that this private aspect of the pupils' lives must give way to the paramount right and duty of school officials to maintain proper decorum and a favorable learning atmosphere in the classrooms.

Recent decisions make one realize that school administrators would do well to review their thinking on this issue. If they do have a restrictive dress code for the school it better have the weight of student decision behind it or trouble will develop.[35] The U.S. Supreme Court has ruled that wearing of antiwar armbands by students as a manifestation of political expression is protected by the First Amendment to the Constitution. At the same time they added, "The problem posed by the present case does not relate to regulation' of length of skirt or type of clothing, to hair style or deportment." [36] However, a U.S. District Court has upheld the right of a student to determine his own hair length.[37] The trial judge rejected as unsupported and insufficient the administration contentions that (1) long hair on male students created a safety hazard in shop classes or athletic activities, (2) long hair on male students is distracting to other students and thus disrupts the educational process, and (3) indifferent or eccentric dress is often correlated with a negative academic attitude.

The court relied on other recent cases in making its decision. Richards v. Thurston, 424 F 2nd 1281 (1st Cir. 1970), among others, found that restrictions on hair length violate the due process clause of the Fourteenth

[35] Tinker v. Des Moines Independent Community School District, 393 U.S. 503 (1969).
[36] Ibid.
[37] Berryman v. Hein, 329 F. Supp. 616 (D. Idaho Feb. 17, 1971).

Amendment. Another, an Idaho Supreme Court case, held that "hair length was a matter of personal taste protected by the Ninth Amendment.[38]

A case in Florida really put the principal on the spot. The Federal District Court ruled that Timothy Pyle was expelled by the principal improperly in that he was denied prior written notice of the school administration meeting in which he was expelled and the right to be heard or to present evidence of testimony on his behalf in violation of his rights under the due process clause of the Fourteenth Amendment. The court ordered Pyle's reinstatement deleting from his records all previous suspensions, reprimands, and expulsions. It further cautioned the school against expelling students in the future because of long hair. Then, the court ordered the principal of the school to pay Pyle $100 compensatory damages in addition to $182 for costs and expenses incurred.[39]

As a general proposition courts have leaned toward the view that school boards have power to adopt "reasonable" regulations governing student dress and deportment. What is causing so much difficulty is the determination of "What is reasonable?" Courts have varied so much in the determination of this question that students armed with judicial precedents have successfully challenged a variety of school-promulgated rules and regulations as interfering with their personal freedom and basic rights as citizens. In reviewing many cases one gains the impression too often rules and regulations of schools are somewhat irrational because one has difficulty balancing educational and disciplinary requirements and health and safety standards against students' rights.

The following general principles might be gleaned from the review of case law in school dress and grooming controversies.

1. Dress and grooming codes should have the weight of student opinion behind their development along with general community acceptance. They should meet the standard of fairness and general acceptability.
2. Dress and grooming standards should be written in simple straightforward language avoiding imprecise and vague terminology.
3. It is reasonable to establish specific grooming standards to cover particular activities; for example, when working in industrial arts shop, homemaking, or chemistry lab or participating in band or athletic events. (Authorities should be able to demonstrate through expert opinion and experience such dress requirements are necessary.)
4. Implementation and enforcement of dress and grooming standards should be applied uniformly throughout the school.
5. Due process procedures should be available to all students threatened with discipline for violating dress and grooming standards.

[38] Murphy v. Pocatello School District No. 25, 94 Idaho 32 (1971).
[39] Pyle v. Blews, No 70–1829–J.E. (D. Fla. March 29, 1971).

Right to Graduate

In a number of cases administrators and boards of education have attempted to enforce rules and regulations under threat of withholding a grade for a course or not permitting the student to graduate. Courts have consistently ruled that the board has a legal duty to issue a diploma to any pupil who has met the requirements. The classic case cited in this regard is Valentine v. Independent School District of Casey, heard back in 1921.[40] The court ruled that the school authorities may determine if and when a pupil has completed prescribed courses entitling him to a diploma. Once the pupil has successfully completed all required courses, the issuance of a diploma is a ministerial act the school officials must perform. Refusal of a pupil to wear a cap and gown at a graduation exercise may justify nonparticipation in the proceedings. However, such conduct on the part of the pupil will not justify withholding of the diploma.

E. Gordon Gee and David Sperry establish some excellent guidelines for school officials in regard to graduation and issuance of diplomas.[41]

Guidelines for School Officials

In view of the legal decisions regarding diplomas, it seems reasonable and supportable to suggest that:

1. If there are no constitutional or statutory directives to the contrary, the governing boards of local school districts may establish the course of study that must be satisfactorily complied with in order for a student to be eligible for a degree or certificate of completion. The exercise of this authority is discretionary in nature and subject only to basic requirements of reasonableness.
2. Course of study requirements necessary for the issuance of diplomas ought to be made available to all students and their parents.
3. Determination of whether students have met all the prescribed conditions entitling them to a diploma rests with the governing board of the local school district. In the performance of this duty, the board exercises quasi-judicial authority which must be conducted in a nonarbitrary manner.
4. School districts have an implied duty to issue written evidence of graduation in the form of a diploma to those who have satisfactorily completed a prescribed course of study.
5. School officials may not deny students their school records or other information pertaining to their graduation status.
6. After a student has completed the requirements prescribed for the diploma, the issuance of the diploma becomes a ministerial act involving no discretionary authority.
7. A student need not participate in graduation ceremonies to be considered a graduate. A graduate is one who has honorably passed through the prescribed course of study and has received a certificate to the effect.

[40] 191 Iowa 1100, 183 N.W. 434.
[41] E. Gordon Gee and David J. Sperry, op. cit., p. D 14.

8. A student who participates in a graduation ceremony, even at the invitation of school officials, but who has not successfully completed the course of study requirements is not entitled to the benefits of a diploma even though a document of some type may have been awarded.

Married Students and Pregnancy

A very common source of litigation was withholding of a diploma because of marriage or pregnancy of a student. While there appears to be an implicit desire by some to punish the girl who has transgressed, like Hester Prynne in *The Scarlet Letter*, recently court decisions have caused schools to reassess their attitudes, policies, and practices regarding married students and pregnancies.

A more complete discussion on student marriages and schoolgirl pregnancy is presented in another section of this book; however, the sign of the times is depicted in a 1971 federal court decision in Massachusetts.[42] The court ordered reinstatement of Miss Ordway despite a school committee policy that excluded pregnant unwed students and stated:

> In summary, no danger to petitioner's physical or mental health resultant from her attending classes during regular school hours has been shown: no likelihood that her presence will cause any disruption of or interference with school activities or pose a threat of harm to others has been shown and no valid educational or other reason to justify her segregation and to require her to receive a type of educational treatment which is not equal of that given to all others in her class has been shown.
>
> It would seem beyond argument that the right to receive a public school education is a basic right or liberty. Consequently, the burden of justifying any school rules or regulation limiting or terminating the right is on the school authorities.

Massachusetts State Commissioner of Education, Neil V. Sullivan, in advising all boards of education in regard to the case stated,

> The Ordway decision reflects a widespread and growing concern with the denial of equal educational opportunity that results from exclusion in these situations. There is also increasing recognition that the long run community interest is not served by excluding a student from school, diminishing her opportunity for education and inflicting possible psychological damage, thus affecting her future ability to support and care for herself and her child. In conclusion, I believe that this federal court decision should prompt all of the schools of the Commonwealth to hereafter recognize that students, married or not, may not be excluded from school solely because of the fact they are pregnant. Naturally, the privacy of any student who prefers to remain at home during her pregnancy should be respected. . . .[43]

[42] Ordway v. Hargraves, North Middlesex Regional High School.
[43] National School Public Relations Association, *School Girl Pregnancy: Old Problems, New Solution* (Washington, D.C.: The Association, 1972), pp. 15–16.

Other states have reviewed their rules regarding pregnant and married students. For example, Maryland passed legislation that says that a pregnant student cannot be excluded from the educational program. The Michigan State Department of Education adopted new rules governing pregnant students in June 1971, concluding with this warning: "School authorities or other school personnel shall not order a pregnant girl against her will, nor coerce her, to withdraw from a regular school program."

In the same general category the married student in many school districts faces the possibility of ostracism and denial of rights that other students enjoy. The courts have been in general agreement that when a teenager marries he/she is emancipated and is no longer amenable to the compulsory attendance laws.[44] In addition, there is overwhelming agreement that marriage in and of itself is not a valid reason for suspension or expulsion from school.[45] The area of major controversy today centers around many board of education policies against married pupils' participation in extracurricular activities, including leadership in school organizations, athletics, scholarship activities, band, glee club, social events, etc. Until recently courts were inclined to uphold the boards in this regard by asserting "the government and conduct of public schools, in general, is committed to the discretion of the school board. Courts will not interfere with the board's exercise of such discretion unless it appears the board has acted arbitrarily or maliciously." [46] In the last two or three years, however, courts are beginning to question the reasonableness of such decisions. Many are citing the Michigan Attorney General's intervention in Cochrane v. Board of Education of Mesick.[47] In this case two boys were denied the right to play football because of their married status. The courts upheld the school policy. However, the Attorney General intervened, contending, "They are entitled by law and public policy to the respect and security of community acceptance in their married status, as well as to all the benefits of equal access to all public educational facilities, including their earned status in cocurricular activities."

The Michigan Attorney General's intervention challenged the long-standing assumption that school officials have a right to discourage student marriages by limiting or prohibiting participation of married students in school activities solely on the grounds that they were married. Beginning in 1972 a series of federal and state court cases solidified the position that school boards should not place restrictions upon the school life of married students.[48] While the practice of discouraging teenage marriages is prob-

[44] State v. Priest, 210 La. 389, (1946).
[45] Board of Education of Harrodsburg, Kentucky v. Bentley, Ky., 383 S.W. 2nd 677 (1964).
[46] Casey County Board of Education v. Luster, Ky. 282 S.W. 2nd 333.
[47] 360 Mich. 390 (1960).
[48] Holt v. Shelton, 341 F Supp. 821 (MD Tenn 1972); Davis v. Meek, 344 F. Supp. 298 (ND Ohio 1972); Moran v. School Dist. No. #7 350 F. Supp. 1180 (D.C., Mont. 1972); Houston v. Prosser 361 F. Supp. 295 (N.D. Ca. 1973); Bell v. Lone Oak School Dist., 507 S.W. 2nd 636 (Tex. Ct. App. 1974).

ably desirable, it is highly questionable whether schools can legally establish any regulation that arbitrarily discriminates between married and non-married students.

Sex Discrimination in Recreation and Interscholastic Competition

There has been a growing amount of litigation concerning the participation of female students in recreational and sporting events. The trend in the courts has been to move rapidly against any area dealing with sex discrimination. In Brenden v. Independent School District 742 [49] two talented female students in Minnesota sought to overturn a regulation that prohibited them from participating in athletic events sponsored by the Minnesota State High School League. The federal court found the league rules arbitrary and violative of the Fourteenth Amendment's equal protection clause. The case did not deal with contact sports; however, it did set precedent for girls having the same equal opportunity as boys to participate in recreation and athletic events.

The equal opportunity rule also applies to elementary age children. Numerous cases dealing with little league play have affirmed the right of girls to participate under the rights of the Fourteenth Amendment. The federal government has added strength to this concept through various Health, Education, and Welfare regulations that deny federal funds to any public elementary or secondary school practicing discrimination "under any education program or activity." [50] The following are some of the specifics of the regulation:

1. All schools must treat their students without discrimination on the basis of sex, including access to and participation in curricular offerings, extracurricular events, and school organizations.
2. Sex-segregated physical education courses are not allowed, but sex separation can occur when contact sports are engaged in during physical education classes.
3. Male and female students must be insured equal opportunity to participate in athletic activities. Teams that are established on the basis of competitive skill and/or contact may have either separate teams for males or females or single teams open to both sexes.
4. Facilities, generally, must be equally available to both sexes. When separate housing, locker rooms, and showers are provided they must be comparable facilities.

[49] 477 F 2nd 1292 (8th Cir. 1973).
[50] HEW's Regulation Under Title IX of Educational Amendments of 1972: Ultra Vires Challenges, 1976 B.Y.U.L. Rev. 133, pp. 169–82.

Summary

Statutes, school codes, school policy, and the interpretation of these by the courts are a firm source of authority upon which every school administrator can rely. Of course the laws cannot specify the what, where, and why of every possible condition; therefore there must be a wide range of implied powers in order to permit a reasonable exercise of legislated expressed powers. Implied powers because of lack of specificity are sources of much litigation. On the other hand, they allow progress, growth, and experimentation for the dynamic and imaginative administrator.

The schools have been described as reflections of our democratic society where individual worth and rights are paramount and where children learn to be sensitive, productive citizens. Yet, when one reviews the litigation regarding the governing of children in school the conclusion is that rather than serving as models of a democratic institution with great reverence for individuals' rights, schools are too often restrictive and repressive. Although few people will openly embrace the old-fashioned philosophy of spare the rod and spoil the child, a great deal of suppression of a student's rights takes place under the guise of proper order and operation of the school. Too many school authorities assume that the discipline of the school will break down unless children recognize that the teacher is the master whose rule is absolute. Uniformity rather than individuality is the major order of the day in many schools.

We often think of our courts as conservative stabilizing elements in our society; however, to observe the changes in the interpretation of our laws as they relate to the rights of the individual guaranteed in both our federal and state constitutions is to observe the upholding of the basic rights of people. These same cases, however, make one concerned about the impact of our schools because it appears that schools lag behind in their administration of justice to the individual. There is no litigation because schools go too far in upholding rights of the individual—it is always just the opposite, and case after case reveals a record of schools being quite arbitrary in the suppression of unpopular and minority viewpoints. It becomes even more a matter of concern when one recognizes that most students and parents never litigate and are simply silenced by the plenary power that school authorities exercise over their lives.

For Further Thought

1. Is there a distinct dividing line between educational opinion and legal opinion? Illustrate.
2. Is it true that every administrative action must be taken within a specific legal framework? Give some examples.

3. Why do practices started under the authority of implied powers so often become expressed powers and laws?
4. How should elementary and secondary school principals participate in the development of laws affecting education?
5. The statement has been made that schools have generally lagged behind in their upholding of the rights of the individual. Debate this statement.
6. Make a summary of all the educational legislation passed in your state in the last two years. What effect has this legislation had on school curriculum? On teaching personnel? On school services?
7. What do you think is the best way for principals and law officers to work together on cases where students may be involved in breaking the law? What cooperative preventive measures might be taken?

Part II

Improving Learning in the School

The overriding philosophy of this book is the very simple but often neglected principle that instruction of the students and learning by the students is the supreme reason for the school's existence. Organization and administration must then be considered as means and not ends. In the development of this point of view the teacher becomes the most important agent in carrying out the educational process. Therefore, a principal's most important function is to help establish, develop, and maintain a teaching staff who will provide the best possible opportunities for teaching and learning. He/she then ministers to the teachers and students so that the teaching–learning environment and climate are of the highest order.

Chapter 8   The Principal's Major Task

It is clear that there is a discrepancy between what principals see as their major task and what they actually do. As noted in an earlier chapter, the professional staff, the board, and the community expect the principal to be a leader. Yet, we find the principal spending an inordinate amount of time on activities other than that set of activities most groups including principals see as the major task, that of *providing educational leadership* to improve learning.

A cursory glance at the history of the superintendency and of the principalship will show that these roles resulted from the fact that things had to be done, records kept, data gathered, and reports made. Campbell and co-authors show the development of the role of the superintendent evolving through three stages: (1) clerk, (2) educator, (3) business manager, to a fourth emerging stage of chief executive and professional adviser.[1] Stage two emphasized the role of the administrator as a teacher–educator. But this role seems to have disappeared. Silberman agreed with Nyquist, Commissioner of Education for New York State, that the term "principal" should become an adjective again. He further stated that restructuring of goals should occur so that principals can return to the role of principal teacher.[2]

Trump has suggested that the secondary school principal should devote about three fourths of his time to improving instruction.[3] Statements such as this have been semantically altered to mean many things to many people. To those who wish to spend time on accounting and acquisition functions, it means that a smoothly running accounting system for all funds, supplies, and equipment, and getting teachers the things they want improves the

[1] Roald F. Campbell, et al., *The Organization and Control of American Schools* (Columbus, Ohio: Charles E. Merrill Publishing Co., 1970), p. 203.

[2] American Association of Colleges for Teacher Education, *Power, Authority and Decision Making in Education* (Washington, D.C.: AACTE, 1971), p. 38.

[3] J. Lloyd Trump, *A School for Everyone*, National Association of Secondary School Principals, Reston, Va. (1977), pp. 66–71.

instructional program. To those who operate on a trouble-shooter level, ready for all comers, it means that devoting time to "protecting" teachers from outside troubles allows them to teach and, hence, improves instruction. These things do contribute to the educational enterprise. But should the principal concentrate on these at the expense of more direct involvement with the quality of instruction in the school?

There is little question that much administration consists of organizing and managing things, some of which are detailed, repetitive, and even mundane. This does not mean that these tasks are not important, for it is by the efficient accomplishment of these tasks that a case for administrative credibility can be made. If monies are not properly accounted for, if non-teaching technical and production work is not provided for the teachers, or if the maintenance and safety features of the building are not attended to, then other leadership activities, however well planned, will lose their impact. Such impact will be lost initially because of the administrative credibility gap. Innovations must have effective resource support if any stabilizing effect is hoped for. Even if the support is merely a well-thought-out scheduling of space, the lack of such support can create a barrier or at least an excuse for not pushing ahead with the logical next steps in the plan. The question is not whether or not careful attention should be paid to this aspect of administration. The question is, Should the principal first be held responsible for the accomplishment of these management tasks if he/she is *primarily* expected to exert educational leadership?

A recent study of an influential group of parents gives a resounding "No!"

Parents Emphasize Instructional Leadership

Questionnaires were sent statewide to local parent–teacher association presidents, to state Congress of Parents and Teachers board members, and to council presidents.[4] The respondents were asked to prioritize by importance ten sets of five statements that reflected possible duties and responsibilities of a principal. These parents chose the following as high priority for the principal:

1. Initiate improvements in teaching techniques and methods.
2. Make certain that curricula fit the needs of students.
3. Direct teachers to motivate students to learn at their optimal levels.
4. Afford teachers the opportunity to individualize programs.
5. Direct teachers to coordinate and articulate the subject matter taught on each grade level.

---

[4] This study by T. L. Drake was co-sponsored by the Indiana Congress of Parents and Teachers and by the Teachers College, Ball State University, 1978.

It is very clear that these parents' priorities focus upon the principal's responsibilities in improving curriculum and instruction and upon directly exerting influence upon students. This becomes even more clear when contrasted with the five items the parents saw as having relatively low priority.

The least important items were:

1. Becoming involved in community affairs.
2. Maintaining a school maintenance schedule.
3. Scheduling the activities of the school.
4. Maintaining school records.
5. Performing other administrative duties assigned by the superintendent.
   The total responses are represented in Table 8.1.

It appears that parents' groups may be viewed as advocates for the idea that the principal should be primarily an educational leader focusing on instructional matters as opposed to administrative detail.

Another study conducted by the author in 1977 indicates that role perception is viewed as a hindrance in spending the time desired on certain job tasks. Table 8.2 shows the supervisory task, percentage of principals responding who wish to spend more or less time on that task, and the percentage of the respondents citing role perception as the hindrance.

Only the last task noted in Table 8.2 was viewed as having another type of hindrance greater than role perception.

Preventing Means from Becoming Ends

Too often carrying out necessary support tasks leads to the distortion of the goals of the job of the principal. The support tasks become the main goal and instructional leadership is worked in, wherever there is time. Such behavior on the part of the administrator reinforces those who work with him/her to give priority to secondary goals—hence, the running-a-tight-ship or keeping-school becomes the distortion of the goal of educating children. Again, the support system or means becomes the end. The profession must protect the role of instructional leadership from becoming a secondary goal. The person incumbent in such a position must be given the means to maintain his/her role as instructional leader as well as not allowing the support tasks to be unattended or less effectively done.

It is obvious that the size of the school is a factor that influences the balance of support tasks and leadership tasks. A small school of eleven teachers and two hundred and fifty pupils will not demand the same amount of support tasks as a school of six hundred and a staff of twenty-six, or a high school of two thousand students. In several communities the small school is the order of the day either by design, tradition, or both. It is possible that the principal can be expected to carry out both sets of tasks equally well. Practice would indicate that over a period of time this may

TABLE 8.1 *Principalship Priorities Questionnaire. Breakdown of Responses into Percentages for All Five Categories*

	A Instructional Programs	*B Student-Related Activities*	*C Community Affairs*	*D Staff Development*	*E General Administrative Duties*
1. Most Important	44.5%	15.9%	9.5%	19.6%	10.7%
2. Second Most Important	21.3%	14.6%	22.7%	29.3%	11.8%
3. Third Most Important	18.8%	19.9%	26.4%	23.1%	12.1%
4. Fourth Most Important	10.3%	28.5%	20.2%	18.7%	22.4%
5. Fifth Most Important	5.1%	21.2%	21.2%	9.3%	42.9%

TABLE 8.2. *Supervisory Tasks Needing More Time for Which Role Perception Was the Identified Hindrance.*

Task	More Time Needed	% of Respondents Citing Hindrance of Role Perception
Defining program goals and developing strategies to achieve them	38.1	33.3
Assessing educational needs of students and identifying learning outcomes	34.7	54.5
Evaluating teachers	7.1	50.0
Selecting and assigning staff	25.0	37.5
Assisting teachers to analyze individual teaching performance	34.7	25.0
Coordinating inservice training to enable teachers to extend teaching competencies	34.7	25.0

not be the case in that one set of tasks tends to become quite dominant, and of course it is that set with which the principal feels most comfortable or for which central administrators hold him/her primarily responsible.

In the larger schools, particularly in larger systems, day-to-day support tasks demand priority so that the institution functions. This has traditionally fallen upon the principal to oversee.

What provisions might be made so that the primary responsibility of educational leadership is not displaced by "clerking" functions?

An Assistant Principal Is Not the Answer

No one has worked out a good solution to the problem. If size seems to warrant it, common solution is to appoint an assistant principal. The rationale usually includes the experience that can be gained by the person so appointed that is valuable to his or her preparation for a principalship.[5] This kind of training experience may very well be the reason it is necessary to write about means becoming ends. Is it really necessary for a person who holds or is working for an advanced degree or certificate to spend several years dealing with the support tasks to learn how best to effect instructional leadership? Should not the selection process for prospective principals be centered upon behaviors exhibiting orientation to people, to optimizing, to motivating, to innovating? Are these going to be developed

[5] For a discussion from an association of school boards' viewpoint, see W. Jack Peterson, "The Assistant Principal—A Member of the Management Team?" *The Hoosier Schoolmaster*, Vol. 19, No. 2 (Indianapolis: Indiana Association of Junior and Senior High School Principals, Winter 1977), pp. 8–9.

by providing the prospective principal with a job that of necessity must be oriented to support tasks that are systems and control-oriented? Viewing it from another vantage point, does this tack provide the principal with the most effective and efficient way of handling the support tasks? Would not a person specifically trained in these tasks and interested in performing them be a wiser use of human resources?

In fact, do many of the tasks require a certificated educator to perform them? A single Services Coordinator might be assigned responsibility for supporting services in two or more smaller schools while the larger schools could require the full-time duty of a coordinator.

The Services Coordinator would work as a team member with the principal and the faculty, providing the best possible system of support services in all areas. He or she would not necessarily be required to be a certified teacher, but he/she would certainly be more effective if he/she were conversant with the educator's point of view of the day-to-day operation.

The coordinator position would be regarded as a career-type position, but should not be viewed as a "dead end" by the system or the incumbent. The purposes of such a position would be:

1. To free the principal for instructional leadership activities.
2. To develop more effective and efficient means of providing supporting services.
3. To assist in operational planning.
4. To provide needed day-to-day operational services to the instructional staff.

The roles of the principal and of the coordinator would mesh in long-range planning and day-to-day operation such as portrayed in Table 8.3.

Differentiated Deployment of Resources

The principal can no longer continue to be all things to all people all the time. It is imperative that different patterns of assigning responsibilities for the myriad of tasks in any school must be tried. Below are some alternatives designed to allow the principal to be held responsible for his/her major task of educational leadership.

The Services Coordinator

The first edition of this text proposed the establishment of a position(s) in each school district that might be given the title of Services Coordinator. The persons assigned to these positions would be held directly responsible by the central administration for the supporting management services necessary for the effective operation of each school within the district. He/she would be accountable to the central administration for the proper

TABLE 8.3 *Possible Tasks of Principal and Services Coordinator*

Principal	Services Coordinator
Instruction	*Instruction*
Objectives development	Data gathering and reporting
Staff development	(development of needed systems)
Program evaluation—	Maintenance of media equipment
development and interpretation	and ordering
with staff, students and	
community	
Media development	
Curriculum	*Curriculum*
Development/innovation	Materials acquisition and
Research	accounting
Materials development and	Materials production
research	
Students	*Students*
Direct involvement	Data gathering/analysis
	Reporting to central office
	Activities scheduling
Faculty	*Faculty*
Selection	Local school responsibility for
Assignment	records and reporting
Development	Communication of personnel
	information to faculty
Community	*Community*
Planning and executing two-way	Materials production
communications programs	
Involvement in community affairs	
tangent to educational concerns	
Finances	*Finances*
Planning with central staff	Accounting for all income and
Budget preparation with	expenditures
coordinator	Operation of cost system
Approval of internal projects	Budget preparation with principal
Space	*Space*
Establish programmatic priorities	Scheduling/utilization
Planning new and renovated space	Maintenance
	Clearing house operations

operation of these services on a coordinated, districtwide plan, and at the same time would be accountable to the principal of the school to which he/she is assigned to see that the school is receiving the services efficiently.

The services coordinator would therefore be accountable to the central office administrator for those services, procedures, and reports dealing with the business functions of the schools. For salary, tenure, or promotion consideration, he/she would be under the central office; however, the principal's recommendations as to his/her effectiveness should have a major influence upon the decision.

He/she would be accountable to the principal for the effectiveness of his/her work in facilitating the instructional program. If any conflicts

FIGURE 8.1 Organizational chart showing utilization of a services coordinator.

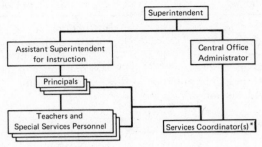

*One Services Coordinator might serve several small schools.

occurred that appeared to be unresolvable between the principal and the services coordinator, they could be resolved between any of the next higher positions, keeping clear that the business stream is a service to instruction. Clearly delineated areas of responsibility will minimize misunderstandings. The organizational chart could look like Figure 8.1. Variations on this would depend upon how many schools could be serviced. A large school would require 100 per cent of the time of one coordinator.

The individual school or system could decide how best to communicate needs and receive services from the coordinator. His/her function would be strictly a staff function and would not have line authority over any professional staff in the individual buildings.

It is the intent of the foregoing to place the major responsibility for educational decision-making upon the principal and relieve him/her from being held accountable by the central administration for supporting services and management detail. It returns to him/her the role of educator so that he/she no longer is swamped with demands not directly related with the learning of children—nor can he/she use those demands as excuses for not being directly involved.

Similar kinds of positions are described by Trump.[6] It is interesting to note that the principal in these models is devoting 75 per cent of his/her time to improvement of instruction and 25 per cent to management. Trump suggests a building administrator (not the principal) to supervise general offices, the cafeteria, facilities, transportation, and so on, along with other roles in larger schools.

Other Possibilities

The principal must not be forced into choosing between being a manager–procurer–scheduler or being an educational leader. Yet, forces continue

[6] Trump, op. cit.

FIGURE 8.2.   Organizational chart for small school utilizing executive secretary and part-time personnel.

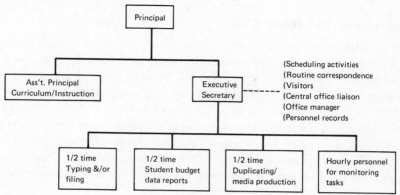

to push toward making that choice. Again, the "ends" serving the "means" problem comes to the forefront in that the person responsible for the quality of instruction in the school is boxed into serving the central office support system. If the principal is to approach spending the majority of time in instructional improvement activities with classroom teachers and specialists, another person(s) must assume responsibility for the management details.

The positive aspects of hiring permanent parttime help to do specific tasks are being documented by business at an increasing rate. Scheduling, data gathering and analysis, completion of report forms, materials ordering and maintenance answering routine correspondence, conducting and maintaining inventories, and many other functions may best be done by persons trained in these specific tasks. A highly efficient administrative assistant or executive secretary could head a services team of full-time and/or part-time people. Figure 8.2 suggests how this might work for a small school. Certificated or licensed personnel are not needed for many of these functions.

All of the above are suggested to re-allocate the principal's time to a set of activities to improve instruction. There is another set of considerations.

Exploring Alternatives to Free Personal Time (Management by Exception)

As noted in an earlier chapter, the principal's time is demanded by many, but a most insistent set of voices demand that time be spent on administrative detail. These voices are so loud that principals do indeed spend most of their time on details rather than upon the main function of the school.

It is not necessary to note the amount of time spent on administrative detail, but it may be functional to examine which of those tasks might actually be done as well or better by another person, or by changing central office procedure. Perhaps the task does not need to be done at the building level.

Reorganizing One's Own Time

Often it is easier to put up with time-wasting meetings, dozens of forms, and having everything "go-through the principal" than it is to face the hard work and in some cases potential risk in attempting change. Obviously it is more difficult for a principal of a small elementary school of two hundred with ten teachers to seek additional help than for a principal of a twelve-hundred-student junior high school. However, in many instances, it may be a matter of re-arranging assigned responsibilities rather than hiring additional personnel. The following may stimulate the reader's thought regarding means to free time for instructional leadership through the management by exception principle.

1. What details are required of principals by the central office that could be changed? The group of principals in the school system may wish to prepare a staff study that identifies the possible changes, how they might be changed, along with a plan that shows what should be done with the time gained. Some areas that might be examined are noted below.

    (a) Many meetings concerned with details and reports are called requesting the presence of the principal when both central office and the individual school would be better served if the assistant principal, a faculty member, or a secretary could attend. Everyone likes to have the chief at the meeting, but it is obvious that there must be a reasonable limiting of time spent this way.

    (b) When reports are required, correspondence and telephone calls often are made directly to the principal who then is required to relay instructions and provide personal direction to the staff. This consumes time. *The central office likes to delegate but they often don't recognize the necessity for delegation within the school.*

    (c) The principal is often required to sign (or often insists on signing) all reports and correspondence that are sent from the school. There is no real reason why this needs to be done if the school has an involved staff and procedures and policies are established to give them proper direction.

2. Learn to delegate authority and responsibility to the staff. Delegation can be the key to maximizing the contribution of employees and the output of your school. Theodore Roosevelt once said, "The best executive is the one who has sense enough to pick good men to do what he wants done and then the self-restraint to keep from meddling with them while they are doing it."

There is a real art to the process of delegation. If a person fully comprehends and is given instruction relative to the details of assignment, is given proper resources and authority to complete it, and then is given credit for a job well done, one can very soon build and develop a confident staff having the competency to carry on business to the point that only matters of exception or special concern need to be referred to the principal.

Often the principal will say, "But I don't have an assistant." Secretarial and clerical personnel can be as effective as educationally trained persons in handling most noninstructional reports and detail, and often more thorough in many aspects.

3. Gain the confidence of the central office in relation to your reporting procedures and the delegation thereof. This can normally be done by the following:

   (a) Learn the expectations of central office personnel in relation to reports and management detail.

   (b) Develop carefully written procedures relative to each report and/or management detail.

   (c) Make specific assignments to staff.

   (d) Provide for the proper training of the person assigned the task.

   (e) Establish a checklist of action control process for person assigned.

   (f) Develop a calendar control process for supervision and evaluation. Conduct periodic checks during slack periods such as summer.

4. Introduce staff to various personnel of the central administrative office dealing with their assignments to encourage direct contact and confidence in an acceptance of delegation process. The typical central administration consists of ten–fifteen different divisions or units. The administrator for these units (Personnel, Plant, Payroll, and so on) appropriately believes his/her work is most important and invariably wants to deal directly with the "boss" of the school, the principal, thinking this is the best way to get things done. This viewpoint can be changed as long as these administrators can be assured details important to them are being properly handled. Often, as proper relationships are developed the requesting unit will help in training the staff member to handle the details exactly as they want them.

To accomplish whatever set of tasks chosen, the principal will be dealing with many variables. The number of variables will change from building to building and from time to time in any one building. Since it is fact that there are options wherever there are changing variables, it is also fact that alternatives can and must be developed. The principal needs to optimize the human and material resources available, including those of his/her own personal behavior.

Resource Variables [7]

People

The most important of all the resources is human. People—pupils, staff, parents, patrons, and "outsiders"—are the essence of a school. This fact alone provides the principal with an almost endless variety of alternatives. The principal who feels "locked in," or in some way prohibited from initiating and implementing worthwhile changes is kidding him- or herself. The school is a system and as such a change in one part causes changes elsewhere in the system. If changes are made in one of the people variables, the other people are affected as well as time, information, program, and so on.

A simple listing will suffice as an example of the variety of people variables with whom the principals can work in developing alternatives.

1. Pupils.
2. Classroom staff.
3. Specialized staff
   (Counseling, health, and so on).
4. Central office staff
   (Information services, budget, data analysis, and so on).
5. Community resource persons
   (Artists, musicians, civic planners, and the like).
6. Professional consultants
   (state department of education, university, organizations, private resource persons and so on).

A decision to utilize community resource persons will raise a host of other questions that, when answered, will affect the use of time, space, and possibly materials and money. For example, shall community persons be relegated the role of guest speaker, or shall they become true resources working alongside the faculty? Do they work with faculty independently or with students or both? Shall they assist faculty to interpret the school's effect upon out-of-school time as well as the in-school impact of pupil–pupil and adult–pupil interaction?

It is obvious that changes will occur if community people begin to work in the schools. Changes resulting in the reallocation of more time to the same kinds of activities may not be a qualitative improvement in the lives of either students or teachers.

How shall specialized staff be utilized? Direct service to referred pupil clients only? A dual role of consultant to teachers and direct service to

[7] For another view of resources, see Francis P. Hunkins, "The Resources, the Decisions," *Educational Leadership*, 30, No. 2 (November 1972), pp. 103–106. The majority of this issue is devoted to the utilization of available resources.

pupils? Are their opinions to be used only when sought or shall the specialists' inputs be formally planned in decisions about pupils?

Time

The use of time is one of the cost items over which the principal has the most control. The state laws and regulations usually fix a minimum school day and school year. Teacher contracts often state maximums in terms of time. States, accrediting agencies, and institutions of higher education set minimum times students must spend to meet graduation or admission standards. Yet, within these parameters the principal and his staff have many alternatives available to them. The utilization of time in the school day should be considered an expenditure item for the pupil as well as for the faculty. Is the school giving the *pupil* his/her time's worth? To listen closely to the real messages behind the usual static, the pupils seriously question if their time is being spent wisely. The principal may find it useful to study the expenditure of time among the pupils, and faculty.

Is it possible that the options available to students for the expenditure of their time contributes to their change in attitudes toward school? One junior high school principal states that the school demands that the students "sit quietly there in that unmoved movable desk and listen to our hang-ups and our bombast. And if you [students] dare to be anything but with us or passive, we'll wither you and shrivel you with scorn." [8] What kinds and how much interaction occurs among students of the same age or different ages? Between adults and students?

Information

The principal is continuously faced with the need for the use of information. It is important to determine what information is necessary in what format regarding individuals, groups of individuals, budget, costs, community resources, and so on.

Information is usually thought of as a necessary ingredient in making decisions. But it is also important in making friends—or at least in not maintaining what occasionally appear to be enemies. Take the press as an example. How many "one-sided" news stories or "misinformed" reports might have been offset or avoided completely if an aura of sharing information with the writer had been fostered instead of reinforcing the enclosed system image? Does the education editor of the local paper know the principal personally? Is information gathered, analyzed, and written in easily digested format for quick distribution? Is information volunteered (with proper central office clearance if required) on locally "hot" issues?

[8] Arnold Rosenberg, "An Angry Principal Speaks Out," *Learning*, 1, No. 3 (January 1973), p. 28.

The planned sharing of information with various community/parent patron groups is an opportunity not only to gain support in attitudes, but a means to discover and tap resources. Clearly stated facts in lay language (as opposed to pedajargon) in short, well-prepared pieces distributed at "rap sessions" in the community could go far to dispel the negative feelings generated by the appearance of hiding information.

It is almost equally important to eliminate the generation and recording of superfluous data. Principals need to be alert to the all-too-common practice of the same data being gathered by different offices on different forms. This applies both internally and from central administrative offices. Certainly time spent duplicating information reporting is not optimizing resources.

Programs and Materials

There is an almost endless variety of combinations of programs and materials as is obvious at any display area at almost any educational convention. The principal's concern is effecting the right matches between these combinations and the people who use them, both faculty and pupils. The principal will ascertain the consistency of these matches with the goals and objectives of the school. For example, an objective may be that instruction shall be individualized according to needs, interests, and individual learning rates. The principal is alert to the possibility that many "individualizing" programs are merely focusing on individualizing rate. Still others may be highly structured "scripts" for teachers to insure that all the children participating are doing so at approximately the same rate. The principal cannot make the best decisions about these matters in isolation. He/she must involve others.

Money

Too often the lack of money is blamed for the lack of innovative teaching–learning situations. It is true that more money can make a good program better by providing more alternatives to the users. Yet, many of the variations mentioned above do not require more money. They may merely require the reordering of priorities. It is recommended that the individual school be given as much budgetary independence as possible. This does not reduce accountability; rather, it increases the principal's accountability to use it wisely toward the improvement of the specific learning situations in the school.

The idea of reallocation of resources within buildings is not new, but with the increasing crunch of inflation and tax limitations, the practice will become more common. The responsibility for reallocation of resources among department, service, or materials centers, or various offices should rest with the principal. But to optimize the available resources the principal will wish to involve as much as is practical in terms of their time and interest, those affected by the decisions.

It would be expected that the principal will also be involved in the district level reallocation decision-making process. He/she should be well prepared with facts, probably beyond those data required by the central office, to support claims for reallocated funds.

Space

The utilization of available space is often controlled by tradition. The principal will wish to explore the effective utilization of walls, plants, outdoors areas, and community space resources such as parks, arboretum, craft center, and so on. The creative use of existing floor space is important. Of course safety regulations should be observed, but hallways, stages, and other underutilized areas could add to the flexibility of the school program.[9]

Optimizing the Options

As stated, the principal optimizes the utilization of available resources to improve the teaching–learning situations within the school. Two guides are suggested to enhance the optimization process: (1) Eliminate the compartmentalization and segmentation of the school, the community, and even the lives of the students; and (2) view selection of alternative solutions to problems as a process involving those people affected by the decisions.[10] The principal is not the fulcrum used to pry loose the solution to a problem. The principal is concerned as much about the "people" of the problem as about the nonpeople aspects of the problem. Figures 8.3 and 8.4 partially illustrate the differences. The principal does not ignore budget restrictions, time problems, policies, and so forth. To do so is to act irresponsibly. But such things are not the essence of his/her job, nor a cudgel with which he/she reinforces his/her status position. They too should be viewed as aids to reaching the optimum solution. In some instances, effecting change in the nonpeople aspects of the problem may be the best solution, but often

FIGURE 8.3. Principal-centered process.

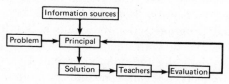

[9] See Ch. 19 for further details concerning the creative use of existing facilities.
[10] The reader is referred to Robert R. Blake and Jane S. Mouton, *The New Managerial Grid* (Houston: Gulf Publishing Co., 1978). The authors discuss the relationships between organizational goals, personal goals, and managerial emphasis.

FIGURE 8.4. Problem/people-centered process.

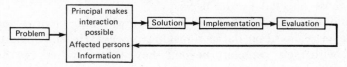

those merely serve as scapegoats or as devices to avoid facing the real problem.

A good example of the problem people-centered process is illustrated by the case conference committee process noted in Chapter 12.

Regardless of the shape of the organizational chart, *we find the principal working with people.* In the multi-unit school the principal works with unit leaders; the traditional high school with department heads, assistant principals, and so on. The important consideration is the emphasis of the work with them. If the management of things (attendance, accounting, supplies, reports, and the like) is the usual bill of fare rather than the improvement of the learning of individuals and groups of individuals, it is not hard to see why the image of the principal is as it too often is. Nor is it difficult to understand why *Up the Down Staircase* was written.

Throughout this chapter the educational leadership role has been emphasized with direct involvement with staff and students. The principal should be concerned about administrative detail and the support roles only as exceptions to the rule. The concept of management-by-exception should be subscribed to seriously. Some alternatives have been proposed, and there are predictable objections.

Objections Anticipated

The Principal Must Be in Charge of All

The old objection is anticipated. To be effective and to be held accountable, the principal must be in complete charge of the building and everything that goes on in it. The authors reject this reasoning in that the principals could be held accountable for educational matters alone. Furthermore, practices throughout the country fly against the old "complete charge" idea. Often personnel and programs operate within a building quite independently from the principal or with allegiance to program objectives and to administrators other than the building principal. Examples include some federally funded projects, special remedial programs, adult community programs, or even maintenance programs. Indeed, the principal would be remiss if he/she did not have some basic understanding of the educational implications of these programs and how they could work with his/her own to improve the educational impact upon the community, but to hold him/her absolutely accountable for them would be in error.

The authors feel the principal ordinarily need not be "in charge of all," and should primarily be held responsible for educational improvement. There is evidence that strong support for this can be found among teachers, parents, and principals themselves.

One Cannot Serve Two Masters

If a position such as the services coordinator is staffed, an out-dated objection that might be proffered is that the services coordinator cannot be responsible to the principal and to a central office administrator. Again, practice will show that this not only can be done well, but in many cases results in improved services to the unit concerned. Specialists such as reading, speech, or social work personnel are responsible to the principals of the buildings they serve as well as to a director of special services. Clearly understood objectives, procedures, and channels of communication will alleviate problems, should they arise.

Such a division of responsibility should fix the priorities on instruction and learning. Central administration staff should see themselves more in the role of providing service to that function, working through the building principal.

Negotiated Contracts Will Preclude the Principal's Involvement in Instructional Leadership

A review of organizational literature does not substantiate the truth of the myth that negotiated contracts will preclude the principal's involvement in instructional leadership. In fact, statements occur in resolution form that imply the opposite. Given the positions of parents and teachers, it is unlikely that principals would be allowed to hide behind that myth even if they wished to, which is not the case. See Chapters 10 and 11 for additional discussion focused on evaluation.

Summary

The major function of the principal is to exert educational leadership to improve the quality of life of each individual within the school. He/she must be viewed by the community, by the faculty, and by the students as being primarily accountable for achieving this function. To accomplish it effectively he/she must be freed to direct his/her time and energy to that task rather than having time and energy drained away because of being held responsible for other pressing tasks. It has been proposed that a services coordinator responsible to the central administration through the business stream of the organization be held accountable for supporting services and accounting functions of the school. If such a position is not staffed, then re-assignments of responsibility must be made with development of strong liaison with central office administrators.

Roles can be redefined. Interaction patterns can be changed. Options can be identified, alternatives developed, and, hopefully, restricting the principal's role to just keeping school can become a thing of the past.

Focusing upon instructional leadership and being freed to do it certainly has implications for the competencies needed by a person proposing to be principal. But it is time—indeed, long past time—we make the move.

For Further Thought

1. Do you agree that the principal should retain veto power over faculty decisions?
2. If a school uses community resource persons in addition to the regular teaching staff, other than certification and salary, what distinguishes the professional staff from the community resource persons?
3. How would you expect the duties of the principal of a small high school to differ from that of a large high school?
4. How would you defend the idea to a school board member that the principal is not the primary contact for every situation?
5. Why is it that occasionally a teachers' group will suggest that the position of the principal could be eliminated with no loss to the quality of the educational program?
6. If a good administrative secretary could do many of the things the principal does, why doesn't she/he?
7. Successfully attending to detail can enhance the principal's credibility to expert leadership. What safeguards can be set to avoid the attention to detail from becoming the main task?
8. Do not principals for the most part do those things they really *want* to do?

Chapter 9 Organizing to Improve Learning

Each of the fifty states has a different pattern of school district organization. Few have uniform arrangements even within the state. There are over sixteen thousand different boards of education for the some sixteen thousand school districts throughout the United States, each with a great deal of freedom in managing its local schools. Volumes have been written on the powers and duties of boards of education throughout the United States, and it would require an encyclopedia to document the absolute differences in control and structure of these boards.

The traditional conception of American educational institutions suggests a highly diverse educational system, each school district having its own unique approach to the business of providing education to its youth. The traditional conception also suggests a doctrine of local responsibility and autonomy, with broad and varied educational opportunities for children and youth. Actually, the basic organizational and instructional pattern of schools throughout the United States is startlingly similar, and the options, while there, are extremely limited.

Similarities Are Universal

There may be diversity in a relative sense when American schools are compared to European schools; however, considered nationally, variations are minor. In general, the similarities are so universal that there are certain aspects of organization, structure, teaching procedures, and learning processes that apply to most schools throughout the United States: (1) Classes are graded rather than nongraded; (2) students are taught each subject by a single teacher rather than by a team or series of teachers; (3) class periods are of a uniform duration such as forty–sixty minutes; (4) the school year consists of approximately 180 days; (5) the formal school is held spring, winter, and fall and closed during summer months; (6) aca-

demic subjects are given an equal amount of time throughout the school
year, no matter what the subject; (7) the academic courses in the school
curriculum are essentially the same; (8) the student is expected to complete
four years of high school before graduation; (9) all classes begin at the
beginning of the semester or school year and end at the end of the semester
or school year; (10) the formal school day begins at a certain time for
students and ends at a certain time for students; (11) students generally
remain in school for twelve to thirteen years; (12) an evaluation system
(usually by letter grading) is provided for pupils that compares them with
the group rather than themselves; (13) most schools have some semblance
of a college preparatory, vocational education, and general education track
system for students; (14) the school building and the classroom is where
formal education takes place; (15) schools have a superintendent, a principal, and a teacher hierarchy; (16) all schools have a board of education
and are part of a state system, and so on. One could go on with a score
of other similarities.[1]

Observing these universal patterns throughout the country, it could be
concluded that there are indisputable laws of learning and unimpeachable,
noncontroversial teaching principles that force the above-mentioned characteristics upon our schools. Such is not the case; in fact, in many instances
what is known about learning is inconsistent with patterns that have become
so popular. The conclusion emerges that custom, tradition, and the demands
of managerial simplicity have had more impact on the way schools are
organized than anything else. In a sense a voluntary bureaucracy and
structure has emerged throughout the nation, reinforced by accrediting
bodies and federal, state, and local educational systems. Throughout the
United States boys and girls are installed into similar types of school
systems that are highly structured and organized. They are programmed
into a college preparatory, general studies, or vocational curriculum. If they
cannot adapt to that system and rebel through overt or covert behavior,
and if they are in a school system with enough resources, enough concern,
and enough leadership, a special program will be provided for them. While
a limited number of school systems do provide a broad flexible program,
it is clear that before a child becomes eligible for most of these special
education programs or before some type of alternative school is provided
it requires a declaration of failure, an unusual problem, or a special
handicap.

The present pattern of showing national concern after people have become problems is unfortunate. It is time for more school systems to
incorporate diversity, flexibility, and a variety of options and· learning
places in the school and in the community so that each pupil can find
learning strategies that suit him/her best and can move forward with
success in terms of his/her own talents and interests.

[1] See Alfred Lightfoot, *Urban Education in Social Perspective* (Chicago: Rand Mc-
Nally, 1978), pp. 36–37 for more specific universals in curriculum and instruction.

Grade Organization and Grouping Patterns

Historical evolution and tradition created the various ways of organizing grades in schools of the United States. Following the Civil War the trend was for children to start school in an eight-year elementary school beginning at age five or six and continuing to age thirteen or fourteen. A few of the better students would then go to secondary education in a four-year high school from ages fourteen to eighteen.[2] This organization, known as the 8–4 plan, was the base for most types of grade organizations that attempted to take into account the particular schooling needs of different age groups of children and youth within a particular school district.

Today the four-year high school is still the most common; however, with the rapid growth of the junior high school in the twenties and the middle sixties, a great variety of organizational patterns is in evidence in the elementary and middle grades. There does not seem to be any evidence, however, that these different organizational patterns are based on any systematic research.[3]

Table 9.1 compares data from districts of varying sizes—small, medium and large—in 1971.

It appears that the 6-3-3 organization pattern prevails in the larger com-

TABLE 9.1 *Patterns of School Organization and Percentage (Not Including Kindergarten or Nursery)* *

Grade Organization	School Population			
	300– 2,999	3,000 24,999	25,000 and above	Total
6–3–3	11.6	36.6	62.3	18.8
6–2–4	17.4	21.3	10.2	18.2
8–4	21.1	10.4	9.6	18.2
5–3–4	8.7	11.9	7.2	9.5
7–5	1.2	1.9	3.6	1.4
6–6	22.7	3.7	1.8	17.5
4–4–4	2.1	1.1	.6	1.8
other	15.3	13.1	4.8	14.5

* NEA Research Division Data Bank, collected 1971.

[2] The four-year high school was probably influenced by the first public high school in the United States, which was established in Boston in 1821 as the English Classical School and then renamed the Boston English High School in 1824. This school originally began as a three-year school and soon adopted the four-year pattern. There followed half a century of trial and error in other states with three-, four-, and five-year high schools but following the Civil War the four-year program emerged as the most popular.

[3] William T. Gruhn and Harl R. Douglass, *The Modern Junior High School* (New York: The Ronald Press, 1971), p. 10.

munities, while the 5-3-4 organization is more common in the smaller size communities; however, a wide diversity of patterns may be seen.[4]

The National Center for Educational Statistics analyzed the grade spans in secondary schools and discovered that 96 per cent of the high schools having a twelfth grade show grade spans as follows: grades 9–12, 7–12, 10–12, and 8–12, listed in order of their frequency.[5] Projected statistics indicate that the order remained the same in 1979.

Grade Span	Numbers	Percent of Total H.S.	Attendance Average
Grades 9–12	7,616	45.4%	968
Grades 7–12	4,868	29 %	468
Grades 10–12	3,150	18.7%	1,180
Grades 8–12	784	4.7%	643
Other	376	2.2%	—
	16,794	100 %	

An analysis further reveals a decided transition in organization of the intermediate grades. Obviously, the middle school movement and continued experimenting with grade levels in the junior high school made this a highly dynamic situation. Table 9.2 shows the great variety of organizational patterns in existence throughout the intermediate grades.

TABLE 9.2. *Grade Span of the Schools Housing Intermediate Grades in the U.S.**

Grade Pattern	Number
Grades 4–6	644
Grades 4–7	101
Grades 4–8	249
Grades 5–6	303
Grades 5–7	101
Grades 5–8	563
Grades 6–6	182
Grades 6–7	93
Grades 6–8	1,334
Grades 6–9	124
Grades 7–7	104
Grades 7–8	2,436
Grades 7–9	4,898
Grades 8–8	85
Grades 8–9	174

* Roy Nehrt, op. cit.

[4] N.E.A. Research Division data bank.
[5] Roy Nehrt, National Center for Education Statistics, Unpublished Study (Mimeo), 1972.

Just as at the turn of the century, when educators recommended a smoother transition from elementary school to high school on the basis of the physiological, social, and intellectual needs of the adolescent, rather than on results of research into the effectiveness of various grade organization or grouping schemes, today's educators are making similar recommendations—this time for the middle school—in the belief that today's adolescents experience the onset of puberty earlier than did their parents.[6] Once again, however, the immediate reason for establishing middle schools was probably to relieve crowded conditions in other schools, a reason, Alexander warns, reminiscent of the one that signaled the junior high school movement.[7] Other reasons cited by principals for establishing middle schools are as follows: "to provide a program specifically designed for students in this age group, to better bridge the elementary and the high school, to provide more specialization in grades 5 and/or 6, and to remedy the weakness of the junior high school." In addition, a strong emphasis is reported on allowing individual progress in a wide range of exploratory activities facilitated by flexible grouping and scheduling.[8]

Grouping

The concept of grouping within a grade level appeared when critics of graded classrooms challenged the lockstep organization, charging that it was too regimented for students. In our high schools today, cross grade grouping by ability, team teaching, and nongraded grouping [9] appear to be the most prevalent practices dedicated to the pursuit of flexibility and increased efficiency in teaching/learning situations.

Since 1922 researchers have been observing and comparing various grouping practices in high schools; however, the results have been highly inconclusive, leading experts to warn that generalizations are impossible.[10]

Ability grouping per se, the topic of a massive amount of research at both elementary and secondary levels, has been found to be generally ineffective in improving academic achievement. This ineffectiveness, it is believed, is due in large part to lack of control of variables such as curriculum content and teacher competence.[11] Teacher attitudes, also, are

[6] Luela Cole and Irma Hall, *Psychology of Adolescence,* 7th ed. (New York: Holt, Rinehart & Winston, 1970), pp. 68–76.

[7] William Alexander, et al., *The Emergent Middle School,* 2nd ed. (New York: Holt, Rinehart & Winston, 1969), Ch. 9.

[8] James J. Fenwick, "Insights into the Middle School" *Educational Leadership,* (April, 1977) pp. 528–535.

[9] B. Frank Brown, *The Non-Graded High School* (Englewood Cliffs, N.J.: Prentice-Hall, 1963).

[10] Walter Borg, *Ability Grouping in the Public Schools,* 2nd ed. (Madison, Wisc.: Dunbar Educational Research Service, 1966).

[11] Warren Findley and Miriam Bryan, *The Impact of Ability Grouping on School Achievement, Affective Development, Ethnic Separation.* USOE, 1970 (Ed. 048–382. JM 000.502).

important, particularly if they foster a self-fulfilling prophecy.[12] Several reviews concluded that there are no consistent findings.[13, 14, 15]

Unfortunate Overemphasis

Perhaps it is unfortunate that so much concern and study was spent on how the grades should be grouped and classes organized for the education of children. This created a great deal of strong discussion and preoccupation on assignment of children within grades according to age groups, in many cases causing educators and the public at large to overlook the possibility that a class or grade system of organization might have been wrong in the first place. One could hazard the hypothesis that overemphasis on grades K–12 and the assignment of children to these grades according to age has done more to retard proper learning than perhaps any other factor in school administration.

As far back as 1913 Dr. Frederic Burk, President of the San Francisco State Normal School, made a strong indictment of the traditional class system: [16, 17]

> The class system has been modeled upon the military system. It is constructed upon the assumption that a group of minds can be marshaled and controlled in growth in exactly the same manner that a military officer marshals and directs the bodily movements of a company of soldiers. In solid unbreakable phalanx the class is supposed to move through the grades, keeping in locked step. This locked step is set by the "average" pupil—an algebraic myth born of inanimate figures and addled pedagogy.
>
> ❋ ❋ ❋
>
> V. The Class system does permanent violence to all types of pupils.
> (1) It does injury to the rapid and quick-thinking pupils, because these must shackle their stride to keep pace with the rate of the mythical average. They do so, usually at the price of interest in their work. Their energy is directed into illegitimate activities with the result that in the intermediate grades a large portion of them fall into the class of uninterested, inattentive, rebellious, and unmanageable pupils.
> (2) The class system does a greater injury to the large number who make progress slower than the rate of the mythical average pupil. Necessarily they are carried off their feet by the momentum of the mass. They struggle

[12] Robert Rosenthal and Lenore Jacobsen, *Pygmalion in the Classroom* (New York, Holt, Rinehart & Winston, 1968).

[13] Walter Borg, op. cit.

[14] Ruth B. Eckstrom, "Experimental Studies of Homogenous Grouping: A Critical Review," *School Review*, 69 (1969), pp. 216–226.

[15] Larry W. Hughes and Gerald C. Ubben, *The Elementary Principal's Handbook*, Boston: Allyn & Bacon, 1978, Ch. 12.

[16] Frederic Burk, *Remedy for Lock-Step Schooling*. Monograph for Department of Education, State of California, 1913.

[17] In using the term "class system" he was referring to assignment of children to grades or heterogenous assignment of pupils to classes within grades.

along, with greater or less pretense, but eventually they are discovered and put back into the next lower class. . . . By setting the pace of a mathematical average, education for nearly one half the class is made impossible. *They are foredoomed to failure before they begin.* . . . This policy is, of course, as inhuman as it is stupid.

* * *

Could any system be more stupid in its assumptions, more impossible in its conditions, and more juggernautic in its operation? Every one of its premises is palpably false; every one of its requirements is impossible and every one of its effects is inefficient and brutal. Nevertheless this system has endured and has been endured for centuries.

The "best organization" war raged on in the battlefield of grouping grades into appropriate units. William T. Gruhn and Harl R. Douglass, in their excellent discussion of the junior high school,[18] point out that the importance of pupils as individuals had been given little attention in organizing schools in the nineteenth century. They cite Eliot's address of 1892 as a recognition of the individual's importance:

Every child is a unique personality. It follows, of course, that uniform programmes and uniform methods of instruction, applied simultaneously to large numbers of children, must be unwise and injurious—an evil always to be struggled against and reformed so far as the material resources of democratic society will permit.

As further noted by Gruhn and Douglass, the National Education Association as early as 1902 stated their position on the

arrangements of courses of study, that they may be adapted to the pupils to be instructed, rather than that pupils should be adapted to a fixed course of study in an inflexible system of grading.

Possibly the most succinct statement about the controversy is the oft-quoted

Best organization? Let fools contest.
Whatever works best is best.

The concern for the external organization of schools within a school district so that children would be placed in the best overall learning environment is a concern to be admired but unfortunately the concentration has been on the grouping of children for the best administrative organization rather than on the individual child and what was the best way for him/her to learn. In all cases grades, classes, constant schedules, fixed classrooms,

[18] W. T. Gruhn and H. R. Douglass, *The Modern Junior High School* (New York: The Ronald Press Co., 1971), pp. 35–36.

and textbooks were constant structures that could not seem to be eliminated when attempts were made to focus on the individual.[19, 20]

Early Teaching–Learning Strategies

Looking back over the past fifty years of educational development one can observe constant attempts to focus on the individual child. Research in child development and theoretical and scientific contributions in educational psychology, sociology, and philosophy were clear indicators that each child is an individual and that learning cannot be neatly categorized, nor do children learn at the same rate and in the same way. Taking cues from these studies from the twenties on, a great variety of new plans were developed by "cutting edge" educational thinkers and practitioners to adapt the new principles to learning for children. New names were coined for various teaching–learning strategies; some were named after the person who developed them, such as Montessori. Others related to the city or town in which they were developed, such as the Dalton Plan and the Winnetka plan, but more often than not they were named after the teaching approach or method such as: project method, unit method, activity program, contract plan, child-centered school, ability grouping, homogeneous grouping, independent study, experience curriculum, common learning, core curriculum, life adjustment programs, etc.

Most of the studies and programs were related to elementary education. This is generally true because it is easier to establish new approaches at this level because elementary education is almost exclusively responsive to the local community and its school district, while secondary education was restricted seriously by controls of state and regional accrediting, college requirements, and the state department of education. In 1932 the Progressive Education Association contributed immeasurably to changes in secondary education through the Eight Year Study of their Commission on the Relation of Schools and Colleges.[21]

The study, generally approved by colleges and universities in 1932, established an effective cooperating relationship between them and thirty secondary schools for the eight-year period of the study. It permitted and encouraged the participating schools to go ahead and radically reconstruct their secondary curriculum to serve more nearly the needs of youth regard-

[19] Irvin K. Rice, "School Structure, Competency and Accountability" NASSP Bulletin (October, 1978), pp. 5–11.
[20] Elizabeth Cohen and Eric R. Bredo, "Elementary School Organization and Innovative Instructional Practices", pp. 133–151 in G. Victor Baldridge and Terrace E. Deal, (Ed.), Managing Change in Educational Organizations (Berkeley, Calif.: McCutchans, 1975).
[21] Progressive Education Association, The Story of the Eight Year Study (New York: Harper Bros., 1942).

less of whether they were going to college. The Commission and the schools held that:

1. Success in the college of liberal arts does not depend upon the study of certain subjects for a certain period in high school;
2. There are many different kinds of experience by which students may prepare themselves for successful work in college;
3. Relations more satisfactory to both school and college could be developed and established upon a permanent basis;
4. Ways should be found by which schools and college teachers can work together in mutual regard and understanding.

A careful examination of the findings can leave no one in doubt as to the conclusions that must be drawn:

First, the graduates of the Thirty Schools were not handicapped in their college work.

Second, departures from the prescribed pattern of subjects and units did not lessen the student's readiness for the responsibilities of college.

Third, students from the participating schools which made most fundamental curriculum revision achieved in college distinctly higher standing than that of students of equal ability with whom they were compared.[22]

The overall effect of these new approaches to teaching–learning certainly did much to break the lock-step of the traditional school, broaden the curriculum, and encourage a remarkable increase in special services such as audiovisual, library, curriculum materials, guidance, work experience, school lunch, transportation, school health, and recreation.

Looking back over these early years of educational development, it is clear that the most radical changes in program and outlook have taken place in the elementary levels. This is true in the teaching approach and the concentration on the individual child. At the secondary level, the changes have been essentially on broadening services and offering more courses rather than on the teaching processes. The middle school and the junior high school have reaped some benefits from both levels but can be characterized generally as being influenced more by the senior high school than by the elementary school.

Reflecting on these movements historically, one can trace development and emphasis starting in the twenties through the leadership of John Dewey, Frederic Burk, William Kilpatrick, Carleton Washburne, George Counts, and many others who could be classed as part of the progressive education and life adjustment movement. This movement began to fall into disrepute in the late forties and early fifties. Particularly with the advent of Sputnik there was a strong swing back to traditional teaching and schooling with an emphasis on the "basics." Then, in the sixties and seventies major problems of the cities began to make themselves felt. With the problems came the realization that schools were not really geared in action or philosophy to meet the needs of certain racial minorities and disadvan-

[22] Ibid.

taged children; thus, a new movement developed that encouraged new approaches to teaching and learning and even suggested some alternative forms of schooling that would be radically different from the normal public school. [23]

The Emphasis on Change and Innovation

While social forces pressed for new thinking in regard to education, action by the federal government through the U.S. Office of Education was instrumental in popularizing the emphasis on innovation and change. The landmark Elementary and Secondary Education Act of 1965 especially recognized inequalities in American education and provided special funds to correct these inequities where there was a concentration of poor people. Head Start, Upward Bound, and Follow Through had similar objectives. Title III programs in particular stimulated new thinking and a turn-about attitude in regard to traditional approaches that weren't working. New and appealing schemes for teaching and learning began to spring up and in the early seventies change-oriented educators were advocating new approaches, incorporating such terminology as team teaching, open education, integrated day, alternative education, differentiated staffing, independent study, experimental schools, and so on.

A general criticism of this period could be that in too many cases there was innovation and change just for the sake of change. Characteristically, America was rediscovered many times over again by the young and uninformed because there was no knowledge of similar experiences and programs, developed in the 1920–40 period, and no attempt to learn from successes and failures of experiments in the past. Despite these negative generalizations, the period did develop some exciting new approaches and it has created an environment that is conducive to change. The time is now ripe for the type of leadership that can stimulate change. The truth may hurt but:

1. We do not teach as well as we know how, now.
2. We have not generally developed school environments that provide the best kinds of learning situations.
3. We still teach the textbook and subject matter instead of the child.
4. We teach classes and groups instead of individuals.
5. We still operate schools as if all teachers are the same and all children learn the same things at the same rate in the same way.
6. We still teach as if the school is the only place a child can learn.
7. We still teach as if children can learn only from adults.

[23] R. Freeman Butts, *Public Education in the United States—From Revolution to Reform* (New York: Holt Rinehart, Winston, 1978).

In other words, the thinking educator knows that there are many areas of needed improvement in our schools. Our excuses for not incorporating these improvements have been many. Now the time is here that we no longer need to make these excuses.

Alternative School—A Movement That Encouraged Options

The growth of alternative schools in the early seventies represented a protest against organizational and curricular inflexibility of the traditional public school. We have always had protest schools in the United States. These have been generally represented by the private schools, which are a recognized part of our total educational system and have educated over the past few years approximately 10 percent of our school-age children. The alternative school movement of the seventies, however, was not part of that pattern; rather, it appeared to run parallel and correspond with the general social upheaval of the times. The movement encompassed both private and public education and it forced school officials to realize that our school systems should be more flexible and responsive if they were to survive.

Alternative schools emphasized a spirit of freedom: freedom of individuals to learn and to grow, to follow their natural curiosity, and to do what they felt necessary to meet their needs. Essentially, these schools de-emphasized the usual structure, organization, and formality of the regular schools and emphasized flexibility and openness. They prided themselves on responsiveness to human need and an ability to reform and reshape themselves to meet the challenge of the times.

Both public and nonpublic alternative schools were established at all levels—nursery, primary, elementary, secondary, and college. They were called counter schools, cool schools, schools without walls, experimental schools, free schools, street academies, independent schools, as well as the more conventional title of alternative school. Thousands of such schools were established in the early seventies, and, according to Harvey Haber, founder of the New Schools Exchange, two or three new "alternative" schools were born every day, and every day one died or gave up its freedom.[24]

At first the alternative schools appeared as a movement counter to and in competition with the regular school, many groups establishing their own schools with private funds and private energy. Soon these groups, many representing minorities, developed into potent political forces demanding to be heard. Thus, the story of the alternative schools merging as a part of the regular school establishment makes an interesting case study of sub-

[24] Donald W. Robinson, "Alternative Schools: Challenge to Traditional Education," *Phi Delta Kappan*, 51 (March 1970), 374.

dominant power groups taking on the established dominants and winning. Reviewing discussion in Chapters 1 and 3 provides examples of subdominants shaking the very foundation of a traditional social order on which so many schools tried to stand.[25]

Although many of these alternative schools were established as counter-movements to the public school system, it is interesting to note how many were actually sponsored and even supported by the public school system. These became special schools within a particular school district or within a particular school itself. Often the alternative school started as a way of preventing dropouts or in ghettos and inner cities where the public school system decided to turn a portion of education over to minority groups in order to satisfy their demands for immediate action in reforming the educational system.

The California Continuation school is often given credit for stimulating alternative forms of secondary education. California attacked the dropout problem in 1965 by enacting legislation ordering all school districts to establish and maintain continuation schools. These schools have taken many forms. There are the "open campus" to accommodate working students; alternative learning centers for small groups of students with handicaps; street academies for any dropout who walks in the door; vocational career development centers for both young adults and sixteen–eighteen year-olds; and formal continuation teaching of vocational and academic subjects for dropouts and potential dropouts.

The California Commission for the Reform of Intermediate and Secondary Education (RISE Commission) indicated the need for full-scale reform of the California schools to "make the schools more effective, more enjoyable and more conducive to a continued interest in learning." [26] Through the commission's support an Alternative School Bill was passed in the California legislature that encouraged and authorized the governing board of any school district to establish and maintain alternative schools.[27]

California discovered early what school districts in other states discovered later about dropouts and disenchanted youth; that is, not much can be accomplished by just manipulating programs and offering remedial classes.[28] A whole new pattern of teaching and learning has to be emphasized, a new atmosphere created that emphasizes relevance, choice in learning, and involvement. Among the movements giving impetus to the alternative

[25] Many educational innovators considered alternative schools failures or "dead" when they became more closely aligned to the regular school organization. See Terrance E. Deal, "Alternative Schools: An Alternative Post Mortem", pp. 482–501, in J. Victor Baldridge and Terrance E. Deal, *Managing Change in Educational Organizations* (Berkeley, Calif.: McCutchans, 1975).

[26] *Report of the California Commission for Reform of Intermediate and Secondary Education,* Sacramento: California State Department of Education, 1975.

[27] The bill became effective on April 30, 1977, and stays in effect until July 1, 1980.

[28] Wilson Riles, "Alternative Education: Choice as a Way of Learning," Sacremento: California State Department of Education, 1977.

secondary schools in public school systems were the career training emphasis, the Elementary and Secondary Education Act, USOE Dropout Prevention Program in 1969–70,[29] the schoolgirl pregnancy problem,[30] the tensions arising from racial militancy in schools beginning in 1965–66, and the general liberal-radical movements of 1968–71.

The rambunctious alternative school movement of the early seventies may well settle down into an optional school movement of the mid-eighties. Philosophically, the idea that there should be greater flexibility and a variety of learning options for each boy and girl has been generally accepted even though it has not yet been generally implemented.

Estimates for the 1978–79 school year would be that there were at least ten thousand alternative public schools in operation representing approximately one third of the sixteen thousand school systems. According to Vernon H. Smith, specialist in alternative education at Indiana University, alternatives serve approximately one million children in the United States.[31] That is roughly two per cent of the elementary and secondary enrollment. These schools may be found in every size school district; however, they are more likely to be found in the larger ones with twice as many being in secondary education.[32]

All evidence indicates the optional school movement is continuing in popularity. It is not as radical and unique because it is no longer on the fringe, but it has become an important phase in the planning of many school districts and its significance is definitely impacting on the mainstream of educational thinking.

The types of alternative schools may be generally categorized as alternatives that focus on: [33]

1. *Instructional styles:* Montessori schools, open schools, behavior modification schools, individualized continuous progress schools, and so on.
2. *Different curriculum:* performing arts schools, career centers, environmental schools, centers for international studies, and so on.
3. *Different clients:* dropouts, multi-cultured, pregnant, highly motivated, gifted, and so on.
4. *Resource facilities:* schools-without-walls, learning centers, educational parks, and the like.

---

[29] National School Public Relations Association, *Dropouts: Prevention and Rehabilitation* (1972), p. 27.

[30] National School Public Relations Association, *Schoolgirl Pregnancy: Old Problem, New Solution* (1972).

[31] National School Public Relations Association, *Alternative Schools: Why, What, Where, and How Much* (Arlington, Va.: The Association, 1977).

[32] NASSP *Curriculum Report,* "A Decade of Alternative Schools and What of the Future," (Reston, Va.: The National Association of Secondary School Principals, October, 1978).

[33] *Changing Schools, Newsletter,* Bloomington, Ind.: School of Education, Indiana University, March, 1977.

5. *Administrative structure:* satellite school, magnet school, minischools, and so on.

School Within the School

The school within a school approach represents the largest increase in any category of significant school organizational change in the past two decades.[34] The concept began experimentally during the booming school enrollment period following World War II. As schools increased in size throughout the country because of the rapid growth in population and population shifts, there came an increasing concern and awareness that some of the intimacy, individual contacts, and personal interaction between students, teachers, and administrators were being lost. As a result, particularly in larger cities, a number of plans were advanced that divided the large school administratively, organizationally, and even instructionally into a number of smaller units. The basic purpose of such plans was to establish more or less self-sufficient operating units within the larger whole that should give the individual pupils opportunities for full participation, individual attention, satisfactory interpersonal relationships, a sense of belonging, and an opportunity to participate in a full variety of learning activities that is characteristic of the small neighborhood school. Other names for organizations established for this purpose are "unit school plan," "little school plan," "house school plan," and "clusters."

Ideally these operating units would be established with a size of from three hundred to six hundred pupils. They would be assigned their own administrators, counselors, and basic faculty, and housed in a specific wing or location of the building. Students assigned to this "little school" or unit would take their basic courses together and work and play together in all of their regular and normal activities. Only where it was necessary to have special classes and unusual or advanced programs would the student be scheduled on a schoolwide basis. At the same time major facilities such as library, auditorium, and gymnasium would be shared by several units.

Figure 9.1 shows a relatively common way to organize secondary schools into smaller units. Variations on this theme extend upward into university settings where the smaller units are identified with living units, dormitories, or combinations of living units. In the other direction, middle schools are often large enough to be concerned with creating workable, "family-like" units within a larger setting. Figure 10.5 (see Ch. 10) is an illustration of the organization of a middle school based upon an Individually Guided Education (I.G.E.) design by the Wisconsin Research and Development Center. The purposes of this organizational structure go far beyond simply

[34] National School Public Relations Association, op. cit., p. 32.

FIGURE 9.1. Illustration of a school within a school organization.

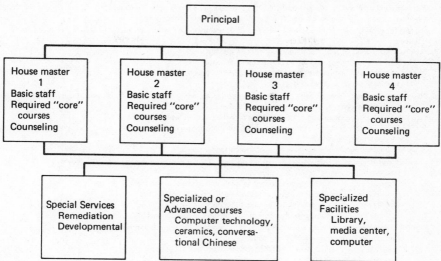

creating smaller units, but it is an illustration of at least one organizational variation feasible in an elementary school.

One of the model schools selected by the National Association of Secondary School Principals for 1979 was the Independence High School of San Jose, California (Fig. 9.2). This school is built as part of an educational park emphasizing the concept of a large school–community center with educational, recreational, and social service components designed for widespread community use. In addition it was internally decentralized into six independent operating units known as "villas."

The Independence High School statement of purpose summarizes the advantages of the school within a school.[35]

Modular or Flexible Schedule

The modular schedule is an attempt to develop flexibility in the teaching–learning pattern and to break the straight-jacket of the forty–sixty minute class period that is scheduled day after day, week after week, month after month throughout the semester and year. This schedule is usually built upon short modules of time, usually ten–fifteen minutes. Thus, each day or week a schedule can be built so that a varying number of modules can be allocated to different subjects and pupil activities, depending upon the learning needs of the pupils and the time needed for presentation and preparation of the subject.[36]

[35] Statement of Purpose, Independence High School, San Jose, California, 1979.
[36] Barbara S. Powell, "Intensive Education—The Impact of Time on Learning," *The Education Digest*, March, 1977, pp. 6–10.

FIGURE 9.2.   A statement of purpose for the villa.

We believe the small school concept consisting of a principal, counseling staff, 15–20 teachers, 600–700 students, and attendant clerical staff, can have a greater impact than a traditional school in the following areas.

Student Identity—Because of the number of Villas (6–7) and their size and organization, the Villa concept can do the following:
  —Stress individualization or uniqueness of the individual.
  —Provide a vehicle for interaction between staff and students.
  —Provide identification with a small group within the larger setting of IHS.
  —Eliminate the callousness of large size.

Student Achievement—Because of the small school organization and staff teams, the Villa concept can do the following:
  —Facilitate integration of teachers into the counseling process.
  —Facilitate interdisciplinary communication regarding student achievement needs.
  —Encourage teachers to explore teaching methods that will help students to learn how to learn and gain the desire for continuing education.
  —Facilitate interdisciplinary team approach to curricular needs.

Student Involvement in Activities—Because of the number of Villas (6–7) and the opportunities provided by this small size, the Villa concept can do the following:
  —Organize and maintain numerous student councils with representation from all groups.
  —Include a larger number of students in planning or formation or activities.
  —Provide experience and training for inclusion in more complex structures.
  —Promote involvement of larger numbers of students in the decision-making process.

Student Conduct—Because of the small size of the Villa, the Villa concept can do the following:
  —Promote individual responsibility for actions.
  —Facilitate parent involvement in student behavioral problems.
  —Provide additional alternatives for coping with disruptive behavior.

Communication with Community—Because of the number of Villas (6–7) and their small size, the Villa concept can do the following:
  —Provide greater numbers of parent groups and broader contacts with them.
  —Promote broader contact between school and agencies.
  —Promote shared decision-making by providing for increased advisory functions.
  —Broaden communication base, promote intergroup and community involvement, broaden counseling base.

(Independence High School of San Jose, California)

Figures 9.3 and 9.4 illustrate some of the differences between a traditional schedule and a modular schedule for a tenth-grade boy.[37]

Of course no human being could handle all the variables of a schedule composed of fifteen-minute modules over a six–seven-hour day with possibly each day being different. Thus, it can be said that the computer has made

FIGURE 9.3.   Traditional schedule.

		Mon.	Tues.	Wed.	Thurs.	Fri.
	1	Sci.	Sci.	Sci.	Sci.	Sci.
	2	Eng.	Eng.	Eng.	Eng.	Eng.
	3	Math.	Math.	Math.	Math.	Math.
PERIODS	4	A B C		Lunch Lunch Lunch		
	5	Art	Art	Art	Art	Art
	6	P.E.	P.E.	P.E.	P.E.	P.E.
	7	Soc. St.	Soc. St.	Soc. St.	Soc. St.	Soc. St.

[37] This sample is from a Washington Northeast School District (Montpelier, Vt.) publication, "Flexible Scheduling: Ten Questions and Answers," p. 2.

FIGURE 9.4. Modular schedule.

Per.	Day 1	Day 2	Day 3	Day 4	Day 5
1	A	A	A	A	A
2	G(LG)	G(IS)	G(LG)	G(IS)	G(LG)
3	Sci. LG IV	Eng. LG III	Sci. LG II	Sci. lab IV	Eng. LG IV
4	SS SG I	FL lab III	FL lab III	Sci. lab IV	FL lab III
5	SS SG I	Arts LG I	Arts LG I	Sci. lab IV	IS
6	Eng. lab III	Eng. lab III	Arts LG I	SS LG I	Eng. lab III
7	Eng. lab III	Eng. lab III	Arts LG I	IS	Eng. lab III
8	Math LG IV	Math LG IV	Lunch	Math LG IV	Math LG IV
9	PE LG II	Lunch	Math LG IV	Math lab IV	SS LG I
10	Lunch	SS LG I	Math lab IV	Lunch	Lunch
11	FL lab III	IS	Eng. SG III	FL SG III	Sci. SG IV
12	IS	IS	Eng. SG III	FL SG III	Sci. SG IV
13	IS	IS	IS	Eng. SG III	Math lab IV
14	Arts LG I	IS	PE lab II	Eng. SG III	PE lab II
15	Arts LG I	PE lab II	PE lab II	Arts LG I	PE lab II
16	Arts LG I	PE lab II	IS	PE LG II	IS

MODULES

A = Attendance at Guidance
IS = Independent Study
LG = Large Group
SG = Small Group

possible the modular or flexible schedule. The computer can begin with the time–subject needs for each student's day of learning, and in a matter of minutes it can generate a minimum-conflict schedule for each student in the school with classes relatively balanced, and students accounted for.

By itself flexible scheduling is only a mechanical system. The important question is why and for whom do we create flexibility?

Its primary purpose is to individualize and personalize learning, freeing the learner to concentrate upon those areas of need and interest and freeing him from time-cells of passive knowledge intake. As such it becomes a tool. However, it is an important tool for opening up the teacher's day and the pupil's day, giving both an opportunity for personal relationships that are essential to good education.

Flexible scheduling demands an extremely enlightened, sensitive, and creative staff who realize that the system will require more work than the traditional schedule in planning, diagnosing, supervising independent work, and meeting with added small groups. However, a teacher can deliver more help per student through combining resources with other teachers and making better use of teacher aides in the various time allotments.

Properly handled, for the student it can create self-learning, self-discipline, and self-confidence, and provide opportunities for supplemental learning and feed special interests.

Robert R. Gard in an excellent article in the March 1970 *Clearing House* summarizes his feelings on flexible scheduling: [38]

[38] Robert R. Gard, "A Realistic Look at the Flexible Schedule," *The Clearing House* (March 1970), pp. 425–429.

If faculty is contemplating an approach to flexible scheduling, its members should assure themselves:

(1) That planning of the "master schedule" is truly adequate to minimize the number of impossible student schedules.
(2) That students are not scheduled for larger loads than the school can support.
(3) That faculty members expect to work harder and to put in longer hours with students.
(4) That administrators, board members, students, and community recognize the price of reduced control—in absenteeism, failure, and even possible violence to person and property. (The community must be prepared for the cost and unpopularity of firm grounds-control measures should this eventuality prove necessary.)
(5) That ample space is available for study and research—adequate even for the necessary inefficiency of voluntary usage—and to accommodate the one in four who probably will need full-time supervision.
(6) That faculty support measures (aides, supervisors, materials, services) are adequate to leave teachers free to teach and to plan.

Given these six essentials, the large school can enjoy the advantages of the computer's help. The teaching day can be varied to suit individual class needs, pupils can be regrouped at will for instructional purposes, individuals can be reached, and pupils can benefit from experience with organizing their own time and working independently. The school can rejoice in glowing reports from colleges and employers that its graduates know how to "take hold" when they are placed on their own. These are benefits that should not be lost because of poor planning, inadequate explanation, or impossible space and staff limitations.

The Shrewsbury Senior High School lists these objectives of flexible scheduling: [39]

1. To expand curricular offerings.
2. To achieve maximum utilization of facilities.
3. To reduce overcrowded conditions.
4. To increase opportunity for independent study, work study involvement, distributive education experiences, and career experience opportunities.
5. To achieve 100% scheduling of pupil electives.

Minicourses

The minicourse offers another way to provide program flexibility. The minicourse can be almost any length of time less than the usual semester. Variations have included courses as short as one week or as long as ten weeks.

[39] Theodore Plekes, *Flexible Schedule—Extended Day Program* (mimeo bulletin Shrewsbury Senior High School, Shrewsbury, Mass., 1978.

Roberts and Gable trace the beginning of the popular minicourses to a one-week experiment in 1969: [40]

In the spring of 1969, the students of Walt Whitman High School in Bethesda, Maryland, ran a one-week experiment in free form education during which there were no required classes, no grades, and no traditional class groupings. A list of 242 subjects was drawn up and 150 guest lecturers, including many of Whitman's most talented students were asked to participate. Whitman students were then asked to sign up for the subjects they wished to study; these ranged from European archaeology to science fiction. Many of the "courses" were action-oriented. Students interned at local and regional planning offices, worked at newspapers, stores, or served as student aides in classes for the handicapped, helped U.S. Senators with their mail and so forth. It was from this experiment and similar variations on the theme that the minicourse movement was born.

A four-state midwestern survey of principals revealed that the number of schools offering minicourses have been increasing although there appears to be a leveling-off in the movement. Fifty-four per cent of the schools contacted did have or planned to have minicourse offerings in the future. Principals in high schools offering minicourses indicated a high degree of success with the programs, that students and teachers were favorable to them, and that such programs do help provide a humanistic school environment.

The data showed that motivational factors affecting decisions to discontinue minicourses or not to establish them were predominantly programmatic and administrative. Obstacles listed as most consistently troublesome were related to organizational design, implementation, and day-to-day operational and management procedures. These findings are no big surprise to the student of program development and change. Countless successful instructional changes have been dropped in the past because administratively they are too troublesome to manage or because they do not easily fit into the existing organizational operational pattern. As stated in the early part of this chapter, in too many cases the decision to do or not do something is based on administrative convenience rather than instructional merits.[41]

There are many advantages to providing for program flexibility through minicourses. Both students and faculty exhibit high interest in the content. This results partially from the voluntary aspects of the program and the high degree of competence and enthusiasm of the instructors. Students can help other students and the concentration is upon learning rather than evaluative marks. Community resource people can be utilized to teach or

[40] Arthur D. Roberts and Robert K. Gable, "Mini versus Traditional: An Experimental Study of High School Social Studies Curricula," University of Connecticut (mimeographed), 1978.

[41] Patricia Hansen and John Guenther, "Mini Programs at the Crossroads," *Phi Delta Kappan*, June, 1978, pp. 715–16.

to help to teach courses since the time commitment is short. Often there is no cost to the school for their help. The minicourse concept provides a vehicle for real student input into curriculum decision making. Some schools offer minicourses during odd or awkward times on their schedule or between semesters when the doldrums set in after the examination periods.[42]

There are disadvantages, but not insurmountable problems to minicourses. Scheduling can be difficult but experience and computers have minimized this problem. Teacher preparations may increase and if the total curriculum is so organized, it may become difficult for a teacher to know his/her students well. But though these and other problems may appear as difficulties, they must be weighed in a setting of mutual learning between faculty and students and a setting where choice is real.

Careful assessment of ongoing programs is needed, but the minicourse idea is certainly an alternative not to be overlooked.

Open Education

There are many assumptions about informal or open education. The name itself is confusing to many people. Some basic assumptions of open education that would generally be accepted by most open educators are:

All children do not learn best the same way.
All children are not interested in the same thing at the same time.
Children learn better when they can influence their learning environments. Therefore, children should have some say in developing the alternatives available to them.
Learning is a natural outcome of the exploratory behavior of children.

Open or informal education means that the learning environment provides an opportunity for these assumptions to be tested and developed. Openness is not an all-or-nothing situation. Any classroom can be conducted informally. Although the careful arrangement of physical space can be very helpful, even wall-less-ness is not essential.

At its best, informal education is carefully structured to insure student mastery of the fundamentals. And the principal has a crucial role to play—not only in helping teachers and pupils implement openness but in insuring that the implementation helps fulfill the school's educational goals.

Focus Upon a Person

Informal educators look at children and youth as delightful creatures—creative, energetic, inquisitive, full of good humor, and extremely serious

[42] Robert F. Knautz, "End the Winter Doldrums—Think Mini!" *NASSP Bulletin* April, 1978, pp. 115–117.

and responsible when provided with the opportunity. Informal education is based on the premise that a student, by nature, is a learner—not passive as many experimental psychologists would wish him to be. The child does not have to be taught how to learn. Indeed, one of the greatest potential resources is the individual child. A child can often perceive another child's stumbling block to learning and actually become a facilitator of learning himself. The role of the educator is to help the child with direction and resources for the learning that is already taking place.

The Three R's—Back to Basics

Open education is not a rejection of teaching the fundamentals. The pupils are guided to achieve basic skills through their interests and their life in and out of the school. It is intended that content, basic skills, and the business of living be integrated rather than isolate skills and content.

Progress can be reported by using a variety of methods, including cumulative folders of the pupil's work and record sheets noting behavioral patterns, and/or learning progress in areas that appear to be difficult for the pupil. Parent conferences centering upon the accumulated work of the child are held as often as feasible, usually two to four times per year.[43]

The Faculty

Informal education cannot be effected by edict. The principal cannot expect (nor be expected) to bring about instant openness. There are teachers who cannot and probably should not function informally in an open setting. And there are some children who for various reasons should remain in a more "traditional" setting. The principal who would have it "all-or-nothing" is actually violating the essence of openness in that he/she is denying alternatives that might meet real needs. His/her concept of openness is closed. How then can a principal begin implementing informal education?

He/she can *inform the faculty of the theories and practice of informal education.* Some effective ways are through study groups, outside speakers, arrangements for visits to open classrooms, films, and videotapes. Workshops and courses could be arranged for those staff members who want to know more about the concept.

If a vacancy occurs, the principal can *search for a teacher who has successfully conducted or who wishes to conduct an informal class.* Sociologists from the University of Denver pointed out that the occasional failures of open classrooms have been due almost always to the attitudes of teachers.[44]

The principal's role may be as simple as helping one teacher plan an

---

[43] Jerome E. DeBruin, "An Englishman Looks at Open Education in the United States," *Peabody Journal of Education,* April, 1978, pp. 270–79.

[44] Robert H. Anderson, "The Industrialization of Learning, Teacher-Related Problems," p. 46 in Louis Rubin (Ed.), *The Inservice Education of Teachers* (Boston: Allyn and Bacon, 1978).

informal approach in an area where the teacher feels especially comfortable —arithmetic, social studies, language arts, and so on. A continuous effort to make other faculty members aware of what's going on should begin as soon as the teacher or teachers developing the program feel comfortable with it. As other teachers express interest in the "experiment," arrangements can be made for interaction between them and the teachers conducting the informal classes. Visits to informal classes in other schools may be arranged.

The principal can *identify financial resources that can be used by teachers developing informal classrooms.*

As more teachers begin to express interest in informal education, inservice sessions might be developed around such related topics as child development; utilization of community resources; utilization of "junk" (wood, cloth, food mixer, motors, engines, string, canvas, and so on); the integrated day; developing diagnostic skills; children's drama, and a host of other topics that help teachers to develop alternative learning situations for children.

Facilities

Open-space facilities are often confused with open or informal education. A school can have one without the other, although the flexible spaces would be helpful to the informal, open-education process. Extensive renovation costs are not necessary for implementing informal education.

The following features would be helpful within any space, whether the traditional nine hundred-square-feet rectangle, or within an open-space plan:

1. Free-standing, easily-moved dividers that can serve as tack boards, writing surfaces, and vision barriers.
2. Easily arranged furniture. Since the room will be divided into several kinds of areas (mathematics, reading, quiet zone, science, etc.), the furniture should include tables and workbenches.
3. Floor coverings (at least in selected areas) that can be used for sitting. Various soft surfaces throughout the room can serve both acoustical and aesthetic purposes if colors are used well.

The learning environment can also include corridors and other seldom used spots in the building and outdoors.

The Year-round School

The year-round school was being advocated in the late sixties because, along with other benefits, it would allow greater utilization of educational facilities and equipment, thus reducing the need for new construction.

Because of the leveling-off and even decline in school enrollments the pressure from this front has waned. As a result, a portion of the strength of the year-round school movement has been lost.

On the other hand, there are several important programmatic reasons for encouraging the year-round school. One of the most significant benefits of moving into the year-round school is that curriculum planning invites re-evaluation of the total school program and a possible restructuring to make it more flexible and effective. Whether this occurs depends upon how and why the year-round school was implemented.[45]

Atlanta, Georgia, which started its year-round program in 1968, spent one million dollars in federal funds and two years time to prepare the program. Indications are that the plan leads to increased costs. Although it has not saved the taxpayer any money because it was not established for that purpose, it has encouraged dramatic curriculum revision. As stated by Leonard Ernst in his article, "The Year-round School: Faddish or Feasible?" [46]

> More than 800 courses are now offered to Atlanta secondary students each quarter; approximately 70 per cent can be taken in any order desired. Coupled with the option of attending any three out of four quarters (or all four) the curriculum content provides tremendous variety and flexibility for the student.
>
> By planning their programs three or four times a year. Atlanta students have a wide variety of enrichment options. The college-bound, who were locked into a pat schedule under a traditional plan, can get more supplementary courses and more course options. (Two electives per quarter is the maximum,) Students interested in in-depth study of a subject can schedule blocks of course time concurrently, something that is impractical in a regular, two-semester, 180 day program where course offerings are fragmented. And, by enrolling in all four quarters, advanced students can graduate early. The slow learner gets a break, too. A student who fails a course can repeat it the very next quarter or take a remedial course immediately. In the very first year of Atlanta's voluntary four-quarter plan, the percentage of failing students dropped 40 per cent, saving the district more than $40,000.

The Atlanta Program was sound instructionally but unfortunately the Board did not consider it feasible financially. When it became apparent federal funds would no longer be available for this activity the Atlanta School System in 1974 began phasing out their year-round program. As stated by a member of their Central Administration: "It was finally resolved we could not support such an endeavor financially. . . . In the last two years we have only operated one fourth-quarter or summer program

---

[45] The NASSP Bulletin, April, 1975, devoted most of this issue to the year-round school.

[46] Leonard Ernst, "The Year-round School: Faddish or Feasible?" *The Nation's Schools*, vol. 88, No. 5 (Nov. 1971), pp. 51–56.

in the Atlanta School System out of 22 high schools that normally operate September through June." [47]

George M. Jensen is optimistic about the benefits of the year-round school. He lists fifteen ways in which he perceives the year-round school as making sense.[48]

1. Right at the start, year-round school boosts utilization of our multi-billion dollar educational enterprise from 75 per cent to 100 per cent. It reduces classroom and other plant needs by at least 20 per cent; it permits accelerated programs that actually chop time off the number of years a youngster spends in school; it puts education into the twentieth century—the idea of closing the schools in summer was devised when Americans were farmers and youngsters were needed in June, July, and August to help in the fields.
2. Most suggested plans, some of which already have been use-tested, release classroom space through staggered or sequential pupil attendance patterns, or through acceleration, or both. This obviously reduces the need for new construction and lowers the pressure for additional taxes. Less property has to be removed from the tax rolls to provide adequate space when new construction becomes necessary for the district.
3. Most plans invite a complete restructuring of the curriculum to make it more flexible, effective, and relevant. This re-evaluation of the total school program, as Atlanta is demonstrating, can result in far more effective use of our already established capacity to teach. This is one of the most significant of the possible dividends to be expected from any year-round school plan.
4. Virtually all year-round plans make it possible but not mandatory for ambitious, highly motivated teachers—especially men—to be employed twelve months a year at commensurately higher salaries (therefore, of course, not as many full-time teachers will be required to staff any system; result: fewer and, hopefully, better teachers, with the current teacher shortage diminished accordingly).
5. The absence of the father from thousands of inner-city families has created a need, more crucial than ever, for more male teachers in both elementary and secondary schools. It can be met by offering men teachers the full-time employment at full-time compensation possible with the year-round school plan.
8. Most suggested year-round schedules result in lower teacher retirement quarter, two quarters, three or four quarters (in any of the quarter

[47] Letter to the authors dated November 3, 1978, from Sidney H. Estes, Assistant Superintendent for Instructional Planning and Development for the Atlanta Public Schools.
[48] George M. Jensen, "Year-round School: Can Boards Side Step It Much Longer?" *American School Board Journal,* 157 (July 1969), 12.

systems plans, for example) can hardly help but better meet the employment needs of many teachers, especially women, than does the present inflexible nine or ten months contract.

7. Offering year-round employment with full-year teaching loads reduces the number of new teachers who must be trained each year mostly at public expense.

8. Most suggested year-round schedules result in lower teacher retirement plan costs with consequently diminished demand on taxes to support such plans. Current plans attempt to provide comfortable fulltime retirement benefits for persons who annually work only nine months or so. Under a year-round plan only those teachers electing a year-round job would receive full retirement benefits. Others choosing to work shorter periods would be recipients of lower but somewhat comparative retirement benefits.

9. Year-round plans with sequential enrollment eliminate the once-a-year enrollment lockstep by enabling a child to enter school at the beginning of the new period nearest his birthday, thus reducing the wide gap in intellectual development that currently exists at early grade levels and makes for a faulty start in formal education for so many children.

10. Since most subject matter would necessarily be split into smaller segments, the cost of repeating would be less.

11. Most year-round plans offer far better vacation employment opportunities for students than exist under today's nine-month calendar, which floods the youth employment market in June, July, and August.

12. Many juvenile authorities agree that a year-round school pattern would tend to reduce the delinquency that historically crests in the late summer months when all youth are out from under the stabilizing influence of school.

13. Schoolhouse vandalism, which peaks during the long idle summer, would be virtually eliminated in some areas, greatly reduced in others.

14. Acceleration is much more readily accomplished by higher achievers in all year-round plans.

15. Under any plan of sequential attendance, fewer textbooks, reference books, less laboratory equipment, fewer teaching machines and language laboratories are required to serve total enrollment of any district (only 66 to 80 per cent of enrollment would be in school at any one time).

Performance Contracting

Alternatives can be provided through performance contracting. A performance contract is an agreement between a board of education and a contractor (individual, group, or organization) whereby the contractor agrees to improve students' performance in certain skills by a predetermined amount. The contractor is allowed flexibility within broad guidelines as to his/her instructional techniques and materials. If the students achieve according to the contract, the contractor is paid the amount agreed upon; but if the students do not achieve as prespecified, he/she is not.

This is a type of the management systems approach to learning. Applied to the school the product of the system is considered precise, measurable, observable student learning. The input, or "raw material," would be learners at entry into the program. The teacher becomes the learning or instructional manager and classrooms have become learning centers. The emphasis quite often is on programmed instruction and individualized instruction, using a limited number of certified master teachers and an abundance of paraprofessionals and teaching aides. Motivation has been a key and reinforcement theory has been practiced using incentives of almost every description.

While most of the schools hiring outside contractors have done so in elementary grades or for an easily tested skill like a narrowly defined reading skill, contracting could be established at any grade level or for any testable skill or subject.

The performance contractor sells a system of teaching and learning that is well organized and constantly controlled and supervised. He/she has systematized ideas about behavior and learning theory that is applied to children under controlled conditions to effect learning.

In some instances, e.g., Gary, Indiana,[49] a performance contract was signed for a private contractor to run a whole school.

While performance contracting was hailed as a way for the private business sector to show schools how the management systems approach could be applied to learning, evidence from numerous evalutions have been uniformly uncomplimentary as far as results are concerned. The Office of Economic Opportunity (OEO) used three different analysis systems to evaluate the test results of eighteen experimental performance contracting programs. They concluded that generally performance contracting is no more successful than traditional classroom methods in improving reading and math skills of disadvantaged children:

> Not only did both groups (experimental and control) do equally poor in terms of overall averages but also these averages are very nearly the same in each grade, in each subject, for the best and worst students in each sample, and with few exceptions, in each site.[50]

Thomas K. Glennon was generally pessimistic about performance contracting and disclosed that four of the six companies involved in the experi-

[49] For details of how the contractor managed the school, see Susan Boyer, "Performance Contracting: Texarkana and Gary," *Saturday Review of Literature*, 54 (September 18, 1971), pp. 62–65.

[50] As quoted in *Education USA, Washington Monitor*, National School Public Relations Assoc., Washington, D.C. (February 7, 1972), p. 125.

ments have given up performance contracting and five of the companies are involved in disputes with OEO over how much money is due them.[51]

Ellis B. Page commended the OEO's effort to assess the performance contract results by their rigorous research design controlling many of the "gain ghosts" such as regression to the mean, teaching to the test, biased analyses, and so on.[52]

While the results of performance contracting have been generally disappointing it has served as a useful alternative and a way of stimulating greater effort on the part of public schools. In addition, it has contributed to greater flexibility and receptiveness to educational and social reform.

Summary

There are a myriad of organizational plans for grouping age levels, abilities, basic skills, and "cultural imperatives" and "cultural electives." These plans have various labels such as middle school, alternative school, open education, integrated day, dual progress, and so on. Tools to effect such plans include modular scheduling, interage grouping, minicourse curriculum, and a host of others. The means for providing for individual interests and needs are not lacking. Alternatives are available to break away from the patterns reinforced by custom, tradition, and the demands of managerial simplicity. Focusing upon the individual human being who has his/her own needs and potential contributions forces us to seek organizations that are flexible instead of rigid, that can change and thereby strengthen themselves rather than break under the stress of pressure from the outside.

For Further Thought

1. Is developing alternatives for learners compatible with efficient organization? Why?
2. Debate: Ability grouping results in the development of undemocratic attitudes.
3. The focus of organization for instruction is upon learners. What, if any, consideration of faculty and staff should enter into decisions regarding organization for instruction?
4. Are specialized high schools such as vocational and college preparatory a threat to equality of educational opportunity?
5. Should faculty attempt to persuade students to participate in activity programs in which they show no interest?

[51] Ibid., pp. 125–126.
[52] Ellis B. Page, "How We All Failed at Performance Contracting," *Phi Delta Kappan*, 54, No. 2 (October 1972), pp. 115–117.

6. Some critics of our schools charge that we provide too many electives and permit students to take too many courses without gaining any depth of knowledge. What is your reaction to this charge?
7. What does research show about relative achievement in long or short periods? Is this adequate information upon which to base a decision regarding modular scheduling for a school?
8. Set up an organization with proper policies and procedures for using local citizens as resource persons to the school, including the establishment of minicourses.

Chapter 10   Staffing to Improve Learning

The idea of one teacher, one classroom with four walls, and twenty-five–thirty students still pervades the literature, the social structure of the school, and the general thinking of the public. No matter what changes or reforms one proposes in a school system, if the change does not in some way or another fit into this traditional pattern it becomes difficult to implement without traumatic overtones for both the community and the faculty. Yet, this in and of itself is a practice and a concept that is limiting educational opportunities, for we know that the classroom unit is not the only place where learning takes place. Each student as a unique individual with an individual learning style cannot be expected to learn best in a constant uniform class situation.

The major personnel task of the principal today as we see it is not the usual personnel administration detail concerned with salary, job benefits, tenure, social security, and so forth. Rather, his/her responsibility is to help develop a staff that can most effectively and efficiently help the student to learn how to become a productive, self-sufficient individual. That very simple statement may mean a much different staffing approach to teaching and learning than we have had in the past.

A Staffing Concept

Education of the child is the major reason schools exist. To carry out this educational task requires *people* (the school staff) who utilize *time* (school day and its daily schedule), *space* (the school building with its classrooms and laboratories, and the community) and *programs* and *materials* (books, visuals, and other work and learning materials), *information* (data organized and analyzed to clarify decisions), and *money*.

In the early days of America the schooling process became systematized by having a school with classrooms and a teacher in each classroom who was given the responsibility of teaching children certain quantities of subject matter during a regularly scheduled time period. The great majority of American adults have gone through this pattern and to them it is their idea of good schooling, whether they enjoyed it or not. Teacher training institutions have reinforced this pattern. Also the teaching profession itself has reinforced the idea by the stands taken on the basis of the common 1:25 teacher–pupil ratio. Thus, the education system in the United States has become essentially static as far as the teacher–student organization is concerned. The teacher and the classroom with twenty-five–thirty students has become a self-reinforcing system with the teacher's professional responsibilities and authority being built almost completely on this limited role. The majority of proposed staffing alternatives are not actually alternatives at all but merely variations of the same theme based upon the assumption of a teacher with a set number of pupils.

Educational planners appear to be completely locked into this one direction. When considering the question, "What type of education is best for the learner?" the traditional teaching pattern typically dominates their thinking. They really are asking, "What type of education is best for the learner based upon the system of a teacher with a set number of children located in a classroom?"

One can break away from this static, structured role by concentrating on the learner, his/her learning needs, and his/her optimum learning style. For the moment, one must forget teacher–pupil ratio and the teacher's role in front of a classroom and consider the teacher strictly as a professional resource who, working with other teachers, resource people, and auxiliary personnel, plans and utilizes *time, space,* and *materials* so that each student can learn at his/her optimum.

Conceptualizing the education process in this manner one may then end up with the traditional teacher in his/her traditional classroom; however, this learning situation probably will be one of many alternative learning situations for the student. Contrary to many opinions such an approach does not "downgrade" the teacher. Rather, it places him/her in a more respected professional role. It recognizes that learning is a function of the learner and that the teachers are the professionals who engineer and set the tone of the entire learning process by:

1. Setting the various goals for learning of the institution.
2. Diagnosing the learning needs and style of each student.
3. Prescribing programs and various types of teaching–learning situations.
4. Arranging for and implementing the prescription.
5. Evaluating results.

Following this approach the collective teachers' judgments are utilized in regard to the way people learn, and then personnel and material resources are appropriately deployed to meet the unique needs of the learner.

Most school systems of any size have all or most of the resources to carry out these five basic tasks; however, few have organized them into functioning operational units that continuously follow the student through the total pattern. At the same time teachers themselves agree that the diagnosis–prescription approach or a task analysis approach are intelligent ways of creating a productive and satisfying learning situation for the student, but operationally they appear to be afraid to move too far from the safety of their special kingdom, the classroom.

It appears that a new concept of the instructional staff of the school will need to be accepted before much that is significant can be done to create an improvement in the learning process. It will need to be a concept that focuses on instructional teams working together to create the best learning environment possible. On these teams are certified teachers as key persons but also technicians, aides, consultants, counselors, psychological examiners, and so on. Whether they team-teach, have hierarchical titles and complicated differentiated salary schedules is beside the point as far as instruction is concerned. The important point is that all possible learning resources are focused on the learning efforts of the student, whether he/she is in the classroom or some other appropriate learning environment.

A number of systematic efforts to utilize the staff so that more emphasis is focused on the individual learner rather than the classroom have emerged in the last two decades.[1] Among the more formal efforts are: (1) in-school tutoring, (2) use of teaching aides and auxiliary personnel, (3) differentiated staffing, (4) individualized instruction, (5) structured teaching–learning units, (6) teacher interdisciplinary teams, (7) team teaching.

In-school Tutoring

The Lancaster Plan could be considered the first obvious forerunner of modern peer tutoring and even staff differentiation. This was the official system of the Free School Society of New York at the establishment of the Society's first school in 1806. It continued until 1853. The essential feature of the plan was that older, brighter, more advanced children would teach the younger and less competent under the direction and supervision of a master teacher. Perhaps one should not depict a possibly encouraging approach to teaching as an offshoot of the Lancaster Plan since the Lancaster system quickly fell in disrepute because, as stated by Edwards and Richey, ". . . the object was to confer a very limited degree of instruction, at the least possible expense, to the entirely ignorant." [2]

This was a harsh indictment of an instructional approach that has real

[1] Many of these so-called movements are not so much new ideas as currently focal ones. They are often adopted from plans tried many times through the years. Note the Lancaster Plan used in 1806, and the National Society for the Study of Education 1925 Yearbook entitled *Adapting the Schools to Individual Differences.*

[2] Newton Edwards and Herman G. Richy, *The School in American Social Order* (Boston: Houghton Mifflin Co., 1947), p. 266.

possibilities. The Durrell Pupil–Team Learning Concept is a modern approach to peer tutoring. Recent research has shown that tutoring by advanced students, college students, teacher aides, and even student peers when carefully planned, organized, and supervised by the professional teacher can be a successful learning experience for children and youth. It is just another method that often brings results when applied as a prescription to improve learning.

Instructional Aides

Bay City, Michigan, Public Schools and Central Michigan University initiated significant pioneering efforts with teacher aides in a partnership project with financial support from the Fund for the Advancement of Education. The project had the usual "ups and downs." A publication by the American Association of Colleges for Teacher Education observed in regard to teacher aides in Bay City

> the program appeared to be an integral part of a continuing educational system. An assessment of that program by Assistant Superintendent Mark E. Bascom, after 15 years of operation, contains the expression of regret by the Bay City Staff that some of the reports about the experience have been of a "semi-sensational" nature. Bascom observes that some have looked upon the Teacher Aide program as a 'panacea for all ills and problems in education while others have seen fit to condemn the experiment without proper observation or study.' At the time of the report the staff seemed to feel that neither the "overzealous claims or severe criticisms" gave a fair picture of the experimental project.[3]

A significant number of schools throughout the United States have utilized and experimented with teacher aides in one way or another. However, after over twenty years it is still considered an innovative practice and a surprising number of schools eliminated the aides soon after funding from foundations or the U.S. Office of Education was withdrawn. AACTE implies that the slowness in the development of new staffing approaches is because the profession itself is spending too much time arguing over process and techniques rather than outcomes. They identified two major positions that exist in the controversy.[4]

Position I. The stature and security of the classroom teacher must not be threatened by variations of merit pay. The ushering in of subprofessionals to invade teachers' roles or limit their career advancement looms as a menace to the organized interests of the teaching profession.

Position II. It is wasteful to employ professional talent for the perfor-

[3] American Association of Colleges of Teacher Education, *Educational Personnel for Urban Schools—What Differentiated Staffing Can Do* (Washington, D.C.: The Association, 1972), p. 32.

[4] Ibid., p. 3.

mance of so many semiprofessional and subprofessional duties. If dentists find technicians to be valuable aides, and if plumbers can employ helpers to good advantage, why cannot teachers increase their level of professional productivity through the use of auxiliary personnel?

Although we are as concerned as anyone over economy moves that would undercut the teaching profession, it is difficult to see how any gain can be made either professionally or educationally by a "holding the line attitude." Actually all evidence points to the fact that when a school staffs on the basis of what are the identifiable activities of teaching that can be performed by a variety of assistants and what the teacher should do him- or herself, a giant step has been taken in professionalizing teaching. Of course, *the professional* teacher's duties must be carefully defined in order to differentiate what is best done by the teacher him- or herself and what should be done by the aides who play supportive roles by doing the things the professionals do not need to do.

The National Association of Secondary School Principals' Model Schools Project, sometimes called "Schools of Tomorrow," has been experimenting with the utilization of teacher aides along with many other innovative practices.[5, 6, 7] J. Lloyd Trump, director of the project, identifies three kinds of assistants required:

Clerks—to keep records, duplicate and file materials, grade objective tests, and so on.

Instructional Assistants—who can supervise students in independent study and small group work and assist with certain other instructional tasks. These should be persons with preparation in the subject area but not necessarily enough training for complete certification. Such persons come from the ranks of advanced college and university students, housewives, and retired or partially retired persons.

General Aides—responsible persons who can supervise playgrounds, lunchrooms, corridors, help small children with clothing, and perform other services that do not require clerical training or preparation attained by instructional assistants. Mr. Trump estimates that auxiliary personnel such as these can perform tasks that now occupy more than one third of a teacher's time.[8]

Other aides or auxiliary personnel that may be identified are:

Technical or Audiovisual Assistant—a technical specialist in the use of audiovisual equipment, television, teaching machines, computers, microfilm, information retrieval, and the like.

[5] J. Lloyd Trump, "How Excellent are Teaching and Learning in Your School?" Undated mimeo paper, p. 6.

[6] William Georgiades, *How Good Is Your School?* Reston, Va.: Nat'l Association of Secondary School Principals, 1978.

[7] J. Lloyd Trump, *A School for Everyone,* Reston, Va.: Nat'l Association of Secondary School Principals, 1977.

[8] J. Lloyd Trump and William Georgiades, *How to Change Your School* (Reston, Va.: Nat'l Assoc. of Secondary School Principals, 1978).

Laboratory Assistant—who assists in laboratory situations such as science or language laboratory.

Student Teacher or Teaching Intern—a college student in a teacher education preparation program who can assist in any backup or other appropriate situation.

Minicourse or Topic Expert—any responsible youth or adult who through special study, experience, or hobby activities is an expert and can teach, help to teach, or serve as a consultant in a special minicourse or teaching unit.

Parent Volunteer Aide—to assist the teacher in any way his or her abilities will enhance the learning process.

Community Aide—(a successful approach in inner-city or neighborhood ethnic areas) a knowledgeable member of the community who can help to interpret community sentiment and needs, identify and help to contact indigenous leaders, interpret cultural mores, and so forth.

Of course the identification, orientation, training, and assimilation of auxiliary staff into the school system is a long-term, complicated process requiring a great deal of faculty-staff planning. It is difficult and it is complicated but it is more worthy of the teacher's time than some of the routines presently being performed.

Staff Differentiation

The National Commission on Teacher Education and Professional Standards (NCTEPS), which has been an early mover on the differentiated staffing front, defines differentiated staffing as follows:

> Differentiated Staffing is a plan for recruitment, preparation, induction, and continuing education of staff personnel for the schools that would bring a much broader range of manpower to education than is now available. Such arrangements might facilitate individual professional development to prepare for increased expertise and responsibility as teachers, which would lead to increased satisfaction, status and material rewards.[9]

Actually, differentiated staffing in a true sense recognizes that the teaching task requires different levels and variety in experience, expertise, and skill and proposes that this diversity can more efficiently and expertly be handled by a diverse staff who would share the various functions.

James L. Olivera illustrates by chart two typical examples of differentiated staffing.[10] Figure 10.1 stresses a teacher hierarchy with a rather complicated arrangement of providing different ranks for teachers accord-

[9] "A Position Statement on the Concept of Differentiated Staffing," NCTEPS-NEA (May 1969), p. 2.
[10] James L. Olivera, "The Meaning and Application of Differentiated Staffing in Teaching," *Phi Delta Kappan* (September 1970), pp. 38–39.

FIGURE 10.1. Differentiated staff—teacher hierarchy.

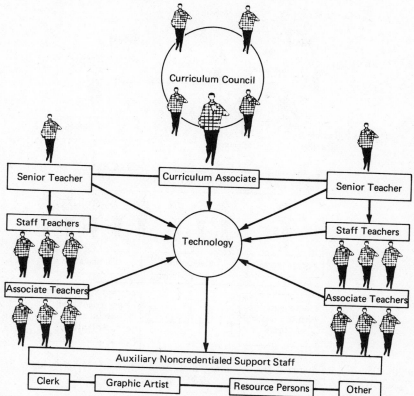

Source: James L. Olivera, "The Meaning and Application of Differentiated Staffing in Teaching," *Phi Delta Kappan* (Sept., 1970), p. 38.

ing to role and function. Figure 10.2 utilizes the master teacher concept but emphasizes teachers and specialists working in a colleague relationship with the help of paraprofessionals.

As illustrated by the Olivera charts, "differentiated staffing" suggests a variety of staffing arrangements and should normally imply operational flexibility to deploy personnel resources in any appropriate way to meet the unique needs of the learner.

However, a major concern, especially of teacher professional and union groups, is that differentiated staffing will create a teaching hierarchy that in a sense sanctions and recognizes differences in ability and quality of teaching. These groups fear that the development of career ladders for positions of varying responsibility could produce an internal hierarchy, merit salaries, and even closer supervision and tighter control than exists at present.

FIGURE 10.2.   Differentiated staff—master teacher concept.

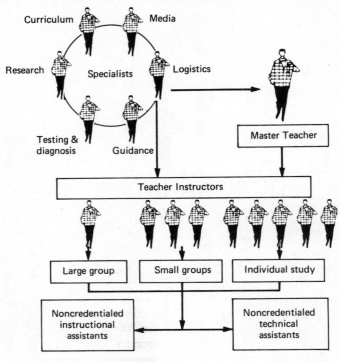

Source: James L. Olivera, "The Meaning and Application of Differentiated Staffing in Teaching," *Phi Delta Kappan* (Sept. 1970), p. 38.

Unfortunately, two school systems, one in Sarasota County, Florida, and another in Temple City, California, that have received the most publicity on their differentiated staffing patterns do place major emphasis on an organizational hierarchy with specified job descriptions and responsibilities related to differentiated pay. The pioneers of this program have done much to promote the idea of staffing options; on the other hand they frighten many educational organizations not only because the controversial issue of "merit pay" is at the forefront in these models but because they see another bureaucracy developing that could be even more complicated and cumbersome than the ones we presently have.

In Temple City the organization is established by placing teaching in the hands of teaching groups or teams. Each group is under the leadership of a master teacher who has a doctorate or equivalent. The master teacher is hired on a twelve-month basis and has staff as well as teaching responsibilities. The group is then tiered down into a hierarchy starting with senior teachers, staff teachers, and associate teachers, each having slightly lower

FIGURE 10.3. Grouping for improving skill development.

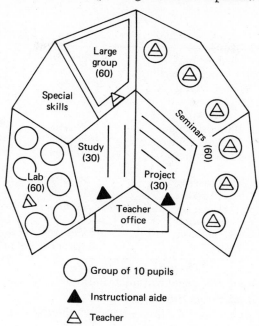

responsibilities, credentials—and naturally salaries. Backing up this teaching group are technical, instructional, and clerical aides.

The Sarasota County, Florida, model that is illustrated in Table 10.1 [11] follows very much the pattern of Temple City. It has essentially the same positions, levels of responsibilities, and benefits according to levels. They merely have different titles.

Although many other models do exist they have not received the same publicity and unfortunately many of the proponents of the California and Florida models are inclined to insist that the only true definition of differentiated staffing is one that would describe their model.

The U.S. Office of Education has stimulated a great deal of experimentation in this area by funding a large number of differentiated staffing and teacher aid proposals. However, they too have frightened many away by advocating the Sarasota and Temple City models. Their stated objective in many instances was to bring different "types" into the teaching profession and to provide careers in teaching for minority groups. Certainly this is a worthy objective; however, this is an instance where in attempting to use the institution of education to achieve a social goal, controversy has

[11] Data for the table were obtained from Richard A. Dempsey and A. John Fioreno, *Differentiated Staffing: What It is and How It Can Be Implemented* (Swarthmore, Pa.: A. C. Croft Inc., 1971), p. 48.

TABLE 10.1   *The Sarasota County, Florida, Model*

Position	Responsibility	Salary	Days Hired	Tenure/ Nontenure
Consulting teacher	Leadership, variable teaching	1.50 ratio	211	Nontenure
Directing teacher	75% teaching 25% supervision and staff	1.25 ratio	211	Tenure
Staff teacher	100% teaching	1.00 ratio	196	Tenure
Instructor	100% teaching	1.00 ratio	196	Tenure
Intern (college student)	100% teaching	.50 ratio	190	Nontenure
Inst. asst.	Asst. teacher	.50 ratio	190	Nontenure
Aide	Asst. teacher	.35 ratio	190	Nontenure
Student Asst.	Asst. teacher and aide	.03/hour	180	
Adjunct teacher	Teacher and asst.	Completely volunteer work— parent or community person		

subverted the important organizational improvement and the profession has shied away from the entire concept.

The foregoing discussion of differentiated staffing was written in the first edition of our book (1974). In the fall of 1978, in preparation for this revision, we wrote to the superintendents of Temple City, California, and Sarasota, Florida, asking for an update on the status of differentiated staffing in their schools. Surprisingly, the two letters we received backed up the observations we made in 1974.

Dear Dr. Roe:

I don't think we have differentiated staffing any more in the manner in which that term has been defined in practice and literature during the past decade. We do have a well-established system of paraprofessionals at several levels, and they are functioning as D. S. intended; namely, to assume duties which do not require professional training, and, of course, to relieve teachers and others of such duties. We do not have a hierarchy within teacher ranks. That is, there no longer are directing teachers, senior teachers, staff teachers by those titles or with *differentiated authority, status, or pay.*

D. S. as a formal model of staffing has disappeared more from natural causes than overt action. I think the primary causes were three: (1) that which I mentioned above—disputes over equity of pay, and competition for resources; (2) the gradual movement during the past decade to conservatism across the nation. My perception from at least our state and local area is that the back-to-basics syndrome and spin-off from it is a phenomenon affecting all parts of society, certainly including governmental services. I think that education is a prime target simply because it is the most accessible to the general public; and (3) the withdrawal several years ago of federal funds to support much of the innovation in general, and D. S. in particular. I think that funds for the pilot projects across the nation were stopped before the concept was strong enough to stand on its own. However, I also believe that the D.S. projects and efforts of the sixties have had some positive effects. We do a better job now of using paraprofessionals, certainly. Also, we are substantially more effective in seeking and using input from employees at all levels in making decisions affecting curriculum and support services. The somewhat jargony phrase of the D. S. era was "shared decision making." I'm sure that the advent of teacher and other employee unions also have brought that into being, but I think that in our school system the effect of D. S. has been greater.

I appreciate your inquiry. I hope that the ultra-conservative swing of the pendulum moves back some; for unless it does, I fear that the next decade or so will find public education stagnating for lack of constructive innovation.

Sincerely,

Gene M. Pillot
Superintendent

The School Board of Sarasota County, Florida
Sarasota, Florida
September 25, 1978

Dear Dr. Roe:

In response to your inquiry as to our current status of Differentiated Staffing—

1. We have some indices of D. S. in our schools—Senates, shared decision making, leadership roles called Senior Teachers, etc.; however, there is little of the formal aspect of D. S. remaining.
2. No, it is not as Croft is describing it.

It will be my thrust, as the new Superintendent, to develop once again those attitudes of involvement and participation from staff that we once knew. We still believe that collegial relationships and corporate attitudes foster greater commitment, which means better experiences for our youth.

Sincerely,

Wesley A. Bosson, Ed. D.
Superintendent
Temple City Unified School District
Temple City, California
August 30, 1978

Differentiated staffing has had its difficulty in a number of school systems. For an interesting case study of a school that abandoned differentiated staffing, read C. Thompson Wacaster's "The Life and Death of Differentiated Staffing at Columbia High School." [12]

Differentiated Staffing at the Top of the World

A description by Albert Haven, principal of the Top of the World Elementary School, Laguna Beach, California, is a good example of a staffing

[12] In J. Victor Baldridge and Terrence E. Deal, (Eds.) *Managing Change in Educational Organizations* (Berkeley, Calif.: McCutchans, 1975), Ch. 24, pp. 467–482.

FIGURE 10.4. Top of the World upper-grade staffing model.

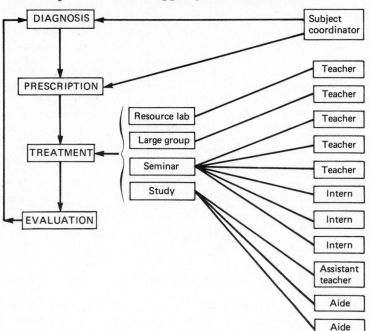

model that is flexible and devised to focus on the needs of the learner
rather than adhering to a particular organizational concept.[13]

> Top of the World School is built in two large pods capable of housing up
> to 240 students each. At present, there are between 210 and 230 students
> in each pod. The total population of each unit is divided into groups of
> about ten; for each subject there will be from 18 to 24 cluster groups
> focusing on specific pupil needs. This number of groups (over a three-
> year-age span) provides opportunity for sophistication in grouping criteria.
> Student learning modes are the primary criteria for forming groups:
> accelerated, remedial, or developmental learners; deductive or inductive
> thinkers; independent or dependent learners; learners who respond best to
> auditory, visual, kinesthetic, or verbal stimuli; shy, compulsive, or competitive
> learners. The important factor is that some identifiable criteria be established
> that can facilitate instruction for a group of youngsters. (Each student
> moves from group to group according to growth.)
> In general, level of skill development, corrected by learning style, forms
> the basic criteria for reading and math groups. Planned heterogeneity is the
> basis for grouping in social studies, interest groups in science, and social
> groups (friends) in art, music, and physical education. The student sees
> himself as a manyfaceted individual: 'Here I have strength, here I need
> help, and here I can help others.'
> In attempting to group by learning styles, we were faced with the same

[13] Albert Haven, "A View from the Top of the World," *The National Elementary
Principal, Differentiated Staffing Special Section* (January 1972), pp. 75–76.

basic problem that confronts any school—a theoretical concept without any reliable, empirical data to provide guidance. But as we probed the problem, we realized that teachers are constantly making subjective judgments about students and how they learn. In fact, this is the heart of the teaching process. It is axiomatic that you can't teach anything to anyone. Learning is a function of the learner. The teacher can only observe the student and make a prediction about how he might learn something. A learning experience is then provided and observation made to determine whether or not the desired learning took place.

There is nothing new and different about this process; it just has never been organized. We have tried to organize teachers' subjective judgments about the way that students learn and to use that data to improve instruction. All of the usual criteria that go into teacher judgments are applied; that is, test scores, cumulative records, parent conferences, psychological testing where needed, pupil classroom performance, pupil–teacher interaction, and the rest.

So far, this is no different from the operation of a traditional school, but combining teachers' observations and judgments about students builds in a correction not available in the traditional model. More than one viewpoint tends to bring objectivity, or, as we prefer to call it, organized subjectivity. All judgments are public and open to question. The arrangement of the groups is flexible, so that new information can bring about a change in instructional mode. Because of the use of different grouping criteria for each subject, each student receives instruction in that subject, according to his/her need. No two students follow the same learning path. Thus, the two main criteria for an individualized program are met: providing instruction appropriate to student need in each subject and no two students following exactly the same program. Yet, the school operates in the group mode—rather than on the classic individualized model—because that mode is consistent with available materials and teacher skills. . . .

At Top of the World School, the upper grade staff in 1970–71 consisted of seven full-time and one part-time teacher, plus two aides. Under the differentiated staffing model, the upper grade staff was reorganized in 1971–72 to include five full-time, one assistant, and one part-time teacher; one full-time and two part-time interns; and two aides–two additional staff positions at a saving of $2,000.

Staffing Units and Equivalents

Job Description	Staffing Unit
Teacher	1
Teacher, part-time	appropriate fraction
Intern, full-time	.5
Intern, part-time	.3
Assistant teacher	.4
Aide	.25

By defining teacher roles clearly, and by grouping students appropriately, teachers can be freed to spend major time on the important aspects of teaching—interaction, diagnosis, evaluation, and goal setting with students. Top of the World School has 16 authorized units. The differentiated staffing organization allows 12 certified staff members to work the major part of their day teaching small groups of students.

Role definition is the critical factor and forms the basis of our program. In most differentiated staffing models, roles do not relate directly to instructional task functions. Rather, they tend to be global in nature; that is, master teacher, senior teacher, junior teacher, and so forth. The major thrust of differentiated staffing too often is confused. In some quarters, it is viewed as a kind of merit pay plan; in others, as a way to pay teachers high salaries and allow them to remain in the classroom; and in still others, as a way of saving tax dollars. The essence of differentiated staffing, however, is a process that allows us to remove some of the constraints on our thinking and enables us to achieve solutions based on the problem rather than on tradition.

The problems faced by education today cannot be solved under traditional patterns of operation. Differentiated staffing, if we keep it in perspective, may provide a viable process to achieve solutions. Concentrating on the peripheral outcomes of differentiated staffing distracts from the purpose and will likely result in failure and abandonment. Focusing on the process of building a staffing pattern to solve individual school needs may open new vistas for public education. All that is needed is the courage to begin.

Present Status of Top of the World

A letter from the present principal of the Top of the World Elementary School indicates this more conservative approach to differentiated staffing has stood the test of time:

Dear Dr. Roe:

Regarding your questions about Top of the World School, the differentiated staff plan is basically the same as it was in 1972, in that we utilize a variety of groupings to maximize benefit from a lower student-teacher ratio. We have organized our instruction to greater emphasize individual academic needs of children, simultaneously focusing on self respect and decision making. I believe we have reached an excellent balance between the flexibility needed to achieve an innovative program and maintain extremely high academic standards for our students.

I hope the above is of assistance to you.

Sincerely,

Michael N. Carroll, Principal
TOP OF THE WORLD SCHOOL

MNC:ak   Laguna Beach Unified School District
Laguna Beach, California
September 1, 1978

Individualized Instruction

Individualized instruction has been a particularly successful teaching process throughout the centuries. Socrates, Comenius, Pestalozzi, Montessori,

Dewey, and many other teacher–philosophers advocated it. Mark Hopkins on one end of a log and the student on the other is often cited as the best example of schooling. Bloom in his book *Human Characteristics and School Learning* presents some persuasive arguments in regard to an individualized form of mastery learning that could change the way we traditionally view teaching and learning in school.[14] Bloom contends through this approach it is possible for 95 per cent of our students to learn all that the school has to teach, and all at near the same level.

Karen Harvey and Lowell Horton in their review of this book indicate that flexibility is crucial if we are to implement Bloom's model.[15]

> The school would need to allow: 1) flexibility of time—time to accommodate different tasks and different learners; 2) flexibility that allows space to be utilized for economical large-group instruction, small-group instruction, and individual work; 3) flexibility in grouping, not only in group size but in composition—children clustered together because of need or purpose, not age; 4) flexibility of materials—a wide range of teaching tools and resources for the achievement of learning tasks; and 5) flexibility of staffing patterns. Highly trained, skilled specialists with competencies that require advanced degrees may well be needed for certain functions, while perhaps volunteer parents, paraprofessional workers, or students could adequately handle other jobs. It is critical also to consider differing teaching styles, for teachers and administrators know that teachers teach better and find greater satisfaction in their jobs when encouraged to develop a comfortable teaching style. Mastery learning requires schools to be flexible: expert planners will need to use this flexibility carefully to maximize learning.

Although Bloom's theory has not been developed into a full-fledged plan, other systems that have been implemented and tested are closely allied to Bloom's ideas. The most well-known systems of this type are: The Westinghouse Learning Corporations "Planning for Learning in Accordance with Needs" (PLAN); individually prescribed Instruction (I.P.I.) and Adoptive Environments for Learning developed by the Learning Research and Development Center of the University of Pittsburg; the Individual Guided Education program developed by Herbert J. Klausmeier of the University of Wisconsin and further refined by Lloyd Trump and the Kettering Foundation.[16]

The I.G.E. program has developed the most sophisticated organization and staffing pattern as a means of implementation. It has been arranged organizationally so that IGE can be the main thrust of instruction for the

[14] Benjamin S. Bloom, *Human Characteristics and School Learning* (New York: McGraw-Hill, 1976).

[15] Karen Harvey and Lowell Horton, "Bloom's Human Characteristics and School Learning," *Phi Delta Kappan*, Nov., 1977, p. 192.

[16] For information on the development of these and other individualized programs see Harriet Talmage (Ed.), *Systems of Individualized Instruction* (Berkeley, Calif.: McCutchan Publishing Corp., 1975.) A National Society for the Study of Education Series on Contemporary Educational Issues.

FIGURE 10.5. Stoughton Middle School.

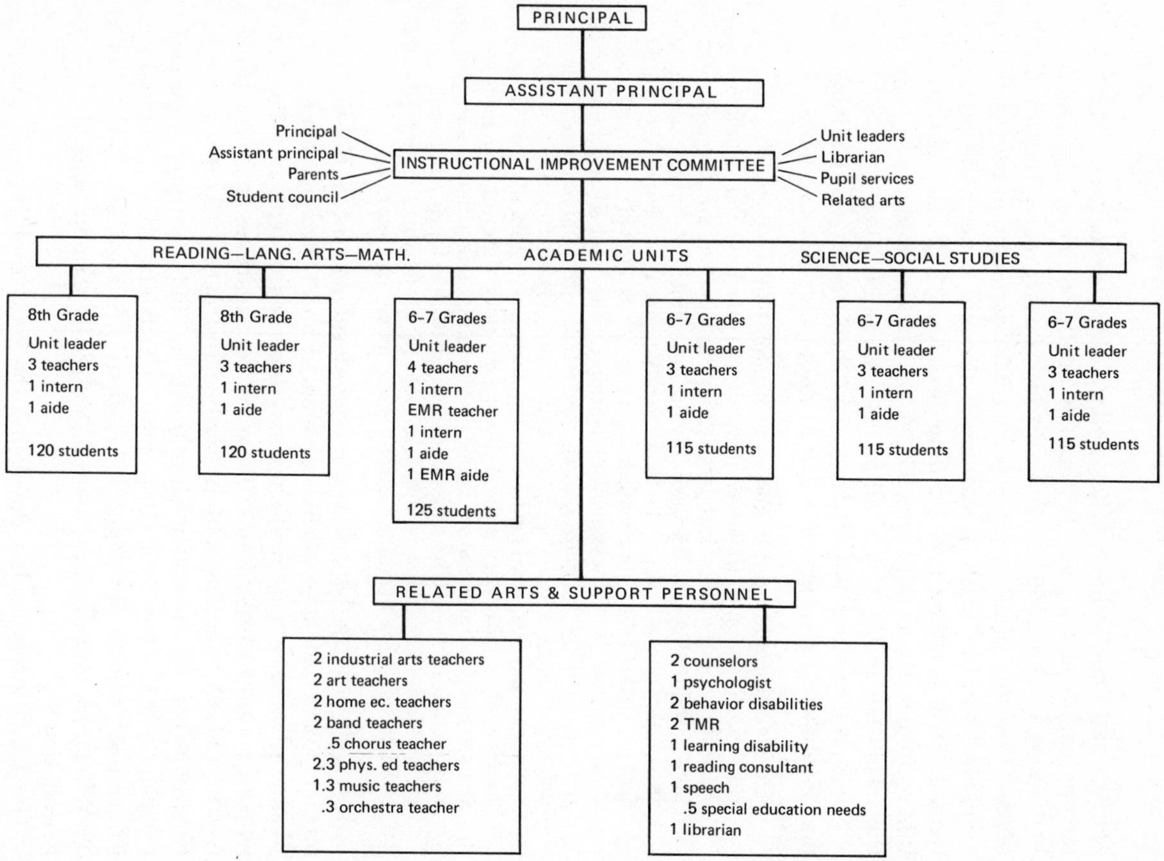

PRINCIPAL

ASSISTANT PRINCIPAL

INSTRUCTIONAL IMPROVEMENT COMMITTEE

Principal
Assistant principal
Parents
Student council

Unit leaders
Librarian
Pupil services
Related arts

ACADEMIC UNITS

READING—LANG. ARTS—MATH.

8th Grade
Unit leader
3 teachers
1 intern
1 aide

120 students

8th Grade
Unit leader
3 teachers
1 intern
1 aide

120 students

6–7 Grades
Unit leader
4 teachers
1 intern
EMR teacher
1 intern
1 aide
1 EMR aide

125 students

SCIENCE—SOCIAL STUDIES

6–7 Grades
Unit leader
3 teachers
1 intern
1 aide

115 students

6–7 Grades
Unit leader
3 teachers
1 intern
1 aide

115 students

6–7 Grades
Unit leader
3 teachers
1 intern
1 aide

115 students

RELATED ARTS & SUPPORT PERSONNEL

2 industrial arts teachers
2 art teachers
2 home ec. teachers
2 band teachers
.5 chorus teacher
2.3 phys. ed teachers
1.3 music teachers
.3 orchestra teacher

2 counselors
1 psychologist
2 behavior disabilities
2 TMR
1 learning disability
1 reading consultant
1 speech
.5 special education needs
1 librarian

entire school system or a process of instruction for just one portion of a school. As an example the Stoughton Middle School of Stoughton, Wisconsin, which in 1978–79 was cited by the National Association of Secondary School Principals as a model middle school, is organized as an IGE school.[17]

Team Teaching

Team teaching is a method of teaching whereby a group of teachers plan, prepare, and help to assemble a variety of teaching materials for a particular course or core of courses and then utilizes the best talents of the group in teaching the various aspects of the course. The heart of the team idea is the strong collaboration of a group of teachers who are expert and talented in the area being taught and utilizing this talent to the best advantage in the teaching–learning situation.[18]

Team teaching breaks down the individual teacher–student classroom relationship and encourages teachers to share teacher know-how and provide a variety of alternative teaching–learning situations presented from different perspectives and by different teachers.[19]

Dr. William R. Boren, Superintendent of the Weber School District in Utah, has these points to make in relation to his experience in team teaching:

1. The principal of the school needs to make a firm commitment to the effort and lend his/her full support.
2. Teachers need opportunity to develop a rationale for teaming and to plan programs and to plan how to effectively implement programs.
3. Teachers and principals need to work out an open system of communication, wherein teachers will be honest and forthright with one another in a truly professional fashion.
4. Teachers need to develop acceptable ways of constructively criticizing one another and to develop a willingness to accept criticism.
5. The team should seek help from experts who have developed the skills necessary for successful teaming.
6. The team should accept the fact that their procedures can and should change as they gain experience.
7. The team should recognize that *team teaching is not turn teaching.*

[17] Adapted from information presented by H. J. Klausmeier, "I.G.E. in Elementary and Middle Schools," *Educational Leadership*, Feb., 1977, p. 330.

[18] Daniel C. Lortie, "The Teacher and Team Teaching," in J. Victor Baldridge and Terrance E. Dean, (Eds.) *Managing Change in Educational Organizations* (Berkeley, Calif.: McCutchans, 1975), Ch. 12, pp. 250–79.

[19] For a more negative point of view about team teaching read Robert E. Rose, "Elementary Teaming, Learning Improvement or Administrative Ploy," *Peabody Journal of Education*, April, 1978, pp. 265–270.

FIGURE 10.6. A plan for organization of I.G.E.

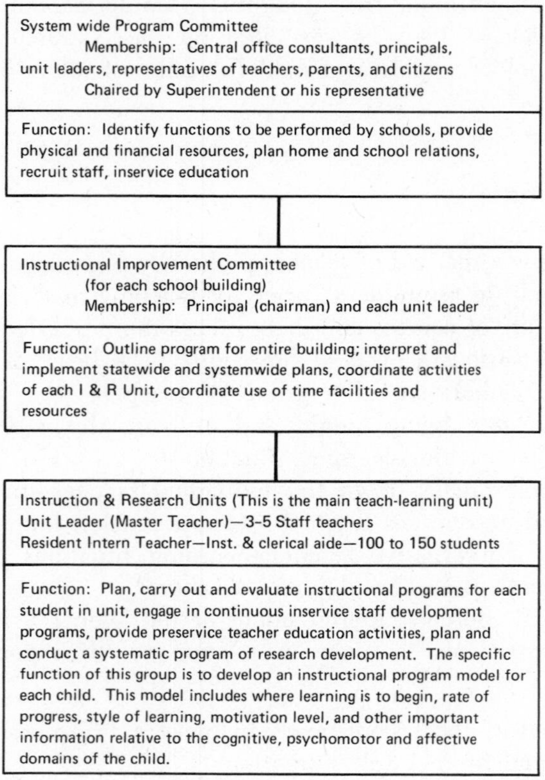

Adapted from information presented by H. J. Klausmeier, "I.G.E. in Elementary and Middle Schools," *Educational Leadership,* Feb., 1977, p. 330.

8. The team should give special attention to individual students and small groups (2–8) of students.
9. School facilities that house teaching programs should provide space for a variety of activities.[20]

Varnell Bench, member of the social studies teaching team in the Walquist Junior High School, identified three types of team teaching concepts, varying from simple to more complex, which would generally characterize the more prevalent types of team teaching. In the first type, Team Teaching Concept A (see Fig. 10.7), the teachers plan a curriculum together and then teach this curriculum in their separate classrooms. In the second type, Team Teaching Concept B (see Fig. 10.8), the teachers plan together, share the teaching of major concepts to large groups and then automatically

[20] W. R. Boren, "Team Teaching: How to Incorporate It into Our Schools," *Team Teaching,* Weber County Schools, Ogden, Utah, Vol. 2, No. 1 (Sept. 1967), p. 1.

FIGURE 10.7.   Team teaching Concept "A."

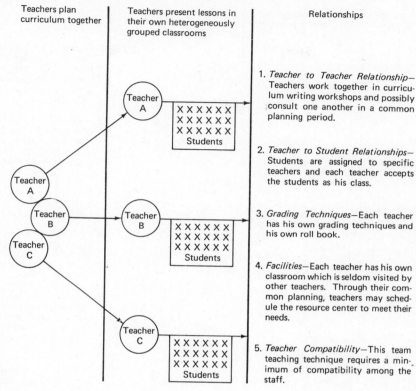

Teachers plan curriculum together

Teachers present lessons in their own heterogeneously grouped classrooms

Relationships

1. *Teacher to Teacher Relationship*—Teachers work together in curriculum writing workshops and possibly consult one another in a common planning period.

2. *Teacher to Student Relationships*—Students are assigned to specific teachers and each teacher accepts the students as his class.

3. *Grading Techniques*—Each teacher has his own grading techniques and his own roll book.

4. *Facilities*—Each teacher has his own classroom which is seldom visited by other teachers. Through their common planning, teachers may schedule the resource center to meet their needs.

5. *Teacher Compatibility*—This team teaching technique requires a minimum of compatibility among the staff.

Source: These three models are from Varnell Bench, "Concepts of Team Teaching," Weber Country Schools, Ogden: Utah Center for Team Teaching, DHEW. ERIC file #ED 033 068, pp. 1 and 2.

work with their own students in smaller groups. In the third type, Team Teaching Concept C (see Fig. 10.9), teachers plan curriculum together, share large group lecture presentations, and then work together with students on an individual basis and in small groups without reference to a class of their own.

Teacher Interdisciplinary Teams

A number of schools are using interdisciplinary teams of teachers to work with groups of students to help personalize education and integrate the disciplines into a "relevant learning whole." It is a process that attempts to utilize the staff to combine the benefits of team teaching, school within a school, core curriculum, and flexible scheduling. Robert Roth, principal

FIGURE 10.8. Team Concept "B."

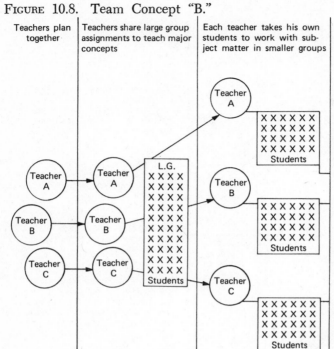

Teachers plan together	Teachers share large group assignments to teach major concepts	Each teacher takes his own students to work with subject matter in smaller groups	Relationships

1. *Teacher to Teacher Relationships*—Teachers must have a similar frame of reference, be confident with one another, and accept criticism.

2. *Teacher to Student Relationship* — The student identifies himself with one teacher although he gets a brief exposure to other teachers.

3. *Grading Techniques* — Each teacher can maintain his grading technique.

4. *Facilities* — Facilities are shared during large group instruction after which teachers return to *their own classrooms.*

5. *Teacher Compatibility* — Teacher compatibility depends on time spent in large group instruction.

of Dunham Junior High School in St. Charles, Illinois describes their system.[21]

> Each team is composed of four teachers—one each for science, mathematics, social studies, and language arts. There are 125–130 students per team, and each teacher team is responsible for its students' total academic program.
>
> The teacher team meets daily for planning, and discusses particular students' self-concepts, interests, capabilities, home situations, and other variables that can affect learning. Once a week, the principal, guidance counselor, and learning disabilities teacher join the team meeting where special stubborn problems may be aired.

Teams Plan Social Activities

> In addition to academic projects, teams of students and teachers are socially active. They hold open house for parents as well as conduct student picnics, and other activities. Each student team also meets one hour daily with the four teachers. The primary purpose of this time block is for the teachers to get to know the students personally and to serve the students in a "helping" relationship.
>
> We have also recognized other advantages of interdisciplinary teams at Dunham Junior High. Time is saved for both staff members and parents

[21] Robert Roth, "Teacher Teams Help Junior High Students Learn, Socialize," *NASSP Bulletin*, February, 1976. pp. 112–13.

FIGURE 10.9. Team teaching Concept "C."

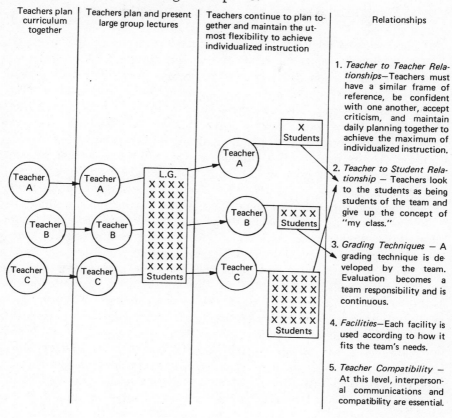

Source: U.S. Department of Health, Education and Welfare, Office of Education. (This document has been reproduced exactly as received from the person or organization originating it. Points of view or opinions stated do not necessarily represent official Office of Education position or policy.)

by having parents meet with a *team* of teachers rather than with teachers individually. In addition, some joint teaching is developing as a natural outgrowth of teachers who are cooperating in solving student learning problems.

The team situation has also increased professional growth. For example, our teachers are presently enrolled in a graduate seminar to improve their capabilities in using behavior modification techniques. Additionally, teachers' own strengths and weaknesses are exposed and, when teachers provide each other with feedback and mutual support, improved teaching results.

Finally, because teams design their own teaching schedules within blocks of time, student movement is staggered. The entire student body does not move from class to class at the signal of a bell. Because Dunham is a modified open space school, having many small groups of students moving through the building rather than large mass movements seems to create a better learning climate.

Use of Structured Teaching–Learning Units of Instruction

The popularity of television has done much to encourage media experts and instructional experts to collaborate in the development of structured materials of instruction that have become course ware, learning guides or learning systems for students for a particular session, a unit, or for a course for an entire semester. The way these systems are used requires a variety of staffing patterns and in many cases changes the teacher's role from providing direct instruction to planning, designing, and organizing learning experiences. The potential for multiple use of audio, film, videotape, television, and computer goes well beyond the typical schools use through language laboratories, computerized teaching processes, educational television, and videotape information retrieval. However, the real potential is yet to be realized. The vast capabilities inherent in recently developed communications media, new audiovisual mechanisms, computerized devices and procedures make possible kinds of learning that were virtually impossible when teachers were forced to rely on their own efforts and the limited audiovisuals available to them. William C. Norris, in a provocative article in *Phi Delta Kappan,* asserts the new technology will usher in a new era in education. He names the electronic technologies most applicable as: television, radio, audio, videotape and discs, computers, computer conferencing, cable TV, microwave and satellite transmission, and of course computer-based education. Norris envisions utilizing computer-based education in a network of learning centers located strategically throughout the United States. These centers would operate twenty-four hours a day seven days a week.

> The system is computer controlled and the main method of delivery is computer-aided instruction with integrated terminal subsystems that include video-discs, audio input and output, and touch input. Structured computer conferences of up to forty students can be held, or a single student can interact with another student or instructor as desired. The key to this system will be computer-aided and computer-managed instruction, but other types of media will be offered as appropriate.[22]

Not a Panacea

Those who are advocates of staffing on the basis of learning rather than one teacher for one classroom generally list the following as advantages:

1. It makes individualized learning programs for students more feasible.
2. It provides greater variety in the instructional process.

[22] William C. Norris, "Via Technology to a New Era in Education," *Phi Delta Kappan,* Feb. 1977, p. 451.

3. It brings greater resources to bear on a particular unit or subject area.
4. It continuously builds greater creativity in the system.
5. The teacher is best utilized according to talents, interest, and skill.
6. Salary and rank are based on levels of work and responsibility.
7. It insures more time and talents devoted to the planning process.
8. It provides more choice by teachers of roles they may take.
9. It establishes different career patterns in teaching, recognizing the necessity for continuous professional development.
10. Its establishment provides a new entrée to the reform of teacher education.
11. Its establishment provides a new entrée to the reform of present school organization and teaching patterns.

As with most of the special innovative approaches in education, different staffing patterns are often claimed by many as a panacea for all the ills of American education. Observing the advantages we have listed one could pose them in the negative and say that these are all the important things wrong with education. It is obvious that different staffing in and of itself is not able to bring about all the listed reforms.

Rather, staffing is only another alternative that may help to solve some of our problems.

Research has repeatedly indicated that it isn't the system, the organization, the facilities, or the finances that are the key to improvement in the learning of a child. Rather, the key is the relationship between the teacher and learner. It follows then that a school will be successful as far as the student is concerned if his/her learning style and learning needs can be diagnosed and a teaching–learning environment established according to an individual's needs and style. The school will be successful if the school principal can locate the best teachers possible and then create a type of organization and environment where their talents can be used to best advantage.

Certainly the teachers' talents are not used to the best advantage if they are bogged down with clerical and nursemaid-type activities, or if all teachers are expected to assume the same general role and duties. Certainly the most talented will not stay in teaching if the planning and decision making always comes from above and if rewards are the same for all regardless of ability and responsibility. Certainly a school cannot maintain a dynamic professional staff unless it has a planned process of utilizing different talent in the system and the community.

For Further Thought

1. Do you agree that the principal should retain veto power over teachers' decisions as to the way they should teach? Discuss.

2. If a school uses community resource persons alongside the regular teaching staff, other than certification and salary, what distinguishes the professional staff from the community resource persons?
3. How would you expect the duties of the principal of a small high school to differ from those of the principal of a large high school in regard to developing a positive teaching–learning environment?
4. How can the principal begin to know the values of persons in the school's attendance area?
5. What "safeguards" can the principal set up to avoid the attention to detail becoming his/her main task, especially when successful caring for detail can enhance his/her credibility to expert leadership?
6. Take a position with regard to one of the staffing plans to improve learning. Present a paper substantiating this position through reference to research studies.
7. Analyze the Sarasota, Florida, and Temple City, California, models of differentiated staffing. Compare with the Top-of-the-World model. Why do you believe the latter has stood the test of time?

Chapter 11 Provision for the Exceptional Student[1]

Individuals who differ from what is perceived as "normal" in our society meet with rejection. This rejection takes different forms, such as being segregated, ignored, or treated in special ways that emphasize the differences. Among schoolchildren this rejection has been found to be associated with such diverse factors as intelligence, achievement, skill, personality characteristics, physical appearance, socioeconomic level, and race.

Another reaction to children who are different is to "pigeonhole" them by applying labels. Such terms as mentally retarded, emotionally disturbed, learning disabled, handicapped, and exceptional have been employed. "Exceptional" is a term employed to refer to those children who differ to such a degree in physical or psychological characteristics that programs purportedly designed for the majority of children do not afford them opportunities for optimum adjustment and progress, and who, therefore, need special instruction and/or environments.

Society, through its agency, the school, identifies additional exceptionalities. The actions and reactions of persons in the school constitute judgments as to the social value of certain characteristics of individuals within the school. Such judgments can, and too often do, create and maintain handicaps for these individuals. Most schools place such a high value on academic achievement that a child with the slightest limitation in this area is quick to be noticed and devalued. The students might place a high value on a particular style of clothes. A child in this school whose parents could not afford such clothes would be more noticeable and more apt to be handicapped.

Two terms, disability and handicap, frequently are used interchangeably. It is almost assumed that they are inseparable; that a disability cannot exist without a resulting handicap. Yet, each one of us is disabled, probably in several ways, but since our disability is not viewed as important, and

[1] We wish to express our appreciation to Dr. Robert Seitz, Professor, Ball State University, for his contribution as a co-author of this chapter.

since we do not call attention to ourselves as a result of our disability, we usually avoid devaluation. That is, we do not develop a handicap. For example, a child who lacks the sense of smell has an objectively measurable disability, but it will not be noticed by others and is not particularly valued by society. Thus, the child will not have a handicap unless he/she later decides to become a chef.

Why the Principal?

The principal is looked upon by the community, the board of education, the central administration, and the teachers as the person responsible for exercising leadership in his/her attendance center. He/she is the allocator or withholder of resources and information that can make a difference. He/she is the one who can encourage or discourage; free or inhibit; exercise positive leadership or drag his/her heels. The principal reinforces or dispels attitudes that can create and/or reinforce handicaps. Even if the principal attempts to avoid directly facing the issue of the handicapped, the status quo that may create handicaps is reinforced.

The principal must operate within a framework already established by laws and individual school district policies. The principal can exert influence in the development of local policy, and can work with the staff in the implementation of policies so that the least harm is done to individual children.

It is the principal who is in a position to aid the staff to break down the handicapping process that is occurring in the minisociety of the school, or at least to intervene at appropriate points in the process. Therefore, as the larger society begins to question why many more children are considered "different," "exceptional," or "handicapped" in the school than are identified before or after the school years, the *accountability buck* begins to come to rest in the hand of the principal of the minisociety that is creating and maintaining the handicaps. Since the attendance area community holds the principal responsible for the learning environment in the school to which they must send their children, there is scarcely anyone to whom the principal can pass the buck.

What Can the Principal Do?

The principal should be primarily concerned with the quality of education for each child in the school; therefore, the focus is upon human interactions and the instructional program that serves as the framework for these interactions. The following are steps that the principal can take to enhance providing for the handicapped:

1. Clarify a personal understanding of handicapping conditions and why the school should make provisions for the handicapped.
2. Become thoroughly familiar with the controlling laws and regulations and their implications for implementation at the building level.
3. Analyze the instructional program in terms of "excluding" practices and materials and identify where school personnel can intervene in the handicapping process.
4. Examine the organizational structure for instruction to determine possible rearrangements of staff and resources to provide for a greater range of individual differences.
5. Establish working cooperation with local, regional, and state special education personnel with an eye toward developing resources for the instructional staff.
6. Institute a staff development program, including preservice when appropriate.
7. Develop with the staff learning alternatives for children.
8. Conduct an inventory of facilities to determine architectural barriers and better utilization of interior and exterior spaces to avoid emphasis upon handicaps.

Clarifying Understanding

To reduce successfully the probability and possibility of his/her school creating and perpetuating handicaps, the principal should understand the process of handicapping. To give a perspective, some views of disabilities and handicaps follow.

A disability may be thought of as an objectively measurable impairment or dysfunction in terms of performance in a particular society.

A child with a physical disability *is* limited in physical ability and *may* be limited in the kind of activities in which he can participate. His parents, other adults, and his peers *may* treat him differently. He *may* feel he is different and also feel he is less worthy. That is, he does have a disability and he *may* have a handicap.

Some limitations on behavior are not disabilities, but socially imposed handicaps. For example, in our culture a female has for years been disqualified from jobs that are well within her capacities, or, until recently, from sports such as racing in American Motorcycle Association events. Skin pigmentation has been a disqualifier from entry into certain job groups. A handicap might be thought of as an arbitrarily imposed, relative position in a particular society.

A disability stimulates certain expectations for behavior. It is difficult to escape from these stereotypes, particularly for those having the more noticeable disabilities. Such expectations may be used to assign the disabled to certain social roles. To a great extent, the expectations of others will shape the disabled person's self-concept and will determine what he/she can do and how he/she will behave.

Mention also should be made of the relationship between a disability and an emotional handicap. No disability requires a psychological maladjustment. If an emotional handicap exists in a person with a disability, it does not stem directly from the disability, but has been mediated by social variables. A full discussion of this topic is beyond the scope of this text, but an explanation of this process and an example, both drawn from the comprehensive and very interesting work by Meyerson,[2] should be instructive. The mediation between a disability and psychological behavior occurs as follows: (1) a person lacks a tool that is required for behavior in his/her culture, and knows that he/she lacks it, (2) other individuals perceive that he/she lacks an important tool and devaluate him/her for the lack, and (3) the person accepts the judgment of others that he/she is less worthy and devaluates him- or herself. The (1) (2) (3) sequence is a unit. If (1) or (2) do not occur, (3) does not occur. If (3) does not occur, there is no emotional handicap.

Cawley[3] illustrates the process of handicapping as follows: A child is born to parents who are poor.

1. The family, including the child, lack a tool for participation in society—in this case the tool consists of financial resources.
2. The family is devalued by the dominant group—in this case the haves—because he/she lacks the tool.
3. The family recognizes the perceptions directed toward them—frequent headlines relative to welfare, unemployment, and so on, communicate these perceptions—and they are accepted by the nondominant group or individual.
4. The family conveys these to the child—who has them amply reinforced in school (e.g., teacher says, "Here's your free lunch ticket" or "Title I is to help you to read better.")
5. The child devalues him- or herself because he/she lacks the tool— and, he/she is handicapped.

It is clear that there is a process, a series of steps, that can create and perpetuate a handicap. Thus, the handicapped are often those persons who are victimized by other persons. External characteristics such as cerebral palsy, obesity, black-skin, ill-kept or cheap clothing, and so on, and labels such as retarded, disturbed, learning disabled, and the like, convey sets of misinformation, fears, and expectations. These sets are translated into almost inescapable expectations about how "those children" will perform, and the phenomenon of the self-fulfilling prophecy reinforces the precon-

[2] Lee Meyerson, "Somatopsychology of Physical Disability," *Psychology of Exceptional Children and Youth*, 2nd ed., William W. Cruickshank, Ed. (Englewood Cliffs, N.J.: Prentice-Hall, 1963), pp. 1–52.

[3] John F. Cawley, "The Handicapped Child: Who, Why, and What," The University of Connecticut, 1971, 19 pp., mimeographed.

ceived fears. The fact that certain characteristics and/or behaviors are present does not mean that the child's whole set of abilities, values, needs, aspirations, and ability to learn are also so different that he/she does not belong, or that he/she cannot profit from being in a "regular" classroom. The fact that a child's language pattern may be different, as is the case with some inner-city children, does not mean that he/she is innately low in verbal ability or that he/she cannot or does not wish to communicate effectively. The child will not wish to communicate with someone who "puts down" his/her language pattern as inferior, however. Such devaluation behavior on the part of the teacher, the school's grading system, and/or other reward systems will constitute an arbitrarily imposed relative position in the school society—hence the establishment of a handicap.

A student enrolled in an academically oriented high school that sends 80 per cent of its graduates on to college may be "handicapped" by certain teachers and students.

A child with a motor disability that impedes his/her negotiating stairs or that simply slows progress down long corridors can also experience such devaluation. The many exclusions from activities, and the "special treatment" received call attention to the disability and increase the chances that a handicap will develop.

While it is true that special treatments must be effected, it is also true that special treatments can accentuate differences and thereby perpetuate handicaps. Thus, in providing special programs a principal should weigh all possible alternatives to select those that would minimize the likelihood that they would make the child's difference more obvious.

Even given current laws, there are many attitudes and practices that transcend the "letter of the law" and can result in not so subtle hostility or at best benign neglect to those pupils and/or parents who seek proper education for their children.

The following summarizes the discussion thus far:

1. A disability or a handicap must be thought of in relation to a particular society.
2. A handicap is *imposed* upon a human being by other human beings.
3. A disability stimulates expectations of the behavior of the handicapped.
4. There is an identifiable sequence of steps in creating an imposed handicap.

Practicalities for the Principal: An Overview

In the educational ferment of the past decade, perhaps no other identifiable element of public education has experienced changes as far-reaching and significant as educational programming for the handicapped. Perhaps the foremost change has been the articulation and establishment of the right to education for all handicapped children through the public schools. As has been true in much of the history of American public education, the forces and influences producing this and other changes came from outside the educational profession.

Parents, advocacy groups, and handicapped persons themselves have provided the major impetus to the instigation of change. It is true that during the decade professional educators of the handicapped evidenced strength and a voice for the profession through the Council for Exceptional Children and provided informational and other resources, in cooperation with the nonprofessional advocacy groups and were successful in asserting education as a basic right for the handicapped.

Prior to 1970, only a handful of states mandated special education for the handicapped. Some states operated limited programs under permissive legislation and many states had no statutory language of any consequence on this issue. For years parents and advocacy groups had attempted to bring about increased educational services to the handicapped via lobbying in the state legislatures, but this proved a slow, uncertain, and disappointing approach except in those states with well-organized and well-funded lobbying machinery. With the civil rights movement of the sixties, advocates noted the success of other minorities in claiming certain fundamental rights before the federal courts, and so, borrowing upon this model, parents and advocacy groups began litigation in federal courts asserting the violation of basic constitutional guarantees. Most cases were class action suits articulating specific complaints and invoking such constitutional bases as right to due process and freedom from discriminatory treatment in denial of basic rights. By 1976, more than forty cases of this fundamental nature were heard and in no case did the plaintiffs lose. Also in no case did defendants, which were usually local and state boards of education, administrators of public schools and institutions, and sometimes professional practitioners such as school psychologists, appeal the verdict or findings of the courts.

Concurrent with the activity in the federal courts, legislative activity in the Congress began to lay groundwork affirming the inclusion of the handicapped under all civil rights guarantees derived from the Constitution. Section 504 of the Rehabilitation Acts of 1973 addressed the right to education for the handicapped but it was not until 1977 that HEW promulgated the regulations to activate the legislation. However, in 1975, Congress passed "The Right to Education for All Handicapped Children's Act," PL 94-142, which, in effect, became the vehicle to spell out in detail the intent of Congress regarding the earlier Section 504 of the Rehabilitation Acts of 1973, and also included provisions for funding. Again, it was not until August, 1977, that the final regulations regarding PL 94-142 were published, but these two major pieces of legislation represented a "new order" for the organization and administration of educational programs for the handicapped, with the primary responsibility for implementation resting upon the public school systems of the nation.

The major elements of current legislation that have impact upon program organization and operation are:

1. Represents a federal commitment to insure that *ALL* handicapped children are provided with a *FREE* and *APPROPRIATE* education.
2. Incorporates *FULL DUE PROCESS* rights for children and parents into the referral, evaluation, and placement procedures.
3. Requires an *INDIVIDUALIZED EDUCATION PLAN* for every handicapped child.
4. Requires *REGULAR REVIEW* of each handicapped child's plan.
5. Requires consideration of the *LEAST RESTRICTIVE ALTERNATIVE* concept in placement of handicapped children.
6. Requires that *TESTING AND EVALUATION* materials and procedures used for the purposes of evaluation and placement of handicapped children must be selected and administered so as not to be racially and culturally discriminatory.
7. Extends *PROGRAM SCOPE* into what has been traditionally viewed as pre- and postschool age groups.
8. Requires *COOPERATION* between local, state, and federal levels to assure compliance with the law.

Even a casual perusal of these items reveals concepts that, though not new to education in every instance, have never seriously been implemented in practice on a broad scale. While many administrators may view the regulations as excessively detailed, laden with parental prerogatives in educational decision making, and limiting to administrative discretion or educational professional judgment, it seems unlikely that there will be major revisions in these concepts since basic constitutional grounds undergird the entire document. In this regard, it appears that school administrators would be prudent to master the content of the law and to recognize the implications for program planning, organization, and operation, and then to mobilize resources for implementing education for all handicapped children that will reflect effective, quality programming. The authors will cite in general terms several implications of the major elements noted here, but the reader is urged to apply each to the local state practice.

There Is a Federal Commitment to Insure That ALL Handicapped Children Are Provided with a FREE and APPROPRIATE Education

While the basic policy statements and procedures regarding implementation of this mandate will be formulated at the board and central administrative level, the fulfillment of the mandate will occur at the building level.

This means that the principal should be prepared to work cooperatively in the development of delivery systems of special services for handicapped pupils in the building. In the past, when the dominant mode of special education was the full-time self-contained special class, not all buildings housed such pupils, but the inclusion of least restrictive alternative and parental prerogative clauses in the law now eliminate this likelihood. While full-time self-contained classes are not eliminated by the mandate, the clear intent of the law is that as many handicapped pupils as possible be served in regular buildings and in contact with nonhandicapped peers. It appears that the "appropriate" education concept will be most nearly satisfied when it can be demonstrated that a flexible educational delivery system for handicapped pupils is functional within a building. Provision of instructional space for special itinerant or resource personnel, facilitating communication between such personnel and regular classroom teachers, coordinating time schedules for pupils and the various instructional or supportive staff members serving them, or the housing of a full- or part-time class may all be tasks that require the principal's planning, implementation, and monitoring.

Perhaps more fundamentally, the federal mandate to serve all handicapped children eliminates the option of local boards of education and administrators at all levels to arbitrarily exclude handicapped children from school enrollment and access to education. Even when no state statutes or official local policies addressed this question, it was not unusual to find building principals exercising judgment as to a handicapped child's admissability to school based only upon the child's physical appearance and the principal's private interpretation of implications for education. It was precisely such practices that led to the enactment of the federal legislation guaranteeing the right to education for all handicapped children. The principal is now obligated to accept all children being presented for enrollment, and, in the case of visible and more severe handicaps, to communicate immediately to parents the steps that the school and parents cooperatively must follow to assure that an appropriate educational plan will ensue. The principal will then initiate the referral process as a first step to mobilizing the service system.

Furthermore, the lack of financial resources, facilities, staff, or existing program cannot be invoked by the schools as an excuse for not providing an appropriate program, for placing students on waiting lists, or otherwise delaying the evaluation and placement process.

In addition to the above implications, it is required that the public schools show positive efforts to identify and locate all handicapped children within the school district. These efforts have sometimes been organized as specific systemwide programs operating under such designations as "Childfind" or "Operation Search" or terms with similar connotations. The focus of search activities is usually a public information thrust seeking to reach every home in the community, and may include newspaper publicity, radio and TV spot announcements, billboards, posters, and talks before community groups. The principal may be asked to disseminate flyers to the homes of all pupils in the building and to schedule opportunities for speakers before the PTA or PTO.

FULL DUE PROCESS Rights for Children and Parents into the Referral, Evaluation, and Placement Procedures

Perhaps the most challenging regulations pertain to the full due process rights for children and parents as they apply to the referral, evaluation, and placement procedures. Undoubtedly, these regulations, in addition to relevant state and local regulations, will be incorporated into a single set of operational procedures for the local program of special education for the handicapped by the board and central administration. It is also probable that in most school systems a central office administrator will have responsibility for the overall functioning of the special education program, including monitoring to assure compliance with the federal, state, and local regulations. Depending upon the size of the school system, there may even be a cadre of supervisors whose duties include the monitoring of special aspects of the referral, evaluation, and placement procedures. Nevertheless, the actual processing of pupils through the entire set of steps takes place most frequently at the building level and requires that the principal be aware, informed, and ready to participate in any way that will facilitate the processing in a legally correct manner.

The importance of the regulations cannot be overemphasized because they demand rigorous attention to procedures that have often in the past been handled in an informal and loosely structured manner. Because certain rights of parents and children are so clearly defined, the school system becomes very vulnerable to complaint procedures available to parents if they believe any such rights have been violated. While the legally required steps to referral, evaluation, and placement are detailed, time-consuming, and therefore cost producing, it would seem prudent to make a commitment to their implementation as a part of standard operating procedure rather than seek shortcuts that are potential sources of litigation. In this respect, the principal must know the detailed steps of the entire procedure, communicate them to his professional staff, solicit their commitment and cooperation, and monitor those that may be specifically a responsibility of his/her staff or his/her own office.

Principals and regular classroom teachers must both be aware that the due process considerations become effective at the moment a pupil is suspected of educational problems that may require behavioral evaluation beyond the observations that the classroom teacher makes of all pupils assigned to the room. Before any diagnostic staff or instructional specialist personnel may pursue data collection pertinent to determining the nature and significance of the problem, the child's parents must be informed of the suspected problem by written notice and must give informed consent in writing for pre-placement evaluation. The notice must include a full explanation of all the procedural safeguards available to the parents under the federal regulations. The notice must be written in language understandable to the general public, or in the native language used by the parents, unless it is clearly not feasible to do so, in which case it must be translated orally or by other mode of communication. These initiating tasks for pupil referral will usually rest with the principal and his/her staff, although it may be evident from even this cursory look that there may be a need to request assistance for communication in unusual cases, or the need to invite the presence of a consultative diagnostic staff member to assist in the explanation of the assessment procedures, instruments, or tests appropriate for pre-placement evaluation.

Once parental approval has been obtained in writing, responsibility for scheduling the evaluative process usually resides at the central administration level. However, the evaluation itself will probably be carried out in the building and the principal will need to arrange for appropriate space or spaces in which this may be done, and to coordinate time schedules and communicate with the teacher in the event that the pupil assessment is carried out in sessions on different days or by a variety of diagnostic team members.

After the relevant diagnostic data has been assembled, a second conference must be scheduled to include the parent and child, if deemed appropriate, all personnel participating in the evaluation, the child's teacher, and an administrator of special education representing the superintendent's office, and other individuals at the discretion of the parents or the school system. While the principal is not mandated to participate by the language of the act, and in many school systems will not have responsibility for convening the conference, principals may be assigned the role of the administrator acting as the superintendent's designee. In most instances, principals will be invited, will probably have to schedule space, and will in most cases wish to participate inasmuch as the findings of the evaluative process will be shared and an individualized education plan formulated for the child.

Aside from input the principal may wish to offer at the conference, there is a need to be aware of the educational plan developed for the child and a readiness to cooperate in the implementation of the plan. It is important to note that the child's placement in special education or need for special services may not be predetermined by any professional staff member connected with the case, and must take place within the case conference with final written approval by the parent before implementation may occur.

If the parents are in disagreement with the recommendations of the case conference, the findings of the evaluative procedures, or agree to placement and later change their minds, they have the right to request a hearing before an impartial hearing officer if differences of opinion cannot be resolved with the professionals acting for the school.

The specific elements of parental rights are:

1. The right to written and timely notice of the place and time of the hearing.
2. The right to review all information and records the school has compiled on their child.
3. The right to obtain an independent evaluation at the expense of the school.
4. The right to be represented by counsel.
5. The right to bring witnesses.
6. The right to present evidence.
7. The right to cross-examine witnesses.
8. The right to a complete written report of the hearing proceedings and findings.
9. The right to appeal the decision.

There is little doubt that these rights as enumerated represent an unprecedented legal intrusion into educational procedures previously assumed to be matters of policy to be determined by state or local boards of education, or by administrative regulation. The potential impact of these rights upon the principal seem self-evident, and may be significant to the extent to which such procedures are invoked by parents. Generally, the steps leading to the arrangement of a hearing will be responsibilities at the central administration level with counsel from the board's attorney. However, principals can expect to provide assistance in preparing the school's case and should be prepared to testify at the hearing with the recognition of a strong prospect for being cross-examined as a part of such testimony.

The many innuendoes of due process rights have by no means been exhausted in this brief review, but the considerations enumerated are primary ones that relate to the fundamental steps of referral, evaluation, and placement of pupils into programs of special education and services and the rights of parents to participate in decision making in each step. While even these may seem imposing and legally excessive to educators, it would seem prudent to have the entire professional staff totally aware of them and to implement operating procedures taking them into account. Once the school system has made the necessary adaptions in procedure, the likelihood of parents invoking the complaint procedures should be considerably diminished. Over a period of years, the schools have an opportunity to generate a record of credibility with the community in such issues so that most parent concerns can be resolved on the basis of communication, mutual trust, and respect.

FIGURE 11.1. Generic checklist of procedures specified or implied in federal law and regulation.

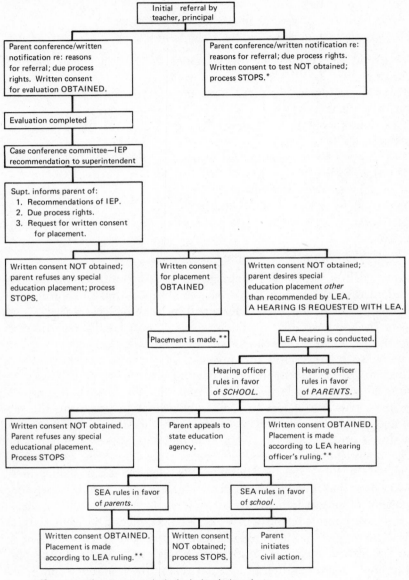

Initial referral by teacher, principal

Parent conference/written notification re: reasons for referral; due process rights. Written consent for evaluation OBTAINED.

Parent conference/written notification re: reasons for referral; due process rights. Written consent to test NOT obtained; process STOPS.*

Evaluation completed

Case conference committee—IEP recommendation to superintendent

Supt. informs parent of:
1. Recommendations of IEP.
2. Due process rights.
3. Request for written consent for placement.

Written consent NOT obtained; parent refuses any special education placement; process STOPS.

Written consent for placement OBTAINED

Written consent NOT obtained; parent desires special education placement *other* than recommended by LEA. A HEARING IS REQUESTED WITH LEA.

Placement is made.**

LEA hearing is conducted.

Hearing officer rules in favor of *SCHOOL.*

Hearing officer rules in favor of *PARENTS.*

Written consent NOT obtained. Parent refuses any special educational placement. Process STOPS

Parent appeals to state education agency.

Written consent OBTAINED. Placement is made according to LEA hearing officer's ruling.**

SEA rules in favor of *parents.*

SEA rules in favor of *school.*

Written consent OBTAINED. Placement is made according to LEA ruling.**

Written consent NOT obtained; process STOPS.

Parent initiates civil action.

*State statutory language may permit school to instigate further action to facilitate proper placement.

**The principal should be aware tht parents may request a change in placement at a later date.

Figure 11.1 provides the reader with a generic checklist of procedures specified or implied in federal law and regulations. The reader must check the details of the state and local variances in such areas as appeal routes, initiating changes in previously agreed-upon placement, and so on.

A great majority of parents will accept the school's evaluation and educational plan for their children. There are a few exceptions in which the parents, though full of good intentions, react irrationally and emotionally to the news that their child may need special help. They can refuse special placement and programming and in some instances seriously affect their child's welfare. At this point the school is faced with a problem. It is our opinion that the principal or other administrators would be under moral obligation to initiate further hearings on behalf of the child. Hopefully, the school would not need to press charges under child-neglect laws or other appropriate laws. It is anticipated that such a situation will, and possibly should, occur if regulations continue to be overloaded in favor of one "side" or the other to the possible negative effect upon the student.

An Individualized Education Plan for Every Handicapped Child

The concept of providing educational opportunities and experiences for individual learners according to the unique abilities and needs of each is not new to education. It has generally been recognized as the educational ideal toward which teachers should strive in organizing for instruction, even though the public schools have traditionally been organized on a mass-production model with the individual being first identified as a member of a group employing age or grade-level designations. Concerns over the needs of the individual versus the realities of group instruction and management have occupied a central position in educational philosophy and practice over many generations, but the language of legislation takes this question out of the realm of speculation and debate for the education of handicapped children. The federal mandate requires an Individualized Education Plan (IEP) for each identified handicapped child before special services or placement may occur. This plan must be formulated in an individual case conference to include the parents and child, if appropriate, to the educational personnel enumerated in the previous section. The conference must generate a written plan that is agreed upon by the participants and attested to by the signature of each. The formal content of the IEP includes the following:

1. A statement of the child's present levels of educational performance;
2. A statement of the annual goals;
3. A statement of the short-term instructional objectives;
4. A statement of the specific special education and related services to be provided to the child;
5. A description of the extent to which the child will be able to participate in regular educational programs;

6. Projected dates for initiation of services and the anticipated duration of the services;
7. Appropriate objective criteria, and evaluation procedures and schedules for determining, on at least an annual basis, whether the short-term objectives are being achieved.

Presumably the case conference to consider the above content must meet as long as necessary to reach agreement, or may be reconvened at another session if time constraints so dictate and the time deadline of forty days between referral and the pre-placement conference is not violated. While the principal may have only indirect responsibilities relating to scheduling the conference, the ultimate content of the IEP generated in the conference may require considerably greater involvement. The extent to which this is true is dependent upon the nature and number of special education personnel and programs housed in the building. If a pupil's IEP calls for full-time special class placement in a room located in the building, the principal's task in implementing such a transfer may be relatively simple. If the child is to continue in the regular class and receive services from itinerant personnel or a resource room teacher, the principal's task in coordinating suitable time schedules for the teachers involved, and assuring that the requirements of the IEP are met, may be more complex. These arrangements may also include the consideration of any specific statements in the IEP regarding least restrictive environment as noted in item five above. Accountability for most other elements of the IEP will reside in the roles of instructional and supportive personnel connected with the special education program.

Regular Review of Each Handicapped Child's Educational Plan. It may be asserted that regular review of educational progress has long been practiced in American schools as manifested in report cards to parents at periodic intervals and administration of system-wide achievement tests at selected grade levels. Nevertheless, the regular review of the handicapped student's plan involves more than the reduction of complex learning and behavior to marks on a report card, or the obtaining of norm-based achievement scores. The review refers specifically to the IEP discussed in the previous section and represents an evaluation of its contents. The word "regular" had been interpreted as "not less than annually," and the review process requires a conference to include the parents, the child if appropriate, all instructional personnel in contact with the child, and any supportive or diagnostic staff deemed necessary to a thorough review. The primary objective data to be compiled in advance of this conference, often called the annual case review conference, will in most instances be quantitative and relate to the criterion measures of goals and objectives stated in the IEP. If the objectives are written in behavioral, and, therefore, measurable terms, the major basis for judging the adequacy and appropriateness of the handicapped pupil's educational plan can be more readily attained. However, this conference must also allow for observations and considerations that may be more subjective in nature, including such items as a look at the child's physical growth, the need for contact with an older social group, or social–emotional maturation that might presage readiness for increased exposure to a regular classroom experience as opposed to continued full-time special class placement. Certainly the principal may wish to offer input on such items or others that relate to least restrictive environment, readiness for assignment to another setting within the school, or advancement to an older age group in another building.

Once a handicapped child has had an IEP that has been implemented through an academic year during which evaluative data has been gathered, the annual case review can serve the dual purpose of the mandated regular review and also the conference during which the next academic year's IEP can be generated. The principal should be aware, too, that even though most IEPs will be based on the academic year and will prove adequate for that time period if well written, the parent or teachers associated with the child have the right and may request a review of the child's progress and program at any time during the year.

Least Restrictive Alternative Concept in Placement of Handicapped Children

The consideration of least restrictive environment in the educational placement of handicapped children represents a marked departure from past practice in the provision of special education for the handicapped. The traditional practice of serving most handicapped children in full-time self-contained classes had undergone considerable challenge and resistance from parents and advocacy groups prior to the passage of PL 94-142, and this influence undoubtedly has shaped legislation so as to include the concept of least restrictive alternative. This concept presumes that the regular classroom, undifferentiated on the basis of the personal characteristics of the pupils assigned, is the most normal school environment and one in which all pupils have a right to participate. Any instruction or service provided to handicapped children outside of this setting requires those steps already discussed under due process, with particular note of the parental approval required. Implementation of this concept necessitates that schools greatly expand the range of delivery systems by which handicapped children can be served.

Figure 11.2 indicates a continuum of theoretically desirable/undesirable combinations of educational services provided to the handicapped.

It is obvious that on any continuum there are many shadings and Figure 11.2 is no exception. The alternatives that may be developed can fall in between many of the above environments and types of personnel, but the intent is that the principal see the potential combinations. The principal and staff need to supply the realities upon which the decisions about the best combination of services for each student are decided.

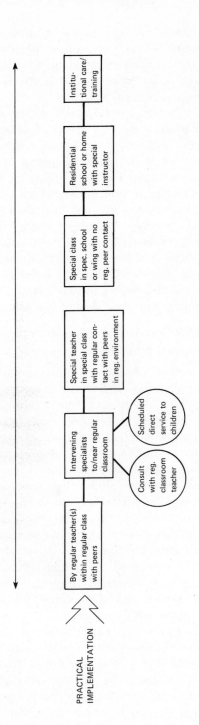

FIGURE 11.2. Theoretical and practical continua for the implementation of educational services illustrating the concept of the least restrictive environment.

THEORETICAL PREMISES

Least restrictive
Optimal setting
Basic right of all children
Can serve mildly handicapped

Some movement from regular class
Flexible alternatives
Use to meet individual needs
Serves most mildly and moderately handicapped

Most restrictive
Self-contained settings
Use only as necessary
Serves severely handicapped

PRACTICAL IMPLEMENTATION

By regular teacher(s) within regular class with peers

Intervening specialists to/near regular classroom

Consult with reg. classroom teacher

Scheduled direct service to children

Special teacher in special class with regular contact with peers in reg. environment

Special class in spec. school or wing with no reg. peer contact

Residential school or home with special instructor

Institutional care/training

216

In effect, it is presumed that the regular classroom and the full-time special classroom represent polar extremes of a continuum, with the regular classroom being the optimal environment for children and the full-time special classroom or special school the least desirable. Remember, that in the case conference to develop the IEP, it is necessary to address the question of the extent to which the child's special needs can be served with minimal movement or time away from the optimal setting. The practice of reintegrating identified handicapped pupils who had earlier been segregated, or maintaining newly identified handicapped children within the regular class setting to the maximum extent, has been popularly referred to as mainstreaming.

As could be anticipated, the attempt to reverse the practice in which the significantly different pupil was identified, referred, and placed from regular education to a parallel and frequently separate system called special education, has sometimes been met with anxiety, frustration, and dismay by many teachers and administrators. Admittedly, not all special educators are convinced that the premises underlying the least restrictive environment concept are educationally, socially, or psychologically defensible, and, from a legal point of view, may have the weakest constitutional basis.

In addition, there is simply no empirical data to show that educational, social, and emotional benefits to the child derived via mainstreaming equal or exceed those derived via the more traditional delivery system. Nevertheless, regardless of professional and academic arguments questioning the merits of this provision, the present requirements of the IEP and due process safeguards will have to be observed in order to be legally correct.

Principals involved in any degree of mainstreaming realize that information to the regular class teachers and a readiness on the principal's part to play a strong supportive role are essential to successful mainstreaming efforts. Informing the staff requires more than a note in the end-of-year bulletin in June to the effect that handicapped pupils are to be integrated or reintegrated in regular classes the following September. Ideally, inservice experiences to cushion the shock of the idea, and time to incorporate the concept of cooperative relationships that may ensue from the presence of a newly defined delivery system and new professional special education staff, would be desirable. Practically speaking, that ideal was not an option for most principals who had to implement much of the mainstreaming concept without any significant lead time because of the short time lapse between the promulgation of the federal regulations and their becoming effective. Nevertheless, it is not too late to pursue an inservice information-giving process if for no other reason than to offer perspective to teachers who may feel very bewildered and slightly resentful because of the "new order" that may have been imposed upon them.

In addition, the clarification of roles and lines of communication between regular, special, supportive, and administrative staff may need continued attention over a long period of time.

The supportive role alluded to earlier may be manifested by the need of the principal to act as a facilitating third party in smoothing the course of staff relationships until, hopefully, both regular classroom and special education or supportive staff have developed trust and mutual professional respect. In this instance, as in so many other educational situations, the need to practice and reinforce positive human relationships and continued communication efforts cannot be overemphasized. Pragmatically, these considerations must also extend to the parents and to the children whose welfare must be the primary common interest of all the adults involved.

Certain responses can be rationally anticipated. Parents of moderately, severely, profoundly, and multiply handicapped children will generally be aware of the nature of their child's needs before the age of school admission, and are often fairly realistic regarding educational options, goals, and aspirations. Most of these parents will understand that physical management, fire and other safety considerations, limited communication skills of the child, the level at which learning experiences must be structured, and numerous other individual needs may render the concept of least restrictive alternative of only academic interest. For all aspects of the child's growth, development, and sometimes simple survival, a self-contained setting may be necessary and acceptable from both the school's and parent's point of view.

On the other hand, children who are mildly handicapped in such areas as limited general intellect, learning disabilities, emotional disturbance, undiagnosed sensory defects, or special health problems are often unrecognized until the nature of the problem is manifested by lack of progress in school. In these cases the school becomes the "bearer of bad tidings" to the parents and, therefore, the object of maladaptive psychological responses from some parents who may then demand unreasonable, or even nonexistent, educational solutions to their child's need. Some of these demands may include the insistence that all of the identified needs be resolved within the regular classroom or with only the most minimal removal from it. Here, again, the human relations and communications skills of the principal and the entire case conference team may be put to the test in attempting to resolve an IEP that will give maximum priority to the child's needs and lesser concern to the psychological needs of the parents. Indeed, the above generalizations should be treated with caution, but may provide some general perspective for the principal's operational frame of reference.

Testing and Evaluation Materials and Procedures Used for the Purposes of Evaluation and Placement of Handicapped Children Must be Selected and Administered so as Not to be Racially and Culturally Discriminatory

This policy and the local response to it will probably be developed at the school board level and monitored through an office of the central administration. The principal must be aware of the federal requirements and associated policies and procedures and should communicate these to the building faculty before possible violations occur.

Since most group and individual tests in the field today are subject to criticism on the basis of having racially and culturally discriminatory items, it would seem wise to allow only the use of assessment approaches stated in broad policy or those permitted to professional diagnostic staff. The general rule governing evaluation of children for handicapped services permits the use of testing or evaluative tools without parental approval as long as such assessment is made of all pupils in a classroom, or at designated age or grade levels by official board policy. The use of any diagnostic approaches or instruments utilized only with selected students, and not covered by the above general policy, requires parental consent in the framework of the due process guarantees discussed earlier. So, while the content and implementation of a testing program may rest outside of the principal's direct responsibility, the need to be informed and to monitor the activity of the building staff in this area will be a tangential responsibility of that office.

Program Scope Extended into What Has Been Traditionally Viewed as Pre- and Post-school Age Groups

It is required that a free appropriate public education be available for all handicapped children aged three through twenty-one.

An exception in these requirements is possible for those aged three, four, five, eighteen, nineteen, twenty, or twenty-one years in those states having legislation, practice, or court order addressing education for the handicapped and the age groups to be served. No exceptions are made in the federal law for pupils aged six through eighteen. Additional interpretation also asserts that local and state past practice becomes a criterion for determining age eligibility for special educational services.

For example, a local school system that has practiced a policy of operating kindergartens for five-year-olds or nursery, headstart, and similar programs for younger children is obligated to serve handicapped children in those age groups even though the state statutes do not include these children in the laws pertaining to education for the handicapped. The principal, then, must be aware of the content of the federal and state laws on this issue, and of the implications of past practice beyond what state laws may address regarding age groups to be served. Thus, the principal with a kindergarten program for five-year-olds should expect to cooperatively participate in program planning for handicapped five-year-olds in his/her building or by some alternate arrangement even though in the past these children may have been arbitrarily, or by board policy or state law, excluded from such participation. Most of the earlier discussion on the right to a free and appropriate public education is germane to this topic also.

Cooperation Between Local, State, and Federal Levels
Assures Compliance with the Law

The burden of proof regarding compliance with mandates rests with the local education agency, and a commitment to rigorous documentation is fundamental to such proof. It is required to have a legally correct set of records to which one may refer in case of parental questions or disgruntlement that may lead to a hearing or litigation. Further, it is necessary to have a detailed record of professional activity that may be important in the long-range planning, management, and evaluation of the educational program for handicapped pupils.

Administrators may anticipate that monitoring for compliance will undoubtedly move in the direction of program audit by on-site visitation, either by state or federal audit teams, or possibly in combination. The likely pattern to emerge will be program audit by the state on a one-, two-, or three-year rotating schedule for all LEAs in a state, with the prospect of unannounced follow-up spot check audits by federal teams on an irregular basis. One may expect that program audits will be fairly rigorous.

Implications of the above discussion will probably vary for principals from one building to the next, depending upon the extent to which numbers of students may be involved in special education and the nature of the special education services delivered in the building. Certainly all principals will need to stock certain standard forms such as referral forms for parents or classroom teachers, and should maintain a file of written communications to the parents and, though it may seem excessively cautious, a log of phone conversations initiated either by the principal or parent and pertinent to a child referred or receiving special education services. In addition, principals should make certain that their responsibilities in the total process of referral, evaluation, placement, and review of individual handicapped pupils are well defined and that a complete file of documentation through these steps is maintained for each pupil served in the building. Only in this manner can principals be prepared to assume appropriate accountability that may relate to individual pupil progress, program audit, or parent-initiated complaint procedures leading to hearings or litigation.

Summary Observations

The features addressed in this chapter are not to be viewed as comprehensive nor is the commentary to be viewed as legal opinion. The attempt has been to present key elements of federal legislation that represent a mandate to the states and localities, together with consideration of the impact this may have at the building level for the principal's administrative tasks. There will undoubtedly be continuing interpretation regarding some of the language and differences of opinion in those interpretations as viewed by various constituencies affected by the law. Because legislation regarding education for the handicapped is intended to redress discriminatory practices of the past and safeguard opportunities for the education of handicapped children, it often appears to invite complaints on the part of parents by detailing the procedures that are required of the schools. Parents individually or in organized groups can be expected to watchdog the local programs and are especially likely to direct questions and expressions of dissatisfaction to the principal of a building in which a child is being served. For these reasons, the principal is in a key position to mediate some of the initial concerns of parents and defuse many problems that may become time-consuming and potentially costly if the hearing process or litigation is pursued.

It can be anticipated that some parents will make unreasonable demands upon the school and expect unrealistic services for their children through participation in the IEP case conferencing and case review procedures. In view of all these irksome potentialities, principals can easily fall into an attitude of defensiveness, and, either subtly or overtly, convey to parents the feeling of resistance or an adversarial stance. Despite the experience of certain stresses and frustrations in attempting to work through the initial problems in delivering services to handicapped children, and in meeting the many requirements, it would seem the path of administrative wisdom to demonstrate a genuine openness in parental communication and maximum efforts to promote teamwork with parents.

It will be obvious to principals that practically everything about the federal act has implications for the utilization of time, and ultimately personnel, whether professional, paraprofessional, or clerical. The principal will be challenged to prioritize time use to supervise or monitor new activities within the building as well as the direct participation in case conferencing, telephone communications, or other responsibilities that may emerge as programs develop. Principals must also provide for the participation of both special and regular classroom teachers in IEP conferencing and case reviews. These required activities may take hours and days for significant periods of time, depending on numbers of children served in the building.

The necessity for documentation noted in earlier discussion also has implications for the use of professional staff time and administrators cannot expect to impose these added tasks upon existing role definitions that include a full instructional day, without the risk of creating serious morale problems or possibly violating working conditions agreed upon in bargained contracts with the instructional staff. Principals must be alert to such developing needs and be ready to communicate them to the central administration with requests for the human and materials resources required if a quality program is to ensue.

Again, the principal is found in a pivotal role in the process of personal and professional growth that has challenged all educators to maximum adaptability throughout a continuing era of rapid social change.

Other Exceptionalities

Thus far we have been focusing upon providing for those who find difficulty in functioning "up to" the normal range of physical or intellectual performance. It may be that our society, particularly the educational sector, may be suffering from this concept of normality to the point that we do not expect a great variation among us. Certainly the provisions for children who can perform exceptionally well are not commonplace. Notable exceptions seem to be made for athletes, but getting to ride in the school station wagon to the state contest seems to be sufficient for the truly gifted pianist or vocal soloist. Seldom does the school seek the well-known ceramics artist in the community, or the interior designer or other talented persons to provide time for a truly gifted pupil to observe, or ask questions or work with that person as part of the educational experience. Such activity seems to be much more acceptable for "work-study" office jobs, or those associated with the industrial arts.

It seems impossible to say that an adequate educational program has been provided for exceptional students if the prevailing attitude is, "We can't provide for everyone; besides, those kids will make it, anyway." Those exceptionally talented young people are many of the ones who can enrich our own lives and those who live long after us if we do not almost force them to conform to the mean. Certainly we have been remiss if we do not provide instructional experiences and flexible structures that will enhance the quality of school life for the exceptionally gifted. It is hoped the schools will take the initiative to provide for these exceptional children so that another constraints-oriented federal system of educational procedures does not have to be legislated. In October of 1978 beginning legislation was passed that recognized the need to develop this critical human resource, the gifted and talented youth of our country.

Analysis of the Instructional Program

Unfortunately, many opportunities exist to reinforce the idea that human variance is a negative thing, even variance toward genius. Although most persons involved in the instructional program will give strong verbal support to the idea that differences must be provided for, facilities, materials, and practices may be implying something else. Because of this dichotomy between verbal assent and actual practice, the principal might find the following assumptions and questions helpful in looking at the instructional program, and in further developing his/her own sets of assumptions and questions:

Some Assumptions:

1. Because of the wide variances in human beings, an instructional program of truly individualized instruction would best provide for the exceptional child.
2. To deal effectively with a wide range of differences, the regular teacher will need to extend his or her conversance with instructional competencies needed for meeting a wide range of human variance.
3. Close liaison between special and regular classroom teachers is not only desirable, but essential.
4. Individualization is not possible without definitive knowledge of where each child is in terms of the competency in question, and a continuing assessment of each child's progress.

Some Questions

1. Are the materials available to the teachers distributed in quantities that assume all the children in a given bloc (a classroom) to be at the same level of competency? What additional resources are readily available on a practical basis to each teacher?
2. Does the way the children spend their time on designated activities encourage compartmentalization of "subjects"? Do all the children in a bloc have "X" number of minutes for reading, "Y" minutes for arithmetic? Does this assume that all children get the same amount of learning by spending the same amount of time on a given topic?
3. What diagnostic techniques are used by the teacher for individual students? What instructional provisions are made as a result of the use of these techniques?
4. What opportunities are afforded children to interact with other than their own class or age group?
5. What opportunities are afforded students to interact with adults in roles not connected with the schools?
6. What specific objectives do the teachers have for individuals in their classes? What measures do the teachers use to determine if the objectives have been met?
7. Are handicapped children "excused" from performance objectives?
8. What provisions are made for exceptionally talented students to extend themselves, or are they limited to doing more of the same until others catch up?
9. What is the nature of the referrals of teachers to get special help for children?

10. What specific provisions are now being made for the handicapped? Do such provisions tend to identify a group and tend to fix that group identification in the perceptions of teachers, students, and community?
11. What instructional strategies are employed in support of the fact that children learn as well or better from other children as they do from adults?

Developing Cooperative Resource Bases

As the allocator of resources in a given school, the principal has at least two tasks in providing for exceptional students: (1) He/she should be continuously assessing the use of resources, and (2) he/she must develop new resources.

In the first instance, the principal must keep in mind not only physical inventories of materials and supplies, but human resources of skills and time. Often the students' time is overlooked as a valuable resource. It would be appropriate, particularly in considering exceptionalities to assess the utilization of students' time. This might be done most effectively as a cooperative study between the teacher, the principal, and observers knowledgeable about the behavior of exceptional children.

The principal is faced with the problem of maximizing "*task*" and "*people*" dimensions while at the same time integrating the two for both sides of the artificial dichotomy of special education and regular education. This is somewhat like the problem of putting together those four blocks of red, blue, green, and white sides so that they all appear to be alike. When all seems right on one or two sides, they are completely out of line on another. A promising tack for the principal is to increase the interaction of the more people-child-oriented teachers with their counterparts in special education concerning a current instructional problem identified by the teachers that deals with providing worthwhile learning experiences for exceptional children.

Not only should the principal be very familiar with existing and probable legislation dealing with exceptional children, he/she should have a face-to-face working relationship with local, and as much as possible with regional, and university special resource persons. Such a relationship should provide the school with direct service to children, inservice education for teachers, resources for materials, assistance in planning, and continuous up-dating about many aspects of providing for exceptional children. He/she should also encourage trying different staffing patterns that have been found effective in similar situations such as teaming with one member of the team being special-education trained; utilization of a resource teacher; inservice–preservice education teams, and so on.

A Staff Development Program Leading to Alternatives for Children

The specter of inservice-programs-past wafts through the corridors, leaving the stench of old tobacco and stale coffee as the most lasting impact of some efforts at staff development. Even with this gloomy given, the principal still has the responsibility to improve the instructional program to provide for all children, and to do this, must be involved in staff development. Focusing upon providing for the handicapped, such staff development might occur in a staff study of handicapping conditions and an examination of practices that develop and reinforce imposed handicaps.

The whole-staff approach is productive in some instances, but often greater impact can be realized by working closely with individuals and small groups of teachers to solve their instructional problems in providing for exceptional children, thus meeting both task and person needs. A vital key to such an individualized approach is the principal's knowing the instructional needs and being able to bring resources to bear upon the needs.

The natural outgrowth of an effective staff development program is the increased "copeability" of the teachers to recognize and to provide for wide ranges of differences among the children they work with.

Providing for Each Student

If provision is made for each student, the result is education for all and the labels "special education" or "education of the exceptional child" are redundant. Until such time as we societally do not include or exclude on the basis of variance from the norm, the principal needs to be sensitive about the curricular and instructional provisions for all; developing resource bases; and continuing staff development. Time spent on providing for each student is the center of the principal's major task. It would seem appropriate that an individualized educational plan should be prepared for each child, not just those fitting under some legal provision or for whom extra funding might be obtained.

The principal can exert much influence upon the educational attitude of a school toward eliminating school-imposed handicaps by exposing them for what they really are. It is the authors' belief that it is imperative that he or she make every effort to do so.

For Further Thought

1. Why is the principal a key person in influencing the educational attitude of a school toward providing for the exceptional student?

2. Is it conceivable that a family name can serve as a handicap to a child? How can such an occurence be minimized?
3. A group of parents of "normal" children are aroused about the large expenditures of funds for a very few children draining away dollars from their children. Outline your response to this group.
4. How can the expectations of others shape a disabled person's self-concept both negatively and positively and help shape what the person can do?
5. Debate the resolution that it takes unequal spending to provide equal opportunity.
6. Does mainstreaming restrict the alternatives for the exceptionally able student?
7. Should every child be entitled to a personalized educational plan?

Chapter 12   A Framework for Evaluation

Evaluation: The very term itself causes a variety of responses ranging from fear through avoidance through partial acceptance on to eager utilization in the decision-making process. Closely associated with evaluation and decision making is the term "accountability." Although accountability and evaluation are not the same, they are practically inseparable. The principal of a school is at the center of each process. In this position, the principal may again be found in between expectations of the school board, central administration, organized groups, and/or allegedly aggrieved individuals. Yet, evaluation is essential to the continuous improvement of the quality of life of each individual within the school, including both pupils and teachers. It is the purpose of this and the following chapter to give the principal a frame of reference about the evaluation process and some insights regarding initiating and implementing the process. It is not within the scope of these chapters to make the reader an expert evaluator; however, the reader will find several references that will be of help in developing evaluation concepts and skills.

The two chapters are organized as follows: Chapter 12—A Framework for Evaluation is subdivided into General Guidelines, What Is to Be Evaluated, What Means Are Available, and Considerations for Presenting Evaluation Results. Chapter 13—Evaluation of Individual Performance treats The Evaluation of Teaching and Evaluation of Student Progress.

It will be helpful to the reader to select a specific educational program with which he/she is familiar and to use this as the context for the first of the two chapters. This may be some "regular" program or a special innovative project; however, the reader should be thoroughly familiar with the total program and its operational parts.

The purpose of evaluation in education is to help the educational process better relate to the client's needs. Evaluation does not stop at the point of inspecting to see if something occurred or did not occur. Evaluation is a continuous process focused upon improving the effectiveness of reaching the school's goals and objectives. This view links the evaluation process with decision making, for improvement cannot result from evaluation unless changes are implemented. These changes may be the development and utilization of selected instructional skills or the reordering of priorities, of purposes, and/or resources, or dropping or adopting alternative means to accomplish specific objectives. It is at this point the school fulfills the concept of accountability in that it goes beyond a description of what is and develops supplemental or corrective actions.

The evaluation process may well be viewed as showing concern for students, faculty, and even the community itself. It need not be a fearsome, oppressive checking to see if goals have been efficiently met and, if not, the setting of the stage for an inquisition. Rather, the evaluation process should be thought of as the clarification of purpose, generation of data, and analysis thereof in meaningful information to determine next steps toward improving current practice.

While the process must really yield the foregoing information, evaluation implies that judgments will be made. Ordinarily, these judgments are best made by those who must implement corrective or supplemental action decisions. Seldom is any evaluation effective as a unilateral, solo effort.

The judgments made usually will be focused upon the teaching/learning process and the supporting environment of that process. The valuing or judging process is represented in Figure 12.1.

It is clear that one type of comparison may not be sufficient to make judgments about a specific program. To provide resources confidently to a

FIGURE 12.1.   A representation of the judging/value process.

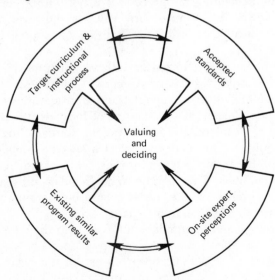

FIGURE 12.2. Steps in utilizing evaluation for making decisions.

program that appears to be "better" than any similar program in surrounding schools may be extremely naive, and, in fact, irresponsible if based on one comparison. On the other hand, to discontinue a program because it does not meet some standards of excellence, e.g., upper quartile on some national norms, may be equally naive and irresponsible. The evaluation process will yield data and information that are useful to those making decisions about the programs evaluated. Decisions, then, may be viewed as a product of evaluation. Figure 12.2 is a representation of the steps toward making decisions based upon the information resulting from evaluation.[1]

General Guidelines

The evaluator will wish to keep the following in mind as he/she reviews past evaluations and plans the evaluation processes that relate to the programs being evaluated and to the audiences interested in the evaluation:

1. Those persons involved in the educational activity being evaluated should be involved as meaningfully as feasible in the design of the evaluation.
2. In designing an evaluation program, one should include a listing of possible outcomes that could result from the evaluation.
3. *One single piece of data or information will seldom provide a sufficient base for evaluation, nor will data from a single source ordinarily be sufficient.*
4. *Programs, processes of data generation, treatments, and type of data or instruments are not always rigidly good or bad. There are continua of relative degrees of appropriateness in nearly all cases.*
5. *Ordinarily there is no one single audience for the results of the evaluation.*
6. Possible/probable influences external to the evaluated educational activity should be examined.

Information Considerations

Evaluation is based upon information. It is important to consider what is meant by the term "information" as opposed to the term "data." A bit

[1] For an expanded discussion of decision making in the evaluation process, see Daniel L. Stufflebeam, et al., *Educational Evaluation and Decision Making* (Bloomington: Phi Delta Kappa, Inc., 1971).

of information is usually derived from data of some sort. Information clearly describes and/or differentiates among things according to a set of values. Data merely reflect the status of a variable or set of variables within a situation. For example, the fact that absenteeism rises sharply at an almost predictable rate from April 1 to the end of the school year in three or four schools in a particular section of a city is not really information. Nor is the fact particularly revealing that 20 per cent of the schools' enrollments are children in families that work in certain agricultural regions during crop-planting and harvesting times. Another fact about attendance in these schools is that there is a relatively low rate of student attrition, that is, when a student enrolls in one of these schools, he usually "graduates" from the eighth grade. A search to find if these data are related is obviously necessary. Many other data will need to be collected before the picture is clear. Once this is done, the investigator can form a piece of information that will be helpful in making some decisions.

There are very few situations that can be evaluated, using one piece of information, particularly in education where the human variables are almost limitless, not to mention the social, political, and economic factors. Any program results from a plurality of reasons and the same program will have a plurality of outcomes. Therefore, a single piece of information will fall far short of really evaluating a program.

By the same token, to look at just one outcome may bias the results to the point of making decisions about the program with a piece of information that points the opposite direction from the direction of all the other pieces of information. For example, let us look at a device employed by a teacher to teach some middle-grade students the multiplication tables. Several audiotapes were made with multiplication table drills and answers on them. Each morning the first ten minutes of class were spent with the tape recorder, the drill tapes, and class responses to the tapes. If one piece of information were used to evaluate the program, decisions might be made to expand it to other areas, publicize it to other teachers, or at least continue it with future classes. If the only question asked was, "Did the students learn their multiplication tables?" the one piece of information would yield an unqualified, "Yes." However, there were other data of interest. The number of times the tape recorder was used for other purposes decreased. Tardiness for that particular room increased alarmingly.

The evaluator then is faced with another reality. All the data about a program or project cannot be collected and analyzed. The evaluator should see that a hierarchy of the importance of certain outcomes is established. The principal should be involved in this process with the teachers as they evaluate their efforts and with "outside" evaluators as they work in the school. If a decision is to be made regarding the tape recorder technique for drill in the multiplication tables, the ordering of one set of outcomes in relation to another set is necessary.

Use of "Outside" Evaluators

If "outside" evaluators are to be used, it is important that their role be defined and clearly understood before the evaluation process begins. Such clarification is important to offset misunderstandings on the part of faculty, administration, pupils, the community or other potential users of the evaluation. There appear to be two "camps" of evaluators when it comes to viewing their roles. One group wishes to gather data, analyze it, and present it to the consumers in as value-free a way as possible. Another group wishes to take valuing responsibility and write up the results as being "good" or "bad" and often going on to recommending action. Occasionally, not having clear understandings about the roles to be played by all on the stage can result in not only losing the impact of the plot, but could seriously injure the directors and producers.

Another area of needed clarity is the responsibility factor. To whom is the outside evaluator responsible—those persons implementing the educational activity being evaluated or to decision makers outside the activity? Who owns the data and information generated?

The caution here is not that outside evaluators are suspect and something to be avoided. The caution is that carefully developed prior agreements should be made and that these agreements be made known to those involved in the evaluation.

Sources of Data

To seek data from one source can create a distorted picture even though several kinds of data are collected. Few programs or projects affect only one group. An experimental program in the teaching of journalism in the high school may appear to be excellent if information is sought from only the students, or from only the teachers. There may be many other groups that should provide information input to the evaluation. There may be administrative problems with scheduling teachers' time or pupil time, or facilities. If a field-based program, there may be serious accountability, safety, or even insurance problems.

A shift in pupil–teacher load may be necessary. Per pupil expenditures may be much more. Parents may have concerns. The local press may react. In short, the principal should identify key groups affected and concerned.

Selection of the Most Appropriate Data

There are very few instances in which educational situations or selected facets of those situations are either all good or all bad, completely unquestionable, or completely unacceptable. The evaluation process inherently has many possibilities of relative goodness or badness, appropriateness or inappropriateness. The important consideration for the principal is that the relativity of these evaluation techniques or treatments applies to programs, data, and instruments used.

Almost every program or project has both positive and negative features. The evaluator should be concerned with finding information regarding both good and bad features.

On occasion, controversy rages regarding the usefulness of subjective data versus objective data. Some people would have nothing to do with subjective data. They regard such data as being totally bad. On the other hand, there are others who view objective data as being too narrow, rigid, and incomplete in scope to be very useful in making decisions about subjective human beings. The fact is that both types of evidence can be important. The use of both types can often give a more complete picture of the situation being evaluated than can one exclusive of the other. To return to our multiplication tables example, the teacher may have been wise in also gathering subjective data about the feelings of individuals about the taped exercises each morning. The more subjective the data, the more evidence or data should be gathered. As with any other data, when planning to gather subjective data, the evaluator should have planned how he/she is going to analyze and store the data prior to gathering it.

What Is to Be Evaluated?

Ideally, the goals and objectives of the program project to be evaluated are clearly specified at the beginning of the program. Such a situation eases the task of the evaluator. In the likely event that specific objectives are not stated, the evaluator must assist those responsible for the activity to clarify and to state goals and objectives in definitive terms. The principal's role in this regard is crucial. He/she should be continuously aiding faculty and staff to develop clear objectives. Timing may force the evaluation of an existing program before the staff has had time to review or to rewrite their program objectives. Already the evaluation process has a finding and a recommendation, namely, objectives need to be developed. The evaluation really cannot proceed much further without them.

How can the evaluator aid in identifying program objectives? An analysis of all program documents and appropriate materials is a beginning point. The evaluator should be alert to the consistency or inconsistency among materials used in the program or between the materials and stated program objectives. For example, it is not uncommon to find faculties stating their goal as being the individualization of instruction so that pupils can learn according to their needs and interests, and at their own rates. The program and materials may be designed to individualize only the learners' rate.

The evaluator can also ask the faculty to identify the program objectives and its key features. It may be helpful to have the faculty prioritize the objectives so that the evaluation can focus upon the most important and thereby be manageable and practical.

The evaluator will wish to look at more than student outcome objectives if he/she is working in an ordinary situation where there are many audiences. Student outcome objectives alone can be misleading and may not provide the kind of decision-information needed at some other level. The principal is cautioned not to use techniques focusing upon selected microcomponents of the school to determine the effectiveness of the total program.

Stating Goals and Objectives

Much heat has been generated regarding the stating of objectives. Semantic difficulties provide most of the fuel for the heat, and these difficulties seem to hover about the words "behaviorally stated," "performance criteria," and similar phrases describing objectives. Is there a differentiation between goals and objectives? Again much heat can be generated. Generally, goals are defined as long-range, broad aims of an institution or program. Objectives are more short-range aims with specific time frames, ordinarily related to the broadly stated goals in that they specify steps toward achieving the goals.

One can become hopelessly bogged down in the "objectives" quagmire. Arguments are offered that highly specific behaviorally stated objectives tend to focus on trivia to the point that important educational outcomes are ignored. Others have the behaviorist-phobia response (which in itself seems to be quite Skinnerian) that performance objectives seem to degrade all their instructional intentions into narrow, Pavlovian terms. Yet, defensible objectives are important guides for programs and people as well as for evaluators. Popham has provided an excellent discussion of the use of instructional objectives in the evaluation process.[2] He points out the possibility that over-precise goals may be too insignificant to pursue and thus impractical from several points of view. But he provides the reader with some attributes of useful objectives such as:

—Objectives should effectively clarify the instructional intention.
—Objectives should have content generally, that is, describe a generalizable class of learner behaviors.
—Objectives should have criteria for adequately judging students' constructed responses ("constructed" as opposed to "selected" from among choices).

[2] W. James Popham, *Educational Evaluation*, Englewood Cliffs, New Jersey: Prentice-Hall, Inc., 1975, pp. 45–74.

—Objectives should have the important conditions associated with the objectives incorporated in the objectives.
—Objectives ideally should have well-defined performance standards.

There are key words one can look for in objectives. For example, examine the following objectives:

To teach history so that the students will *appreciate* its impact upon today's society.
To teach poetry so that the students will learn to *like* it.
To develop *understanding* of the basic principles of geometry.
To conduct class so that the pupils *behave better* in class.

It becomes quickly obvious that if the evaluator is to determine whether the program has succeeded, he/she must develop some way to measure the students' appreciation, liking, understanding, or behaving. An effective way to check an objective when reading or writing it is to ask the question, "What *evidence* is there to substantiate the reaching of this objective?" If there is no clearly indicated evidence in the objective, it should be re-written, or additional subobjectives should be written. For example, the last of the illustrated objectives could be rewritten to read, "To organize work so that the pupils are out of their seats fewer times per day than they are now," or "To provide learning opportunities in which they are interested so that there are fewer interpersonal clashes between pupils per day than there are now." In some situations, these may be either very appropriate objectives, although in others these could lead to rigid, stultify-ing classroom conditions. Again, the evaluator should be careful not to base evaluation on one piece of information.

Carefully prepared objectives for any enterprise are important for those engaged in the activity as well as for someone trying to determine if the activity is achieving its intent. But as with the usual household funds, even though the objectives are all praiseworthy, there comes a time when priorities enter in. Thus, it is not only the principal's role to help develop clear objectives, but to also assist faculty and staff to prioritize objectives. Just as the time, energy, even the emotion expended by faculty preparing specific objectives are cost items the principal must take into account, so is the cost of prioritizing objectives. The forest can easily be lost because of all the trees obstructing one's vision.

What Means Are Available?

It is not within the scope of this chapter to detail the instrumentation process, but rather it is the aim of the discussion to provide the principal with some general considerations, definitions, and references regarding the instruments that are used in evaluation.

General Considerations

When selecting or developing an instrument, the evaluator should consider the validity, reliability, comparability, and practicality of the instrument. These are defined as follows:

Validity—The instrument measures what it is intended to measure.
Reliability—The instrument is consistently valid.
Comparability—The instrument is valid and reliable when administered to different groups, that is, it measures the same thing for both groups.
Practicality—The investment of time, money, and expertise should be such that the returns to the school decision-making process are worth the expenditures.

Prepackaged or Homemade Instruments?

Obviously the answer to such a question is, "It depends." It depends upon the need for generalizability versus specificity; upon the availability of the prepackaged instruments; upon their applicability to the local situation; upon costs; upon the expertise of available persons to develop instruments; and upon a host of other factors. If there is a need for supporting evidence to be compared to some sort of norms, decisions must be made regarding (1) what set of norms, (2) availability of norms, and (3) practicality of generating local norms.

"A major defect with using norm-referenced measures for purposes of educational evaluation is that there is often a substantial lack of congruence between what the test measures and what is stressed in a local curriculum." [3] It may be that a combination of prepackaged and "homemade" instruments would be most appropriate.

The evaluator must determine if there is a match between what the test measures and what the curriculum is to teach. Popham continues by pointing out the fact that if a large percentage of respondents to an item answered correctly, the test publisher would discard the item because it did not produce a reasonable degree of response variance. Thus, the typical norm-referenced instrument is "relatively insensitive to instruction." [4]

So You Wish to Design a Questionnaire?

There are several steps regarding the construction of a questionnaire that the principal and/or evaluator must consider. The first step, frequently passed over lightly, is carefully and very specifically defining what is to be measured, and how the resulting information will be used in making decisions regarding the educational program. If either or both of these

[3] Popham, op. cit., p. 107.
[4] Ibid., pp. 108–109.

continue to be rather hazy, it might be best not to develop an instrument until the haze is dissipated.

A second concern is deciding how you wish the respondents to indicate their answers. Should they respond on a scale from one to five, answer "yes" or "no," or check one column out of several specifically named columns? Should the items be open-ended for essaylike responses?

After the questionnaire is written, it should be field tested prior to general distribution. Obviously, the group selected for the field trial should be as nearly representative of the total group of respondents as possible. There should be provision for documented feedback as the respondents attempt to complete the questionnaire. This may be done in the margins or by encouraging the respondents to "think out loud" as they encounter each item.

Examination of the results should give insights into construction, semantic, or ambiguity problems. If certain items are responded to exactly the same by everyone, the evaluator might question the need for the item in that it does not seem to differentiate between respondents. The respondents should be given the opportunity to suggest missing parts.

Carefully planning and executing the steps of (1) defining what should be measured, (2) scaling, (3) item-writing, and (4) field-testing are important. The final revision should then provide information with which the decision maker will feel more comfortable.

Analysis of Data

Deciding the method of analyzing the data is not a last step. It is concurrent with deciding exactly what is to be measured and with the selection or development of instruments to gather the data. It is not to be left to the last so that the evaluator is faced with the problem of having data but wondering what to do with it.

In assessing achievement, growth or other kinds of change, the evaluator is faced with the following set of questions, among others:

1. Do I wish to compare one group to itself over a period of time?
2. Do I wish to compare one group to another group?
3. How are those groups alike or different?
4. Do I wish to describe merely the present status of a group?
5. What external factors other than program or instructional activities may be affecting the data, e.g., a rapid population shift or an emotionally ladened controversial issue in the community, and so on?

If two or more groups are to be compared, it is obvious that the groups should be alike as possible at the beginning of the program. Obviously, matching each possible variable is impossible. Various techniques are available to the evaluator to solve this problem partially and to determine how alike the groups really are. The reader is encouraged to study references such as are cited for this chapter in the selected readings.

The authors do not believe in the inherent goodness or badness of "hard" evaluations versus "soft" evaluations. Often truly objective data generated in an experimental design and analyzed via inferential statistics (hard evaluation) is either impractical or impossible given the real world of the school. Yet, we should not be satisfied with evaluations always being near the other extreme of nonexperimental, subjective, or "soft" evaluations. Figure 12.3 provides the reader with a matrix showing the range of design-data-analysis mixes the evaluator can use.[5]

Comparing "Gains"

Cautions are raised in comparing units of change, or "gain scores." An example might be given in the gain scores of the times of two groups of ninth-grade students running the mile. Let us assume that the criterion for effectiveness is how much improvement in time has been made. The data are to be gathered by measuring the times for each group at the beginning of the semester and at the end of the semester. The gains in time will then be determined and the two groups compared. For sake of the example let us assume one group ran an eight-minute mile at the beginning of the semester and a six-minute mile at the end of the semester. The other group's times were six minutes and four and one-half minutes. It is obvious that the first group had the greater gain, that is, two minutes as compared with one and one-half minute. As is obvious to any jogger, it can be reasonably argued that the second group had the greater gain, even though the "gain score" might not be as large. It is much more difficult

FIGURE 12.3. Components involved in hard and soft evaluations.

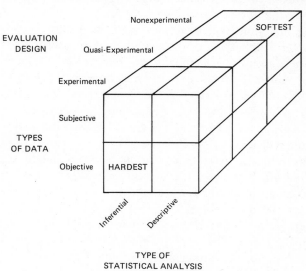

[5] Scarvia B. Anderson, *Encyclopedia of Educational Evaluation* (San Francisco: Jossey-Bass Inc., Publishers, 1975), p. 193.

and requires more training and conditioning to match the second group's "gain" than to match the first group's gain. Which group deserves the higher grades—if that is a consideration? Or which coach the merit increase?

Of course, another set of questions might be raised. Of what value is increased speed? What overall effect might the increased speed have upon general physical fitness, or the lack of gain upon self-image?

The above appears to be more straightforward than it is. Gain scores are generally derived from measures less than 100 per cent reliable; hence, the gain score is even more unreliable. "Borich cites the example '. . . if the correlation between pre- and posttest is .70 and the reliability of each is .80 (coefficients that in practice are fairly common), then the reliability of the gain score would be .33.' " [6]

The phenomenon of regression to the mean, the subject of our following discussion, also affects the reliance the evaluator can place on using gain scores.

Using Norms

If a group's scores are to be compared to some norms, the appropriateness of the norms must be examined. The group used to develop the norms should be similar in many ways to the group being compared to the norms. The recency of the norms should be checked. The conditions under which the data were gathered should be similar.

The measurement phenomenon of regression to the mean should also be considered. For example, imagine any group that widely deviates, either above or below, from the mean average for similar groups in a given skill. If they are measured in this skill a second time, shortly after the first time, their scores will tend to regress to the mean. That is, those who scored very low the first time will tend to score higher the second time. Those who scored very high the first time will tend to score lower the second time. Suppose a group is selected for the reason that they are very low in their reading scores. The mean on the first time they are tested may show that they are four years below grade level. If nothing different is done and within two weeks they are tested again, the mean will tend to show an increase. To illustrate further, if a child has two unusually tall parents, his/her height will tend to be closer to the mean than that of the parents because there is not a perfect correlation between height of parents and height of children. If a special treatment in reading instruction had been given to one group of children who were four years below grade level, we could not state that the rise in their scores was attributable to the treatment. It could merely be the function of measurement and the tendency of regression to the mean. The principal should be aware of these tendencies in reviewing data and designing new evaluation programs.

[6] Gary D. Borich, *The Appraisal of Teaching—Concepts and Progress* (Reading, Mass.: Addison-Wesley Publishing Co., 1977), pp. 51–52.

Criterion-Referenced Measures

An alternative to the predetermined norm-referenced tests are criterion-referenced tests. These tests are usually homemade with the attendant weaknesses. Criterion-referenced tests are costly to construct and require sophistication in measurement technology. There are, of course, commercial prepackaged C-R tests. The principal should approach these with caution, given the current state of the art. However, they do tend to match the curricular emphases of the school's program and they tend to be more sensitive to change, but not without cost. The reader is referred to Popham's discussion.[7]

Parent Participation in Evaluation

Parent participation in the evaluation process is often overlooked, sometimes by design, but more often it is simply oversight. Parents' input is usually sought in determining needs and in describing the current situation. On occasion parents are involved in targeted valuations such as the desirability/undesirability of a certain offering, e.g., health sciences, sex education, and so on. Certainly the opportunity exists for increasing understanding about the school and its purposes.

As in any evaluation, the school may wish to design special feedback instruments, may wish to purchase ready-made inventories,[8] or to seek the service of a consultant to design or adapt an instrument. The reader is referred to an ERIC bibliography for a listing of selected articles on parent evaluation of schools.[9]

Considerations for Presenting Evaluation Results

Again, planning for this step is not to be left to the end of the evaluation process. It should be planned concurrently with the other steps so that relevant data are collected, and so that the information produced is meaningful to the recipients.

A question that should be answered at nearly each step of planning an evaluation is *who* needs to know *what,* relative *to what kinds* of *decisions?* As this question is answered, the ways the data should be collected and stored will emerge. It will also begin to point toward the various kinds of reports that may be necessary.

[7] Popham, op. cit., pp. 126–162.

[8] An example of an inventory that can be cross-referenced with responses from other groups such as teachers or students is the *Parent Opinion Inventory* published by the National Study of School Evaluation, 1976.

[9] "Parent Evaluation of Schools," The Best of ERIC, No. 35, March (1978).

The evaluation design, collection of data, and the treatment of the data may be beyond question, but yet there is one sensitive step to take—presenting the results to the intended, and often unintended, audiences. Seldom is there a single audience; therefore, seldom does one type of presentation suffice. The complexity of the evaluation process would dictate against a smorgasbord approach to reporting the results. Whether *à la carte* or complete dinner, the report should be prepared for the specific consumer. The following may serve as guides for the evaluator:

1. *The impact of the evaluation upon the people and the program must be a consideration.* The mere fact that a program is being evaluated stirs up different sets of emotions and expectations of the people implementing the program as well as external observers who may conjecture why the evaluation was necessary in the first place.
2. *No audience, even a small group of teachers, will identically interpret and utilize the data presented.*
   The pitfalls of misinterpretation should be anticipated and the presentation, written or oral, should guard against misuses.
3. *The sophistication of the audience's understanding of data analysis, or even raw data, will dictate the amount and type of audience preparation needed.* If the presentation includes differences between sets of scores, yet only a few of the differences are statistically significant, there are certain questions the presentor should ask. Do the readers or listeners know the meaning of "statistically significant?" If not, will they be able to differentiate after a brief explanation? Should the picture be confused by showing all differences?
4. *The information, written or oral, will remain in one form or another for quite a long period of time and will likely be related by someone to new information presented at a later date.*
5. *The limits of applying the findings and of generalizing from the findings must be dealt with carefully.*

The principal should not overlook the possibility of retaining the services of a professional writer to prepare reports for general consumption. The result should increase clarity, diminish jargon, and possibly even raise some pertinent questions for further study.

A well-planned evaluation can lose much positive impact by careless handling of the results. Whatever form the presentation takes, care needs to be taken that the "consumer's" misuse of, or overgeneralizing from, the information presented is minimized. This is not to imply that information be withheld, but rather that only information pertinent to the audience's needs be presented and then with the limitations of its application clearly defined.

Chapter 13 Evaluation of Individual Performance

Informal evaluation is continuously occurring. Pupils evaluate teachers; parents evaluate the maintenance of the building; teachers evaluate the principal; and so on. Often these informal, subjective evaluations are irrational and can be harmful unless there are formal, data-based evaluations to add substance and objectivity to the scene. No planned program of evaluation is going to change this informal, subjective, and almost unconscious evaluation process; however, misconceptions may be alleviated through a carefully designed and executed evaluation of individual performance. It is essential to develop, maintain, and document quality learning environments and experiences for pupils. The principal shares the responsibility for the evaluation of individuals and groups of individuals. It is only through the behavior of persons and the interactions between persons that the purposes of the school, or any organization, are achieved. It is mandatory that these behaviors be evaluated in terms of the achievement of the school's purposes.

Evaluation of Teaching

There are many problems associated with the evaluation of one human being by another human being. Indeed, this may be the crux of the problem, namely, that evaluation is perceived as deciding a person's worth. His/her relative worthiness becomes a matter of official record. Often the arguments are used that one cannot properly assess the teaching act, and that there is no proven relationship between many personal characteristics and good teaching. It would appear to be appropriate to reduce the emphasis upon the person by focusing upon the results of his/her work. The argument that the salesman can be easily evaluated by the number of sales, or the piece worker can be evaluated by the number of pieces of work produced might also be applied to teaching. Indeed, several states have mandated the evaluation of teachers.[1]

A few states have mandated that pupil progress and growth are to be part of the annual evaluations of teachers.[2]

As if the emotional overtones and the state of the measurement science were not enough, the negotiated contracts and recent position statements of organizations have added to the difficulties of the evaluator.[3] A review of teacher organization resolutions reveals an acceptance of the evaluation of teaching as part of improving instruction. The stipulation by most contracts that the evaluator must not be part of the bargaining unit does not negate the fact that teachers look to the principal as a resource for improving teaching performance. On the other hand, some school board and administrator literature seems to interpret state mandated evaluation as limited to determining which teacher goes and which one stays. The principal once again is in the middle. It is important that evaluation be approached cautiously, realizing the complexity of the teaching-learning situation.

A model for evaluating teaching is provided in Figure 13.1 for the reader's consideration.

An assumption made regarding this model is that specific, measurable objectives have been determined and that valid means of measurement are available. Another assumption that should be examined if the evaluator applies this model is that those objectives are in fact the important ones and inclusive enough to approach the total impact of the teaching–learning situation being considered.

Two other approaches to evaluating teachers are via the instructional

FIGURE 13.1. Teaching evaluation model.

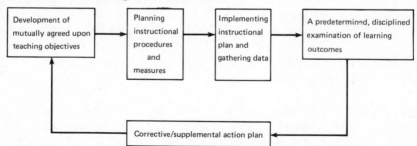

[1] For an overview of some of these mandates by state legislatures see George B. Redfern, "Legally Mandated Evaluation," *The National Elementary Principal*, 52, No. 5 (February 1973), pp. 45–50.

[2] *Education U.S.A.*, Washington, D.C.: National School Public Relations Assoc., July 17, 1978, p. 342.

[3] It is reported that 71.8 per cent of 375 systems studied have a group-negotiated agreement covering evaluation. See *The School Administrator*, AASA, Vol. 35, No. 9, October, 1978, p. 14.

acts performed by the teacher, and the personal indicators of a successful teacher. In the first instance, it is assumed that definite relationships have been established between certain types of teaching behaviors and learning. Medley and Mitzel raise serious considerations regarding judging a teacher's skill simply by watching him/her teach.[4] Yet, behavior is manageable in that it is at least observable. Some cautions regarding observations of teaching performance are noted later in this chapter.[5]

At least one danger is present in limiting evaluation to determining the presence or degree of specific behaviors. It is possible to limit one's considerations to only those behaviors that are easily identifiable and/or measurable. To do so limits the concept of the teaching act or art to only the "safe" areas, or those areas with which the evaluator feels comfortable. This can lead down the same well-traveled road used by some researchers that if it can't be measured, it is not worth researching. Many important considerations can be discounted or avoided by applying this simplistically.

The personal characteristics that seem to be related to student learning are also quite limited. Barr and co-authors present a cogent discussion of some of the problems associated with the personal qualities or traits approach:

> First of all, it should probably be observed that qualities such as considerateness, cooperativeness, ethicality and the like are not directly observable but inferences drawn from data. These data may be of many sorts arising from the observation of behavior, interviews, questionnaires, inventories or tests. Whatever the source of information, judgments about the qualities are inferences and subject to all the limitations associated with inference making, including the accuracy of the original data upon which the inferences are based, and the process of inference making. Beyond this there is a most difficult problem in semantics arising out of the problem of attaching common meanings to the term employed.
>
> . . . .
>
> Are the techniques of teaching that are presumed to grow out of learning theory encompassed by the personal qualities associated with personality traits, or are the behaviors found in the techniques of teaching something different?[6]

It is apparent that the evaluation of an individual's performance must be carefully planned. It is also clear that no one approach will be sufficient, but neither will unrelated bits and pieces form a clear picture.

Not only is it the professional obligation of the principal to evaluate faculty and staff, it is each teacher's responsibility to evaluate his/her own performance. There should be a congruence of concern between principal

[4] D. M. Medley and H. E. Mitzel, "Measuring Classroom Behavior by Systematic Observation," *Handbook of Research on Teaching* (Chicago: Rand McNally & Co., 1963), p. 257.

[5] See also Borich, op. cit.

[6] A. S. Barr, et al., *Wisconsin Studies of the Measurement and Prediction of Teacher Effectiveness* (Madison: Dembar Publications, 1961), pp. 10–11.

and teacher regarding the effectiveness of the teacher's behavior as it relates to student learning and behavior.

The Evaluation Process Must Be Consistent with the Philosophy of the School. It is easy to lose sight of the philosophy of the school as applied to pupils when teachers are under consideration. A common philosophy expressed in some way by most schools is that people are different from each other and provisions should be made accordingly. It has been established that attitudes and behaviors exhibited at one level of the organization will tend to be reflected at the next lower level. Therefore, it is not unreasonable to expect that if the evaluation of teachers reflects no consideration of human variability, the teacher's evaluation of pupils could be affected accordingly.

Another example of a school's philosophical commitment is the idea that each student should grow to the limit of his/her capacities. While much semantic quibbling can occur regarding such a statement, it is clear that the intent of the statement is that no individual should be denied the opportunity to develop his/her strengths. Such a philosophy holds implications for the teacher evaluation process in that the evaluation process should identify strengths as well as weaknesses, and should result in determining ways to capitalize upon those strengths.

The Evaluation Process Must Encourage Growth. To avoid deterioration to the role of inspector, the principal can plan the evaluation program so that each individual will be encouraged to study and develop skills each may now have in embryo stage or not at all.

To do so implies growth on the part of the faculty that results in improved teaching. Sergiovanni and Starratt point out that ". . . school clients grow and mature as the professional staff develops. Self-fulfillment for students is little more than an educational pipe dream if we deny self-fulfillment to teachers."[7] Such an approach is consistent with the idea of maximizing the meeting of both the individual's needs and the institution's goals.

A further implication of individual growth resulting from the evaluative process would be that the development of the process itself should be on a cooperative basis. If the process is to have real meaning to the one being evaluated, he/she should invest in the development of the process.

If the focus of evaluation is upon the growth of individuals, it is not intended to narrow performance into greater conformity. The emphasis will really be upon the many options that can be developed rather than upon uniform behavior.

---

[7] T. J. Sergiovanni and R. Starratt, *Emerging Patterns of Supervision: Human Perspectives* (New York: McGraw-Hill Book Co., 1971), p. 151.

The Purposes of the Evaluation Should Be Developed Cooperatively.
A clear understanding of the purposes of the evaluation is necessary to
reduce the tensions or threats that could result. The teacher can more
readily identify with the goals of the school if he/she helps to develop the
goals and is involved in the process of assessing contribution toward
achieving those goals. One is reminded of the country marksman of some
renown who never missed the center of the bullseye. Upon observation
it was discovered that he merely aimed at an unmissable object, found the
hole where the bullet had hit, and then drew the concentric circles of the
target around the hole. By involving the teacher throughout the evaluation
process, the teacher will not feel that a target was drawn around the
evaluator's findings.

The Criteria for Assessing Performance Should Be Clear Prior to Evaluation.
It is generally accepted that evaluation must be related to objectives
concerned with the learning of the students. It follows that the criteria for
assessment must be related to what happens to and with students and how
these things affect the academic and social behavior of students. As with
the purposes of the evaluation, the assessment criteria are best developed
cooperatively, between the evaluators and the evaluated. This is not to
say that there are no prior givens. The community's, the board of education's, and parents' expectations are important inputs. They are important
considerations for the principal and the teacher as they relate the performance criteria to the purposes of the school.

Evaluation Should Be Continuous. Evaluation cannot be conceived as
consisting of a flurry of half-hour, or even half-day, visits twice per year,
mostly clustered in the spring semester. Professional growth does not
flourish according to a visitation schedule. The overall evaluation plan
must be continuous throughout the calendar year and there should be
continuity from year to year.

*The Results of Each Stage of the Evaluation Should Be Recorded and
Reported.* If the parts of the evaluation process have value to the point
where an expenditure of time and effort is made, it is important enough
to record the results. Board policies, law, and/or negotiated contracts may
influence this process and the principal is reminded to be familiar with
each of these guides. Also, if the real purpose of teacher evaluation is to
improve students' learning, it is important that the teacher have feedback
throughout the process. Evaluation is not the filling out of a sterile checklist,
but rather part of a learning process itself. Feedback also should be continuous, not an accumulated list of strengths and weaknesses to be revealed
at a witching hour in spring, prior to contract time.

Means of Evaluating

The purpose of this section is to acquaint the reader with

1. some available techniques and procedures for collecting data and analyzing it;
2. some basic considerations regarding rating and observation techniques;
3. an approach to utilizing the information gained from the techniques and procedures.

As noted earlier, there are various levels of the organization and community that receive and utilize the results of evaluation procedures. This particular section is concerned with the building level professional staff as they seek to improve instruction.

Studying What Is.   It is important to know some background information and what data base has already been established prior to developing an evaluation system. The principal has many data already available. While some of it may need to be reorganized for study, most schools will have data concerning individual faculty, achievement of students, and previous evaluations. Often annual reports or outside survey team reports are available.

Studying the Faculty.   The principal will wish to study the faculty as a whole to see what groupings or patterns may exist. Data are available in placement folders, personnel files, transcripts, and previous evaluation reports. As the data are sorted into meaningful information, the principal will find not only a base from which to develop an evaluation process, but probably many searching questions for further investigation.

The following are examples of questions that may help the principal develop pertinent information about the faculty as a whole.

FIGURE 13.2.   Age and experience ranges within the school.

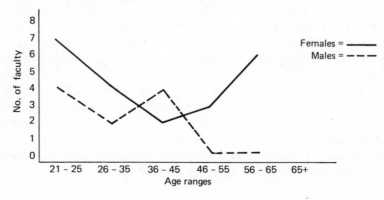

The Total Faculty:

1. What are the age and experience ranges within the various parts of the school? Does this show a curve skewed to one side or the other? (See Fig. 13.2 for an example of this.) Are there hiring or reassignment implications?
2. Where do the faculty live in relation to the school and the attendance area the school serves? Is there an obvious reason for this pattern if one exists? What implications does this pattern have in terms of community interaction and impact?
3. What teacher education institutions are represented on the staff? Is there a balance of input from this point of view?
4. What is the tenure pattern of teachers within this school? Is the turnover rate typical for the district? Is the turnover balanced in terms of age groups, disciplines, educational backgrounds?

Individuals:

5. What special strengths in preparation does this person have? What potentials for future development of expertise?
6. What do previous evaluators regard as this individual's strengths? Are previous evaluations consistent?
7. Are any outside interests evident that could contribute to the program of the school?
8. What has been the professional growth pattern? Planned program of study? Summer courses? What type of courses?
9. Are there any "outside" influences that might hinder professional activities or growth?
10. What additional professional contributions have been made? Organizational work in local, state, or national organizations? Research? Articles?

The principal is *preparing* for evaluation, therefore, he/she is not placing value upon the answers to questions such as the foregoing at this time. It is sometimes difficult to avoid asking, Is there a *proper* balance of this or that? However, this would be inappropriate at this point.

During the course of gathering data, the principal will wish to be alert to various groupings of persons. These groups may emerge as he/she analyzes the faculty by age, by institutions, by grade level or subject matter and institution, and so on. Such information may be helpful in planning inservice work, organizing for instruction, or many other possible changes.

Studying Achievement. There are many data available regarding student achievement, and it is important to know what the total picture is regarding his/her achievement. The achievement of pupils may be viewed along at least six strands: standardized test scores; teacher grades; behavior anecdotes; feedback from followup studies; relationships with others; and contributions such as art work, volunteer work, clubs, class offices, and the like. Again, the following list of questions serve to aid the reader to develop questions pertinent to his/her own school.

Standardized Test Scores:

1. What is the testing pattern using what tests? Every other year?
2. What are the ranges of growth between one testing time and another for each specific area? Is this consistent from one year to the next?
3. Are the ranges of growth we have mentioned consistent with the intervals at which the tests are given?
4. Does an analysis of growth by teacher indicate any significant variations from the typical or average growth increment for that area? What obvious factors contribute to any variation? Is the variation consistent from one year to the next?
5. What norms are typical for these tests in schools similar to yours?

Teacher Grades:

6. Does the individual teacher's distribution of grades approximate a normal distribution curve?
7. Are the distributions of grades relatively consistent throughout the faculty? Within departments? Within grade groups, e.g., primary, middle, etc?

Behavior:

8. Are the anecdotal comments of the teachers about student behavior consistent? Are they discriminating or essentially the same by some teachers?
9. Do school records show any pattern of behavior problems apparently concentrated in one grade, class, subject, and so on?

Follow-up:

10. Using a sample, or the total population, what grades by subject do the students receive at the next higher level? Is the distribution typical of the schools they are attending?
11. How do the students feel about their preparation?
12. Do the follow-up studies give an integrated picture of pupil achievement or do they yield unrelatable lists of data?
13. What follow-up is attempted with those pupils not attending a next higher level of formal education?

Relationships with Others:

14. What interaction patterns exist across age groups, racial groups, and so forth?
15. What evidence is available regarding out-of-school interactions? Are there patterns of interaction between the community at large and certain groups of students?

Pupil Contributions:

16. What sorts of contributions do the pupils make to the school and to the community? Is there any indication of volunteering for these contributions?
17. Do the contributions appear to come from just one or a few groupings of students, e.g., socioeconomic group, grade or subject matter area, etc.?
18. From what sources do the opportunities to make contributions come?

The above listing of questions is clearly not exhaustive, but rather illustrative of many that the principal should answer in a systematic way in preparing to design or assist in designing an evaluation of and with the faculty. With information gained from answering such questions, a base can be developed to relate the evaluation of teaching–learning acts to student achievement.

Observation of the Teaching–Learning Situation

There is a multitude of evaluation forms, scales, and other devices. Also, many of these devices are not really designed as purely observational but are expected to serve a dual purpose of recording data about the teaching–learning situation being observed while also placing value upon those observations.

Classroom observation has a long tradition that is generously sprinkled with examples, and magnified rumors, of misuse, abuse, and general ineffectiveness. Reaction to these examples have taken many forms, including well-rehearsed show lessons to rigidly written sections of negotiated contracts. Much of this type of reaction can be avoided or alleviated by delineating the part classroom observation is to play in an understood cycle of improving instruction. This idea is later expanded under the heading Analysis of Data and Information. In addition, limiting observation to those techniques designed only to yield objective, reliable, and valid data without value judgment will aid in keeping this facet of evaluation in the "improve" camp rather than the "prove" camp.

The principal is aware that his/her presence or that of any "outside" observer does have an effect upon the class and teacher being observed. He/she may find it helpful to discuss this effect with the staff involved prior to observing so that mutual understanding is developed as well as means employed to minimize this effect.

Formalized Observation Techniques. There are observation devices available for recording selected behavior of teachers and pupils, and interactions between them.

They range from relatively narrow, often simplistic devices to horrendously complex, costly processes requiring multiple, trained observers.

Given the current status of negotiated contracts, the use of many of these complex instruments may be precluded. Regardless of contract language, the faculty should be involved in the decision to use and in the selection of the observation instrument(s).

The reader is cautioned not to adopt any techniques without careful consideration of how the data are to be gathered, analyzed, and utilized.

Before selecting an observation technique, the following should be considered:

1. "If an observation technique can be used successfully only by a trained observer, it has limited usefulness." [8] Much suspicion can be cast upon the results because of the adequacy or inadequacy of the observers' training.
2. An observation technique should be employed only if it really shows differences in behavior and not just a recording of impressive behavior.
3. An observation technique should not be used as a single source of data upon which to base the evaluation of a teacher's performance.
4. Data should be generated about important behaviors and should be recorded in such a way that it can be analyzed by persons other than the recorder.
5. There are few studies that relate observable teacher behavior and actual measures of students' achievement. [9]
6. Many "unobserved" factors may enhance mediocre performance or negate outstanding performance. For example, attitudes conveyed by body posture, tone of voice, selection of words with negative or positive connotations can all contribute to the effectiveness or ineffectiveness of a specific, observable, recordable behavior.

These limitations are not intended to discourage the reader from using observation techniques. They are intended to give perspective on the use of preprepared techniques and to the evaluators' own observational procedures.

[8] D. M. Medley and H. E. Mitzel, "Measuring Classroom Behavior of Systematic Observation," *Handbook of Research on Teaching* (Chicago: Rand McNally, 1963), p. 279.
[9] Barak Rosenshine in Borich, op. cit., p. 115, notes that there are too few correlational and experimental studies of the relationships between classroom events and pupil outcomes to support policy decisions about desirable teacher behavior.

Locally Developed Observation Procedures. The principal will wish to analyze current observation procedures to determine if they are yielding data regarding important behaviors, that they do not ignore nonverbal behavior, and that they do not concentrate only upon teachers or only upon pupils. Procedures can be developed by a local staff but Cogan warns that there are few staffs competent to develop their own instruments.[10]

The use of a predetermined set of categories and definitions of descriptors is desirable in that distractions do not enter into the results as readily, but more importantly, the data can be more specific and objective. A disciplined approach to observing can actually lead to noting behaviors or situations not usually observed. For example, it might be decided cooperatively between the teacher and principal to count the number of praise versus censure statements directed toward individuals in the class so that a frequency chart could be established showing this information for a certain period of time. The teacher might discover that a large percentage of his/her praise statements were directed toward two students and an equally large percentage of censure statements were directed toward one student. Gathering these data two or more times over a period of two weeks or even two months might be very instructive for the teacher. There are many such counting procedures the principal, supervisor, department heads, or trained observers may use to help the teacher evaluate his/her performance. Some suggestions include:

1. How much time does the teacher spend talking versus listening to students?
2. How many times does the teacher give directions to the whole group as opposed to individuals or to small groups?
3. How many times does the teacher interrupt working with a student or students to correct the behavior of another student?
4. How much time does the teacher spend lecturing versus questioning?
5. How many questions are recall-facts type and how many questions are designed to elicit responses requiring application of knowledge?

The principal should attempt in all instances to relate his/her observations of teacher performance to student behavior and the results of teaching. The purpose of an observation should be to form an accurate *description* of the classroom situation. We would question the accuracy of the description if it is based on an isolated, posed snapshot once or twice per year. The description should be as free as possible from the placing of value upon the data. It is only as the data are compared with the specific objectives the teacher had set for the period of time the data cover that they become part of the evaluation process. If the evaluation process is to be useful to the teacher in improving competencies, he/she should be involved in planning

[10] M. L. Cogan, *Clinical Supervision* (Boston: Houghton Mifflin Co., 1973), p. 162.

that process by clarifying instructional objectives, by indicating what data might be helpful, and by aiding in establishing interpretive criteria to the results of the observations.

Rating Procedures

The rating of teacher performance serves administrative accountability purposes but, more important, provides positive direction for improvement. These purposes need not be at odds with each other, and if the principal is to realize his/her role as an instructional leader, they cannot be mutually exclusive. Rating for administrative accountability purposes might be conceived as a point along a continuum of process evaluation for instructional improvement purposes as illustrated by Figure 13.3. The number of times necessary to rate an individual's performance for administrative accountability purposes would probably be dictated by local policies.

Before You Rate.   There are pitfalls in the rating process. Several studies have shown that there is little or no correlation between raters' judgments about the same teaching–learning situation. Part of this problem is caused by the limitations of the real measuring devices—namely, the individual raters. Remmers reminds us as follows:

> Note that the measuring device is not the paper form but rather the individual rater. . . . ratings are limited by the characteristics of the human rater—his inevitably selective perception, memory and forgetting, his lack of sensitivity to what might be psychologically and socially important, his inaccuracies of observation, and, in the case of self ratings, the well established tendency to put his best foot forward, to perceive himself in a more favorable perspective than others do.[11]

Lack of the rater's knowledge of self limits the accuracy of rating. Raters tend to overlook defects like their own, and they tend to rate those

FIGURE 13.3.   Rating for administrative accountability as an integral part of rating for instructional improvement.

[11] H. H. Remmers, "Rating Methods in Research on Teaching," *Handbook of Research on Teaching* (Chicago: Rand McNally, 1963), p. 329.

persons they like higher than those they do not like. A history of out-standing incidents can positively or negatively affect the rating of a current teaching–learning situation.

Rating forms have been in use for a long time and there seem to be enough of them to boggle the mind of the evaluator. They range from simple environmental checklists to heavily value-oriented scales.[12] The forms them-selves are limiting factors. Although there appear to be as many forms as there are evaluators, Stoops and Johnson suggest that essentially all of them focus upon the following areas: [13]

> Classroom management and disciplinary control
> Knowledge of subject matter
> Teaching techniques and instructional skills
> Working habits, dependability and record-keeping
> Personal characteristics: appearance, punctuality, tact, voice, cooperation, sense of humor, initiative, enthusiasm, and good grooming
> Personal fitness
> Human relationships with pupils, parents, other members of the staff, ad-ministrators and the community
> Professional conduct and ethics
> Evidence of professional growth

While recording observations on predetermined items aids the evaluator to cover items that are important to him/her, and also provide an instant record of the evaluation, there are several cautions regarding the use of such forms.

Too often such forms emphasize personal characteristics and physical environment. While both are real factors, they tend to de-emphasize the learning of the students as the prime consideration. It is obvious also that a teacher could score very high in many of the areas (e.g., punctuality, record-keeping, poise, good grooming, personal fitness, and so on) and the students would still be achieving very little. The opposite is also possible. It is not intended to discount these areas or to devalue the use of forms, but rather to give the reader a perspective in the selection and use of forms. It has been pointed out that scores on rating forms tend to be indices of compatibility between rater and rated. This may also apply to the items selected for rating in that the rater will tend to select those items or rating forms that emphasize those items with which the rater feels most comfortable. This can be a serious indictment if, as Bolen states,

---

[12] The reader might be interested in knowing that a sixteen-point diagnostic rating scale was developed and used by T. L. Torgenson in 1930. The scale included items on types of criticism, individualization, on-task behavior, behavior control, and remedial instruction. It was used for self-evaluation, and supervisor evaluation with follow-up confirming observations. How far have we come in a half century?

[13] Emery Stoops and Russell E. Johnson, *Elementary School Administration* (New York: McGraw-Hill Book Co., 1967), p. 291.

the instrument designed to evaluate instruction, "in fact, becomes a statement of educational philosophy." [14]

Rating scales may be judged as measuring devices according to the
following: [15]

1. Objectivity—The data yielded is not a function of the rater and is re-
producable.
2. Reliability—The same values will result under the same conditions.
3. Sensitivity—The data will show as fine distinctions as are typically made
regarding the behavior selected for rating.
4. Validity—The items selected for rating should be relevant to already
established area of investigation.
5. Utility—The yield should be in balance with the expenditures of time
and labor.

The use of number ratings, e.g., 1–5, without further description can
cause misinterpretation later in the event the data are used in dismissal
proceedings. Rund [16] provides the following example:

Professional image displayed	5
Punctuality	3
Attendance	4
Professional advancement	5
Teaching effectiveness	2
Discipline	1

The key is 5 = Excellent and 1 = Poor.

Rund describes the outcome as follows:

The above teacher is a nice dresser who is working on her masters degree
as she must, and has fairly good attendance, but is occasionally late for
school, can't teach worth a hoot, and the class is in a constant state of
disruption. Yet the hearing examiner averages the rating and determines that
the teacher's overall rating is 3⅓, or 'higher than average.'

The example is sufficient for the reader to examine what could occur in
his/her own situation given the current rating forms in use.

Involve Those Being Rated. If the purpose of rating is primarily the
improvement of instruction, then it is important to involve those being
rated in selecting the items to be rated and the criteria to be applied. This
is spelled out in the majority of systems by the negotiated contract. The

---

[14] J. E. Bolen, "The Dilemma in Evaluating Instruction," *The National Elementary
Principal*, 52, No. 5 (February 1973), p. 75.

[15] These five criteria are taken from Remmer, op. cit., p. 330. The reader is encouraged to study this source for additional clarification.

[16] Robert W. Rund, "Seven Evaluation Syndromes to Avoid," *Indiana Elementary
Principal*, Fall, 1978, p. 5.

principal will find the following steps helpful in implementing this facet of evaluating individual performance.

1. Clearly state the purposes of the evaluation as related to policies and contractual agreements.
2. Delineate the procedures to be employed and the criteria to be applied.
3. Wherever feasible, develop the items we describe with the staff.
4. Plan cooperatively to evaluate the evaluation. Make clear feedback channels.
5. Throughout the process emphasize the diagnostic usefulness of the evaluation.
6. Assist the staff in utilizing the information for self-evaluation.

Self-Evaluation

It is reasonable to expect that a teacher is interested in assessing his/her performance as a teacher. The principal can encourage this interest by creating threat-free vehicles whereby the teacher may assess his/her work. A plan can be worked out cooperatively to obtain feedback from students and even from colleagues. The teacher may wish to develop a checklist for his/her own observation of the students to try to determine his/her effect upon the classes. A self-evaluation checklist of the teacher's feelings about individual performance may be useful to bring to the surface new considerations. Using some rating scale (e.g., 1–5, or "excellent" to "needs improvement"), the self-evaluation checklists usually include the following areas of concern:

1. Relationships with students in regard to their behavior, sensitivity to their needs, and utilization of their interests.
2. Utilization of a variety of materials, media, and aids.
3. Involvement and interaction with students regarding topics studied.
4. Initiative and responsibility of students for their own learning.
5. Reality of topics studied to the students.
6. Effectiveness of evaluation of student's work.
7. Relationships between students.
8. Relationships with colleagues.
9. Evidences of self-improvement.

The teacher should be encouraged to discuss the results of the self-evaluation with a colleague, the department head, or the principal.

Pupil Input to the Evaluation Process

Pupil evaluation of the teaching–learning situation has caused much emotional reaction. All the arguments against it need not be repeated here except to point out that they generally center around any person's reaction to another judging personal worth. This may well be the key to redirecting the focus to the more neutral turf of the learning environment and learning outcomes than upon the teacher. Certainly in no instance should an evaluation consist of just student input. Glass [17] suggests the following as appropriate elements of a larger observational–judgmental system:

—Judgments of teacher behavior to at least corroborate other ratings.
—Judgments of the learning environment.
—Reports on the state of basic human decency prevailing in the classroom.

Can younger children really make judgments about the preceding? Several writers apparently feel they can and should. For an interesting instrument for this purpose see Hughes and Ubben.[18] Can older students really make judgments that are helpful to the teacher and for the evaluator? It would appear that the most productive use of the student feedback can be made by the teacher in a self-evaluation mode. It has been found to be helpful to make available to the teacher a second viewpoint to confirm or to question some of the conclusions he/she may have drawn.

Some work done with older students has identified four factors to which students respond: (1) teaching skill, (2) rapport, (3) organization, and (4) difficulty.[19] A rating form should include at least these kinds of items for student response. It should be noted that teaching skill was the most powerful factor of the four.

Given their time investment, it seems logical that when feasible, the students' opinions would be of assistance in the evaluation for improvement of instruction.

Analysis of Data and Information

The placing of value judgment upon the data and information gained by the use of observation techniques, rating, and self-evaluation is the most important step in the whole process. It is at this point that positive change can be effected. Here too the persons being evaluated must play an active part. A supervisory practice being more widely employed to involve the persons being evaluated is clinical supervision. The emphasis is upon identifying and interpreting patterns that emerge in the teaching–learning acts observed. Cogan distinguishes between general supervision and clinical supervision by stating "*general supervision* subsumes supervisory operations that take place principally outside the classroom . . . activities like writing and revision of curriculums . . . units and materials of instruction. . . . In

---

[17] Gene V. Glass, "Teacher Effectiveness," *Evaluating Educational Performance* (Herbert J. Walberg, Ed.) (Berkeley, Calif.: McCutchan Publishing Corp., 1974), p. 28.

[18] Larry W. Hughes and Gerald C. Ubben, *The Elementary Principal's Handbook* (Boston: Allyn Bacon, Inc., 1978), pp. 175–178.

[19] *Criteria* (Ann Arbor, Mich.: Center for Research on Learning and Teaching, University of Michigan, June, 1976) p. 4.

contrast, *clinical supervision* is focused upon the improvement of the teacher's classroom instruction." [20]

A major outcome of analyzing the data and information with the teacher(s) is the teacher becoming adept at self-evaluation of his/her performance. If the principal works in the classroom directly with the faculty he/she will be assisting them by showing them how to develop questions or hypotheses about their performance, how to generate data relevant to those questions, and means to analyze the data. If the school is very large and/or departmentalized, the principal may find it more productive to work with department heads or level coordinators in a clinical fashion, thus not only meeting his/her own responsibilities effectively, but enhancing the department heads' effectiveness in improving instruction within their own departments.

The following are essential to the effective analysis of the teaching–learning acts:

1. The emphasis must be understood by both supervisor and teacher(s) to be upon developing the strengths of the teacher(s). Obviously there will be some occasions in which weaknesses are prohibiting pupil learning to the point that they must be dealt with immediately, but these should be viewed as exceptions.
2. Data should be so recorded that both teachers and supervisors can analyze them separately as well as together; patterns of behavior can be identified; and the data can be reviewed later if necessary.
3. The interaction between the supervisors and the teachers should be relatively threat free and not focus upon the value of the job performance except as it pertains to the pupils' behavior and learning.

Current organizational patterns that put faculty into "teams" holds much promise for an enriched clinical approach to the improvement of instruction.

Dismissal and/or Suspension

When one considers evaluation and accountability of personnel the enlightened approach for the administrator is to see the process as a positive one. In other words, the process should be considered a diagnostic tool to assess strengths and weaknesses of the school and individuals working for the school. It should provide clues and means to correct the weaknesses and buttress the strengths.

Unfortunately, there may come a time in every school when the only legitimate recourse in correcting a weakness is to dismiss an employee. If it is necessary it should be done as simply, fairly, and effectively as

[20] Cogan, *Clinical Supervision*, loc. cit., p. 9.

possible without attendant public controversy, which can do so much to harm a teacher professionally or shake the confidence of the public in the school. Analyzing the hundreds of court cases that developed as a result of suspension, dismissal, or attempted dismissals one discovers controversy and the resultant lawsuit invariably occurred because of lack of proper procedures by the board of education generally and school administrators specifically. Procedural deficiencies fall within three broad headings:

1. The school district did not have written guidelines that would give teaching personnel direction as to dress, speech, general behavior, and appropriate teaching mode.
2. The school district and its administrators did not maintain specifically detailed written records of anecdotal nature delineating questionable behavior and teaching deficiencies.
3. The school district did not have an established written administrative procedure for suspension and dismissal of personnel that adhered to local contractual agreements regarding dismissal, state statutes regarding dismissal, and/or nationally accepted "fundamentally fair" procedures that recognize the constitutional rights of individuals.

Written Guidelines

There are thousands of school districts throughout the United States representing a full spectrum of possible viewpoints from ultra-conservative to ultra-liberal. Each district has a basic right to establish its own rules and regulations regarding the behavior of its personnel as long as it operates within the law and the state and federal constitutions. If there are basic norms of conduct, dress, or general behavior and especially if there are accepted teaching and student discipline and relationships modes, these should be specifically spelled out and made available to teachers in the system.[21]

Teachers cannot be dismissed for exercising their constitutional rights but dismissal can occur if professionals fail to meet the high standards and expectations of their profession.[22] These high standards and expectations can be those generally held by the profession itself or specifically held by the district in which the teacher works.

The major reasons for which discharges and suspensions are allowed are incompetency, insubordination, immorality, and for "good cause." Of course, these words are so general that a school board is obligated to define what it actually means when using such words and specifically what

---

[21] The authors believe that such guidelines for conduct should be developed jointly by teachers, administrators, board members, and citizens. However, the point of this discussion is that no matter how developed they should be written as specific policy of the district and made available to each teacher. See Lucia Duggan, 303 F. Supp. 112 (D. Mass 1969) for further discussion on this point.

[22] Fickering v. Board of Education, 291 U.S. 563 (1968); Keyishien v. Board of Regents, 385 U.S. 589 (1967).

the defendant did as examples of action or lack of action to trigger the boards proceedings.

Thomas Flygare, discussing this in his "Fastback Bulletin," makes the point that policy or regulation about classroom conduct and general teacher behavior are very important in a court's decision relative to a school district's dismissal rights. He further declared that a teacher has a greater chance of winning the suit if the "guidelines are vague and overly broad." [23] Lest one be lulled into a sense of false security by the absence of guidelines, Flygare reviews an interesting case in the Tenth Circuit Court of Appeals that held "that even in the absence of guidelines teachers could be discharged for employing unconventional teaching methods particularly when more competent teachers are available in the labor market. Adams v. Campbell City School District (1975)." [24]

Detailed Written Anecdotal Records

The time is long gone when a teacher can be dismissed on generalized negative observations of an administrator. Records of a teacher's deficiencies must be specific, detailed, and recorded over a long enough span of time so that they cannot be classed as incidental behavior. In serious situations the supervisor should have observations verified by a responsible second party. Further, the supervisor should have available as a matter of record a description of efforts to apprise the teacher of deficiencies and suggested methods for correcting said deficiencies.[25] Information of this type is considered privileged information. As long as it is not indiscriminately broadcast and is released only to those who have a right to receive such information, the administrator need have no fear of charges of libel.

An illustration from a court case in Illinois helps emphasize this point. A school administrator made statements before the board of education to the effect that a certain teacher left the classroom unattended, lacked ability as a teacher, and did poorly in certain courses at a teachers' college. The teacher brought suit for damages, alleging that the statements were untrue, and since they formed the basis for her discharge, that they were defamatory in nature.

The court did not agree. So long as the administrator (1) had made the remarks in line of duty (2) to persons having the right to receive such information, and (3) without malice or harm intended, his/her communication was conditionally privileged (McLoughlin v. Tilendis, 253 NE 2nd 85 (Ill. 1969).[26]

[23] Thomas Flygare, *The Legal Rights of Teachers*, Fast Back 83 (Bloomington, Indiana: The Phi Delta Kappan Foundation, 1976), p. 11.

[24] Ibid., p. 11.

[25] Bott v. Board of Education, etc., 392 N.Y.S. 2nd 274 (New York) Court of Appeals of New York. February 8, 1977.

[26] National Association of Secondary School Principals, A *Legal Memorandum*, (Reston, Virginia: The Association, April 1974), p. 5.

Established Written Administrative Procedures

Specific procedures for suspension or dismissal are usually described in a local bargaining contract, state legislation, and/or in State Department of Education Regulations. Above and beyond this, of course, are the basic constitutional rights of any individual. These are generally referred to as "due process" rights given to every citizen by the Fifth and Fourteenth Amendments to the U.S. Constitution. The courts through their interpretations of these rights have defined the rights of citizens and the circumstances under which these rights may be restricted and at the same time guaranteed to each citizen an opportunity to refute any attempts by government to deprive him/her of substantive rights. A school district should use these as the base but beyond this it is desirable to detail more specific procedures appropriate to the local situation to give the administrator clear direction in suspension and dismissal cases.

Generally accepted procedural standards for termination and suspension cases were developed in the Goldberg v. Kelly case.[27] The defendant should be given:

1. "timely and adequate notice detailing the reason for a proposed termination."
2. the opportunity to be heard "at a meaningful time and in a meaningful manner."
3. the opportunity to "confront and cross-examine witnesses."
4. sufficient time to present arguments and evidence "orally as well as in writing."
5. "the right to retain an attorney."
6. a hearing before "an impartial decision maker." (The school board would normally act as a hearing board unless actual prejudice or bias can be shown.)
7. a hearing and resultant decision based "solely on the legal rules and evidence addressed at the hearing."
8. a statement by the decision maker of the "reasons for the determination and of the evidence relied upon." [28, 29]

Any action followed by the hearing must meet the procedural and substantive guarantees provided by their administrative code for all discharge proceedings.

[27] 387 U.S. 254 1975.

[28] See Rubin, *The Rights of Teachers,* American Civil Liberties Union Handbook 155, for further recommendations.

[29] Experience to date indicates that like the medical model when documenting evidence for litigation, teachers are held responsible for what knowledgeable and skilled teachers *do.* Results are not guaranteed.

Summary

In the meeting halls of administrators' conventions one hears story after story of the flagrantly incompetent or immoral teacher who "beat the rap" when the school district tried to fire the teacher. The personal and professional good name of a teacher is a precious thing to that individual. Our system of government recognizes this and has made every effort to see that one's good name will not be carelessly or capriciously smirched through unfounded accusations. If the truth is actually known in most cases the incompetent or immoral teacher did not "beat the rap" as much through ineffectiveness of our system as through poorly designed personnel processes, or the ineffectiveness of evaluation procedures and/or administrative practices.

Evaluation of the Principal's Performance

It is expected that the principal will wish to conduct a self-evaluation as well as have feedback from his/her hierarchical superiors. Ordinarily the latter follows the goal setting/procedures/analyses/outcome conferences format. Individual performance objectives are agreed to by the principal and the evaluator. Schmitt[30] suggested these could be related to system-wide goals and objectives, specific areas of responsibility in the job description, or personal growth. In this process a self-appraisal and the evaluator's appraisal are part of the determination of a performance rating that determines salary increment for the following year.

Evaluation of Student Progress

Many stones lie in the path of persons evaluating student progress. One of the stones easily tripped over is finding oneself evaluating the student rather than evaluating the student's work or progress. The problem is obvious, and, as mentioned earlier in this chapter, applies to evaluating the work of any human being. Others may be the inappropriateness or narrowness of evaluation instruments, the interpretation of results, the reporting procedures, or as will be discussed, the lack of relationship between the evaluation and the program objectives. Mandated competency further complicates the picture. The evaluation of competencies have all the inherent advantages and disadvantages of criterion referenced tests discussed earlier. But such evaluation has additional emotional overloading that has resulted in the flood of literature and some litigation surrounding

[30] Norman J. Schmitt, "Appraisal of Administrative Performance," *Salary and Merit*, Massachusetts Assoc. of Elementary and Middle School Principals, November, 1977.

the subject. The reader is referred to Chapter 15 where the topic is treated as an issue.

Evaluation Should Assist the Student.   The principal should assist the faculty in developing this concept regarding the evaluation of the students' work. A mere recording of the relative goodness of a student's work is not sufficient reason by itself to evaluate.

Whenever feasible, the student should know the criteria by which his/her work and performance will be evaluated. There is little gained, and often much lost, in causing the evaluative process to be viewed as a mystical rite performed by the faculty to put individuals into rank order.

Evaluation Should Provide a Record of the Student's Growth for Longitudinal Study.   Most recording of evaluation is a mark derived from many inputs such as teacher tests, standardized tests, criterion performance, observation, and general interaction between teacher and student. It is appropriate to raise the question of the value of these "grades" as being evidence of student growth that would be sufficient data for longitudinal study. If each evaluator's objectives were the same, measuring devices alike, and criteria alike, then the record would be an excellent device for study. The type of information found in many student "grade" records would only serve to support statements about the student's relative consistent academic performance in a particular school.

Evaluation Should Provide a Means of Communicating with Parents.   Parents insist upon evaluation and upon the reporting of the results. The evaluation program must yield information that is relevant to the student's development and relevant to the parents' frame of reference.

Evaluation Should Be a Diagnostic Tool for the Faculty.   The evaluation of student performance, both short-term and long-range, is valuable to the student if the objectives are being met. If properly designed, the evaluative devices should yield information that would help to determine the adequacy of the methods and materials used. On the short-range basis, evaluation can provide a means whereby individualization can become a reality.

Evaluation Is Sensitive

The evaluation of a student's work is a sensitive area from the student's point of view as well as from the viewpoints of the parents and faculty. One problem that the principal should help the faculty to deal with is the potential of any evaluation program to cause goal displacement for the student. It is equally important to work with the parents in this regard. If the student sees the "grade," the "score," or some other value symbol resulting from evaluation as the main goal or for which he/she perceives his/her parents and teachers want him/her to strive, it can easily become the main goal. The means of assessment can become the end rather than the proposed objectives of that student's education.

Parents wish their children to do well. They want the evaluation program to tell them how well their children are doing. A responsibility of the principal and faculty is to help the parents focus upon the developmental progress of each child rather than his/her relative position on a scale that might be quite unfair and even meaningless. Parents are rightly concerned that the evaluation process is fair. They are also concerned about what the results of the process mean for the future of the child.

The principal and faculty must be alert to the fact that the results of evaluation become a permanent record that can provide a basis for predetermining the student's performance.

Bases for Evaluation

The evaluation of a student's progress should be in relation to his/her own goals and capabilities. In addition, the evaluation of a student's work should be in relation to the objectives of the educational programs in which he/she participates. Carefully stated criteria should be developed to give meaning to the data generated in the evaluation process. Data indicating that a student is able to use grammar skills in a way comparable to the way an "average" sixth-grade student would be able to use them is not particularly informative in and of itself. If this is a reasonable performance criterion for this student in the learning situation, the information becomes meaningful. The principal has the responsibility to develop with the faculty specific objectives for the various learning units or subunits in the school programs. But beyond that, he/she must help them relate the evaluation process directly to these objectives. Each of the methods described below should be designed with program objectives in mind.

Observational data can provide one basis for evaluating pupil progress. Some simple counting devices may be employed. For example, how often does a student volunteer answers? How often does he/she initiate interaction with his/her peers? How often is he/she on-task versus off-task?

The principal can assist the faculty in developing skill in this area by using resources available from curriculum specialists or supervisors, or consultants specializing in these skills. Interviews, both structured and unstructured, often yield important insights regarding the students' development.

Teacher-made tests are useful and have been found to be effective diagnostic tools if properly constructed. Valuable inservice program effort could be well spent in developing skills in test construction and measurement.

Standardized tests should be viewed as but one means of getting the whole picture of a student's development. Caution should be taken that the faculty and public be cognizant of the limitations of standardized tests and of the various problems inherent in interpreting the results of such tests.

The exclusive use of norm-referenced tests really indicate that the school's goals are circumscribed by the items on the test. This might then make interesting copy if the teachers were to teach to the test and thereby prove they had met all the school's goals. Of course, if a large population were to successfully answer all those test items, the test publisher would tend to throw the items out. The principal may wish to develop norms for his/her own school and have norms developed for the system. While it is not within the scope of this volume to review the intricacies of testing and measurement, the principal must have the skills and understandings basic to this area.

Severe limitations are inherent in many of the materials-based tests, e.g., reading level tests associated with basal readers. The principal must be able to work with his/her faculty to clarify the purposes of the testing and to aid them in appropriately interpreting the results of tests.

The author will always remember one instance of the use of the "draw-a-man" [31] device used rather widely with young children. The scoring of the device includes the amount of detail in the child's drawing of a man. The test was usually given in late spring. In this instance, the teacher perceived this as a means of evaluating her teaching effectiveness; therefore, the teacher carefully instructed the children in how to draw a man and she had given them many opportunities to practice for this test with critiques of their work throughout the year. Obviously, the usual means of interpreting the results of this test were useless. However, the anecdote also serves as a reminder to the principal of the varied perceptions possible regarding the total program of evaluating student work.

Criterion-referenced measurement provides the faculty with excellent opportunities to review program objectives as well as review their effectiveness in individualizing instruction. Many publishing houses are now developing their texts with this approach to evaluation of student progress. An important distinction is that this approach focuses attention upon the individual's progress as relating to self rather than comparing his/her achievement with that of other students on either a local basis or on norm-referenced tests. It provides the teacher with specific information about each student's progress and can be directly used in reporting this progress to parents.

There are time limitations to this process, but the faculty may find the time well spent. The teacher who uses this means will have to be committed to the idea, that is, the principal cannot proclaim it as the thing

---

[31] Florence Goodenough, *Draw a Man Test* (Worcester: Clark University Press, 1931). Various adaptations of this test are used in conjunction with other assessments of readiness.

to do and expect it to be effective. One of the greatest problems with criterion-referenced measurement is that the types of behaviors most easily identified and measured are often not the most important. There is a tendency to stop short of an effective assessment program. The reader is cautioned that the criterion-referenced test not be designed for showing short-term success, but that it have functional validity; that is, it measures on a long-term basis rather than for the short term with little or no carry-over into application other than for the classroom situation.[32] A further caution would be to view this as but one means of evaluation.

Work samples collected over a period of time provide a means of evaluating progress as well as reporting to parents. This method is employed in many of the integrated day or informal classrooms in British primary schools as well as in the "open classrooms" in the United States. It is particularly effective in reporting progress to parents of primary-age children and is effective in working directly with secondary students regarding their development in several skills. Samples of work provide the teacher with tangible means to establish a base line of performance for a student.

Reporting Student Progress

The principal must relate the reporting procedures to the total evaluation process. There are several means of communicating with parents regarding the progress of their child: "grade" cards, checklists, narrative descriptions, parent–teacher conferences, telephone conferences, and any combination of these.

Regardless of which means are used, the principal should plan that each step is carefully monitored. Faculty should be given time to prepare the reports. If parent–teacher conferences are used, inservice education in the form of organizing and presenting data might be very helpful. If narrative descriptions are used, analysis of good and poor reporting techniques might be quite useful.

As in reporting any evaluation, the audience must be considered. In the case of parents, they tend to want to hear if their child is performing at grade level or better. Researchers have pointed out the difficulties with interpreting grade equivalents to mean that a third grader who scores 6.0 in mathematics can do sixth-grade work. The reverse is true of reporting a score slightly below grade level but well within the normal range. Additional complications arise in that the compression of scores in the lower grades is much greater than in the upper grades or secondary levels; thus one grade below at one stage is much more a departure from "average" than the other. The principal and faculty might consider reporting achievement to parents in percentile scores.[33] A good rule to follow is offered by

[32] Popham, op. cit., p. 155.
[33] Gary Echternacht, "Grade Equivalent Scores," *Measurement in Education,* The National Council on Measurement in Education, Vol. 8, No. 2, pp. 1–4.

Plas: "A test consumer should always interpret a score through use of that statistic which represents the relationships best understood by the user." [34] As with the total evaluation program, the reporting process should be designed to help the student, and not considered to be apart from him.

Miss Pinkston—A Case Study [35]

Evaluation is viewed as a continuous process to improve the teaching–learning situation. The following case should be read from this point of view. What evidence of agreement on instructional goals between teacher and principal can be found? What effect might a mutually developed program evaluation system have upon the situation described? Is it proper to separate the evaluation of the teacher's performance from the teacher as a "whole person"?

> The twenty-four teachers of the Brandon Elementary School (K-6) are evaluated annually by the supervising principal, Mr. Burke. Individual conferences follow classroom observations with discussion and signing of forms by both teacher and principal. Of special concern are those teachers now completing the third year of successful performance and therefore being considered for tenure recommendations.
>
> Miss Pinkston has taught first grade in this school system the preceding two years and her classroom performance ratings are good, based on Mr. Burke's biannual observations.
>
> Miss Pinkston is unmarried and lives alone in an apartment in the town. She has few friends among the staff members or known friends outside the school. The few invitations she accepts are not returned, and staff members comment that no one has seen the inside of her apartment. At noon hour Miss Pinkston carries her lunch tray back to her own classroom and eats alone. She never takes a coffee break at the provided time.
>
> Mr. Burke expresses concern for her lack of communication or exchange of professional ideas with other staff members and seeks her out for involvement on committees. He also suggests to her that some lively discussions at the faculty lunch table are stimulating as well as relaxing.
>
> On two occasions Miss Pinkston did venture out at noon hour. Once she came into the small, crowded faculty lunchroom and found the table already filled. The group squeezed in closer to provide room for another chair and welcomed the new arrival. Upon being seated, Miss Pinkston placed her unchilled can of tuna fish and a can opener on the table and proceeded to grind away. The pungent odor of warm tuna fish clouded the corner of the room as she devoured the whole can of tuna. One by one, the other faculty members hurriedly finished their lunches and departed, soon leaving Miss Pinkston seated alone in the lounge.
>
> Her evaluation of the first-grade students assigned to her has resulted in many pleased parents experiencing glowing conferences and outstanding

[34] Jeanne M. Plas, "If not Grade Equivalent Scores—Then What?", *Measurement in Education,* op. cit., p. 5.

[35] This case was prepared by Dr. Suzanne V. Drake, Assistant Professor, Ball State University.

grades on report cards at each marking period. The past two years, only the principal and some second-grade teachers have been aware of the phone calls from parents expressing concern about their children suddenly experiencing difficulties in second grade and receiving sharp drops in report card marks.

Of special interest to the principal are the end-of-level tests published by the Basal Reader Company and administered by all teachers at the completion of each reading level. Composite scores for small instructional reading groups within each room are recorded and turned in to him prior to filling book requests for subsequent instructional levels. Over a year's time a first-grade teacher could have almost a dozen reporting sessions in reading. As these test summaries are filed, it appears that Miss Pinkston's group is consistently high. Almost without exception, every child in her room achieves nearly perfect scores.

This year Miss Pinkston has been selected to work with a small group of high-risk first graders. Only eighteen children designated by their kindergarten teachers as least ready for formal reading were chosen for this one room with extended readiness activities recommended.

It is nearing mid-year and six small-group reading reports have been submitted by Miss Pinkston. Mr. Burke notes that these high-risk students have completed the same number of levels as previous groups and with a majority of perfect scores.

To gather additional information, Mr. Burke calls Miss Pinkston's room and requests a conference to go over the actual tests just completed. He explains his special interest in this experimental group and hopes to involve her in decisions concerning grouping procedures.

Upon examination of the test booklets, he sees evidence of numerous erasures on all booklets. On many items with three choices for answers, all three answers have been marked at some time. It is doubtful that the neat, complete erasures were done by first graders since there are no evidences of tearing, wrinkling, or roughing of paper, but only the indented lines from concentrated pressure of first-grade "telephone pole" pencils.

What is the best way to handle this situation with Miss Pinkston? Is this an opportunity for in-service experience in test administration and interpretation? To what extent will it aggravate her obvious insecurities? What is the best procedure for implementing change in her perceptions of evaluating pupils, use of testing instruments, and teaching procedures?

Mr. Burke is faced with several important decisions. He must first determine what is the most appropriate action given local tenure regulations and contract agreements. Next, he must face how this affects Miss Pinkston's recommendation for tenure when the forms are due in the superintendent's office next week.

For Further Thought

1. How is shared authority compatible with the evaluation process?
2. Discuss the implications of the statement: The evaluation process should have a direct relationship with the selection of teachers.
3. What relationships should exist between the evaluation program and inservice education?

4. What steps can be taken to avoid meaningless evaluative statements being recorded in "open" personnel and student files?
5. List ways in which the reliability of the data and information gathered for evaluating teachers' performance can be increased.
6. Programs evaluated by an internally designed evaluation process can be "doomed to succeed." Discuss how this can be avoided.
7. How would you develop a speech to a group of citizens in favor of making high school graduation freely available to all who attend high school and who make a reasonable effort at the schoolwork?
8. Do most of the ways of evaluating schools by state departments of education and other accrediting agencies tend to encourage uniformity or individuality? Which should be encouraged?
9. Is a climate where mistakes are allowable compatible with an evaluation program and accountability?
10. Are the concepts of maintaining and building self-esteem and of holding high performance expectations incompatible? Will not the latter concept, if held to throughout the school years, result in a greater incidence of failure?
11. Is the idea of self-evaluation of the principal incompatible with the idea of a bargaining unit for principals?

Chapter 14 Staff Development to Improve Learning

No matter how the staff is organized, a major responsibility of the principal is to help faculty and staff grow into an enthusiastic, inspired, hardworking, dynamic team. Unfortunately this is a difficult task. The professional person who has been part of such a team knows that it can be the highlight of a professional career. Often it is very difficult to pinpoint what or who inspired the team spirit to develop as it did. Invariably it is a combination of many factors having mostly to do with creative people feeling encouraged to work together on teaching–learning programs and projects in a professional environment where the talents of the staff are stimulated both individually and collectively.

All this depends very much on the principal exercising those magic leadership qualities that are so difficult to describe and teach. Often, in attempting to analyze these qualities and propose steps that will enhance staff development, some of the magic appears to be lost; nonetheless, whether the principal has charisma or not there are some definite steps any principal should take to help create an exciting productive team.

Steps the principal can take to build a dynamic faculty are: (1) select professional people who are enthused and talented; (2) provide a professional environment that will inspire and release talents; (3) stimulate the initiation of inservice programs and projects that will be professionally rewarding; (4) encourage teachers to be creative in their teaching; (5) create relevant opportunities for the staff to work together; and (6) support with enthusiasm, personal attention, and additional resources those teachers who team together to develop and implement ideas to improve learning.

These steps are what staff development is all about. Staff development considered individually consists of all activities and efforts of the school or recognized by the school as contributing to the personal and professional growth of individual employees so that they may perform better and with greater satisfaction. Collectively it is the efforts of the school to achieve unity and the type of teamwork among staff members that will produce a high degree of involvement in and commitment to the school and the total systems goals.

Good staff development then means there is a well-organized personnel management system that ultimately relates recruitment, selection, and placement to each school within the system so that the principals and teachers are involved in the building of their own school team. It then follows up with supervisory practices, personnel policies, and inservice education opportunities that tie in with the goals of each school.

The Total Staff

Whether the principal faces trying to staff a new school with a new staff, or, as is more often the case, finds him- or herself the only new addition to a staff, he/she will need to try to analyze the staff as a whole. There are many viewpoints from which data can be generated about a staff. Some of these are listed below:

1. *Ages.* Does the faculty have a "normal" age distribution as a whole? Are there departments or sections of grades, e.g., primary grades that are quite homogeneous in age? Is there a bimodal distribution of ages toward the ends of the age continuum?
2. *Sex.* Is there an appropriate balance of males and females in the school? Within each department?
3. *Educational backgrounds.* What degrees are held by the faculty? What majors? What proportion of the faculty were educated at the same institution? What evidence indicates current professional growth?
4. *Experiential backgrounds.* How long has each individual been in teaching in the current level and field? Has it been in the same school? Is the faculty made up mostly of persons who have stayed in the community or are they from without the community? If the faculty comes with experience outside the community, what types of schools and systems did they come from? Large? Affluent? Traditionally oriented? Or a mix of those and other characteristics? What evaluation records of past performance are available and what kinds of patterns do they show? How many of the faculty have had outside experience? What kind?

The principal will identify factors that are important and will gather and organize the information to show the current situation. In doing so, certain strengths and weaknesses will become apparent. There may be clear implications for certain selection criteria as attrition or expansion occurs. Reassignments may make better use of certain faculty members' skills and interests. Obviously, a beginning analysis as mentioned is just that—a beginning. Other important inputs are necessary before the needs picture can be considered complete.

The analysis must be continuous to be effective. Like any information system, it needs to be current or today's decisions that affect tomorrow will be made on yesterday's information. The information should be updated at least annually and it should be in readily available form that is easily interpreted. In smaller schools, there is a tendency to keep the information in memory form; however, this can be time-consuming as well as subject to error when certain parts of that information need to be constructed or reconstructed in readable form.

Selection of Staff

Part of staff development is the selection of replacements or additions to the staff. As in any system, a change in one part affects the other parts. The social–professional system of the staff is no exception for every time a staff member leaves or one is hired, the total impact of the school is changed. This important personnel function of the principal is one of the most difficult. In too many cases, particularly in larger school districts, the selection of teachers is removed from the principal's domain. While this function cannot be the exclusive prerogative of the principal, neither should it be completely removed from him/her. The principal and faculty should make input into the selection process based upon the total staff picture, the specific competencies needed, and upon the long-range plans for educational program development. The interview-selection process should also be shared on a carefully planned basis with the principal, the faculty with whom the person is to work, and with appropriate personnel in the central office hierarchy.

Foolproof, predictive data are nonexistent for the selection of staff; therefore, this is probably one of the most frustrating tasks faced by the principal. Yet, there are several sources to which the principal can turn for indicators of success. Records of past performance indicate the relative success of an individual. These can be found in the placement files and received through direct inquiry to persons with whom the candidate has worked. In most instances it is wise to follow up written evaluations with telephone or face-to-face inquiries, particularly when the written recommendations are nebulous or appear to leave out important information. The authors have never seen a really negative set of placement credentials; therefore, such documents must be read carefully and critically.

Within the set of credentials will be evaluative reports of student-teaching performance. Consideration should be made of the type of school in which the student taught, length of teaching, level, and, if available, the training institution's rating policies. One should be careful not to screen out those candidates coming from institutions whose rating scale provides only for "pass" or "fail," "successful" or "unsuccessful."

School Staff Utilization and Development

This is particularly true when receiving credentials from institutions awarding letter grades of "A" to nearly all student teachers and reserving the grade of "B" for those who were weak.

Though not a primary responsibility, the principal should check the certification status of the candidate as to level, subject, any deficiencies, and so forth.

In the case of both student teachers and experienced teachers, when feasible, an on-site visitation may give the principal valuable insights regarding the candidate. Appropriate clearances from the candidate and his or her superiors should be obtained ahead of time.

Additional aids to completing an accurate composite of the candidate's qualifications include structured interviews, examinations, scores on standardized tests (e.g., National Teachers Examination), or other information of record.

It is imperative that the principal regard the selection of staff as a proactive role and not a passive situation. The principal should be involved in the cooperative development of the vacancy announcement, at least to include those competencies and expectations unique to the community and school program. Likewise, faculty should be involved to the point that they too will take responsibility for the new faculty member's success.

Changing Profile of Faculty—Implications for Inservice

From 1942–72 America's school administrators faced unprecedented enrollment increases and thus because of the continued need for additional teachers they had all they could do to maintain an adequate professional staff. The concerns in those years were to develop greater maturity and experience in the staff and to provide inservice education that would supplement preservice training that was generally of "short-cut" emergency quality. H. S. Broudy describes the preservice training of teachers as resembling "the production of automobiles that are designed to go into the repair shop immediately after delivery to a customer." [1] His statement is not entirely facetious. In 1947 less than half of the teachers in the United States had completed a full-fledged teacher training program and had a baccalaureate degree.[2]

Times have changed! While we would argue there is not necessarily an oversupply of teachers based upon quality educational needs, we do have an oversupply based upon the public's willingness and ability to pay. The facts are simple: Elementary enrollment has dropped, secondary enrollment is leveling off and facing significant declines. The surplus, plus changing social and economic conditions, make the older teacher with tenure think long and hard before leaving the school or the profession. The better job

[1] H. S. Broudy, "Inservice Teacher Education—Paradoxes and Potentials", in Louis Rubin, *The Inservice Education of Teachers* (Boston: Allyn & Bacon, Inc., 1978), p. 58.
[2] David B. Tyack. *The One Best System: A History of American Urban Education* (Cambridge, Mass.: Harvard University Press, 1974), p. 274.

in the next school district or in business and industry just is not there today. The profile of today's teacher shows a person with advanced degrees, several years of teaching experience, and often outside work experience. More men than ever before have entered or are now a part of the profession and an unusual number of women who are married and have families have remained as teachers. There are far fewer beginning teachers and a declining percentage of teachers in their twenties. By 1984 it is estimated the average age of classroom teachers will rise to nearly forty.[3] This adds up to a faculty with greater education, experience, and maturity. The situation creates a need for changing the old concepts of inservice education. For the most part these older teachers aren't interested in more course work at the university or a canned professional speech series from visiting experts. But they do need varied and flexible inservice opportunities to sharpen their teaching skills and provide growth above stagnation.

Many bemoan the "graying of the teaching profession." However, a faculty does not need to be young to be dynamic. There are many advantages to the mature faculty. Jean Grambs and Carol Seifeldt in their study of the older teacher concluded that an older teaching faculty is to be prized if the school system can develop policies that weed out weak teachers and retain those who are surplus in their speciality.[4, 5] The financial strain of having the more experienced higher paid teachers would be offset by more acceptable educational productivity and with renewed community confidence and support. They contend research indicates that the older teachers are more involved in professional organizations, more professionally committed, more politically active, profess stronger ties to the community, are more loyal employees, have greater wisdom regarding the experience of teaching and learning, have greater insights into the behavior of the young, are significant informants regarding community expectations, and provide the stability that can eliminate many discipline problems.

Inservice Education [6]

The term "inservice education" elicits a variety of responses for a variety of reasons. Many of the negative responses may stem from past experiences in which the planned program had little or no relationship to the needs of those in the program. An effective inservice educational program is an out-

[3] B. David Delhanty, "Myths About Older Teachers," *Phi Delta Kappan* (Dec. 1977), p. 262.

[4] Jean Dresden Grambs and Carol Seifeldt, "The Graying of America's Teachers," *Phi Delta Kappan* (Dec. 1977), p. 260.

[5] See Ch. 13 for a discussion on how to dismiss the incompetent teacher.

[6] There are many academic discussions over the differences and sameness of the terms "inservice education" and "staff development." We consider inservice education as a part of staff development and do not use the terms synonomously.

growth of perceived needs. It is obvious that the one(s) who perceived these needs can be anywhere on the organization chart, but unless those persons who exercise the competency in question also perceive the needs, the success of the inservice program is on shaky ground.

Inservice education should not be regarded as merely formal, planned programs for a number of grade-level subjects, faculty or even for a total building, or systemwide faculty.

To regard it as such is to compartmentalize inservice experiences as if they had little or nothing to do with application to the realities of helping students to learn. Inservice education should take place as an integral part of the day-to-day operation of the school.

Any school has characteristics and needs unique to itself, as does each individual in that school. The principal must be alert to these differences as he/she proposes inservice programs and reacts to proposals for inservice programs. The principal cannot leave the planning and development of inservice programs to another office or agency, although he/she will find such help valuable. Inservice education is a total faculty responsibility.

The following considerations are important in the development of inservice programs:

1. Inservice education should be directly related to a specific goal and/or objective of the educational program.
2. Channels should be maintained so that inservice needs may be easily communicated and initiated from the faculty.
3. Tangible commitments in the form of money, time, and materials need to be made by the central administration and school board. Commitments of time and energy should also be expected from the teachers.
4. Communications with the whole system is essential to ensure participation by those interested as well as at least partial avoidance of misinformation regarding the purpose, or cause, of the inservice program.
5. A carefully designed evaluation of the inservice program should be considered part of every inservice attempt. The evaluation should be directly related to the effect upon the main clients of the school—the pupils.

Opportunities for Inservice Education

There are many opportunities for inservice experiences for teachers. The following list provides the reader with a beginning for his/her own expanded list:

1. Specially designed courses, with or without college credit.
2. Demonstration teaching.
3. Lectures by fellow teachers, administrators, community resource persons, experts in selected fields, and so on.
4. Technical workshops, e.g., media utilization, computer aids, and so on.

5. Curriculum committee work.
6. Specialized committee work, e.g., facilities provision for the handicapped, mainstreaming, and so on.
7. Visitations to programs and projects of interest within the school or system, or to other schools or agencies.
8. Research and experimental projects.
9. Teacher position exchanges.
10. Involvement with local, regional, state, or national teacher centers.
11. Development of proposals for outside funding.
12. Organizing and implementing different teaching patterns.
13. Planned faculty retreats.
14. Group awareness sessions.

As noted, this is but the beginning of the many opportunities a faculty and principal have for initiating meaningful inservice experiences. Educational travel, conferences, summer institutes, and the like can also prove to be invaluable.

The principal should not think in terms of teachers only when developing inservice programs. Inservice needs may be quickly apparent among fellow principals. In addition, clerks, secretaries, aides, specialized personnel, custodians, food service personnel, and so on can profit by inservice experiences designed with their help.

The College Role in Inservice Education

In days past the essential and usually exclusive role for the teachers college or school of education was to offer courses for permanent certification requirements or provide a program of advanced work toward a graduate degree. These offerings were classroom sessions geared toward meeting college requirements. The past few years has seen a role change in that many higher education institutions have accepted the idea that the college professor should step out of the typical institutional classroom into more direct problem solving situations with teachers and administrators in the field. This growing philosophy has provided a great deal of flexibility to the type of assistance a college and university could provide to local schools. As illustrated in Figure 14.1, universities have developed response systems to meet a great variety of options.

For example, under an ideal relationship a given school system could assess the special professional requirements of their faculty. Following their needs assessment they could contact a nearby higher education institution through the college of education or the office of continuing education for help in establishing a workshop, seminar, or course that would satisfy the needs of the faculty. Or, suppose a school faces a particular problem. A team composed of the teachers and administrators might decide they would like to formally work on this problem in a disciplined way. They could

FIGURE 14.1.   Developing college and university inservice course patterns.

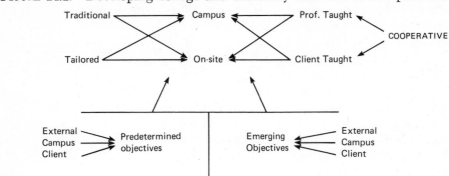

contact the college and plan a workshop so that the professional resources of the college would be made available to the team in finding solutions to the problem. In some states a number of higher education institutions have pooled resources to help local schools solve their problems. One such workshop is described by Thomas J. Switzer.[7]

> One such effort, in which I have been involved for the past four years, calls for such a role change on the part of college professors and attempts to deal with some of the common problems encountered with inservice efforts. Called the Wayne County Interinstitutional Workshop, it is in effect a consortium involving the Wayne County Intermediate School District (Detroit and surrounding areas). The University of Michigan, Michigan State University, Wayne State University, and Eastern Michigan University.
>
> The program works this way: Teams of teachers and administrators from throughout Wayne County indicate to the Wayne County Office that they would like to work on specific educational problems facing their schools or school districts. Enrollment in the workshop is limited to twenty teams of no less than five and no more than twelve members; if more than twelve from a school district wish to participate, two or more teams are formed. Each team designates a team leader who may or may not be an administrator. There is some encouragement to select the leader from among teacher members of the team. Team leaders then attend a preliminary planning session where the purposes and goals of the workshop are discussed and plans are made for the general sessions. The workshop itself consists of fifteen sessions, which start in October and conclude in February. The first two—general sessions involving all teams—focus on team building activities and the presentation of information on the change process, problem development, and necessary administrative matters such as registration. Participants may register with the university of their choice.

[7] Thomas J. Switzer, "An Institutional Consortium: A Model for Inservice," *Innovator* (Ann Arbor: University of Michigan, School of Education, Sept. 1977), p. 10.

Participating universities have agreed to a uniform fee structure for the workshop, and each has agreed to supply at least one staff member. Additional staff members are provided by the Wayne County Office.

During the succeeding twelve weeks participating teams meet once a week for four hours in their own schools or in a location convenient to the team members. Each team is assigned a university or Wayne County staff member who works with the team in its setting. Other staff members are brought in to assist as needs arise.

The final session is a general one at which teams share their experiences. The workshop is evaluated during this session, and staff members exchange grades.

The Teacher Center

One of the maturing concepts in inservice education is the teacher center. Teacher-center education is rooted in the philosophy that a professional person can and should exercise responsibly the initiative for his or her own personal and professional development. The center is a central informal work place where teachers may meet together on their own to generate ideas, information, and materials to help them with their own classroom. Normally, a center does not have a formal ongoing program. However, from the sharing of ideas and the identification of needs, programs may develop such as brain-storming sessions, interest groups, workshops, demonstrations, and even specially arranged seminars and workshops.

There is no one teachers' center that one could point to and say, "That is a model teachers' center!" A model teacher center probably cannot actually exist because each center seeks to serve and fulfill the needs of the teachers in a particular locale. These teacher centers are basically people, people who share common needs in teaching. While they are more of a process than a physical entity, to fully meet needs, some type of physical facility is necessary for a common meeting place and to house, distribute, and even reproduce materials of instruction. This physical facility might be an old abandoned school building or classroom in a school.

Some centers are sponsored by professional teacher groups, teacher collectives, school districts, state departments of education, and some even by colleges and universities. A number of foundations have provided grants for experimental centers and the federal government has provided funds for their selective establishments with the idea they could eventually develop into a national network.

Centers have not been established without some political rumblings. It is easy to see that they could often conflict or compete with the schools' regular inservice program. Many administrators contend that if a center is to be sponsored and funded through governmental agencies then educational officials should play a role in their governance. Too much emphasis on control could kill some of the important elements of spontanity and motivation. Administrators should not control teacher centers. It is important that teacher centers be accepted by the administrator as an honest attempt by the teachers to generate their own professional growth. From the administrator's point of view the concern should not be one of either competition or control, but, rather, how can we utilize, coordinate, and complement the center's activities with the ongoing staff development needs of the school?

Supervision and Staff Development

There may be some question about supervision being a part of the staff development process. The question arises because the word "supervision" has a great variety of meanings. It can mean general overseeing and control, management, administration, evaluation and accountability, or any and all of the activities in which the principal is engaged in "running" the school.

The dictionary describes the supervisor as the "overseer, administrator, the person in charge." In addition, except for supervision experts and members of the Association of Supervision and Curriculum Development, authors of professional literature generally use supervision interchangeably with administration, evaluation, and management. The job descriptions from school districts throughout the country make the principal responsible for supervision of various and sundry activities from accounting for lunchroom money, to athletic events, to teacher behaviors.[8]

Because of the variations in meaning, the more descriptive term "supervision of instruction" will be used when discussing supervision as part of staff development. Used with this specificity it has a deeper and more sophisticated meaning, becoming the process through which the principal attempts to work with teachers in a positive way to achieve the major goal of the school, superior teaching and learning. Our description of the principal's role in supervision of instruction is: those leadership activities in which the principal engages cooperatively with teachers and other staff members to improve teaching and learning in the school. When instructional supervision is used in this way it is inextricably tied in with leadership and staff development.

Even with this more specific and definitive use it is recognized there are contradictions and conflicts that are inherent in the process of instructional supervision.

1. Can the principal separate supervision and evaluation?
2. Must the principal in the instructional supervision role take the stance that he/she is more knowledgeable about teaching and learning on all subjects than the teacher who is a specialist?

[8] National Association of Secondary School Principals, *Job Descriptions for Principals* (Reston, Va.: The Association, 1976).

3. How does the principal deal with supervision and the supervisor (consultant) from central administration?
4. Does the principal have the time to accept major responsibility for instructional supervision?

Supervision and Evaluation

If supervision of instruction as we have defined it is to succeed, it must be considered as a process separate from evaluation even though they are both important responsibilities of the principal.[9] The supervision process in the "old days" may have meant inspection and evaluation, telling how and what and then inspect to see if it was being done. Today, in dealing with teachers as knowledgeable professional people, our understanding of theory and research should make us realize that much more can be gained by professional stimulation and cooperation than by force and coercion. In fact, force and coercion will hamper cooperation and creativity.

Instructional supervision then must be threat free. The principal as designated leader of the school, of course, must accept responsibility for encouraging and stimulating activities that will help the teacher improve teaching and learning in the classroom. In this sense he/she acts as motivator, initiator, and change agent. Rather than telling the teacher what to do, the principal and teacher discuss as colleagues and peers how to improve teaching and learning. They exchange ideas, brain-storm, trade experiences, discuss alternatives. The principal having broader contacts may identify other resources to help and provide them as necessary but avoids whenever possible any implications of judgment of criticism based upon his/her organizational position in the administrative hierarchy.

Instructional supervision is at its best when:

1. The teacher can openly share concerns with the principal, when there is free communication, and each can react and disagree without fear of hurt feelings or reprisal.
2. There is a genuine feeling that the teacher and principal are solving professional problems as colleagues.
3. There is realization that expertise is a function of knowledge and experience and the administrative position does not by itself make the principal an expert.
4. The teacher recognizes the principal values his/her worth as a person and is concerned about both personal and professional growth.
5. There is recognition of the teachers' professional competence by the helpfulness of feedback and the supportive way it is given.

[9] Evaluation as a separate process is discussed in Chs. 12 & 13. The authors are strong advocates of the need for evaluation and accountability. The best teachers should be retained; poor teachers should be released. Processes should be developed to handle this effectively, objectively, and humanly. However, the processes should be separated from instructional supervision. See pages 257–260.

6. There is recognition that the infinite variability in human beings makes universal applications in teaching and learning questionable. Teaching can be risk taking and failure in some experiment or new venture is not a sign of incompetence.
7. The teacher feels professional freedom in that he/she may experiment with teaching procedures and seek help in many different directions without being made to feel inadequate.
8. There is an understanding that teaching is both rational and emotional and that discussions of feelings and interpersonal relations may be as important as talking about the teaching process itself.

The Principal as an Expert

It is a serious mistake to assume because the principal is administratively responsible for instructional supervision, he/she is and must be the expert in any and all fields represented in the school. Nor can the principal be the determiner of educational method or specific teaching procedure, for it is a myth that there is one best universal method. Along with providing motivation and support as a professional colleague to improve teaching and learning the principal's supervisory function is to develop instructional teamwork. If a school is to be something more than a group of uncoordinated classes the faculty needs to go through the process of identifying group goals and then each teacher be committed to accept responsibility for tying individual subject matter goals with those of the entire school. The principal then can help each teacher coordinate teaching with the goals of the school realizing that his/her teaching is part of a cooperative enterprise.

It is true the principal can gain much support through the expertise exhibited but the expertise should include broader technical, human, and conceptual skills such as:

1. Expertise in motivating teachers to improve, to be creative, productive teachers belonging to a unified working faculty.
2. Expertise in ability to place the school in perspective with the local, state, and national educational enterprise.
3. Expertise in marshaling a great variety of resources that can help the teaching–learning situation.
4. Expertise in working with the community and central administration to gain the necessary support for the teachers and the school.
5. Expertise in working with students to wield them into an effective productive community.

Supervision—the Principal and the Central Office

A possible conflict often exists with central administration over the supervision function, particularly if there is a strong staff of central-office supervisors, consultants, subject matter specialists, or coordinators. Many instances exist where the central office influence is so strong or the principal's instructional leadership so weak that the principal becomes the management mechanic. The school, then, rather than being a unified team, has a faculty individually oriented who gains incentive from "on high," the central office. Situations like this exist for the most part from custom and tradition rather than actual organizational policy. In investigating the situation the authors discovered that the overwhelming majority of supervisors are staff personnel rather than administrative. The principal, on the other hand, is by board direction the administrator of his/her building and responsible to the superintendent and the board for all activities (including instructional supervision) carried on in the building to which he/she is assigned. Thus, it is the principal's responsibility to utilize the central administration supervisor as a resource to the school faculty individually and collectively. They are part of the team but they neither control or administer and they work through the principal's office. They should work alongside the principal with the faculty to develop internal policies and procedures so that the fullest advantage can be made of all possible resources. The expertise of the principal should be evident in the exercise of ability to utilize central administration supervisors as part of the school professional team.

The Principal and Time for Instructional Supervision

The major purpose of a school is teaching and learning. If a principal doesn't have time for instructional supervision, priorities need to be readjusted to find time.

In a Point Counterpoint Series on whether principals can be instructional leaders, B. J. Fallon stated that the multiplicity of duties assigned principals provides an ideal basis for the rationalization: "I don't have time to be an instructional leader!" He adds, however, "There is always a lingering hunch that principals find a modicum of security in concentrating on 'countables' and tangibles and go out of their way to look for these kinds of things to avoid one of the toughest jobs in the world—assessing teaching–learning situations and suggesting ways of improving them."

In the counterpoint view Gilbert R. Weldy asserted principals *are* responsible for instructional leadership. They have no choice! "In this period of declining student achievement, wavering public confidence in schools, and demands for financial accountability, principals must furnish instructional leadership whether they want to or not. If they don't know how, they must learn. If they don't have time, they must find time." [10]

Trump and Georgiades in their description of model schools throughout the country indicate the principals of these schools spend three fourths or

[10] NASSP Bulletin (Point/Counterpoint) Berlie J. Fallon, "Principals are Instructional Leaders, Hit or Myth?"; Gilbert R. Weldy, "Principals are Instructional Leaders."

more of their time directly on the improvement of teaching and learning.[11] These principals found time through the "Management by Exception Theory" propounded by the authors, although they did not recognize it as such. "Other persons saw salesmen, arranged athletic schedules, policed corridors, took care of the physical plant, etc., so principals left their offices more to be where teaching and learning occur." [12] Finding time is more often than not a matter of organization, delegation, desire, and especially establishing priorities.

Teacher Improvement Through Clinical Supervision

The clinical approach toward supervision has proved to be an important inservice education process. It produces a self-directed teacher who analyzes and seeks solutions to his/her own teaching problems with the help of another professional. Clinical supervision emphasizes teacher growth in that the supervisor talks with the teacher as a colleague to identify and clarify problems and then observes the teacher in a classroom situation to provide feedback on possible solutions to problems identified. In a sense the clinical supervisory process causes the teacher to develop his/her own needs assessment with the help of the supervisor, and then with the help of the supervisor work out a plan on how to satisfy these professional needs. The solution to the identified problem or need may often require taking formal course work, forming workshop or study groups with teachers having similar problems and needs, or just special individual study and practice.

A strong flexible inservice education program is imperative for clinical supervision to operate effectively. If a teaching weakness or special need is identified but the school has no resources available to help, then a frustrating debilitating situation is created rather than a positive one!

Charles A. Reavis listed the various steps to clinical supervision.[13]

1. *Pre-observation conference.* To establish rapport, obtain orientation to students and lesson to be taught, agree on what aspects of teaching the teacher would like feedback. This should take place several days prior to the observation.
2. *Observation.* This should be neutral and nonparticipating. The purpose is to record as objectively what goes on in the lesson particularly in relation to teacher-identified needs.
3. *Analysis and strategy.* This is a carefully thought-through plan by the supervisor as to how feedback is to occur and how to identify the teacher needs.
4. *Supervisory conference.* This is specific feedback on the lesson observed based particularly on pre-agreed upon items. In this step the supervisor

[11] J. Lloyd Trump and William Georgiades, *How to Change Your School* (Reston, Va.: The National Association of Secondary School Principals, 1978), p. 53.
[12] Ibid., p. 33.
[13] Charles A. Reavis, *Teacher Improvement Through Clinical Supervision* (Bloomington: Phi Delta Kappa, 1978), pp. 11–16, Fastback III.

may help the teacher plan the next lesson incorporating identified improvements. (It is at this stage certain more formal inservice education experiences can be worked out to improve the teacher's competency in certain areas.)

5. *Postconference analysis.* This represents an inservice training for the supervisor to review strategy and results of the experience to consider how it could be improved and to identify helpful ways of working with the teacher in the future.

As stated above, from the viewpoint of inservice training and growth Reavis could add an additional step, which would be having the various supervisors of the school get together to review the needs identified by teachers and then work out with the teachers certain inservice activities that the school could sponsor in order to satisfy some of these needs.

Summary

Not so long ago administrators had as one of their major concerns the hiring of a sufficient number of teachers to fill the classrooms each school year. If the qualifications and competencies of these teachers were deficient they could rely on experience on the job, occasional speeches, and more college courses to make up the deficiency. This roughly was the inservice education program. Now the problem of acquiring a sufficient number of teachers has dissipated, rapid turnover has decreased, and with the development of a more mature experienced permanent staff, it is time schools move on to a higher order of inservice needs. This higher order approach should be a coordinated ongoing staff development program developed with full participation of the faculty. Its major objections should be twofold (1) individually to contribute to the personal and professional growth of employees so that they may do their work better and with greater satisfaction, and (2) collectively achieve unity and teamwork among staff members and a high degree of commitment to and involvement in the schools systems goals.

For Further Thought

1. Give some examples of social, economic, and political problems of society affecting personnel problems in an individual school.
2. How can you best determine whether a person has personal qualities that will make for success in teaching?
3. To what extent can "off-the-job" personal problems of employees be considered personnel problems? How much should the principal become involved in them?

4. Is there any difference between training and indoctrination as far as inservice education is concerned?

5. Should the teacher center be under the jurisdiction of the central administrator? Discuss.

6. Utilizing the points of view of some of the experts in the field, determine the fine distinctions between "staff development" as we are beginning to understand it and "inservice education" as we used to know it.

7. It is a proven fact that the teaching profession is becoming older, less mobile, and more expensive. What implications does this have for the principal and his/her role?

8. Many educators contend the present leveling-off of supply and demand for teachers will be good for the profession in that it will encourage emphasis on quality rather than quantity. Is this happening? Discuss.

9. Visit the college placement office. With the help of placement officials identify school systems with the most effective recruitment procedures. What makes them more effective than others?

10. Some contend the purposes of administration, supervision, and evaluation are such that the principal can never be a part of the "team" in working with teachers to improve teaching and learning. Discuss.

Part III
Special Problems and Issues

A continuing challenge to the principal is determining strategy for resolving problems and issues related to the school. Many of these problems and issues never seem to "just go away." They are always with us to some degree or other. For many, such as "discipline" or "teenage pregnancy," there appears to be NO absolute solutions. However, if we cannot entirely eliminate the problem there are approaches, strategies, and attitudes that can eliminate much of the trauma (both to the school and the student) accompanying the problem.

An important part of the preparation program for a prospective principal is to help him/her to understand the perennial problems facing each school and to have the "know-how" to work with students, faculty, and the community in dealing with them in a way appropriate to that particular school community.

In a study of exemplary principals throughout the nation, problem solving was considered one of their most effective and important abilities both by the principals themselves and their "significant others." In fact, most principals cited as exemplary were rated four or five in ability in this area on a scale where five was the top score.[1]

Problem-solving methods used by many of these effective principals were identified as being basically intuitive; however, much of this so-called intuition had an experiential and educational base. Two specific approaches toward problem solving emerged when studying their methods, one emphasized process, the other personal qualities.

The principals who tended to utilize principles and steps of problem

[1] National Association of Secondary School Principals, *The Senior High School Principalship, The Effective Principal*, Vol. II (Reston, Va.: The Association, 1978) pp. 35–42.

solving, when confronted with a problem, listed the following as part of their process. These principals described how they:

1. *Investigated* and *diagnosed* the factors that seemed to be the cause of the problem.
2. *Identified* and *assessed* the various alternative means of resolving the problem; looked creatively for that third or fourth or fifth alternative.
3. *Met* with a variety of people, particularly those who were to be affected by the problem or its resolution.
4. Utilized *mediation, counterproposals,* and *compromise* in their approach to problem solving.
5. Selected a proposed resolution of the problem only *after considerable analysis and thought.*
6. Planned carefully and thoughtfully the *implementation* of the proposed solution.[2]

A number of principals emphasized the importance of the personal qualities in problem solving. The personal characteristics they felt to be most important were:

1. Being a good listener.
2. Not becoming defensive or emotional.
3. Being able to take pressure or tension.
4. Staying "cool."
5. Being fair and reasonable, but firm.
6. Showing stick-to-it-iveness.

On the basis of a nationwide survey of the current educational literature, the authors developed a list of persistent high priority problems that face our schools today and will continue to do so in the years ahead. The problems were then reviewed with a national sampling of principals, teachers, parents, and students to verify their importance and high priority. The result was a list of high-priority problems and issues facing every school. Every principal should have a master plan for handling these problems and issues. What is yours? How would you develop it? It is questionable whether you can have a strong viable school unless you have the ability to work closely with teachers, students, and parents in attempting to resolve these problems and issues.

The following identifies twenty-one of the high priority problems and issues that emerged from our survey. Many have been discussed throughout the book. Eight of them are starred, which indicates we are dealing with these problems specifically in the next two chapters by defining and delineating them on the basis of our knowledge and point of view.

Discipline (classroom management and general school behavior) *
Vandalism and violence *

[2] See Ch. 4 for a list of logical problem-solving steps that are more specific.

Absenteeism—the attendance battle

Minimum competencies and declining achievement (the basics issue) *

Alternative programs—alternative schools

Desegregation and busing

Mainstreaming

Staff development (variations in teacher's dedication, interests, and abilities)

Assessments and accountability (student, teacher, and principal evaluation)

Bilingual/bicultural education

Collective bargaining and negotiating—its effect on the principals' role *

Substance abuse (the drug scene) *

Student rights and responsibilities (school code)

The unmotivated-doubters, delinquents, and dropouts

Parent–citizen involvement in the school

Sex, sex education and teenage pregnancy *

Student involvement—participation and positive school climate

Enrollment decline and reductions in force

Dealing with abused or neglected children *

Communications

Sexism *

We have presented these starred problems in two separate chapters, one entitled Society-Related Problems, (Ch. 15) the other School-Centered Problems (Ch. 16). It is not possible to draw a neat, clean line between what might be considered a school problem and society's problem. Certainly both could share responsibility for its existence as well as its solution. Nonetheless, it may be seen that many of the problems in the school are more a by-product of society than of the way a particular school operates.

Chapter 15 Society-Related Problems

The problems discussed in this chapter are identified as society-related problems because they have emerged as major by-products of our society. We believe schools make a serious mistake in shouldering *complete* responsibility for either the assessment or solution of these problems or accepting blame for their existence. However, the school as an important social institution can and should take appropriate leadership in alerting the community to the problem and work as a cooperative team member with the broader community in seeking solutions. In addition, they must develop specific procedures for dealing with these problems when they emerge in the school itself. This chapter focuses on vandalism and violence, child abuse, substance abuse, and school girl pregnancy (sex and sex education).

Vandalism and Violence

School vandalism and violence became a national headline in 1975 with the release of a preliminary report by the Congressional Subcommittee to Investigate Juvenile Delinquency. The report, entitled *Our Nation's Schools—A Report Card: "A" in School Violence and Vandalism* brought to public attention the results of a nationwide survey that attempted to determine the extent and trend of violence, vandalism, and related problems. In July of 1976 the subcommittee followed up with two volumes containing over sixteen hundred pages of testimony, statements, and articles concerning the nature of the problem.[1] In 1977 they issued a final report with a more helpful approach by emphasizing various strategies and models useful to schools in reducing violence and vandalism.[2]

[1] Subcommittee to Investigate Juvenile Delinquency, "School Violence and Vandalism: The Nature, Extent, and Cost of Violence and Vandalism in our Nation's Schools," and "School Violence and Vandalism: Models and Strategies for Change" (Washington: U.S. Government Printing Office, 1977).

[2] Subcommittee to Investigate Juvenile Delinquency, "Challenge for the Third Century: Education in a Safe Environment—Final Report on the Nature and Prevention of School Violence and Vandalism" (Washington: U.S. Government Printing Office, 1977).

While the extent of violence and vandalism seems to have peaked, and may even be declining, the nationwide cost is still in the range of 200 million to 500 million depending upon whether one wishes to listen more closely to the Congressional subcommittee estimates or those presented by the *Safe School Study* of the National Institute of Education.[3] No matter which stance one takes—"Viewing with alarm," as the subcommittee did, or the more conservative, slightly defensive approach of the National Institute of Education—one must admit that this problem is taking its toll on education through the excessive expenditure of time, money, energy, and concern that could much better be expended on more positive aspects of education. The problems of violence and vandalism seem to be spread evenly among urban, suburban, and rural schools when considering numbers of seriously affected schools; however, when considering percentages the urban schools are clearly in the lead. In the random interviewing of secondary school principals at their 1978 Convention in Anaheim, California, urban principals were almost unanimous that this was a problem of which they had to be constantly aware and on guard about even though many did not consider it a major problem. Vandalism, particularly after school occurrences, appeared to be a natural possible constant occurrence that was handled rather matter-of-factly by all-school security. Violence, however, seemed to always be lurking in the background as a threat, thus the need for establishing constant safeguards. On the other hand, rural and suburban school principals did not consider these a constant threat that needed to be guarded against. They were inclined to downplay the idea that violence and vandalism were major issues that should elicit their concern. One Connecticut suburban principal who was interviewed on the airplane going to the convention was exceedingly outspoken about these not being major issues. He contended we were not only "beating a dead horse" by pursuing this as a problem area in our textbook but were furthering a negative image that was a disservice to administration. Consider his chagrin when he arrived at his hotel and responded to an urgent phone call message to discover that his school had been broken into the evening before with an estimated twenty-five thousand dollars worth of damage by vandalism.

Education U.S.A., in reporting on the National Institute of Education study, stated:

> Typically, one school in four is vandalized each month, with an average cost of repairs at $81. Further, one school in ten is broken into at an average cost per burglary of $183. "School crime (and especially vandalism) is not just an urban problem," the study states. In fact, the per capita cost of school crime is higher in the suburbs than in the cities. But violence among students

[3] National Institute of Education "Safe School Study" (Washington: Department of Health, Education and Welfare, U.S. Government Printing Office, 1978).

increases with the size of the community and the school. Generally there is less crime in rural areas.[4]

The study does show that in large cities 26 per cent of the high schools, 18 per cent of the junior high schools, and 12 per cent of the elementary schools indicate they have serious problems while 6 per cent of the rural, 8 per cent of the suburban, and 11 per cent of the small cities report "serious" problems.

Even though the lightning does not strike every school, every school principal has an important stake in this issue for at least two important reasons: (1) The principal's leadership is necessary to help the public understand the nature of this national problem; that the solution to crime in the school does not lie solely within the schools. These are social problems that lie deep below the surface with roots in the very foundation and structure of our society. (2) The central conclusion of all the studies read on the subject seems to be that the principal's leadership is one of the strongest factors in reducing school vandalism and violence.

The subcommittee to Investigate Juvenile Delinquency concluded a solution to the problem required the combined effort and participation of the entire educational community, including parents and citizens at large. They then recommended a checklist that could be accomplished by individual schools under the direction of the principal: [5]

> The subcommittee's intention is to provide some initiative and direction to stimulate a simple yet vital ingredient in the effort to reduce school crime problems—the involvement of all elements of the educational community.
>
> *Individual Schools, Principals, Teachers, Students, and Parents*
> —Principals should establish uniform and clear disciplinary practices to insure that all teachers and students know and understand school rules and the procedures for enforcing them.
> —Principals could form a committee of students, teachers, parents and administrators to draw up a proposed written code of rights and responsibilities which in turn can be submitted to the school community for adoption.
> —An antitruancy committee consisting of a parent, a counselor, and a student could be formed to visit the homes of truants and potential dropouts and encourage them to return to school.
> —Teachers and principals could hold discussions with student groups on violence, vandalism and related problems in the schools. Students should be encouraged to provide suggestions to alleviate the problems.
> —Principals could visit the homes of people who live in the neighborhood and request their help in keeping watch on the school building when it is not occupied.
> —Custodians could conduct a complete tour of the school facility for new students each year in order to make it a more familiar and welcome place.
> —School officials should meet with police officials to reach a clear under-

---

[4] National School Public Relation Association, *Education U.S.A.* (January 16, 1978, Vol. 20, No. 20), p. 145.

[5] Subcommittee to Investigate Juvenile Delinquency, *Final Report,* op. cit., pp. 89–90.

standing concerning the circumstances in which police will be called on school grounds and how such an operation will be handled.

—Principals and teachers might telephone parents with news of good grades or some other accomplishment on the part of their children. Some parents complain that the only time they hear from the school is when their children are in trouble.

—A Student Advisory Committee could be formed to help reduce violence and vandalism by enlisting student support and assistance.

—An overall school safety committee could be formed made up of student custodians, teachers and parents to present suggestions to the principal on methods of controlling problems.

—Alternatives to suspension for non serious offenses such as behavior contracts or cool off rooms could be instituted.

—Parents could be encouraged to provide active assistance to principals and teachers during the day.

—Custodians should keep extra materials available to effect rapid repairs and avoid the epidemic effect of vandalism.

—Principals should develop clear understanding with both the Superintendent's Office and the individual School Security Officer as to their respective responsibilities and authority.

—School officials should seek out isolated areas of the school where problems are likely to occur and close them off or provide for increased supervision or activity at critical times.

—School officials should meet with teachers to insure that they understand school policy in critical situations such as a fight in a classroom or a crowded hall.

—Peer group counseling groups could be formed.

—Telephone campaigns could be initiated to encourage parents to attend PTA meetings.

—The school could establish a vandalism reduction fund.

—Students and teachers should be encouraged to promptly report intruders on school grounds.

—Principals might contact the local police department to set up a police-liaison program.

—A counseling program might be initiated to provide assistance to students or teachers who have been the victims of assaults.

On the basis of sifting through the findings of hundreds of studies, including their own, the *Safe School Study* concluded a school could reduce its level of violence and vandalism by: (1) increasing efforts in student governance and rule enforcement, (2) treating students fairly and equally, (3) increasing alternative opportunities for attaining an education, (4) improving the relevance of subject matter, making it more appropriate to students interests and needs, (5) having smaller classes with teachers instructing a smaller number of different students.

They then developed a profile of a hypothetical model school that would have a low crime rate.[6]

Throughout this analysis, the data point to the principal and the school administration as the key element. An effective principal who has developed

[6] National Institute of Education, op. cit., p. 137.

a systematic policy of discipline helps each individual teacher to maintain discipline by providing a reliable system of support, appropriate in-service training for teachers, and opportunities for teachers to coordinate their actions. This means that the teachers themselves are in a more secure position and are more likely to take effective disciplinary actions to control their own classrooms. Teachers are also more likely to recognize that they have a responsibility in establishing school-wide discipline. Students will respond favorably when this occurs; they will see the system as fair, will understand better what the rules are, and will be less likely to feel that the school is capricious and despotic. The effective school also finds ways to provide positive incentives to all students. The honors of the school go to many students, regardless of social class or academic ability. The school is sufficiently comprehensive to offer something of value to all of its students.

Child Abuse

Concern about child abuse is not new to popular media or to professional literature. The first child protective case was recorded in 1874. Literature focusing upon this problem has been accumulating rapidly, particularly since Kempe's paper, "The Battered Child Syndrome," in 1962.[7] The statistics are alarming; the problem appears to be widely distributed; and the consequences are long term. The following is not an appeal that again the schools take over a neglected area in family or societal responsibility. It presents the facts about the situation and suggests that school personnel assume their places alongside others in exercising moral and legal responsibilities.

Dispelling Myths and Stereotypes

The following might be representative responses to an inquiry about child abuse and the school's responsibility. Yes, there is child abuse in certain large city slums, but not here in this neighborhood. The incidence is so low that it is not a major concern of the schools. Nothing is really ever done if a case is reported. There is really little the schools can do to help, and besides, it is the welfare authorities' responsibility, not ours.

What are the facts regarding the distribution and incidence of child abuse?

> It is impossible to categorize the abuser according to the color of his skin, ethnic heritage, religious preference, where he lives, or what he earns. . . . Child abusers have two characteristics in common: They hurt their children, and they need help.[8]

In 1963, DeFrancis stated that newspapers reported 662 cases during 1962. Of these 26.8 per cent died. In 1970, in one state, 315 child abuse

---

[7] C. Henry Kempe, et al., "The Battered Child Syndrome," *Journal of the American Medical Association*, 181, No. 1 (July 7, 1962), pp. 105–112.

[8] Brian G. Fraser, *The Educator and Child Abuse* (Chicago: The National Committee for Prevention of Child Abuse, 1977), p. 5. For additional information, see Fraser, op. cit., 1977, or contact the National Committee for Prevention of Child Abuse, 111 E. Wacker Drive, Suite 510, Chicago, Ill. 60001.

cases were investigated, and in 1971, following the passage of a mandatory reporting act, 512 cases were investigated. In 1977 statistics were reported out of a study conducted by the Children's Division of the American Humane Association.[9] The total number of child neglect and abuse cases found to be valid after investigation was 136,504. The ratio of neglect cases to abuse cases is about 2:1. These figures must be tempered with David Gil's 1973 testimony before the U.S. Senate Subcommittee on Children and Youth on the Child Abuse Prevention Act in which he said ". . . there is no connection whatsoever between the statistics and reality on this particular issue." [10]

The term "child" often is misleading. The literature on child abuse usually refers to "child" as being from age zero to eighteen. The estimated figures are astronomical, but based upon cases dealt with, it is estimated that 50 per cent of all abused children are over six years of age and about 20 per cent are teenagers. In the 1976 *Proceedings* of the First National Conference on Child Abuse and Neglect, it was reported that of forty-seven thousand reports in which age was identified, seventeen-thousand (36 per cent) involved children between the ages of twelve and seventeen. Clearly, child abuse is an area of concern for educators at every level. As the school's responsibility is extended downward to include younger children, the percentage of cases rises. Though not presently documented, the number of cases investigated or officially reported are merely the tip of the iceberg. Aside from the many unnoticed situations, some are ignored and avoided by persons not wishing to "become involved," others are incorrectly reported, and still others carefully concealed by the abusers.

Who abuses children? Two thirds of the child abusers are parents of the children and the remaining one third are nearly always family members or people with access to the home.

Spinetta and Rigler reviewed the literature regarding abusers who willfully inflicted physical injury to children.[11] They state that abusing parents were themselves abused or neglected, physically or emotionally, as children. The implications of this for school personnel are clear. Aiding in correcting a problem of child abuse is not just solving the problem at hand, but also possibly aiding in preventing occurrences in the next generation. Another message can be heard. What positive role can the school play in providing for children an emotional environment rich in love, tolerance, and example?

Abusing parents can be helped as well as abused children. The school

[9] Vincent DeFrancis, "American Humane Association Publishes Highlights of National Study of Child Neglect and Abuse Reporting for 1975," *Child Abuse and Neglect Reports,* June, 1977.

[10] S. J. Cohen and A. Sussman, "The Incidence of Child Abuse in the United States," *Child Welfare* (June 1975), Vol. 54, No. 6.

[11] John S. Spinetta and David Rigler, "The Child Abusing Parent: A Psychological Review," *Psychological Bulletin,* 77, No. 4 (April 1972), pp. 296–304.

must enter into an active partnership with other community agencies to make homes safe for children.

DeFrancis pointed out that "battered children are not peculiar to any socioeconomic group in the community." [12] Nor are the abusers teenage mothers since nearly two thirds of the mothers in one group of cases studied were between twenty and thirty years of age. Spinetta and Rigler found that "only a few of the abusing parents showed severe psychotic tendencies." [13] They further cited research that indicated that some abusing parents expected and demanded much from their children prematurely.

The foregoing studies deal with physical abuse as conveyed by the concept "the battered child." Sex crimes are another concern. The incidence is high and widely distributed. In most cases the offender is known to the victim and may be a relative or close friend of the family. Incestuous relationships occur with far more frequency than often suspected. DeFrancis conservatively estimated the incidence of sex crimes against children in New York City to be three to four thousand cases annually.[14] The projection of these figures is staggering. One of the authors was aware of two pregnancies resulting from incest in a two-year period in a one to eighth grade school. Frequently the mother will not report such a relationship even though she may be aware of it.

Legal Responsibilities of School Personnel

The moral obligations are clear, but often easily avoidable because if a problem is everybody's business, it can be easily left to the next person, thus becoming nobody's business. Legislation has been passed in all states but one. These laws outline mandatory reporting of suspected physical injury inflicted by other than accidental means, maltreatment, sexual molestation, cruel punishment, or deprivation of food, clothing, or shelter. Anyone can report cases of child abuse but the law REQUIRES medical personnel, school principals, teachers, social workers, clergymen, and police officers to report such cases. Those who report suspected abuse in good faith are granted immunity from civil or criminal liability. It should be noted that one need not have "proof," but rather it is only necessary to have reason to believe a case of child abuse in order to file a report.

School boards have adopted policies in accordance with this legislation. It is conceivable that professionals could be prosecuted for not properly reporting suspected cases of child abuse. As the public becomes more conscious and conscientious about dealing with the problem, school personnel will be expected to play an active role in reporting and in supportive

[12] DeFrancis, op. cit., p. 8.
[13] Spinetta and Rigler, op. cit., p. 299.
[14] Vincent DeFrancis, *Protecting the Child Victim of Sex Crimes* Children's Division (Denver: The American Humane Association, 1945), p. 2.

roles with agencies following up actual cases of child abuse. In nearly all cases, the follow-up agency will focus upon the parents. An important partnership link can be effected if school personnel can give support to the abused child or his/her siblings. The support might take several forms but would include providing an environment of acceptance, opportunity for successes, recognition of those successes, and continued observation of the situation for any negative recurring symptoms.

Recognition of Child Abuse by School Personnel

The principal will wish to alert faculty and staff to some of the common signs of abuse and neglect of children. Although the largest proportion of child abuse occurs in children who are below school age, it is nevertheless true that mandatory attendance at school may be an abused child's first regular contact with the outside world. The first professionals to see an abused child may be elementary school teachers.

Child abuse is a familial problem; therefore, recognition of child abuse in a school age child may lead to detection of abuse in younger siblings—possibly enabling these younger siblings to survive to reach school age.

What should alert school personnel to become suspicious of child abuse? What signs or types of behavior in children or parents should warn school personnel to look further or report the case? How may a teacher or school administrator or school nurse recognize child abuse? What should they look for?

The following guidelines for recognition of suspected child abuse were prepared by a physician and distributed by the Connecticut Child Welfare Association Child Advocacy Center in Hartford, Connecticut. These guides for recognition of abused children and abusing parents will aid school personnel as they come into contact with children.

Guidelines for Recognition of Child Abuse: [15]

1. Clinical Signs of Physical Abuse and Severe Neglect in Children
   Professionals responsible for child care and child welfare in the home, school, doctor's office, or emergency room should be on the alert for the following:
   a. Injuries which are not appropriate for the child's age and maturational level: e.g., fractured extremities or skull in a child not yet walking, burns, etc. (Small scars or marks on the extremities which would ordinarily be concealed by clothing may well be secondary to cigarette burns.)
   b. Bruises or wounds in various stages of healing, implying repeated exposure to trauma (or repeated injury inflicted), especially in the region of head or neck.

[15] These guidelines were prepared by Suzanne M. Sgroi, M.D., and distributed by the CCWA Child Advocacy Center, 1040 Prospect Avenue, Hartford, Connecticut 01605. For additional information, see Fraser, op. cit., 1977, or contact the National Committee for Prevention of Child Abuse, 111 E. Wacker Dr., Suite 510, Chicago, Ill. 60001.

    c. Physical evidence of undernutrition and/or water deprivation: e.g., poor skin tone, abnormalities of mouth and mucous membranes.

    d. Overt evidence of neglect of physical needs of young children (presence of more than "surface dirt"): e.g., diapers which are rarely changed; ears, nose and fingernails which are never cleaned, etc.

    e. Unexplained tenderness or overt evidence of trauma to the mouth or perineum. In cases of sexual molestation, even a young child may exhibit signs and symptoms of venereal disease. A sexually molested child will almost uniformly deny the true source of injury, especially if a parent was the molester.

2. Some Characteristics of Abusing Parents

  In cases of suspected abuse, interview of the parents may elicit the following:

    a. Lack of emotional response at the time when assistance is being sought for the child. These parents may appear noncommittal and unconcerned about the child's condition in the doctor's office or emergency room.

    b. Unconvincing explanation of the child's injuries, sometimes with marked discrepancies between the history offered and the child's actual condition. If interviewed separately, the parents may give contradictory explanations. Abusing parents often "doctor-shop," seeking aid from a variety of sources in order to avoid detection.

    c. Expectations and requirements of a child which are unreasonable in view of his age and maturational level. For example, abusing parents may expect a very young child to follow a rigid and arbitrary feeding, sleep, and play schedule, thereby requiring him to meet their needs instead of the reverse. Such behavior reflects emotional unpreparedness to accept the responsibilities and demands of parenthood.

    d. Unwarranted belief in the efficacy of physical force to promote acceptable behavior and "teach the child to mind." Abusing parents have been known to spank a 3-week-old child to "teach him not to cry."

    e. Past family history of physical abuse. Abusing parents tend to have been abused themselves in childhood and perpetrate a vicious circle when they employ violence in rearing their own children.

3. Some Characteristics of Abused Children

    a. Refusal to admit that abuse has occurred. Most abused children will not volunteer the true cause of their injuries, especially when the abuser is a parent. When questioned, they usually concur with the parent's explanation of the injury.

    b. Passive, accepting, frightened behavior. Children do not ordinarily express hatred or vindictiveness toward abusing parents. Instead, the child, if old enough, is likely to feel guilty about the supposed misbehavior which precipitated the abuse and will actively seek love and forgiveness from the abusing parent.

Where to Turn

There are several sources of help available to the schools. These agencies and services have different names from state to state, but are ordinarily easily identified once the task is begun. It is suggested that the reader try the steps suggested in Figure 15–1 with a hypothetical case to see if there

FIGURE 15.1.   The steps in reporting a *suspected* case of child abuse.

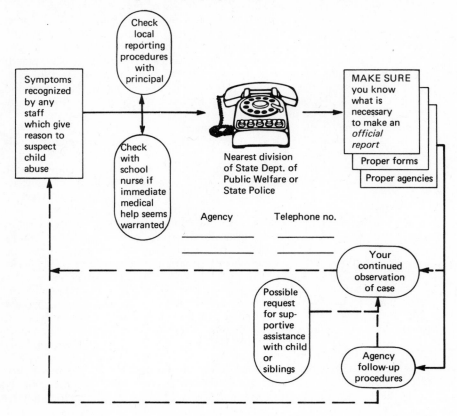

are local reporting procedures and what names and telephone numbers should be filled in the blanks provided. In other words, try it. You'll learn it. Listings under the headings of county, city, or state welfare agencies may include names such as the following:

Child Welfare Department: Child Protective Services
   Registry of Child Abuses
Society for the Prevention of Cruelty to Children
   Children's Division of the American Humane Association

The above are merely representative of the services available in the reader's area. It is possible that leadership is needed to increase the communications between local services as well as the public. As a community leader, the principal can exert influence to effect increased communications.

Suggestions for Implementation

The following will be of assistance to the principal considering a proper role in meeting the problem of child abuse.

1. *Learn to recognize signs and symptoms of child abuse in pupils.*
2. *Know enough general background about the phenomenon to feel comfortable in explaining it to school personnel and local officials.*
3. *Alert the staff to the clusters of indicators of child abuse.* As noted above, there are various sources of help for educating professionals. Often specially targeted projects have developed programs and have speakers available for this purpose.
4. *Know what community and state resources are available for investigation, follow-up, and treatment of child abuse, and how to report to them.*
5. *Familiarize him- or herself and the school staff with their legal responsibilities and local policies governing the implementation of those responsibilities.*
6. *Develop definite communication channels for all staff to report suspected cases of child abuse.*
7. *Proper, current reporting forms should be available in the school office.*

The end point of these communications should result in proper reference and reporting of the case to appropriate agencies. Too often oversights in the reporting procedure result in no further investigation.

Summary

Prevention of further injuries to children is unquestionably right. Yet, taking steps to do so has been avoided by many professionals for many reasons, including lack of follow-up cooperation and sanctions imposed by the community. Forward-looking legislation is beginning to change this by making it mandatory for professionals to report suspected cases of child abuse. Like legislating love, the results of such legislation will be but token behaviors until the reality of the problem is internalized. The principal is in a key position to help in this regard. The effort expended is well worthwhile if one child can be spared further injury, and if as a result a next generation can be spared.

Substance Abuse

For centuries various substances have been used for the pursuit of pleasure. Opium has a long history of inducing feelings of well-being. An ancient Sumerian clay tablet refers to "the joy plant," thought to be opium. The hemp plant has been known as producing a kind of "high" since before Christ. Recently a combination of influences have created a compelling environment so that abuse and experimentation have rapidly increased, particularly among the young. Farber notes the irony of concerned adults who do not see their ingestion of alcohol, aspirin, cigarettes, coffee, and other chemicals as being an integral part of a drug society.[16] Whether it be a combination of perceptions about these influences that lead to the comment, "If you're booked for a cruise on the Titanic, why not go first class," or any other real or unreal set of factors, the reality of the drug scene cannot be questioned.

In 1969 representatives from the Office of Education, the Bureau of Narcotics and Dangerous Drugs, the Department of Justice, the National Institute of Mental Health, and the Office of Economic Opportunity met to discuss this serious problem. An Interdisciplinary Panel of professionals was formed to review curricula developed by some systems. This panel viewed the situation as follows:

> The problem of drug abuse is not a new phenomenon. Man's use and abuse of drugs dates back thousands of years. In recent years, however, the dimensions of the problem have reached frightening proportions, raising the specter of societal suicide. Contributors to our current concerns have been the easy accessibility of a myriad of drugs, a tense, stressful social environment, thrill seeking and escapism, among others.
> In addressing itself to so complex a problem the discipline of education must go beyond mere dispensing of information and make a stronger effort to effect student attitudinal and behavioral change. The more traditional teaching methods will be inadequate to do the task. This implies the need for broadscale teacher training and retraining in new approaches and techniques. Periodic reinforcement will be needed if the operational style of the classroom is to change. What is required is a long-range view that will aim at the preparation of health educators and other school personnel who can address themselves to this and other serious health problems.
> There must also be cooperation and involvement of all other segments of the community in a joint effort with the school if the mounting trend of drug abuse is to be reversed. The closeness of the effort needed is a condition that both the school and the community organizations will find unfamiliar, but melding of community effort is essential if the common objectives are to be met.
> The tasks described above will require significant, longterm financial support and commitment. They will also require wise, perceptive leadership from national and state levels.[17]

It must be added that these tasks will require the leadership of the principal and staff to reinforce the efforts of other societal units, and where necessary, to jolt other units from their hope-it-will-go-away attitude toward this pesky problem that "other" people seem to have. It is not the place of the school to accept the sole responsibility for "educating" youth about drug abuse, either in the correction or prevention modes. It is more

[16] Nancy Farber, "Facts Alone Are Not Enough," Learning, 1, No. 4 (February 1973), p. 10.
[17] National Clearinghouse for Drug Abuse Information, Selected Drug Education Curricula.

appropriate that the school actively seek their part and clearly communicate this to other agencies and the public in general.

The limit of the school's responsibility must be more than merely the presentation of facts. The school must be an active partner with all those concerned with the young, particularly parents. The human-to-human interactions that mean so much in shaping and turning around attitudes must not be censuring and implying deserved punishment. Rather, these interactions should be ones of understanding and willingness to help based upon knowledge.

Establishing Perspectives

It is often painfully clear to the pupils, if not to the faculty, that those attempting to provide drug education are much less sophisticated about drug abuse than the pupils. It is true that to teach, or to guide learning, one must begin where the learner is. In this unusual circumstance the pupils are sometimes sharply divided between those who are quite knowledgeable about the illicit use of drugs and those who are quite naive, as naive as the teachers. Hence, it is extremely difficult to touch both without missing both, or without creating a fascinating world that must be enjoyable to be shared with those more knowledgeable. Clarke [18] suggests the following as steps toward relevancy in drug education:

1. The natural but undesirable tendency to use one's own set of acquired experiences as base reference for relevance in drug education must be brought to one's conscious attention.
2. Those who provide educational guides should give more direct assistance in locating the shifting areas of learner relevance and suggest alternative methods and objectives accordingly.
3. . . . there is insufficient use of athletics for a context of relevance . . . .
4. . . . design the unit or course as "drug education" instead of "drug abuse education". Consistency in relevance is easier to come by if the positive tone is fundamental.
5. . . . instead of trying to influence personal decisions for behavior . . . use the approach of "helping others" make decisions.

Perhaps the most effective program against drug abuse is that program that enhances the self-concept of students and aids them to build a sound basis upon which to make decisions about their own behavior. Various programs are being built upon this concept.[19] The school's staff needs to know the effects of drugs upon kids, but to tell if behavior for one student is abnormal, the staff person must know that student as a unique human

[18] Kenneth S. Clarke, "The Relevancy Perspective in Drug Education," *School Health Review,* 3, No. 2 (March–April 1972), pp. 5–7.

[19] Several efforts were reviewed in Farber's article noted previously. See also "Another Revolution in Lexington?" by Glynn in the same issue of *Learning.*

being. Otherwise there is no known base line of behavior from which to note departures, much less to meet the needs prompting the behavior.

An amazing number of youth have at least experimented with or are users of drug and or alcohol. Henriksen et al. reported Jones's 1977 findings that substance usage increased from grades seven to twelve and alcohol was the substance used most.[20] One high-usage area reported that 44 per cent of the seventh-grade students were nonusers of drugs and/or alcohol and only 16 per cent of the twelfth graders were nonusers. Alcohol is a substance used most frequently, by school age youth, yet students generally do not recognize alcohol as a drug. Statistics from community agencies dealing with substance abuse clients show a remarkable parallel between the percentage of adult users and users under eighteen years of age.

The U.S. Office of Education recognized that simply providing information to educators about how to recognize drugs and their symptoms was not enough to deal with the larger problems of substance abuse. As a result the U.S.O.E. Alcohol and Drug Abuse Education Program sponsored special teacher education programs to deal with the alienation, fears, and insecurities of youth that may cause or contribute to substance abuse. These programs focused upon reinforcing nonuse; discouraging experimentation; and preventing or intervening early in destructive use of all substances.[21]

Developing Policies

Every school system should have policies relating to the possession and use of drugs on school property. The beginning point for the principal is the legal basis for action and then the board of education's specific policies that must be administered.

There appear to be at least two starting points from which policies can be developed. The first of these is the viewpoint that a user is performing an illegal act that may bring harm to himself/herself or someone else and should be dealt with as any other person committing an illegal, antisocial act. Another view is that the user is reacting to some type(s) of stress and should be dealt with to treat the problem not the symptom. The latter viewpoint, coupled with judicious use of referrals to treatment-center personnel, tends to reduce the appeal to use alcohol or other drugs as an act of rebellion against authority. To reduce this type of reaction to authority appears to stimulate less the counterculture phenomenon.

Several sets of guidelines are available. One such set has been compiled by educators from eighteen school systems in Connecticut and printed by

[20] L. W. Henriksen, Terry K. Schurr, and Frank J. Sparzo, "Student Drug Usage in Eleven East Central Indiana Secondary Schools" (Ball State University, mimeographed, 1978), p. 4.

[21] James Spillane and Ruth Levenson, eds. *Humanizing Preservice Teacher Education: Strategies for Alcohol and Drug Abuse Prevention*, ERIC Clearinghouse on Teacher Education, Washington, D.C., December, 1977, p. 3.

the Connecticut Mutual Life Insurance Company.[22] Topics covered include the following:

1. Possession: In each school the principal should be designated by the Board of Education as personally responsible for holding contraband materials and for delivering them to the proper public authorities. A receipt should be furnished the owner, if known, and one requested from the officer who takes possession.
2. Search for contraband materials: The rules of a board of education might well stipulate that . . . the maintenance of discipline in the school, an authorized school administrator may have permission to search a student's locker or desk (but not his/her car) under three conditions:
   a. The probable presence of contraband materials poses a serious threat to the maintenance of discipline and order in the school.
   b. There is reason to believe one or more students have contraband materials in desks or lockers.
   c. The students have been informed in advance, that, under school board regulations, desk and lockers may be inspected if the administration has reason to suspect that materials injurious to the best interest of the school are kept on school property.
3. Property use: The board of education should provide well-developed and detailed regulations for the use of school property and be prepared to prosecute offenders. The rules should be designed to control the use of parking spaces on the school property.
4. School personnel responsibilities: School personnel, except those authorized to act for the board of education, should be forbidden by regulation to act in a law enforcement capacity. When a criminal act is suspected by such personnel, they should notify the school administrator who may, at the proper time, call the police.
5. Rights of questioned students: The school is responsible for protecting each student under its control. School authorities should establish effective working relations with the police department, the resident state police, and other law enforcement officials. According to rules of the Connecticut State Board of Education, questioning of a student or teacher in the school or on school premises will be done only in the presence of a designated school official. Every effort will be made to include the parent or guardian of a child in any hearing that carries an implication of the possible allegation of guilt or the furnishing of information leading

[22] *Recommended Drug Policies and Procedures for Local School Systems*, printed by Connecticut Mutual Life Insurance Co., 1971, under the auspices of the Greater Hartford Council on Alcoholism, The Capitol Region Education Council, and the Capitol Region Drug Information Center. Many other companies provide similar material. State departments of education are always a beginning point for obtaining guides for policies and procedures.

to an indictment. The pupil's right to remain silent or to speak through an attorney or parent may not be abridged. The designated official of the school will maintain an informal record of the interview showing the time, place, persons, and summary of discussion and findings. In case of emergency or of clear and present danger, the schools will cooperate with the police.

Emergency Procedures

The recommended policies we cited here continue to concisely suggest procedures in the event of emergencies.

School boards should cause suggested procedures to be developed covering both physical and disruptive emergencies. Such procedures or regulations should be officially approved and all personnel concerned notified to include parents, students, teachers, administrators, and the community.

1. Physical emergencies:
   During any of the following situations:
   a. If the student has been rendered unconscious.
   b. If a student verbally or by his/her actions threatens harm to him- or herself or others.
   c. If a student exhibits abnormal coordination so as to injure him- or herself or others physically.
2. Suggested procedures for school staff:
   The roles of school personnel should include the following:
   a. All personnel—The student at no time should be left unattended. If there is suspicion of the use of controlled or narcotic drugs, be prepared to advise, if warranted by the specific circumstances of the emergency, the school principal or medical authorities. No statement of any type should be released by staff members to the news media.
   b. Teacher—Immediately involve the school nurse, giving her all pertinent information. Be prepared to discuss facts and impressions, carefully distinguishing between the two, assuming an inquiry will be held at a later time. Keep a written record of the incident.
   c. School nurse—Take appropriate steps to notify the student's parents or refer to the building administrator who should do so. If a critical health situation is involved, consult the family physician and/or school physician. Attempt to determine whether drug use is an isolated instance or part of a pattern. If controlled or narcotic drugs are involved, be prepared to advise the appropriate school official with pertinent facts if circumstances so indicate. Keep appropriate records.
   d. School physician—Treat for any medical emergency. Attempt to determine whether drug use is an isolated instance or part of a pattern, whether the matter is a behavior or health problem. Report

circumstances to appropriate school officials. If controlled or narcotic drugs are involved, follow the reporting procedures required by statute.

    e. School principal—In an emergency be sure parents are immediately notified of circumstance. The superintendent of schools or designated officer should be alerted and kept fully informed. Arrange for whatever conferences may be needed. Maintain necessary records.

3. Disruptive emergency:

Occasionally a student may disrupt a school function or activity by an acutely abnormal or bizarre personality display. While no uniform set of procedures can be applied to all situations, the following observations should be kept in mind:

    a. It should be remembered that such behavior may be emotionally, organically, or chemically induced and that immediate differentiation may be impossible.

    b. Immediate assessment of real danger to the student, other students, staff, and property must be made.

    c. If time permits, consultation and/or assistance from pupil personnel services or other personnel who may already know the individual student or have specialized skills in this area may avoid unpleasant and unnecessary complications.

    d. If the crisis persists and no reason can be determined for the obvious and sudden personality change, the parent and/or doctor should be called immediately.

    e. In most instances a referral to pupil services will be indicated to determine the most appropriate long-range plan for the child.

    f. Punitive disciplinary measures are usually contraindicated in these situations.

The principal must prepare to take leadership in the event of emergencies, and should see that all the staff knows the basic policies of the school regarding the use and abuse of drugs. Furthermore, the staff should be knowledgeable about some of the perceived pressures and values that create a climate for experimentation with drugs. The staff will need to know not to "hassle," touch, or threaten the student if he/she appears to be influenced by drugs.

Dealing with drug abuse is a human-to-human process where quality of interaction, not quantity, is essential. Moralizing is not effective. Meeting human needs is effective.

Schoolgirl Pregnancy (Sex and Sex Education)

Digging beneath the surface of schoolgirl pregnancy one quickly discovers that pregnancy is really a noticeable adverse consequence of a much broader social problem. The problem arises because society generally has accepted the idea of greater sexual freedom for consenting adults. Yet for elementary, middle school, and high school youth there is no generally accepted way of helping teenagers' deal realistically with their growing sexuality. Thus, boys and girls are left to face adult feelings without adequate knowledge, maturity, or experience to place them in perspective or to understand consequences of experimentation. There has been general failure to appreciate the problems of developing adolescents within our contemporary society. Our society has a broad range of moral codes, most of which seem to conflict. It provides us with book, magazine, television, and movie heroes and heroines who inspire free sexual behavior. Inevitably this conveys mixed, confused, and inaccurate messages to the young about what they should or should not do.

The statistics and prediction presents in cold figures the extent of a highly emotional and troubled situation that has moral, psychological, physical, and economical overtones. There are eleven million teenagers in the United States who are sexually active. Sixty per cent of all teenagers have sex before they finish high school. More than 1 million girls between fifteen to nineteen years of age become pregnant each year. Thirty thousand girls under the age of fifteen become pregnant and pregnancy in this group is increasing. Eight out of ten who become pregnant before the age of seventeen never finish high school.[23] Between 1972 and 1976 one out of four newly wed women twenty-four years of age or under either had a child before marriage or was pregnant when she arrived at the altar. There are racial differences in this fertility statistic: About 6.6 per cent of white women between the ages of fourteen to twenty-four had a child before marriage compared with 37.7 per cent of black women in the same age group.[24]

The increase in teenage sexual activity has prompted a number of predictions that also foretell growing problems for the school. Princeton University's family planning expert Christopher Tietze predicts that if teenage sexual behavior doesn't change by 1984 approximately 40 per cent of today's fourteen-year-olds will have been pregnant at least once. In addition to the 21 per cent who will have given birth, 15 per cent will have had a legal abortion and 6 per cent a miscarriage or stillbirth.[25]

Pregnancy is not the only physical consequence. It was reported in 1978 that there were three million new cases of venereal disease. Most of these cases were contracted by youth under age twenty-four with the highest rate of increase in children between eleven to fifteen years of age.[26]

[23] National School Public Relations Association, *Education U.S.A.* (Washington: The Association, July 3, 1978), p. 331.

[24] Special Census Bureau Report on "Fertility of American Women," 1978.

[25] Planned Parenthood Federation of America, *Family Planning Perspectives: (Teenage Pregnancy)* (New York: Alan Guttmacher Institute, 1978), pp. 1–51.

[26] Sol Gordon, "But Where is Sex Education?" *Education Digest*, Feb., 1978, pp. 50–53.

Because we are talking about school age youth, the schools are deeply involved with the problem and they should be. The often crippling health, psychic, economic, and educational consequences do not need documentation here. Yet, what does need documentation is the naive way the schools have in so many instances attempted to solve the problem. They have said that they will offer sex education courses and that will solve the problem. In the first place, just sex education courses have not solved the problem and in addition what has insued in so many instances is community reaction that has created bitter conflict rather than a joining of forces in a community to focus on the problem in a united, flexible way. Sex is an educational issue, Yes! It is also a moral, religious, family, medical, social, and personal issue. It is impossible to reach concensus on sex issues in our pluralistic changing society. We are in error to expect to find one set of acceptible sex behaviors for all adolescents at all times and to then instill these behavior patterns through sitting in a class listening to a lecture.

Like drugs, crime, poverty, and discrimination, this is a broad social issue and it must be dealt with on a broad social base. Educators, no matter how good their intentions, should not assume they can solve this problem on their own. They cannot! The problem is so visible to them, however, that they should take the initiative in helping all segments of their community to realize the extent of the problem and then propose working hand in hand in attempting to find proper resolution of the problem. The question is, What do we seek to resolve? Do we want to simply eliminate unwanted pregnancy by providing contraceptive knowledge and accessibility? Do we seek to eliminate venereal disease by providing treatment or methods of prevention? Do we wish we could eliminate all problems by preaching and teaching nonmarital sexual continence? Should we look for underlying causes and help young people deal with their sexuality in broader, responsible terms? A logical response may be, "All of the above, and more!" Whatever the response, all responsible people and agencies in the community must join forces to face the problem: the churches, the family, social agencies, and the school.

The school should take an extra-special look at its curriculum to see that sex, reproduction, and sexuality are placed in normal context with disciplines being taught. Special workshops should be established to help teachers become more aware and competent in this regard. A special task force should be established to recommend specific action for the school. But above and beyond this is a broad social issue that must be dealt with cooperatively by all segments of the community.

Dealing with Pregnancy in the School

A broad-based approach may be appropriate for dealing with the general problem created by increased sexual activity but when a teenage schoolgirl becomes obviously pregnant the principal must take a specific stance. A simplistic solution has been to treat pregnancy as a moral issue, and dispose of it by isolating the pregnant girl from the rest of the student body as soon as pregnancy is discovered, either by rumor or physical evidence. In many cases the isolation takes place by denying her privileges accorded other students. Others suspend the pregnant girl or force her by social and official pressure to withdraw from school as quietly and unobtrusively as possible.

The day of considering school age pregnancy and marriage as an evil of which we shall not see, speak, or hear is over—even though a large number of school districts still have policies that are archaic and puritanical. First, from a legal point of view, the courts have been looking with great disfavor on the pressure and disfranchisement policies that have been imposed on these students. Secondly, our society is becoming more open in viewpoint about all types of social issues. In the past, sex was something one just did not talk about in mixed company and out-of-wedlock pregnancy was the result of a sin to be hidden and hopefully forgotten. Today the subject can be discussed openly and with candor. Women are becoming aware that they should accept leadership responsibility in forcing school districts to develop more humane and reasonable school policies on this issue.

The review, reassessment, and revision of policies and practices regarding the pregnant schoolgirl fortunately is becoming a national movement spearheaded by the Department of Health, Education and Welfare's Inter-Agency Task Force on Comprehensive Programs for School-age Parents. The new emphases appear to be these: (1) involvement of a broad segment of the community in relation to the problem, (2) provision of continuation of education for all expectant students,[27] (3) establishing flexible, individual programs geared to individual needs, and (4) cooperation with health and social agencies to provide comprehensive services that meet the pregnant girl's education, health and social risks.

The following are some principles that can provide the principal firm ground on which to deal with this issue:

1. Every girl in the United States has a right to and a need for education that will help her prepare herself for a career, for family life and for citizenship. To be married or pregnant is not sufficient cause to deprive her of an education and an opportunity to become a contributing member of society.[28]

[27] For additional information regarding the effect of an "interim education" provision for pregnant girls see R. A. Mayer, *The Postpartum Pupil: Her Educational History, Special Concerns and Relationships with a Secondary School Program,* Unpublished doctoral dissertation, University of Connecticut, 1972.

[28] Policy statement issued by U.S. Commissioner of Education Sidney P. Marland when creating an Inter-Agency Task Force on Comprehensive Program for School-Age Parents, January 1972.

2. The public school should not attempt on its own to establish a policy on a social issue that divides the larger society. The school must take responsibility to alert and educate the community regarding the pregnancy problem and involve them as completely as possible in the policy decision. However, community pressure should not be an excuse for denying constitutional rights to a student.

3. The public school should be considered an agency that develops policies, programs, and attitudes that open futures, not close them. The fact that students are different from the norm, or something happens to them that is unusual, is no reason to exclude them but all the more reason to give them some special help and attention.

4. The school should not attempt to provide all services to the pregnant student. The education function and the needs of students are so complex that they must be accomplished through a number of institutions, agencies, and activities. Strong cooperation and coordinated working relationships with other education and social agencies is essential in the solution of most problems in the school.

For Further Thought

Vandalism and Violence

1. Can we justify having police constantly on patrol in our schools? Discuss.
2. A well-known educator recently stated, "School crime should be handled by the police; school discipline by the school." Is this too simplistic a concept? What do we do about the gray areas in between?
3. What does the school principal do when headlines come out in the paper, TEST SCORES GOING DOWN WHILE VIOLENCE AND VANDALISM IS GOING UP!
4. Develop a master plan to eliminate the possibility of violence or vandalism in your school.

Schoolgirl Pregnancy (Sex and Sex Education)

1. What effect do unwed pregnant students have on the school and other students? Does it encourage promiscuity? Does it reflect on the quality of the school?
2. Is sexual activity of students outside the school really any of the school's business?
3. What do students think of having pregnant students in their midst? Should it be discussed with them? What do parents think? Should the problem be discussed openly with them ?
4. What is the effect on the pregnant student of isolating her? Suspending her? Establishing a special program for her? Allowing her to remain in school with all rights?

5. How strongly does your community feel on this issue? Will each community feel the same? Can this be a topic for community discussion
without creating undesirable controversy and conflict? Should the principal base a plan of action based on the nature of the community?
6. What should be done about the young putative father?
7. Is it unreasonable and unfair to expect the school to serve as an arbitrator
among contending value systems?

Chapter 16   School-Centered Problems

The problems discussed in this chapter are identified as essentially school-centered problems. We agree society helps create them and, therefore, should be asked to participate appropriately in their solution; nevertheless, the school must take the initiative and responsibility in seeking their solution whether or not the school is able to obtain help from the general community. This chapter focuses on school discipline, collective bargaining, sexism and the testing and back-to-the-basics controversy.

School Discipline

For more than a decade discipline has ranked as one of the most serious problems facing our public schools, according to the annual Gallup Polls of Public Attitudes Toward Education. Discipline has been frequently listed by teachers as one of their major problems and their reason for leaving the profession. Discipline is the major concern of the beginning teacher and is most frequently cited by administrators for lack of success of a teacher. Yet, most books on school administration avoid the topic. We believe it an important part of the principal's leadership function and an issue that must be very carefully considered by the school administrator.

Most people agree school discipline is a problem. Issues emerge, however, when one asks certain questions: What is it? Need it be punitive and authoritarian? How do you get it? Is it something an administrator and teacher gets by hiring tough taskmasters? Does one obtain it by demanding obedience and order? Can a school have "good discipline" without the concerted efforts of all segments of the school community? Can an administrator operate the school as a model of democratic society and still have good discipline? [1]

[1] One could get into a rather involved academic discussion over the relationship of discipline, violence, and vandalism. Certainly there is a relationship. We are treating

These are questions that will get as many different answers as the people who are asked. A few years ago the author conducted a series of citizenship workshops throughout the state of Michigan discussing the topic of school discipline. Two words that always emerged in early discussions were "order" and "respect." Few would disagree with these two words as key ingredients in making discipline but many did disagree on how they were to be attained. Viewpoints ran the gamut from strict authoritarianism to democracy to an almost anarchistic viewpoint that self-discipline developed from within by some type of osmotic contact with society. However, the great majority agreed that "order" and "respect" were imperatives for any school system in order for positive learning to take place. If it could not be attained through democratic teaching–learning processes as last resort it must be attained by authoritarian means.

In the 1978–79 academic year two advanced doctoral seminars at the University of Connecticut were given the responsibility of reviewing the research and developing a simple guide for the establishment of "good discipline" in a school. Their review revealed that the processes that create "good discipline" are generally the same processes important in "good teaching." They are as follows:

1. *Clear objectives.* A general comprehension of the purpose of a school and clear objectives for each class (vagueness predicts vague learning and unsettled behavior).
2. *An understanding of desirable behavior.* Desirable behavior must be taught and learned. One cannot assume everyone knows and recognizes desirable behavior (there is a great variety in value systems).
3. *Involvement.* Students should be actively involved in any learning process, including discipline (participation and sharing create personalization, understanding, and caring).
4. *Personal interest in students.* The school staff should be receptive to students' ideas and encourage their interaction with teachers and administrators (let them know someone cares).
5. *Modeling.* Teachers and administrators should serve as models of secure, well-ordered, sensitive, self-disciplined persons (modeling appears to be one of the best teaching–learning processes).
6. *Smooth operation.* Activities should flow in a smooth logical sequence illustrating careful planning and "with-itness" (disorganization causes frustration and confusion leading to discipline problems).
7. *Challenge arousal.* Activities should be planned to stimulate interest, to challenge, to encourage positive, productive thinking.
8. *Overlapping relationships.* Efforts should be made to help students see

these as separate issues because while vandalism and school crime are discipline problems they are abnormal and of such an extreme nature that they can and should be punishable through the regular laws of our society. The matter then is one of degree. In-school discipline is an everyday affair for every teacher and every school. It is an integral part of the teaching–learning process.

the school as a whole and how the various parts (classes and activities) make up the whole in a clear meaningful way.
9. *Accountability.* Students should understand they are accountable for their own behavior; there are rewards for positive behavior and well-understood penalties for undesirable behavior.

These graduate researchers also agreed that reasonable order must prevail in a school for meaningful learning to take place. However, they cautioned that a strict authoritarian process should only take place when emergency measures were needed. They were unanimous in their belief, based upon their review of research, that good discipline is first attained through a teaching–learning process that encouraged active participation and involvement of students as well as the entire school staff.[2]

Meaning of Discipline

There is strong evidence that discipline has become a major school problem and public issue because schools generally deal with it in a piecemeal punitive fashion and consider it essentially an authoritarian process requiring "hands on control." The authors contend discipline should be considered the most meaningful learning experience in the school. In the broadest sense it involves learning to adjust and cope successfully with society. Relating with other people of various ages, intelligence, and background, it becomes the process through which a person discovers not only his/her rights and those of associates but also responsibilities for the proper functioning of the entire group. Through this process respect for the human being is achieved regardless of race, color, sex, creed, intelligence, or age and valuable insights are acquired into the relationship of people and the consequences of positive and negative behavior. Discipline viewed in this sense is the process of helping students to learn to live and work together productively and happily. As such it becomes as important to the teaching–learning process as anything in the school curriculum. It becomes an imperative of learning, one so universal it must be planned as a part of every activity of the school, day or night, in school or out. It warrants the constant cooperative consideration of all school personnel, especially the teachers who are the key agents of the learning process. Discipline is one of the disciplines. It must be learned by every student and made a basic objective of every teacher and one of the broad objectives of the school. When this is done it will no longer be a major problem of our schools.

The authors of *Effective Classroom Management* make an interesting comment about classroom management that expresses our viewpoint about discipline in relation to total school management.[3]

[2] See: National Association of Secondary School Principals *NASSP Bulletin* (February 1979), Vol. 63, No. 424. A large portion of this publication is devoted to discipline.
[3] Carl J. Wallen and LaDonna L. Wallen, *Effective Classroom Management* (Boston: Allyn and Bacon, Inc., 1978), p. 5.

The fundamental reason teachers have problems with classroom management is that they ignore the psychological dynamics of the learning process. Ignoring these dynamics often causes conflicts in the classroom and the failure of students and teachers. Education involves our whole being, not just our intellectual forebrain processes. Merely teaching the three R's cannot be done without taking into account the *whole person*. The intellectual function is influenced by the student's personal traits and emotional responses. The importance of dealing with the whole student is not just a philosophical point of view with which the teacher has an option of agreeing or disagreeing, but rather, is a critical factor in the entire educational process.

The school is a real community—a social system, no matter who runs it or how it operates. Students are placed in this community to live an important portion of their lives. It is possible, when the professional educator places the entire emphasis on the cognitive process of learning subject matter, students may learn that subject but at the same time and the same place learn disruptive and irresponsible behavior from their peers. It is better to realize that in the school learning takes place in every activity and responsible behavior is an important part of that learning process. Thus, each teacher, no matter what he or she teaches must be considered a member of a professional educational team that has accepted collective leadership for developing and maintaining a positive conducive learning climate for all activities of the school, in class and out. Accepting this concept, they would work together as a group to plan activities of both an experiential and cognitive nature that would encourage responsible individual and group behavior. Further, they would plan ways to involve students in the process as an operating part of society and parents and citizens as resources and participants.

The editor of the *NASSP Bulletin* made the following editorial comment to conclude one of the issues devoted to school discipline.[4]

> Those who were in schools as teachers and administrators just 10 or 15 years ago will easily recall that everyone assumed responsibility for keeping the school in order. If we saw trouble we made our presence known—and it did wonders. We were in the corridors, we were in cafeterias, we were all over. Yes, we still had problems of misbehavior, but no where near the proportion we seem to have today.
> What has happened? Many things. So many in fact that we must not be naive and blame any single factor. One thing that did happen was the advent of teacher negotiations. When teachers started negotiating contracts for the first time in the early and mid 1960s, they claimed to be educators, not policemen, and withdrew from making their presence known. And it didn't take students long to recognize this fact.
> What the teachers claimed is right—they are professional educators and have every justification for wanting to be treated as such. What they wanted to avoid was patrol assignment, and to emphasize the point they declined all responsibility for law and order outside their own classrooms.
> The point is that no one associated with the work of schools can abdicate

4 Thomas F. Koener, "Discipline: A Mutual Endeavor," *NASSP Bulletin* (February 1976), p. 124.

this responsibility. Discipline is a required condition for educating and teaching and learning. This means that students (and their parents), teachers, and administrators—the human components of every school—must share in ensuring that discipline pervades the entire school environment.

Model schools have made much of the idea that when students feel good about themselves, they feel good about each other. Thus, they have attempted to develop "school climate" and "tone" to enhance discipline in the school. Their experience is that involvement of the total staff is required to create the positive school climate. It is created through personalized contacts with students, contacts that exemplify courtesy, friendliness, respect, and humanness to show both a model of behavior and a genuine concern for the individual.

Accountability and Punishment

Every person has to be accountable for his/her actions or lack of action. Life in its subtle way begins to make this clear at a relatively early age. Many persons will go to great extremes to avoid accountability but if the rules are clear and reasonable and if when broken the penalty is just and fairly administered, the punishment is accepted in good faith. Weighing the consequences of unacceptable behavior against the rewards of acceptable behavior, each person makes a conscious decision as to a course of action. Each social group, including the school, must determine the behavior necessary for the successful operation of that group. The more numbers of the group involved in determining what the proper behavior is and the penalty for unacceptable behavior the more goodwill there will be in following the rules and accepting the consequences if they break them, for everyone will recognize the rules are for the good of the group and therefore for the good of the individual. In other words, "We have rules and penalties because we care about the group and therefore we care about the individual." However, once the feeling prevails that rules are punitive and not group centered and their enforcement implies the school does not care for the individual then battle lines are drawn. It becomes students against the teachers and administrators. Under this system the more one can get away with unacceptable behavior and the more tolerant one can become of the punishment, the greater the hero he/she can become with his/her immediate peers.

One of the modes of punishment that appears to create special and often irrevocable alienation is suspension from school. This implies rejection and "not caring"; therefore, the common reaction from the student is to fight back and in turn to reject the school. Many incidents of vandalism and violence are performed by students who have been suspended in the past or were under suspension at the time of the incident. The relationship is so noticeable that the Senate Subcommittee to Investigate Juvenile Delinquency stated:

Too often suspensions (in the case of non-dangerous behavior) resulted in an increase of a school's disciplinary problems rather than a decrease.[5]

The courts have also taken a careful look at suspension as a method of punishment. The number of court cases are multiplying where suspension has been challenged as being contrary to the purposes of the school, unreasonable, or violating the constitutional rights of the student. In the only exclusion case to be decided by the U.S. Supreme Court the Court ruled that suspension is a "serious event." The student to be suspended should be given the complete constitutional protection of the "Due Process Clause" and that suspension may not be imposed "by any procedure the school chooses."[6]

Suspension is a negative approach. *First,* it is an overt act of rejection encouraging retaliation. *Second,* when the student misbehaves because of difficulty with schoolwork (which is often the case) upon suspension he/she gets even further behind and often finds it impossible to catch up.

A more positive approach may be some type of in-school restriction where certain privileges are withdrawn and the individual is isolated from the regular group as punishment. At the same time he/she can be given special individual or group counseling to help improve behavior and provided help to keep up and even improve schoolwork during the isolation period.

Many counselors reject problem students because they wish to avoid the impression of counseling being part of punishment to improve discipline. True, counselors should not be the disciplinarians of the school. However, the counselor is avoiding a most important responsibility if he or she does not help the problem student become more disciplined in behavior through proper counseling processes.

Strategies for Improving Discipline

The following is a condensed listing of activities that many model schools have established to improve the orderly functioning of their school. This listing is not intended to be a set of instructions delineating the steps necessary to eliminate discipline problems. Each school and community is unique in that they have their own particular set of conditions that should prompt them to develop their own strategies. However, here are some good ideas that could be adopted or adapted by the administrator within his/her own school system.

1. The school gets together as a community on frequent and regular intervals both in large and small groups to discuss and review the operation of the school as a community of students, teachers, and administrators.
2. A constitution and a bill of rights have been developed and approved

[5] The Senate Subcommittee to Investigate Juvenile Delinquency, op. cit., p. 94.
[6] Gross v. Lopez, 419 U.S. 565, 576 (1975).

for its schools by the board of education that establish a basic legal framework for its operation.

3. There is a clearly written code of rights and responsibilities for the specific school that is available to all students and parents that is frequently confirmed and updated.

4. There are uniform and clear procedures for enforcing the school code with reasonable penalties established for undesirable behavior.

5. Students, parents, teachers, and administrators have worked together to draw up the code and keep it up to date with processes established for continual input.

6. A climate assessment instrument is used frequently to determine the general morale of the school and to determine where special effort needs to be made to realize improvement.

7. The principal and assistants are visible and available throughout the school, actively involved in classroom observation, frequently walking in and out of class and extracurricular activities. They are friendly, open, and supportive with both students and teachers.

8. Special efforts are made to increase the involvement of students in the ongoing activities of the school.

9. Special positive-type reinforcement programs are developed to enhance school spirit, school pride and loyalty, the feeling of belonging, to reinforce positive attitudes, and boost the *esprit de corps*.

10. A special effort has been made to solicit help from parents in creating responsible behavior in the school and to communicate with them relative to efforts of the school to improve behavior.

11. Teachers work with the principal as a unified professional team to moniter and enforce the school code, at the same time involving students in appropriate and meaningful ways.

12. The faculty accepts responsibility, along with the principal, for discipline and order in the entire school enterprise. As teachers they make their presence known as models, and as friendly mentors but, beyond that, as persons of authority and responsibility who are seriously concerned that the business of the school goes on in orderly fashion.

13. Workshops, seminars, and professional inservice efforts have been established for teachers and administrators so that they keep up to date on discipline as a basic part of student learning and the humanizing aspect of the school.

14. Punishment, when necessary, is handled uniformly, fairly, and quickly.

15. Out-of-school suspension is used as a means of discipline only when the student is determined dangerous and incorrigible. In place of the usual suspension a more positive form of punishment is used, such as in-school restriction where the student is isolated and loses privileges but at the same time is given special individual or group counseling to improve behavior and given help to keep up and even improve schoolwork during isolation.

16. Teacher aides are provided in larger schools to serve as building monitors during the school day (at least one male and one female). These aides should be given special inservice training. They may be assigned to the principal's office but should work closely with the teachers and act as teaching guides and mentors rather than as a police patrol.
17. Central administration and the board of education are supportive of school discipline effort and provide the necessary resources to make it effectively operational.
18. The school building and grounds have been studied so that problem areas are identified; the school's class, recess, and activity schedules have been planned so that frustrating situations that spawn discipline problems such as crowding and pushing are eliminated.
19. Custodians are involved with students and teachers as part of a school committee responsible for encouraging and maintaining an environment that elicits pride. In addition, they are provided time and resources so that repairs are made swiftly and graffiti erased immediately.
20. Local police are frequently involved in working positively with students in seminars and assembly sessions on drug abuse, crime prevention, vandalism, and other appropriate topics.
21. Committees of students, teachers, and parents are established singly and collectively to present suggestions to the principal on such topics as school safety, student rights, schedules, and buildings.

For specific theories relative to handling discipline problems in the school, the following will be helpful:

Glasser, William, *Approach to Discipline*, Educator Training Center, 2140 W. Olympic, Los Angeles, Calif., 1979.
Howard, Eugene R., *School Discipline Desk Book*. West Nyack, N.Y.: Parker Publishing Co., 1978.
Tanner, Laurel, *Classroom Discipline to Effective Teaching and Learning*. New York: Holt, Rinehart and Winston, 1978.
Volkman, Christina S., *The Last Straw*. Palo Alto, Calif.: R&E Research Associates, 1978.
Wallen, Carl J. and Wallen, LaDonna L., *Effective Classroom Management*. Boston: Allyn and Bacon, 1978.

Collective Bargaining [7]

A powerful movement was signaled in 1946 as the first teacher strike in the United States occurred in Norwalk, Connecticut. But the "big bang"

[7] The authors are indebted to Gerard Rowe, Associate Professor of Educational Administration at the University of Connecticut who wrote much of this section. Dr. Rowe

took place in 1961 when New York City teachers won collective bargaining rights. Since that time, collective bargaining for teachers has spread throughout the United States. This section will not attempt to incapsulate the wealth of information regarding teacher unionism, but will review some of the effects it has had on the principal.

In 1976, a number of elementary principals were interviewed in an attempt to understand what principals perceived to be their functions and how they felt about their work.[8] One preconceived idea was found lacking: Instead of seeing unionism as impacting upon their work, most principals failed to mention teachers unions when asked, "What forces outside of this office have the greatest impact upon your work?" It was only through eliciting a response that principals responded at all. It could be concluded that the principal *vis à vis* collective bargaining was as a frog, in a pot of cool water, having the temperature raised ever so slightly to its ultimate boiling point for the most part, unaware of what the incremental changes are doing to his or her work.

But this appears to be changing. In 1978, twenty-eight University of Connecticut graduate students went out to collect ethnographic slices of the professional lives of elementary, junior or middle school, and high school principals. In addition to following these principals from the moment they came to school until they left at the end of the day, these researchers went armed with the same questions used by the writer in his earlier work. And this time there was a difference. No longer did most principals (as frog?) need to be prodded for a response. Now they were showing heightened awareness to the impact of collective bargaining.

What has been happening? For one thing, principals have increasingly been pushed out (or they have opted out) of teacher bargaining units. The American Federation of Teachers had never welcomed administrators. The National Education Association once had its "departments" for principals but the close liaison of principals with the NEA was gradually broken with the formation and growing strength of the National Association of Elementary School Principals and National Association of Secondary School Principals. Accompanying these changes was a concomitant state-by-state movement for principals either alone or in concert with other administrators (but not including superintendents) to create their own unions. And this setting apart has stranded the principal, who is no longer the "principal teacher," but in many cases neither is the principal considered part of top management. For proof of this, we need only to look at teacher agree-

---

has been active as a neutral arbitrator since 1969 and also was a school board member for six years.

[8] This research was done by Dr. Rowe as a Visiting Fellow at the Institution for Social and Policy Studies at Yale University, and reported, in part, at the National Convention of National Association of Elementary School Principals at Las Vegas in 1977.

ments or contracts to see that authority that was once the prerogative of principals is often now found in tightly written documents agreed upon by teachers with the board of education. Principals are often not being consulted about the impact these agreements have upon the operations of the school.

The National School Boards Association, in a major study on principals' attitudes, was greatly concerned over the rebellious attitude of principals against the top management of their districts. The general feeling among principals was that "they've let us alone and unsupported while they've signed away everything to the teachers." According to the results of the study, 86 per cent of the responding principals were in favor of state laws that would guarantee their right to bargain directly with school boards and would force boards to bargain in good faith with principals.[9]

A look at selected articles from a prototypic agreement illustrates the range of matters negotiated by the teachers and board in a suburban community: among them, Grievance Procedures; Regulations on Faculty Meetings; Teachers' Salary Schedule; Additional Salary for Special Assignments; Personal and Professional Absences; School Work Year and School Day; Class Size and Pupil–Teacher Ratio; Teacher Facilities. Many of these, of course, drastically limit the amount of discretion left to the principal.

The Changing Role of the Principal

Most principals are hired from within the system where they had been teaching; this has been especially true of, although not limited to, the big cities. These "home grown" principals will need to work especially hard at adapting to the effects of collective bargaining or they may wind up as frustrated persons with lessened effectiveness. For example, take the time-honored forum, the faculty meeting. Often, before unionism, the principal could call nonscheduled meetings in order to discuss an emergency situation in the school, and the teachers were expected to participate. Today in many cases this is no longer possible. The specifics of faculty meetings have been negotiated in most contracts. Many spell out quite specifically how many, how long, and how much notice must be given for faculty meetings. For example, from a big-city contract:

> Faculty meetings shall be limited to a maximum of two per month and shall normally be completed in 45 minutes, but shall not exceed one hour. The faculty meetings shall begin ten minutes after dismissal of the last class of the day . . . Inservice meetings involving the same teachers shall be limited to one (1) per month except that during those months where there are five (5) Mondays or Tuesdays, two (2) Inservice meetings may be held.

As can be seen, very explicit rule-setting by teachers and boards are legitimized in the contract and now principals must conform with no

[9] Mildred Bentsen Galloway, "The Principalship: Death by Ambiguity?" *The Hoosier Schoolmaster,* Fall 1977, pp. 4–6.

apparent room for creativity. And yet, one principal showed some creativity as she considered a contract provision that simply read, "Faculty meetings shall not exceed sixty minutes per month." Her intention was "to call six ten-minute meetings per month" at which she would raise provocative topics during the ten minutes and then "let anyone leave after that if they so desire."

Many principals today are reporting that their job has become more difficult since the rise of teacher unionism. They find that they must become more resourceful in order to juggle schedules of "special teachers," to provide the free time required by the contract, and to make good on the duty-free lunch. On the other hand, teachers report that working conditions have become more effective because the contract limits arbitrary or capricious demands by the principal.

Still other principals are not certain whom to turn to first for advice or support when some emergency occurs, or even for routine changes. The question arises, "Do I check with the central office first, or with the building representative?" This is not an uncommon dilemma. The answer probably is all of the above. The point is that good reasonable working relationships need to be developed for each particular school based upon the people involved, the type of contract, the trust people have in one another, and the operational pattern of central administration.

Union Building Representatives

Some principals, especially from the city school systems, consistently have involved the building representative of the union in discussions of proposed decisions as a way of gaining support for those decisions as well as testing ideas that might not be palatable to the staff. Of special importance was to provide early warning to the building representative if there was a staff member who was perceived as not satisfactory and for whom dismissal might be in order. In effect, if the building representative generally agreed on the ineffectiveness of a particular teacher, preparation for dismissal would continue; and if not, special definitive objective evidence would need to be collected if the principal believed proceedings should continue, anyway.

There is evidence that suggests that in schools with professionally active union-building representatives, teachers feel more involved in the essential decision-making process of the schools. It would seem that the union-building representative can be a key force in shaping the school as a professional organization with dependence on professional standards and a collegial rather than a hierarchial structure. Much depends upon how he/she exercises options. Schools will become more bureaucratized if unions are absolutely rule dependent and militant for militancy's sake. They can become more professional and democratic if they use their increased autonomy to improve professional practice through utilizing theory and research on educational solutions and to make professional diagnoses and prescriptions.[10]

Grievances

It is sometimes difficult to convince board members and the superintendent that a grievance procedure can be a useful process and not something to be feared. When school systems gain experience at various levels with grievance procedures it is generally seen as a mechanism that is good for the health of the school system as well as for its individual members.

A grievance has come to generally mean: (1) a claim based on an event or condition that affects the welfare or conditions of a teacher or group of teachers; or (2) a dispute, arising over the interpretation or application of the provisions of the contract; or (3) an alleged violation of the contract. The purpose of a grievance procedure is to solve problems as close to their origin as possible. Thus, in a high school, for example, most grievances can or should be solved at the departmental level or if that fails by the principal. In the elementary school grievances may often be quickly settled by the union-building representative and the principal. In a large school system, hundreds of grievances are settled rather quietly with little publicity outside of the school system.

The principal obviously plays a key role in any grievance that reaches his or her office—and then continues involvement in those cases that move up the organizational ladder to the superintendent, to the board of education, and/or on to arbitration, if necessary. This takes time, requires new skills, but also has an impact on the everyday decision making and other administrative functions of the principal.

Strikes and Other Sanctions

When teacher unions and boards of education reach an impasse over a new contract (the most common cause for a strike), and mediation and arbitration have failed to resolve that impasse, a strike or other sanctions may result. Prior to 1966 teachers' strikes were infrequent. Only thirty-five were recorded from 1956 to 1966. There were 114 strikes in the 1967–68 school year, and the number of strikes has increased each year up to a record high of 203 teacher strikes in 1975–76. Since that date the number of strikes seems to have leveled off to slightly over 150 per year.[11] Experts have predicted record strike years ahead in the early eighties because of the effects of Proposition 13 and the public's efforts toward tax reform. Virtually all states prohibit teachers unions from striking, but this has had little effect on strike action as a way of bringing things to a head.

[10] See Michael J. Murphy and David Hoover, "Negotiations at the Crossroads: Increased professionalization or Reinforced Democracy," in Anthony M. Cresswell and Michael J. Murphy (Eds.), Education and Collective Bargaining (Berkeley, Calif.: McCutchans, 1976), pp. 476–482.

[11] Richard G. Neal, "The U.S. Teacher Strike Scene, 1978–79," Phi Delta Kappan, December, 1978, p. 327.

The principal often finds him- or herself in a very uncomfortable position when the schoolteachers go on strike. Oftentimes, the school system tries to keep schools open (in part, so that state payments will continue to flow in). The principal usually will have to cross the picket line, and that act alone can create a polarization that may be creating differences that may never be resolved. In addition, more subtle feelings may occur. Experiences related by several principals indicated that their first feelings were that the strike (or other sanctions) were somehow aimed at them personally. Their reasoning went something like this: "If the teachers really respected *me* they wouldn't be doing this". Two examples: Charles reported that in his first year as a city principal he went out to the teachers on the picket line to plead with them, "What are you trying to do *to me?* Come on back into the classrooms." He can laugh at himself several years later, but he perceived the strike as a blow at his chance to make his mark as a new principal. In a suburb, Mary, a veteran principal who regarded her faculty as her family, was convinced that *she* was the target of a sick-out even though the teachers brought her flowers to reassure her that she was not at the heart of the controversy.

In conclusion, Cresswell and Murphy state as follows: [12]

> The outcome of collective bargaining has generally been an increasingly complex body of rules and regulations which explicitly govern teacher behavior, rights and privileges of administrators and teachers, and minimum performance expectations. This codification of organizational authority in a body of rules (written contracts) has several side effects.
>
> 1. Direct authority of administrators and supervisors is reduced.
> 2. Undue emphasis is placed on minimum behavior standards.
> 3. Goal displacements occur, with rules becoming more important as ends than as means. As a consequence the organization may become less adaptive and less responsive to individual students.
> 4. Rules and regulations reduce individual teacher autonomy and the power of professional standards.

There will continue to be adaptions within school systems as collective bargaining becomes a more imbedded feature of our systems. The principal's role will continue to be redefined in subtle ways day-by-day and perhaps in quite profound ones as the years go by.

Sexism [13]

We often unconsciously assume that schools are in the forefront of social reform, that they lead the way in the improvement of our society. Un-

[12] Cresswell, Anthony M., and Murphy, Michael J., *Education and Collective Bargaining*, A University Council for Education Administration and Phi Delta Kappa Publication (Berkeley, Calif.: McCutchan Publishing Corporation, 1976), p. 477.

[13] The authors are indebted to Joan Seliger Sidney, Assistant Professor, University of Connecticut, who assisted with the development of this section.

fortunately there is much evidence to the contrary. Very often schools unconsciously reinforce status quo that may be unfair and actually discriminatory to certain segments of our society. The evidence is mounting that this is true in regard to sexism.

The word "sexism" emerged into general usage within the past decade. It was coined by the women's movement as a parallel term to "racism" to denote discrimination, but in this case, discrimination against the female sex. It has now developed a broader meaning and implies prejudice and discrimination against either gender. School people generally deny discrimination or prejudice of any kind. However, it is impossible to deny that throughout the centuries schools have unconsciously and even arbitrarily stereotyped boys and girls within the system. Research is accumulating that reveals stereotyping can be found in almost every phase of school operation—textbooks, curriculum, athletics and recreation, social activities, and even in school discipline—for the general process of control is predicated on a value system of gentlemanly and ladylike behavior that too often demeans the girl for assertiveness and initiative and praises the boys for the same characteristics.[14] This can be carried to the point of being ridiculous. For instance, a school has been known to be forced to demonstrate that as many girls are spanked as boys.

The women's movement to a large extent should be credited for focusing attention on the disparate standing women have endured in our society, particularly relating to certain occupations, political, economic, and educational opportunities, and even the free social movement within the system. Few would disagree that women should be equals with men. The issue arises when one attempts to spell out the specifics of this equality, for these specifics so often run contrary to long-standing mores, customs, religious beliefs, and value systems. This is clearly illustrated by the heated controversy the Equal Rights Amendment to the U.S. Constitution generated. This was a controversy not just of women against men but of a great mixture of each gender against the other with hundreds of seemingly simple items under contention. This is what the educational leader faces. The school community, being a partial microcosm of our total society, often becomes embroiled in the same type of controversy but sometimes in a more heated fashion because in regard to sexism it isn't just talk but it is here, in this school and this community where the rights must be operationalized. A true educational leader must accept the responsibility to know and understand the rights of people as enunciated by our Constitution and laws. In a low-key unemotional way he/she should explain these rights and then work with the faculty in developing a plan to assure that rights are assured. Unfortunately, as in any controversy this will make some people unhappy.

[14] Pottker, Janice, and Andrew Fishel, Eds., *Sex Bias in the Schools: The Research Evidence* (Cranbury, N.J.: Fairleigh Dickenson University Press, 1977).

Sexism frequently begins with sex-role stereotyping: the assumption that because people share a common gender, they also share common abilities, interests, values, and roles. Not only does sex-stereotyping restrict the achievement of individual potential for both sexes, but it also frustrates those individuals who do not conform to traditional norms. The first step toward equality of education, nonsexist education, requires an in-depth examination of our school. This includes exposing both overt and hidden curricula of sexism that accompany most formal education, sex-stereotyped attitudes, practices, materials, as well as the general school environment.

Title IX

Title IX of the Education Amendments of 1972 has forcibly initiated such an investigation. According to this law:

> No person . . . shall, on the basis of sex, be excluded from participation in, be denied the benefits of, or be subjected to discrimination under any education program or activity receiving federal financial assistance . . . (*Peer* Title IX Regulation Summary, p. 1)

In order to be in compliance with this law, by July 21, 1976, all schools receiving federal assistance were required to have:

1. Completed a detailed self-evaluation.
2. Taken and recorded any steps necessary to eliminate sex discrimination.
3. Adopted and published a grievance procedure to resolve student and employee complaints.
4. Appointed a Title IX coordinator.

Title IX provisions also prohibit discrimination in admission to certain kinds of institutions, in treatment of admitted students, which includes housing, courses or other educational activities, counseling, financial aid, student health and insurance benefits, marital or parental status, and athletics. For employees of covered institutions, the regulation prohibits sex discrimination in all aspects of employment, recruitment, and hiring.

Educators often disregard provisions of Title IX, implying this is another example of federal intervention. Particularly many private schools are inclined to disregard it because they do not receive federal funds and the government's means of enforcing Title IX is to withhold federal funds. A more enlightened consideration of Title IX is that it is a plan for assuring that the constitutional rights of all children and youth are implemented in schools. Although it may not be legally necessary for a private institution to comply specifically with Title IX, it has the moral responsibility of developing a plan of its own that complies with the constitutional rights of human beings in general.

The U.S. Department of Health, Education and Welfare has the responsibility of enforcing Title IX by: (1) investigating school districts and universities not in compliance, and (2) by investigating complaints by individuals or groups.

The federal government reported that as of March, 1977, nearly two thirds of all school districts and colleges receiving federal funds had failed to meet the basic compliance requirements of the Title IX law.

In a recent study to determine how schools about the nation are implementing the Title IX law, Joan Grossman stated: [15]

> Some schools not in compliance indicated they did not receive the requirements from the federal government, that they did not know where to mail the completed information, or that they were not going to comply. Of the schools that did meet the requirements, most seemed to do so in order to meet federal legal requirements rather than to raise consciousness or to benefit children. Many schools complied to avoid losing federal funds, not to eliminate sex discrimination in their districts.
>
> There clearly has been much reluctance to put the Title IX law into effect. The general attitude seems to be, "It'll be ten years before HEW gets to us." Comments such as, "Little has been done," "Movement in this direction has been slow," "It's not a top-priority issue," reveal that little progress has been made.
>
> I discovered that institutional self-evaluations often consist of a simple statement such as, "We don't have any problems in this area." . . . Administrators occasionally described how literature on Title IX had been distributed, workshops held, and staff involved in the self-evaluation. But when teachers in the districts were asked, "What has been happening with Title IX implementation?" they had never heard of Title IX.
>
> Although many school systems had appointed a Title IX official, they made no attempt to help others in the district become aware of the law and its implications. Often someone was appointed as an official because there was no one else available to perform the task. . . . it is the rare school that has put much effort into Title IX implementation. The key factor seems to be the support and leadership of the administration. If the school committee and the top administrators make their commitment clear and let it be known that Title IX is a high-priority issue, then something gets done. The administration sets the tone by mandating change and supporting the efforts of those working for progress.
>
> Why is progress slow? Progress toward Title IX implementation has been slow for several reasons. Many schools, for example, generally resist federally imposed mandates. People do not like to be told what to do by the federal government. Another law also means more paper work and more record-keeping. Some schools wonder if the federal government is serious about monitoring Title IX and enforcing its regulations; they also tend to resist change unless there is a real threat that federal funds will be cut off if they fail to comply.
>
> Another difficulty has been the lack of guidelines and assistance from the federal government. When the Education Amendments of 1972 were passed by Congress, the government planned to minimize its own involvement and leave implementation to the local schools. But the schools wanted direction, materials, workshops, and guidelines. Although schools were supposed to be

[15] Joan Grossman, "A Look at Implementation of Title IX," *The Innovator,* University of Michigan School of Education, Vol. 10, No. 1 (July 1, 1978), pp. 18–19.

in compliance by July, 1976, it was not until the fall of 1976 that the federal government provided training manuals on institutional self-evaluation.

Cost is another factor slowing down progress. No money was appropriated by Congress to aid in Title IX implementation, and school systems wonder where they will get funds to provide, for example, adequate sports programs for both sexes. In physical education alone, more equipment, facilities, and coaches will be necessary to achieve equal opportunity.

Progress has been slowed down because of a difference of opinion as to the role of the school. Is the school supposed to perpetuate society or is it supposed to be an agent of change? Some feel that Title IX encroaches on basic religious tenets. Several church groups (particularly in certain regions of the United States) disapprove of discussions taking place in the school on topics concerned with women; these groups believe the Bible states that God intended for women to remain in the home.

Many schools are presently overwhelmed with problems and issues other than Title IX—integration, for instance. Some use their preoccupation with racial integration as an excuse for not addressing the problem of sex desegregation; others—in Denver, Los Angeles, and Minneapolis, for example—because of their previous work with minority problems and their involvement with integration, feel better able to deal adequately with sexism. Furthermore, sexism is often subtle and difficult to identify. People may not be conscious of their ingrained attitudes, habits, and behaviors or of their inadvertent comments that perpetuate sexism. It is a long road to awareness before change can be accomplished.

Nonsexist Curriculum

Title IX compliance represents only one aspect of eliminating sexism in education. Since this "regulation does not require or abridge the use of particular textbooks or curriculum materials" the principal and staff must systematically examine the materials in use as well as those to be purchased. Consider the following:

1. Are both sexes shown in a wide variety of roles or only in traditional, stereotyped roles?
2. Do the members of both sexes respect each other as equals?
3. Are males and females shown as having a wide range of emotions and responses? Of choices?
4. Are the life-styles depicted realistic? Do they include minority characters favorably delineated in their setting?
5. How many women have been included in the standard texts as compared to men? (Select books that will include representative women in the curriculum.)
6. Are there subtle forms of bias such as white males in power relationships with women in subservient roles, different standards of success, e.g., are women rewarded for their good looks and culinary skills whereas men succeed on the basis of their intelligence and fortitude?
7. Has the use of sexist language been questioned? (Urge publishers to utilize neutral terms in place of male generics, e.g., "human being" or

"person" instead of "man," "human resources" or "workers" for "manpower," and so on.

Staff Inservice

The issue of nonsexist curriculum extends beyond the selection of materials. Inservice education should be utilized in order to help the entire staff function in nondiscriminatory fashion. This includes:

1. Heightening awareness of one's own prejudices and sexist behaviors.
2. Techniques to enable each person to overcome discriminatory behaviors.
3. Training in development of nonsexist materials and in using traditional resources in nonsexist ways.
4. General information concerning nonsexist techniques, resources, research findings, and so on.
5. Encouraging the staff to learn more about the contributions of women to our society.

Consultants can be used advantageously to determine and respond to the specific needs of each school, working closely with the principal, curriculum coordinators, and staff, including custodians, cafeteria workers, bus drivers, and the like. Whenever possible, parents and students should be invited to participate in consciousness-raising and strategy sessions to overcome sexism in their school. The ideal approach consists of the entire educational community working together to provide extensive options for all.

Testing and the Back-to-Basics Controversy

The recent public concern about testing and "back to basics" has provided a spate of negative professional outburst in educational publications, professional organizations, and by the self-styled educational spokesman. The decline in test scores of our students on some of our most well-known and widely used tests (Scholastic Aptitude Tests [SAT], American College Testing Program [ACT], National Assessment of Educational Progress [NAEP]) made national headlines. Couple this with rising delinquency, drug usage, violence, teenage pregnancy, crime, discipline problems, absenteeism, and it is easy to draw an erroneous but pervasive cause-and-effect relationship: for example, the headlines in many daily newspapers, "Test Scores Going Down While Juvenile Crime Goes Up!"

It is truly unfair to blame the schools for a constellation of social factors beyond its immediate control. Knowing this, the first reaction to such headlines is defensiveness. Considering the move a momentary resurgence of conservatism and reaction, many educators are negative about proposed solutions and drag their feet about doing anything specific about improving "basics" or competencies.

Clearly and admittedly, the movement toward basics and competency testing is being pushed by noneducators. To join the movement could create the impression that the schools are indeed at fault; therefore, the developing strategy by many educators is to complicate the issue.

Proliferation of educational jargon in reaction is creating confusion in the minds of the lay person as well as the teacher and administrator who is responsible for the improvement of program. Particularly on competency testing, educational experts are having a field day in conflicting viewpoints. Researchers and psychometricians are disagreeing on "methods of statistical analysis," "limited validity," "questionable reliability," "learner verification," "minimum level of acquisition," criterion reference testing, horizontal and vertical addition. Educational philosophers and humanists are bemoaning "nonhumanistic" trends and emphasis of the "cognitive over the affective," curriculum imbalance, harmful anxiety and social side effects, and "ethnic bias."

The trend toward the basics and accountability, however, has not been nor will it be easily turned. In early 1978 thirty-three states had taken some type of action to mandate the setting of minimum competency standards for elementary and secondary students. All of the remaining states either had legislation pending or legislative or state board studies underway.[16]

Examining the public's attitude toward the public schools as expressed in the Gallup Polls, one discovers there is growing public consensus in favor of requiring high school students to pass a standard examination in order to receive a diploma. This posture by the public is not new and the number advocating it is increasing. A question posed in a 1958 Gallup Poll is the same one as used in the 1976 survey, as follows:

> Should all high school students in the United States be required to pass a standard nationwide examination in order to get a high school diploma?

The findings for the two surveys show:

	National Test for Graduation	
	1958	1976
In favor of such a test	50%	65%
Opposed	39%	31%
No opinion	11%	4%

Sensing a gaining of strength in the "back-to-basics movement" the 1977 Gallup Poll attempted to discover how widely this movement is accepted and to obtain evidence of its popularity. Of the public familiar with the

---

[16] Chris Pipho, "Minimum Competency Testing in 1978: A Look at State Standards," *Phi Delta Kappan*, May 1978, Vol. 59, No. 9, p. 585.

term the question was asked: Do you favor or oppose this back-to-basics movement? All groups in the population expressed overwhelming (83 per cent) approval.

Administrators and teachers must realize that this is not a "flash in the pan" movement that will eventually go away. It is not a subversive trend led by a few political reactionaries who are guising their attempt to lower taxes. It is not something new, an "empty panacea" as implied by many educational writers.[17] Failing to know and understand the history of American education is one of the reasons many educators are losing perspective about competency testing. The real issue is not necessarily testing and basics. Its roots are found deep in our way of life. It is part and parcel of the American tradition of public education. A free public system of education was established at great effort and expense so every boy and girl would have an opportunity to develop into a productive self-reliant citizen. As "people's schools" the public has a legitimate right for assurance that the schools they have established are properly meeting the needs of children and society. To the public the simple tools or needs of children are the basics: reading, writing, and arithmetic. The simple means of determining whether children possess these tools is to test. The public, beginning with the very first public school movement in the seventeenth century, has intended and expected that children would obtain basic skills for learning. They intended and expected that schools would be held accountable for their efforts. From the very beginning of American education, testing as a way of determining acquisition of basics and establishing accountability has been common procedure from grade to grade, from elementary school to high school, from high school to college. More recently we have had State Assessments of Educational Progress and Regents Exams, College Boards, and National Assessment of Educational Progress. It is indeed unfortunate that so many educational leaders are supporting negative positions, remaining impervious to the historical background of our schools. It is this imperviousness that has caused a public counterreaction that has resulted in legislation mandating state achievement tests and pending legislation proposing national achievement testing.

True, there are many more basics and educational imperatives than reading, writing, and arithmetic. True, these basics are very difficult to identify and mean many things to many people. It is true that for a full life each child needs varying physical, emotional, intellectual, and moral enrichments well beyond what we consider basic. It is true testing is only

---

[17] Jim Mecklenburger describes competency testing as "another short and demeaning chapter in American education." Jim Mecklenburger, "Minimum Competency Testing: The Bad Penny Again," *Phi Delta Kappan* (June 1978), p. 697. Chris Pipho stated: "Contradiction and controversy are evident at every turn, but then the minimum competency and testing movement has no parallel in the history of American education." Chris Pipho, "Minimum Competency Testing in 1978: A Look at State Standards," *Phi Delta Kappan,* (May 1978), p. 586.

one of many ways of assessment, that there are many aspects of the cognitive and especially the affective we cannot truly test. It is true that overemphasis on testing can negatively affect the curriculum and create undue pressure on the teacher and especially the child. We also know state and national testing can create excessive bureaucracy and erode local control. However, on the positive side, it is also true a child cannot learn effectively unless in possession of the basic tools of learning and we do not know if he/she possesses these tools unless we test the child. Testing is a useful tool of diagnosis. It is like placing a thermometer under a child's tongue. The results provide a clue to condition; diagnosis and remedial prescription are the next positive steps. As stated in a report by the National Academy of Education ". . . standardized testing in early grades can have a positive influence on student learning by aiding diagnosis of individual student weaknesses and building pressure for school wide improvement of basic skill programs." [18] We also know that requiring reasonable accountability in schools does help improve and maintain academic achievement. For example, "those schools with stable or rising test results in the Scholastic Aptitude Tests (SAT) are characterized by high academic standard." [19]

The problem is to keep the basics and testing in perspective—this is where the efforts of educators should be directed—not in fighting the movement itself for it does represent a public interest and concern in education. The true educational leader will agree there is an important place for basics and testing in the curriculum and then work with the public to help place them in proper perspective. The leader will show the public that formal paper and pencil testing is only one of many processes of assessment, that there are alternative ways to determine students' growth and achievement, assuring the public at the same time that schools stand ready to be accountable for their efforts.

The principal in the individual school can do little one way or another to change the state legislation relative to minimum competency except as he or she operates in professional organizations or exerts leadership through the community sphere of influence. The movement, however, does provide an exceptional opportunity for the principal to develop with teachers professional approaches that interpret and implement the deep-seated viewpoint about accountability of public schools. The discussion could begin by debating the pro and con merits of the following:

1. Every course or subject in the school should have an important measurable impact on both the cognitive and affective learning of a student.
2. Every course or subject should have written objectives that have measureability.

[18] George Neil, "Washington Report," *Phi Delta Kappan* (June 1978), p. 723.
[19] National Association of Secondary School Principals, *Guidelines for Improving SAT Scores* (Reston, Va.: The Association, 1978).

3. Every teacher should accept responsibility for measuring the degree of attainment of objectives by each student.

4. Every teacher should accept responsibility for diagnosing problems students have with achieving objectives and prescribing corrective action.

5. No matter what subject and what grade level, every teacher has a responsibility to help children learn and improve the basic tools of learning especially the commonly accepted 3 R's: reading, writing, and arithmetic.

6. Every course and subject taught in the school should have specific built-in teaching and learning processes that will improve the competency of students in the so-called basics.

7. If the competency tests do not match our curriculum does this mean our curriculum is not or is irrelevant or the tests are inappropriate?

8. Teachers at various levels should develop committees to determine the skills they consider essential for each pupil's success at the next level.

9. How do we square competency testing with equal education opportunity for all? The answer is not more academic selectivity but how do we handle it.

10. An opportunity to learn something predicts a student's achievement score. Does everybody have an equal opportunity to learn reading, writing, and arithmetic and does each level of the school establish processes to build on these skills?

11. How much should parents and community people be involved with what the schools should teach and what is important?

These are fundamentally professional issues relating to the basics and competency testing. They are important professional concerns to be discussed profoundly and with the intent of arriving at some solutions that can be implemented locally.

Actually, when we are talking about basics and minimum competencies we are talking about a basic curriculum for the school that should provide these competencies. Rather than be afraid teachers will teach the test, the curriculum should be such that it will stand the test of its effectiveness in teaching skills necessary for effective citizenship. Of course, we want and expect more than the minimum; we strive for a maximum but the total curriculum must be built on a solid minimum base with more flexible and individualistic maximum competencies growing from this minimum base. The whole issue becomes a very complicated professional problem that the teachers in the school need to solve for their school and their children in the school. Those who teach in the school have a responsibility as professionals to solve the problem. All teachers have a responsibility to identify both the minimum and maximum competencies or outcomes for each course and to be able to defend them to the community. The best advice on testing is to keep the whole thing simple. Develop the basic tests by staff, students, and parents and keep in a dynamic state of revision. Or, select some standardized tests on reading, writing, and math and submit them to strong scrutiny, evaluation, and testing by parents, teachers, and students.

As stated by the Educational Testing Service, "The minimum competency movement is no panacea. But, thoughtfully developed and reasonably applied, a minimal competency program can do much to improve the quality of American education. Given the insight of such a program, a high school diploma would certify that the student possessed the basic skills needed to be a productive adult citizen capable of functioning in a complex society." [20]

Questions Relating to Minimum Competencies

1. What are minimum and maximum competencies?
2. Do basic school skills measure basic life skills (functional literacy, application of basic skills to everyday life problems)?
3. How can we best measure competencies? How many? School product? School performance? Paper and pencil?
4. Shouldn't the effective curriculum stand prepared to be tested on its own merit as regard to competencies?
5. When do we measure competencies?
6. How much do we standardize for the school, state, nation?
7. What do we do with the incompetent?
8. How do we handle the special emphasis on the quantitative that testing may provide in relation to the humanistic?
9. How do we compensate for the special emphasis on the cognitive that testing may provide over the affective?
10. How can we utilize competency testing as a way of improving education without contributing to bureaucracy, excessive centralization, and so on?
11. How can we keep the cost and time of administrative record-keeping and reporting to a minimum?
12. What do we do to help those who can't pass the tests?
13. What processes can we use for early identification and subsequent remediation?
14. What about the child who arrives at the school or the grade level in a disadvantaged state?
15. How can we protect ourselves from being so preoccupied with testing minimums that we lull average or above average into complacency and/or neglect?
16. Competency testing can clearly lead us into more academic selectivity

[20] An ETS Information Report: "Basic Skills Assessment Around the Nation," September 1977, p. 3.

if we are not careful. How do we assure equal education opportunity for all and free access to education without overemphasis on selectivity?

17. What should a student master? What constitutes "functional literacy"? How many competencies are enough?

For Further Thought

Collective Bargaining

1. Negotiable items must include only those matters dealing with salary, fringe benefits, and similar items. Matters directly affecting children and the educational programs should be nonnegotiable. Debate.
2. Professional negotiations might be called the result of inadequate administrative leadership. Discuss.
3. Should principals have their own collective bargaining unit? How would this affect the administrative team concept? What has been the impact in those school districts where principals have had their own collective bargaining unit?
4. Using research and historical data show how teachers' unions and collective bargaining has changed educational administration in the last ten years.

Testing and Back to Basics

1. Many educational writers are asserting the competency testing movement is a new reactionary trend in American education. Make a case for or against the statement: "Beginning with the very first public school movement in the United States the public expected children would obtain basic skills for learning and intended and expected schools would be held accountable for their efforts."
2. Debate: The emphasis on the acquisition of basic skills and on competency testing is undemocratic.
3. If a course or subject does not have known, accepted, and measurable objectives then can we really justify offering it in school?
4. With the recent emphasis on mainstreaming, schools have been struggling with some "policies of exception" for those students who are not intellectually capable of passing minimum competency tests. Is mainstreaming in conflict with competency testing and back to the basics? Discuss.

School Discipline

1. Describe the most serious case of misbehavior you have observed personally. How was it handled by the teacher or principal? What recommendation would you make for dealing with a similar problem?

2. Is student behavior better or worse than it was twenty years ago? Present solid evidence for your answer.

3. The faculty of a school troubled with discipline problems has asserted: "We are not policemen! It is not our job to monitor the halls, lavatories, lunchrooms, and athletic events. We will *not* do it!" Do you agree with them? What could or should you do as principal in this situation?

4. Utilizing French's and Raven's five bases of legitimate power (see Ch. 6) what means should a principal use to work with teachers in improvement of the climate of a school with major discipline problems? Assume the teachers have a strong professional union and a history of effective collective bargaining.

Sexism

1. A school superintendent recently stated: "Sexism often is not a problem until it becomes a problem." Do we often allow injustice to continue until someone fights aggressively for their rights? Has not this happened with many things in our schools? Discuss.

2. It has been asserted that sex stereotyping can be found in every phase of school operation: textbooks, curriculum, social activities, recreation, and even school discipline. Much of this stereotyping affects females negatively, but some also affects males negatively. What is the research evidence in this regard? How do we deal with it?

3. A school principal anxious to correct discrimination against females may become embroiled in situations dealing with strong religious convictions, deep-seated mores, firmly held values. How does one deal with this?

Part IV
Management of Supporting Services

The authors are firm advocates of organizational and operational patterns that relieve the principal of much of the direct responsibility for management detail, thereby forcing his/her major responsibility to be instructional and educational leadership. We realize an executive cannot abdicate responsibility for housekeeping details. Nonetheless, operational and staffing patterns can be established that relieve him/her of much of the daily concern for this detail without sacrificing efficiency or extra cost to the system. Much can be accomplished by the willingness and ability of the principal to properly delegate responsibility. In addition, there needs to be a strong conviction on the part of central administration that this delegation is necessary and appropriate. Thus, central administration will not make the principal feel guilty about delegation nor will they require the principal to attend every meeting in relation to business management activities, to sign every paper, or to personally brief the staff on every new housekeeping development. We believe as a principle the principal's management technique in business matters should be "management by exception"; that is, routine matters would be handled by subordinates and only special and exceptional matters are referred to the principal.

By saying this we do not mean to downgrade the importance of supporting services to school operation. We just do not want the principal to become a housekeeping mechanic! The deployment of supporting services so that they give the instruction staff the necessary resources when needed is an important act of educational leadership and therefore an important portion of the principal's task.

Chapter 17 The School Office: Information and Communications Center

The school office is the communications, information, and production services center for the school. It cuts across organizational channels and community information exchange channels; therefore, its effective functioning is essential to the realization of established educational goals. It is for the school's best interest that the principal strive to develop a strong secretarial and clerical team that is understanding of and dedicated to the purpose of the school.

The public really knows the school through the conduct of its office as much or more than through contact with the teachers. Likewise, faculty members quickly sense attitudes that seem to emanate from the way the school office operates. If supply needs or heavy demands upon the duplication facilities are anticipated and provision is made to reduce the problems that could arise, the principal's credibility is enhanced. If the secretary courteously answers the endless stream of questions and yet conveys the idea of willingness to go the extra step to be helpful, the public is more ready to listen to the message the school has for it. Of course, caution should be raised regarding these means becoming ends.

Roe identified five elements of office management: (1) organization, (2) personnel, (3) facilities, (4) policy and procedures, and (5) control.[1] He cautions that, like chemicals, these elements must be kept in proper balance to be productive rather than harmful. Overemphasis on any of the parts, or omission of any of the parts could lead to serious deficiencies in operation and a lowering of morale. The key is carefully preplanned routines based upon the rational analysis of each separate operation. Office procedures should be so systematic that there is a self-perpetuating repetitive processing with only the exceptions requiring attention of the principal or her/his assistant.

---

[1] Wm. H. Roe, *School Business Management* (New York: McGraw-Hill Book Co., 1961), p. 77.

A Communications Center

The school office receives and sends many communications via mail, telephone, interoffice memoranda, face-to-face contact with parents, teachers, and students, and many other means. It is important that the communications received be accurately understood and conveyed to the intended receiver. The reverse is also true—that the communications sent should be designed to convey the intended messages accurately and effectively.

Occasionally *frequency* of communication is confused with *good* communication. Frequency is not as important as clarity of purpose and clarity of the message. The receiver should have as much information as possible about *why* the communication is directed toward him/her. If he/she knows why the communication has been sent, he/she will more freely accept it and try to understand it accurately.

Communications must also be semantically in tune with the intended receivers. Since the five hundred most-used words in the English language each have approximately twenty-eight separate meanings (a total of about fourteen thousand), the sender must be sensitive to misinterpretation of meaning.

School–Community Communications

The several communities that the school serves make various inputs into the school system and into the individual school. (See Fig. 3.2, Ch. 3.) In turn, they expect certain communications from the school. Report cards, newsletters, presentations at local meetings, announcements of upcoming events, and letters to individuals are communication media from school to community. The quality of these communications conveys as much as the messages they attempt to get across. The principal will wish to see that the office staff and faculty check written communications for accuracy of information, correct grammar and spelling, proper format, and clear duplication when needed.

The school district will have definite policies and procedures regarding the release of information to the public through the various media and through school-produced materials. The principal should become thoroughly familiar with the policies and current practices of the school district regarding communication with the general public and the general plan, if any, for the school's public relations program.

Internal Communications

Internal communications should be routinized, clear, and concise but complete. It is desirable to routinze certain communications so that the faculty and staff can expect to receive a communication at a specific time each day (or on Monday, Wednesday, and Friday, or some other workable arrangement) in a known format so that minimum searching is required for needed information. The order of items presented should be the same each time, e.g., schedule changes, meeting announcements and agendas, professional information, personals, and so on.

Wordiness is not desirable, but the information should be complete enough for proper action to be taken upon the information without need for further clarification.

Mail and Messages

The handling of mail and messages requires precise fail-safe procedures to prevent misplacement, tardiness, or loss. They should be assigned to a specific work station for processing. Routine school mail should be opened, sorted out for priority, and directed to the proper destination with routing slips. Time and date stamps should be used on all incoming mail and messages for future chronological reference. Correspondence that should be directed to the principal's specific attention may be screened and prioritized by the school secretary to include underlining or notation on pertinent information and appending of related correspondences or file documentation.

Information Services [2]

Any organism and any organization is continuously making adjustments to its environment based upon information it receives. Individual human beings receive massive amounts of information at all times; however, much of the information received is ignored or "stored" since it has no relevance to the person's purpose at the time. We are all aware of the effect visual images of food attractively displayed and packaged have upon the prospective buyer's decisions when hungry. Each of us decides upon the basis of information we perceive to be relevant to our purposes at given times.

An organization, through the principal and faculty, makes decisions based upon the information it receives and perceives. They can choose to play a passive role and react to the information that comes its way and interpret that information according to tradition. They can choose to play a pro-active role and seek information and develop meaningful analyses of that information. Information is useless unless it is accurate, in meaningful form, accessible, and relevant to the decisions that need to be made. Much information now being collected in schools does not meet these criteria. Indeed, too much of it meets only the criterion of accuracy. Much of it is kept in the event that it *might* prove useful someday.

Information is not an end in itself in the school setting. It is merely a means to provide a service to the decision-making process. Neither the

[2] John Greenhalgh, *Practitioner's Guide to School Business Management* (Boston: Allyn Bacon, 1978).

information nor the system that generates it is sacred. The information-gathering and analyzing processes must be viewed as modified tools. The process should not determine the way it is used so that only certain classes of decisions can be made because only certain kinds of data are available.

The backbone of the information service should be an up-to-date easily accessible reference shelf. This shelf should include pertinent state department of education bulletins, school board policy guides, administrative regulations, personnel policies, collective bargaining agreements, the budget and related financial documents, operational memos and handbooks, school calendars, data on all other local schools and personnel, local laws and ordinances important to education, and information on governmental and social agencies. Appropriately enough, part of the process of building the expert power we described in the leadership chapter (Ch. 6) is developed through creating the idea that the principal is a quick and authentic source of information on most anything regarding government and education. A good secretary can do much to enhance this idea by serving as a key information source and researcher for the principal's office.

The tendency of the principal to view the school as the center of the information universe with which he/she deals can cause misinterpretation and misuse of the data he/she collects. The objectives of a single school must be considered in a larger setting. A school is one subsystem of many. It is a subsystem of the school district, of the community, of the state, and of the nation. He/she must interpret the information accordingly or he/she will find that his/her decisions are narrowly focused and they may or may not be appropriate to the larger systems. All decisions should take into consideration the total situation, but they will not necessarily be made at the expense of the clients of the school. Rather, it is the educational manager's role to optimize the situation for the clients, while also keeping the objectives of the school in proper perspective with the larger systems' objectives.

Some Prior Questions

There are reasons for some of the bits and pieces of information being collected and stored in schools today, but some of them are weakly based or based only on tradition.[3] As the principal surveys information needs, he/she should ask the prior questions noted by Andrew and Moir: [4]

> What Information Is Needed? . . .
> Why Is the Information Needed? . . .
> How Is the Information to Be Used? . . .
> When Is the Information Needed? . . .
> Who Is to Use the Information? . . .
> Where Should the Information Be Collected or Used? . . .

[3] General Services Administration, *Guide to Record Retention Requirements* (Washington: U.S. Government Printing Office, 1977).

[4] Gary M. Andrew and Ronald E. Moir, *Information-Decision Systems in Education* (Itasca, Ill.: F. E. Peacock Publishers, Inc., 1970), pp. 8–9.

As with almost any facet of educational management, the principle of planning for planning applies. The principal will find it helpful to work out complete answers to questions like those asked above, and is cautioned not to try to develop a complete set of either questions or answers without beginning to involve some people who can generate the information, help to analyze it, and use it.

Mechanical Aids

Most school systems have access to electronic data-processing hardware. Computers are available on a time-share basis, either at the school's central office, or by special arrangements with a bank or industry, and the remote terminal is an integral part of many school operations.

In addition to the large computer, micro-processer based communications and information systems are reshaping office procedures and information systems. Their presence are becoming more evident in the local school office as well as that of the central administration. Each year we see and hear more of telecommunications, small business computers and cheap memories, dictation systems, text editors, photo-composition units, new laser beam technology being used for printing and microfilming, office machine comptrollers, and energy comptrollers. The individual school can profit a great deal by utilizing these aids. The main task of the principal and staff is to determine what is needed and in what form it will be useful, and to show its cost effectiveness.

The time saved by a careful investment of time at the planning stages can be applied toward more direct service to the educational program. As the value of information increases, even the same amount of time spent on the collection and organization of information can yield a much higher return.

The School Secretary

The readers' experiences with the many offices with which they come in contact either by mail, telephone, or in person is enough to remind them of the importance of the secretarial help in an office. The courteous word, the pleasant manner, and the apparent willingness to help can do much for the effectiveness of any office. The conveying of the confidence that everything is under control and that whatever the request may be it will be competently handled is one of the greatest contributions the secretary can make. A national survey that questioned selected exemplary principals on reasons for their success reveals that these principals listed a competent secretary as an important factor contributing to their success.[5]

[5] The National Association of Secondary School Principals, *The Senior High School Principalship: The Effective Principal*, Vol. II (Reston, Va.: The Association, 1978), pp. 31–32.

An Important First Contact

The secretary is often the "voice" of the school to many parents and to personnel of agencies contacting the school. Her/his work represents the school in written form. Accuracy in reports gives the recipients of those reports an impression of the school. The secretary is usually the first person a teacher, student, parent, or any other person meets when contacting the principal. The principal must be sensitive to the "impression" the office makes, and work with the secretary and clerks to develop the best possible contact with teachers, students, and the public both by telephone and in face-to-face situations. A very common cause of poor morale of both teachers and students is the negative way they are treated by the principal's office staff. A secretary should never create the impression she/he is "door guard" or "gate keeper" for access to the principal. However, a tactful receptionist becomes very skillful in carefully questioning the caller to determine if something needs the immediate personal attention of the principal or if some other person can handle the problem.

The principal may want to be contacted on some telephone calls no matter where he/she is, such as calls from the superintendent, the mayor, the school board president. Needless to say, an understanding must be established about certain priority calls and callers. On others, if the principal cannot come to the phone or is not in the office, some assurance should be created that the principal is legitimately unavailable. Nothing implies poor management faster than having a receptionist say, "I don't know where he is," or " I don't know when she will be in." There must be a sincere businesslike response such as "Mr. Jones is in conference" or "Mrs. Smith is at lunch," or "meeting with students" and then a real showing of concern to assist, such as: "She will be back in the office at 2:00. May I give her a message?", "Shall I ask him to call you back?" or "Is there someone else that can help you?"

The principal will wish to review periodically the job functions of the secretary and the clerical staff. Clear, written job descriptions should be developed if they do not already exist. As new tasks are introduced, the total load should be analyzed.[6]

Certain guidelines may be helpful to the principal to avoid creating or reinforcing problems:

1. A clear ordering of priorities for work is important. General priorities can be ordered and the principal can change these as emergencies arise.
2. The services of the office and the responsibilities of the office worker should be made known to the teachers.
3. Office procedures should be periodically reviewed with the total secretarial staff.

[6] David H. Rhone, *Wage and Salary Administration for Classified Staff School Employees* (Chicago: Association of School Business Officials, 1976).

4. Office directives to the professional staff should not go through the secretary.
5. Schoolwide decisions should not be made by the secretary. Plans should be worked out to cover unexpected situations if the principal is not in the school. On other than routine office work, the secretary should have someone to refer to if a new situation occurs.
6. Provide membership for the secretary in a school secretaries' subscription service or, if available, a school secretaries' association.

Inservice Training

It is recognized that the central offices of the school system will probably have a plan for the inservice training of office staff. After becoming familiar with this training program plan, the principal should assess training needs in his/her own office. It is a fact that most principals inherit their office staff, and that the secretaries see principals come and go. Yet, the principal should not assume that all is as it should be in all the operational aspects of the office. A study reported by the Association of School Business Officials [7] indicates that clerical and office personnel are among those on whom the greatest training effort of schools should be expended, and that the training can be effectively conducted at the location of the job assignment. This clearly involves the principal of the building. If there is no systematic plan for this important investment in the human resources of the school, the principal should press for such a plan, and if necessary pilot a demonstration program. The reader may wish to read the ASBO publication we mention for some guidelines regarding inservice training of classified employees.

The most qualified secretaries should be encouraged to seek a formal rating of CPS—for Certified Professional Secretary—that can be achieved by passing a two-day, six-part exam dealing with topics ranging from behavioral science in business to accounting. The tests have been administered since 1951 by the Institute for Certifying Secretaries, a department of the National Secretaries association. CPS review courses are offered in many communities in cooperation with colleges and universities.

More and more schools and companies are recognizing the CPS rating, giving priority in hiring to the more than twelve thousand secretaries who have earned it. There is also an Association of School Secretaries that has done much to develop a strong professional spirit in their members.

Work Simplification

It may be important to assess the work loads and activities of the office workers to determine if their time and energy is being utilized effectively. The complaints about interruptions, materials not available, and so on,

[7] James W. Burns and Donald K. Sorsabal, A Handbook for In-Service Training of Classified Employees (Chicago: Research Corporation of the Association of School Business Officials, 1970).

may be indicators to the principal that steps could be taken not only to alleviate the stated problems but to increase the efficiency of the office staff. Clerks or secretaries may be duplicating tasks, or priorities of one may cause others to be unable to complete their tasks as a result of fragmented assignment of tasks. Littlefield and Rachel[8] cite the U.S. Bureau of the Budget series of questions as having value for the office manager in analyzing task accomplishments:

1. What activities take the most time? Should these take the most time?
2. Is there any misdirected effort? Is any time being spent on unnecessary tasks?
3. Are skills being used properly?
4. Are your employees doing too many unrelated tasks?
5. Are tasks spread too thinly?
6. Is work distributed evenly?

The office staff can keep a simple log of tasks and time spent over a period of one or two weeks. These can be tabulated and summarized by worker, by day or by week, by type of task, and any combination of these. The result should be helpful to the principal in asking questions about the operation of the office.[9]

If the principal has concern about how much work should be expected from a worker performing certain tasks, he/she may wish to discuss the matter with the business manager, business education personnel, or, may wish to refer to various guides that provide work standards.[10]

Office Layout

The principal should give special thought about working with the secretarial and clerical team to analyze the physical characteristics of the office environment, its layout and design. This has become a specialized study by certain management experts. Known as "Ergonomics," it is the behavioral science that studies people's relationships to the physical environment and seeks to adapt the working conditions to suit the task of the worker. For example, sharp-edged desks and tables located in heavily trafficked parts of the office are ergonomically unsound because they present unnecessary hazards.

[8] C. L. Littlefield and Frank Rachel, *Office and Administrative Management*, 2nd ed. (Englewood Cliffs, N.J.: Prentice-Hall, Inc., 1964), p. 72.

[9] Howard, F. Shout, *Start Supervising* (Washington, D.C.: BNA Books, 1977).

[10] As an example of the detail available to a manager who wishes to do a detailed study, the *Guide to Office Clerical Time Standards* (Systems and Procedures Association, 1960) will provide the reader with great detail. One can find that getting up from a chair and starting off takes 0.05 of one minute, or that to address an envelope with 55 characters with a manual typewriter will take .4725 minutes or with an electric typewriter, .4492 minutes.

But beyond this, work stations should be well defined and as self-sufficient as possible. They should be grouped in terms of work flow from station to station. Related tasks should be clustered both physically and according to personnel. Locating the files, equipment, and data concerned with related tasks will save time and energy for the person doing the work. Traffic routes can be established with the careful placing of furniture for efficient channeling of people to discourage undiscriminate sojourns into the work area and to reduce nonproductive conversation. Special consideration should be given to providing a pleasant area for visitors to wait, security spaces for cash handling and confidential records, and isolation for noisy business machines.

The Office Environment

Joseph J. Jones entered the office, approached the China-wall-like counter, and waited for the receptionist to cross the room from her desk. The adding machine and the spirit duplicator seemed to be engaged in a staccato fugue, with the hum from the electric typewriter and copying machine providing a bagpipe-like accompaniment. He told the receptionist that he had come for his 2:30 appointment with the principal, but had to repeat his name since the telephone added its voice to the orchestration. The principal's door was closed.

The receptionist asked him to wait since the principal was engaged in a telephone conversation and she nodded toward two chairs tucked away behind the door and next to the teachers' mail boxes and work pick-up baskets. The teachers certainly seemed to be friendly, but then, close quarters always make for congenial conversation.

An intercom buzzer sounded and within seconds the receptionist appeared from behind the great wall and told him that the principal was free. The principal's door was open and he welcomed Mr. Jones warmly and asked him to make himself comfortable. He closed the door as he followed Mr. Jones into the room, commenting that it was necessary to keep the door closed to keep out the din from all those machines. Mr. Jones was surprised that he was aware of it.

The physical environment is important to persons working in it and to those who visit. The affective impact of the environment can unconsciously, and sometimes consciously, help or hinder the tasks at hand. In the case of Mr. Jones above, noise was affecting his impressions. An average noise level between forty and fifty decibels is reasonable. Johnson and Savage cited a study of noise reduction in offices in which 60 per cent of the respondents cited improved morale; 48 per cent more accuracy in typing and clerical tasks; and 34 per cent noted an increase in the volume of work.[11] Keeping noise at a reasonable level seems to be productive. Sound-absorbent materials and strategically placed objects can at least manage to reduce the noise level. Carpeting and drapes are very helpful. Soft

[11] B. Lewis Keeling and John Neuner, *Administrative Office Management* (Cincinnati, Ohio: South-western, 1978).

material backings at strategic points can reduce noise, e.g., on a file next to a typewriter

A Procedures Manual

Many of the tasks of the school office are routine in procedure, process, time, or all of these. Purchasing procedures, reporting attendance figures, routine maintenance requests, and scores more are tasks for which proper procedures are designated by the central administration. These procedures usually are sent to the buildings in memorandum form, indicating changes, additions, and so on. On occasion the central administration offices will prepare a procedures manual for business-related procedures. If it has not, the principal may wish to inquire about the feasibility of such a manual being developed.

A loose-leaf binder-type manual can be of great help to the secretary and other office workers. It can be divided and subdivided into as many categories as needed for quick reference, e.g., attendance, accounts, purchasing, emergency-medical, communications format, and so on. Copies of forms can be inserted with proper distribution designated. As procedures and forms change, they can easily be replaced. If the principal wishes to add details or categories unique to the building, it can easily be done.

The advantages are obvious: (1) Compiling such a manual often clarifies many procedures; (2) new personnel have a reference from which to work: (3) a procedure is established for keeping information up to date, and (4) it can aid in relieving the principal from having to react to procedural administrivia.

Time Checklist

Certain tasks have to be done regularly, just like paying taxes in the spring. Emergency situations, special reports, illnesses, or numerous other problems may cause regular work to be put off or even forgotten until some terse reminder is made. As part of the office master calendar, or as an insert in a procedures manual, a checklist of routine duties can often avoid missed deadlines and occasional embarrassment. As certain dates are fixed, e.g., budget requests due, program memoranda, and the like, they can be logged in so that all office workers are aware of time demands.

Summary

The school office is vital to the well-being of the organization. It is the communications link, an information bank, and processor of incoming and outgoing contacts. The office personnel, its environment, and its procedures communicate to those who come in contact with it. The communications products of the school office and the information it collects, analyzes, and disseminates do much to enlist internal and external support for the school. Important as it is, however, the office and its operations must remain a means, rather than an end in itself.

For Further Thought

1. How can the school office affect the effectiveness of the teaching–learning environment? Cite specific instances.
2. If you were a newcomer to the community, what words might describe the atmosphere conveyed to you on your first visit to your school's office? What specific changes might be helpful?
3. What is the significance of this statement as far as the school office is concerned?: The executive is always responsible for the work that he/she has delegated to assistants or subordinates.
4. Are there important differences in the principal's personnel administration practices when dealing with teachers as contrasted with clerical and nonprofessional personnel? Be specific.
5. How have significant changes in mechanical aids affected school office management? Give some specific examples.
6. The "Management by Exception" principle has been advocated by the authors as the way to free the principal from spending all of his/her time on management detail rather than instructional and educational matters. We also agree that only a skillful manager can set the proper stage for this type of operation. List some procedures and policies that an outstanding principal should develop before he/she "Manages by Exception."
7. Map out a work flow traffic pattern for the school office utilizing the effective placing of furniture and machines. Have fellow students critically analyze your efforts.

Chapter 18   Business-Related Management of a School

The administration of budget, supplies, maintenance, and similar school-related activities can easily become the main task of the principal. These activities are important in that without their smooth operation the school's efficiency is brought into question. If these areas are operating smoothly, the principal can enjoy the credibility necessary to be effective in other areas. Yet, some principals do find little time to do those other things such as help teachers teach better, work with them with exceptionalities, evaluate programs, develop research, and so on. Kimbrough opined that principals become lunchroom managers by personal choice.[1] The same may be said of any of the business-related functions of the principal. While some may concentrate on an efficiently run accounting system, others may be proud of their ability to keep the supplies inventory at optimum level right to the last sheet of paper used on the last day of school.

It will be important to a principal to concentrate on these areas so that efficient processes are established and responsibilities clearly fixed for implementing the processes. Once done, the supervisory function of the principal should be the extent of his/her involvement. If feedback indicates malfunctions, he/she must initiate steps to correct them. A continuous monitoring plan should be established, but in such a way that a major portion of each day is not spent on these tasks. As stated previously, we believe the principal's management technique in business matters should be "Management by Exception"; that is, routine matters are handled by subordinates and only special and exceptional matters are referred to the principal.

In many instances much groundwork has already been laid in the central administration offices. Utilization of these procedures and information will assist the principal to oversee those management functions for which he/she is held responsible. Cooperative efforts between schools can yield a more

[1] Ralph B. Kimbrough, *Administering Elementary Schools: Concepts and Practices* (New York: The Macmillan Co., 1968), p. 373.

efficient operation of some functions. Technology can provide additional aid in reducing labor in reporting functions and providing continuously up-dated information.

Financial Responsibilities

An overall understanding of school finance and the local tax structure is important because local taxpayers often have questions about the impact of proposed changes on their tax bill. Teachers too occasionally need help in answering these questions.

The principal works with the central administrative offices in the financial matters dealing with budgeting, purchasing, and fund-accounting. He is held accountable for the management of a significant amount of resources provided by the public.[2] To manage efficiently and effectively, the principal must follow a carefully developed financial plan citing projected income and expenditures, which is the budget.

We are not suggesting the principal needs to be a financial expert or accountant. But we do believe a practicing school administrator of today must be knowledgeable about school finance—knowledgeable enough to "keep on top" of the school's budgeting and accounting process, and knowledgeable enough to speak and understand the language and secure enough about it to participate on equal terms with central administration when decisions are being made that depend on the allocation of funds.

In the growth of education, finance has been a shaping and often governing factor. It is no idle statement to say, "Power follows the purse." A person who knows and understands finance has an advantage in dealing with other administrators, business managers, and comptrollers who may be only too willing to allow "money power" to accumulate in their office. The authors have dealt with many superintendants, business managers, and accountants who create the impression that finance is beyond the comprehension of any ordinary human being. They maintain control and power through the ambiguous discussion of funding and when questioned create the impression they are grappling with some mystic, elusive, unexplainable "they." It is not that complicated. An elementary knowledge of accounting and budgeting procedures plus some simple self-study of the state's school finance procedures, the school's classification system for accounting, and the school district's budget over the past five years is all one needs to know about school finance to be an effective principal leader in any school system.

---

[2] Kenneth M. Mathews and Thomas S. Upchurch, "Managing School Fiscal Affairs: Ten Guidelines," *National Association of Secondary School Principals Bulletin*, February, 1978.

Money, or the lack of money, will govern the way an organization is managed and the way it succeeds. An educational activity may be encouraged by increasing its revenue, or it may be discouraged or enfeebled by denying it financial support. Thus, finance can become an instrument of control. From this circumstance, we discover the need of a fundamental identity between school policy and planning and school finance. Left unfettered and uncontrolled finance can, like the slaughterhouse goat, lead the way to destruction. Properly controlled and used as a tool for education, money can serve as the lifeblood for a growing and flourishing school. Thus "budgeting" as the device for translating the educational plan into a financial plan has become a more important administrative process each year. If handled properly, it is an important educational leadership activity and *not* a routine management detail.

The Budget

The budget has been defined in a variety of ways. Bartizal [3] defines it as follows: "A budget is a forecast, in detail, of the results of an officially recognized program of operation based on the highest reasonable expectation of operating efficiency."

Koontz and O'Donnell [4] conceive budgeting as "essentially the formulation of plans for a given period in the future in specific numerical terms. As such, budgets are statements of anticipated results."

Others somewhat facetiously have called budgeting "a method of worrying before you spend, instead of afterward."

The authors would define the *educational budget* as the translation of educational needs into a financial plan that is interpreted to the public in such a way that when formally adopted it expresses the kind of educational program the community is willing to support, financially and morally, for a given period.

Business and industry consider the budget an instrument of control. Making frequent comparisons between budget figures and actual performance enables management to control activities so that all efforts are coordinated toward the achievement of objectives. However, this is a rather restricted view of budgeting. A budget should be basically an instrument of planning and only incidentally one of control. It reflects the organizational pattern by breaking down the elements of a total plan into their sectional and departmental components, allowing costs to be more easily estimated. It then forces a coordination of these elements by re-

[3] J. R. Bartizal, *Budget Principles and Procedures* (Englewood Cliffs, N.J.: Prentice-Hall, Inc., 1942), p. 1.
[4] Harold Koontz and Cyril O'Donnell, *Principles of Management* (New York: McGraw-Hill Book Company, Inc., 1955), p. 435.

assembling costs in a whole so that a comparison may be made with total revenues. This very process requires a kind of orderly planning that otherwise might never take place. Budgeting, then, forces the principal and faculty to plan together on what needs to be done, how it will be done, and by whom.

The benefits of budgeting may be listed as follows:

1. Establishes a plan of action for given periods, long term and short term.
2. Requires an appraisal of past activities in relation to planned activities.
3. Necessitates the development of specific goals and objectives.
4. Necessitates the establishment of work plans to achieve goals and objectives.
5. Provides security for the administration by assuring the financing and approval of a year's course of action.
6. Necessitates foreseeing expenditures and estimating revenues.
7. Requires orderly planning and coordination throughout the organization.
8. Establishes a system of management controls.
9. Provides an orderly process of expansion in both personnel and facilities.
10. Should serve as a public information device.

Budgeting

The budget has been defined in a variety of ways. Bartizal[3] defines it as formed at the local school program level. One of the most difficult tasks the principal faces is making provision for the knowledgeable, positive participation of staff in the budget-making process. The quiet looks exchanged between teachers as the topic of budget is raised speak loudly. The specter of reams of requisitions marching across a desert painted with the business office's REJECT stamp haunts the teacher who spent long, extra hours pouring over catalogs and received only the colored chalk. Worse yet is the nightmare of the teacher who carefully matched program needs to supply and equipment needs and did not receive any hint as to why he/she received only the beakers. For the principal to tolerate such a situation makes faculty participation in budgeting a farce.

Rather than a mechanical management process from the principal's viewpoint the budget process should serve as a way to encourage the teachers and auxiliary staff to plan and work together as a team to implement the goals and objectives of the school. It can be used as a leadership device and also to encourage teachers to take a hard look at the instructional program. The principal is missing an unusual opportunity to develop team work and cooperation if he/she does not operate in this manner.

New budgeting practices focusing on programs may alleviate the principal's task in obtaining faculty support of the budgeting process. The process must intimately involve the principal for this to happen.

Planning, Programming, and Budgeting. To exert educational leadership, the principal must have an impact upon the allocation of resources to the school's programs. The advent of program-budgeting in its various forms provides an important means for the principal to effect progress toward achieving the school's objectives.

Much literature is available concerning Planning Program Budgeting Systems (PPBS). Although the concept has its formal beginnings as far back as 1949, it gained momentum in the mid-1960s through governmental agencies, particularly the Department of Defense. Since that time several states and cities have instituted some form of PPB systems. A number of states have mandated that all school systems convert to such systems. The Association of School Business Officials through its Research Corporation has prepared materials relative to implementing planning programming budgeting and evaluation systems (PPBES), and educational resources management systems (ERMS).

These developments have brought even more pressure upon persons responsible for programs to delineate their objectives in clear, precise terms. These systems are truly systems in that no activity, e.g., budgeting, is considered in isolation. Rather, the total program from objectives to output and its relationships to other programs are considerations.

A number of school districts have found PPBS (Program Budgeting) is too cumbersome and difficult for boards of education and legislatures that normally deal with the traditional incremental-type budgets. Therefore, many schools require program budgets for specific schools and programs and then in their total system-wide budgets convert or provide standard crosswalks from program budget to the traditional budget. The traditional budget then is used by central administration to summarize the costs based on standard classifications while the program budget is a tool to explain costs more specifically and programmatically.

Identifying Programs and Costs. At least two components of PPB and ERM often are overlooked or at least underdeveloped, and yet, these are crucial to the principal as he/she leads the instructional program. These components are identifying alternative programs or methods to achieve the program objectives, and cost–benefit analysis to aid in deciding between program alternatives. The principal is the key to implementing the program budgeting system by identifying programs—those clusters of related educational activities designed to achieve specific objectives and goals. Programs may be organized by grade or level groups, subjects, departments, and so on. It is mandatory that the principal be involved in the process of identifying alternative programs and methods.

While he/she may not be and probably should not be involved in actually manipulating the details of a cost–benefit analysis, the principal should make inputs into the process so that a clear picture of cost trade-offs are given to the analyst. This is one of the chief functions of the principal in the systemwide PPBS development—namely, specifying the real cost areas of the program. As pointed out by Thomas, "Every decision of the administrator, whether or not it involves the expenditure of money, has costs as well as benefits associated with it." [5] As pointed out earlier, time is a resource, and use of someone's time is a cost. The use of a pupil's time is a cost that has been referred to as foregoing other learning. If, as Thomas suggests, the allocation of time is the most important task of the principal [6] the role of the principal is very important to the effective implementation of this budgeting process. It is often overlooked.

Establishing Program Objectives. The principal must work with his total staff, and in some instances the pupils, to establish specific objectives for their school. This includes the total staff—instructional, secretarial, custodial, food services, and so forth. The objectives must be within the framework of the broader goals established by the total system, but in many instances will be unique to the individual school. The process may well include parents and other concerned citizens of the community, particularly those residing within the attendance area.

Each program will have a set of specific objectives. There will be some overlapping because many programs will have an effect upon the accomplishment of overall goals of the school.

There is no doubt that much time is needed to prepare objectives. Commercially prepared materials in subject areas are increasingly including behavioral or performance objectives. This can be a starting point for the faculty. The revision and adaptation to the local situation usually takes much less time than beginning from ground zero. One caution regarding this, however: The principal and faculty should have a clear idea of what broad goals they have prior to selecting a set of preprepared objectives for adaptation.

Specifying program objectives and developing and choosing alternative means to achieve those objectives will aid in identifying materials, supply, and equipment needs as well as human resources. As this process develops, the next important step evolves—establishing priorities.

Establishing Priorities. There are few, if any, school situations with unlimited budget resources; therefore, as the process of relating needs to goals and objectives progresses, certain priorities are established. The principal is the key in this process because he/she must not only aid in relating each component of one school to the others, but keep the inputs from the school's central offices and from the community at large in balance

[5] J. Alan Thomas, *The Productive School: A Systems Analysis Approach to Educational Administration* (New York: John Wiley & Sons, 1971), p. 33.
[6] Ibid., p. 63.

with the "in-house" priority setting. The principal must be aware of the projected budget, including those increases that will cause the most resistance.

Upon completion of the list of needs, it may be advantageous to have faculty and staff assist in establishing priorities. It should be emphasized that suspected budget limits should not dictate what program needs are articulated. Yet, it is important that a high-priority program not suffer at the expense of a lower priority program's demands for some expensive materials or equipment.

Initiating the System.   The machinery for faculty and staff involvement will vary from school to school. While one principal will find the department head structure most efficient and effective, another will find a small committee best. Regardless of the means, it is important to involve the faculty in the budgeting process in a way that is directly related to their functions, thereby positively affecting their responsiveness to the total financial processes of the school.

The processes represented will involve short- and long-range planning and the choosing among alternative plans of action to realize the best utilization of available resources. The Association of School Business Officials indicate the major steps in the process to be: [7]

1. An assessment of the needs.
2. The examination of existing goals and identification of new ones.
3. The establishment of a set of priorities.
4. The tentative determination of major programs.
5. The careful analysis of alternatives.
6. A selection of alternatives.
7. The preparation of a program and final plan.
8. The development of a comprehensive plan for evaluation.

The human element is crucial. The principal has the responsibility to work with the staff regarding every process of the system that directly affects them. Clarifying the process does much to alleviate fears that are commonly found among faculty as a PPB system is developed. There is a particular need to be specific regarding the evaluation procedures. The principal has a dual responsibility of effecting a systemwide evaluation program and of being sure the faculty have proper input into the evaluation process. The partial solution to both these responsibilities lies in the development of objectives. If the objectives are stated properly, the evaluation of the programs are delineated. An objective that has no criterion to determine if it has been reached is really not an objective. The principal

[7] William H. Curtis, *Educational Resources Management System* (Chicago: Research Corp. of the Association of School Business Officials, 1971), p. 30.

should not be willing to accept inappropriate objectives, nor should he/she accept unclear, nonspecific objectives.

The process of planning programs so that they are accountable in relation to the resources used is a vital leadership responsibility of the principal.[8]

Reporting and Accounting for School Funds [9]

A budget is the spending plan for the school or school system. This plan supports the instructional programs of the school. This means that the accounting function is an instructional support system designed to see that the spending is done according to plan. The principal will find some apathy and possibly some negative reactions to the accounting necessities of the school. If the faculty is genuinely involved in the budgeting, these reactions are minimized.

Automated accounting systems are used by most school systems so that the time for reporting and analysis of accounts is minimized. It is important that the processes for receiving and expending monies are understood by all those who are part of the process because the automated systems can be only as accurate as the information provided them. False expectations concerning time saved should not be encouraged at the input point of the system. The initial work of recording information is necessary and takes time, but it is time well spent. The slightest hint of questionable practices with even the smallest fund will bear this out.

Petty Cash Fund. It is common practice to have a small amount of cash on hand to make change, or to purchase small items that might be needed quickly and for which it would be counterproductive to go through the regular requisition procedure.

Petty cash should not be used to thwart or circumvent established purchasing procedures; instead, it is a convenient accommodation to facilitate immediate acquisition of low-cost goods and services in an efficient manner. Only the initial amount of money and the additions or deductions to it are included in this account. The petty cash fund may be in the form of actual cash on hand and may also include a small bank account.

The cash on hand plus the amount in the bank plus all entries in the petty cash book, or on vouchers, should equal the original amount in the fund. The book or voucher should have entries showing:

1. A serialized number of entry or voucher.
2. Person making payment.
3. Amount of money.
4. Account to be charged.

[8] John Greenhalgh, *Practitioner's Guide to School Business Management* (Boston: Allyn and Bacon, Inc., 1978), pp. 15–29.
[9] U.S. Office of Education, *Elementary and Secondary Education Financial Accounting, Handbook* II (Washington: U.S. Government Printing Office, 1973).

5. Purpose of expenditure.

6. Signature of person receiving money.

Other information may be dictated by the central accounting office to insure compatibility with the central accounting system.

Purchases should be kept to a minimum. The cash on hand should also be kept to a minimum and always locked when unattended. Records of receipts and expenditures should be kept separately from the actual cash box or drawer.

Student Activity Funds. Student activity funds deserve special considerations because it is so often neglected and poorly managed, particularly monies derived from extra class fees, athletic contests, plays, concerts, sales, and special programs of all kinds. From these sources even in a small school many thousands of dollars may be handled each year, and in the large school system the money easily reaches six digits and beyond.

There have been many instances in which the question has arisen whether or not this money is really public money and therefore under control of the board. In other instances boards have paid no attention whatsoever to these funds and left their management and supervision to chance.

Some school districts have actually established policies ruling that the money belongs to a student activity or to the athletic department and is therefore beyond the supervision of the board.

The weight of legal opinion is that monies collected as a part of school activities must be considered public money and therefore "the proceeds of these activities belong to the board of school directors and must be accounted for in the same manner that other funds of the school district are accounted for." [10] As far as the courts are concerned, the fund is public in nature if it is produced through public facilities, by public employees as a part of public services for which they are employed.[11] In essence, boards of education in all school districts are required to identify and control the funds of any school-approved and administered student organization or school service agency.

While these funds are without question under the jurisdiction of the board of education they may be handled in a manner slightly different from that in which ordinary school funds are handled. An effort should be made to keep these funds as close as possible to the students, providing learning situations for them, and imparting to them a personal concern and feeling of responsibility for the proper control of money.

The centralized fund accounting system in which a specific person, often known as the activity fund manager, does the accounting of activity funds

[10] In re German Township School Directors, 46 S. and C. 562 (1942).

[11] Petition of Auditors of Hatfield Township School District, 161 Pa. Sup. Ct. 388, 54 A.2d 833 (1947).

for all schools of the district has proven to be a success. The centralization process assures uniformity of procedure and security, and at the same time facilitates reporting, aids in postauditing, and provides uniform data for planning and administrative purposes.

Whether student treasurers are used or faculty or office workers, the general guidelines below will aid in developing a plan for properly handling monies received:

1. All money received should be acknowledged by issuing a type of receipt to the person from whom the money is received. This may be a formal receipt or simply a numbered ticket.
2. A deposit slip should be made out and all money deposited immediately.
3. A receipt should be issued to the person making the deposit.
4. The amount deposited should be recorded in a proper book or ledger under the appropriate fund.
5. The person responsible for the fund should receive a regular (monthly . . .) status report of the fund.

It may be beneficial to have a set of student "books" if a student treasurer is used. The advantage of having dual records to check back on is obvious as well as the instructional advantages for the students.

Sample forms and entries may be found in references such as *Financial Accounting for School Activities*.[12] It would probably be most appropriate to review procedures and forms with the central office business manager.

Expenditures from the activity funds should be handled with at least the following steps:

1. A requisition/purchase order should be initiated by the person in charge of the activity fund.
2. Approval of the central controller in the school (usually the principal or representative) should be obtained.
3. Check issued.
4. Record the expenditure in the proper books or ledgers under the appropriate fund.

Merchandising Activities. Some activities of the school have more than the cash receipts and expenditures to account for. Supplies of various kinds must be inventoried on a regular basis and reconciled with the fund accounting system to give a clear and accurate picture of certain student activities. Concessions at athletic events or school stores are examples.

The principal should make every effort to clarify the process to both students and faculty so that misunderstandings are avoided. The account-

[12] U.S. Office of Education, *Elementary and Secondary Education Financial Accounting Handbook* II, 1973 (Washington, D.C.: U.S. Department of Health, Education and Welfare).

ing procedure can acquire a negative connotation to student activities much as the auditing function can to the principal if either or both parties misunderstand their roles.

Nonstudent Funds.   Tradition has left some school offices with the task of accounting for funds collected and expended by nonstudent groups and organizations such as the P.T.A., booster clubs, and so on. If the principal is in the happy situation of not having such funds, he/she should jealously guard this happiness. Often these nonstudent funds have served to supplement or even maintain certain functions that should have been the responsibility of the community as a whole to support. Continuation of such relationships do not encourage the schools and community to shoulder the responsibility as they should. Rather, it has the opposite effect.

The new principal would be in a most awkward position to try to disavow responsibility for accounting for and handling these nonstudent funds. An educative process is much more productive.

Managing Supplies and Equipment [13]

In the general management process there is a nationally recognized distinction between pieces of equipment and items of supply. Items of supply are like paper, pencils, paper clips, and so on. They are generally inexpensive items that are consumed with use. It is normally more feasible and even less costly to replace supplies with new items rather than set up a system of control, retrieval, and repair. Supplies as expendable items are generally accounted for at the building and departmental level and if they are inventoried it is for the purpose of determining replacements rather than control. Equipment is considered as nonexpendable. That is, its use does not deplete it. Equipment is like desks, chairs, typewriters, and adding machines. It represents an investment of money that makes it feasible and advisable to capitalize the item and control it and if broken after use to repair it rather than replace it. Pieces of equipment are normally integrated into a comprehensive system-wide inventory control process. Supply management as a total process deals with the purchasing, receiving, storing, distribution, and accountability of supplies used in the operation and maintenance of a school. The way this management process is carried out is important; it can create among the public an impression of waste and dishonesty, or of thrift and integrity.

Many improved methods and techniques have been developed in the area of supply management over the past few years. Large city schools are almost compelled by the immensity of their task to maintain a complicated

[13] U.S. Office of Education, *Elementary and Secondary Education Property Accounting,* Handbook III (Washington: U.S. Government Printing Office, 1977).

central warehouse that operates daily. Small schools have begun to look with favor on the centrally administered, decentralized storage method. This plan combines the advantages of both the centralized and decentralized methods of storage. At the same time it provides adequate control by placing definite responsibility on specific people and by establishing a system of records that follow the flow of supplies from the planning and purchasing stage to the expendable stage.

In the end it must be understood that systems are carried out by people. Thus, when developing procedures, administrators must give major consideration to the human element. When complicated reporting and follow-up procedures are required, more may be lost through poor morale and the cost of personnel services than the savings warrant. The real challenge to management is to create in all personnel an appreciation of the proper use of supplies and equipment.

Certain decisions will already have been made concerning the storage and distribution of supplies at the systemwide level. Large school systems will use a centralized warehousing system with an infinite number of variations on the theme. Smaller school systems will probably use some form of centrally administered–decentralized storage supply management. The principal does have the responsibility to know how the system operates, what delivery schedules are available, and so on. He/she also should be alert to any improvements that would be feasible in better supporting the instructional program.

Once the supplies and equipment reach the school, the principal must determine the best way to store, distribute, and account for the supplies and equipment. Equipment must also be maintained.

Acquisition

This aspect of supplies and equipment management is closely tied to the budgeting and purchasing processes of the school. The principal should be familiar with the purchasing procedures of the system and the practices in the school. The idea of "those who share, care" also applies to the purchasing of instructional supplies and equipment. The faculty can easily feel as if they are not part of the purchasing cycle, particularly in giving feedback regarding quality to responsible officials. A sensitive principal can alleviate this problem and at the same time upgrade the quality of the supplies and equipment in the building as related to use and effectiveness. That is, Product A may be judged by certain persons to be superior to Product B, but if the users will use Product B and not use Product A, then B is "better" if it enhances the instructional program.

Certain details of the acquisition process may be incumbent upon the individual school if the supplies and equipment are delivered to the school directly by or from the vendor. In this case, the principal should see that the following steps are included in the receiving of shipments:

1. Check for damage to the outside carton or crates that may have resulted from shipping.
2. Note any damage on the bill of lading before signing for the shipment.
3. Check the contents to confirm that they are the same and in the same amount as those that were ordered and billed.
4. Notify the central office of the shipment and that it should be paid for if all is in order. The process for doing this varies from system to system, but usually consists of forwarding a copy of the vendor's invoice and a local form.
5. Process the shipment for storage and distribution. In the case of textbooks or equipment, this usually means stamping or stenciling with the school name and assigning a coded, serialized number to each item. In the case of expensive equipment, this coded number can be etched on the equipment at various points and the number and equipment description registered with local or state police to aid in recovery if stolen.
6. Record the acquisition of supplies or equipment in the appropriate inventory books or card files. A perpetual inventory system should be maintained so that at any point in time the amount and location of supplies, materials, and equipment can be determined. A periodic check of this inventory should be made. Checks may be necessary for selected supply items each month, others toward the end of each semester. At least once per year all items of supply and equipment should be inventoried.

Storage

Storage space seems to be a perpetual problem. It may be necessary to send nearly all supplies directly to the rooms in which they will be used. There are obvious disadvantages to this, including the fact that few rooms have adequate storage space. In addition, the possibility of the mismanagement of the supplies is much greater. The little bit of "pack rat" or "squirrel" in each of us has an opportunity to develop into a full-blown hoarder. It is desirable to make some provision for central storage space. The principal must then decide whether to have "open" storage or "closed" storage.

Open storage has at least the following advantages:

1. Standard supplies are available on very short notice.
2. It reduces the need to hoard private caches of supplies, thus perpetual inventory figures are more real.
3. It reduces office paperwork and personnel time.

Disadvantages of the open storage include that of a questionable inventory as a result of haste; and added time to the teachers' already busy day. Occasionally it is tempting to send pupils to gather supplies and deliver them.

The closed storage arrangement solves nearly all the foregoing disadvan-

FIGURE 18.1. Supplies requisition—Someday School.

Supplies Requisition Someday School		
Teacher		Date
Quantity	Unit	Item
		Newsprint, 9 X 12
		Newsprint, 18 X 24
	Ream	Newsprint, lined 9 X 12
	Doz	Pencils, #2
	Roll	Cello tape
	Box	Staples

tages. It also ties the diminishing levels of supplies more closely to those involved in the acquisition function. The closed storage can actually save the teachers' time. A simple checklist of available supplies can be mimeographed and distributed to the faculty. (See Fig. 18.1.) A distribution schedule can be set up utilizing custodial or in some instances student personnel so that the teachers know that supplies requisitioned by a particular time will be delivered after a specified time interval, e.g., twenty-four hours, one half day.

Inventories

A perpetual inventory system is recommended. A simple "balance sheet" or card for each item can provide an instant status report of frequently used supplies. A periodic check of the balances will provide information for requisitioning supplies, and if plotted over the year will give the office a means for anticipating the needs for next year.

The principal will be evaluating the administrative processes of the office, and the management of supplies and equipment is no exception. Stoops and Johnson [14] provide a checklist that might be adapted to the local situation to aid the principal in evaluation:

    1. Educational equipment, materials, and supplies are directly related to educational objectives.   yes_____ no_____

[14] Emery Stoops and Russell E. Johnson, *Elementary School Administration* (New York: McGraw-Hill Book Co., 1967), pp. 207–208.

2. The budget provides adequate educational equipment, materials, and supplies to carry out educational objectives.   yes_____ no_____

3. Various personnel are delegated the responsibility for supervising the equipment, materials, and supplies.   yes_____ no_____

4. Record keeping is efficient, complete, and accurate.   yes_____ no_____

5. The selection of educational equipment, materials, and supplies is accomplished by cooperative participation of the school staff.   yes_____ no_____

6. A *Standard Supply Catalog* is used as a basis for requisitioning.   yes_____ no_____

7. Provision is made for emergency and special requisitioning of supplies.   yes_____ no_____

8. The school is equipped according to standard allotments based on enrollment or rooms.   yes_____ no_____

9. Standards for requisitioning are established.   yes_____ no_____

10. Provision is made for the facilitation of placing buy-out orders.   yes_____ no_____

11. Provision is made for prompt delivery of supplies.   yes_____ no_____

12. Adequate storage facilities are provided.   yes_____ no_____

13. Policies are established for the distribution of equipment, supplies, and materials.   yes_____ no_____

14. Equipment, materials, and supplies are readily available to all staff members.   yes_____ no_____

15. An open stockroom is used with proper controls.   yes_____ no_____

16. Provision is made for assisting new teachers with supply management.   yes_____ no_____

17. Equipment, materials, and supplies are efficiently and economically used.   yes_____ no_____

18. Teachers receive instruction in the use of equipment, materials, and supplies.   yes_____ no_____

19. An adequate system is used for inventorying all equipment, materials, and supplies.   yes_____ no_____

20. All equipment is kept in usable condition at all times.   yes_____ no_____

21. Equipment, materials, and supplies are available to meet the needs of *all* pupils regardless of their ability.   yes_____ no_____

22. The school staff and pupils are educated concerning their responsibility for conserving and using wisely all supplies and equipment.   yes_____ no_____

Like most management functions, supply and equipment management can easily outweigh its relative worth if the principal does not guard against such a situation occurring. If he/she can enlist the aid of each staff member in properly evaluating and using supplies and equipment, a good portion of the task is done.

For Further Thought

1. How can budget building become a dynamic educational leadership process? How can it become a deadening blanket to educational improvement? Does either necessarily cost any more?
2. What are some important differences in business management of a school and business management in industry? What are some important similarities?
3. What is the difference between bookkeeping, accounting, and accountability?
4. Do you agree with the following statement: All activity funds regardless of source should revert to the general activity fund at the close of the fiscal year and be rebudgeted. Debate.
5. Should student organizations be encouraged to make money? Discuss pro and con.
6. Distinguish between "Zero based budget" and "Incremental budget" and "P.P.B.S."
7. Within the past few years there has been a number of reactions against "P.P.B.S." Some states and school districts that formerly required it have now changed. How do you account for this reaction? Be specific.
8. Devise a plan so that administration of the activity fund can be a learning and responsibility experience for students and still be properly supervised by the board of education.

Chapter 19   Facilities Management

The principal has a key role in the planning and operation of the school facility. The school facility itself is a communications medium. Its appearance, design, and even the freedom in its use communicates much to pupils and staff. The community receives inputs from the appearance as well as the uses of the building and grounds and uses the same as its own communications medium to visitors and neighboring communities. The principal's tasks of program development, staff development, and community relations adapt to and adapt the building to become a useful tool for people.

Creative Use of Existing Facilities

The principal will receive many inputs regarding the effectiveness of the building from faculty, students, and maintenance staff. If the building is frequently used for community groups, they too will have suggestions. These inputs are accompanied by expectations that the principal will do something about them, if no more than to route them to the decision-making levels at which changes can be effected. To limit "evaluation" to such input places the principal in a reactive role. Rather, an evaluation program should be planned and the other inputs used to supplement it.

Facilities Evaluation

In larger school districts there is often a continuous evaluation of existing facilities conducted by a facilities planner or by a unit of the business administrator's office. Ordinarily, these evaluations are concerned with the safety and maintenance of the building and grounds, and with the pupil capacities of the facilities. Questions to be answered would include at least the following:

1. Are minimal health standards physically provided for first aid care, food service areas, restrooms, showers, lockers, heating, air circulation, and construction materials?
2. Are safety standards observed for the above areas as well as within all shops, gymnasia, outdoor areas, and disaster shelter areas?
3. Are the lighting, thermal, and sonic levels healthful and comfortable?
4. Is the building maintained so that health and safety standards are met and so that the building and grounds are pleasant?

The primary focus of the facility evaluation will be upon the facility's educational adequacy. Specific evaluation questions must be set in the context of the overall mission of the school meeting the needs of the community and society at large. The answers to the questions need to be framed so that they fit into the system-wide planning process and policy development. Examples of some of the questions are noted below.

1. Are the rooms or spaces available adequate for the grouping and instructional patterns throughout the instructional day?
2. Are there nonfunctional areas either within the building or on the grounds? The principal may wish to be alert to dysfunctional areas such as recessed entrance ways, stairwells, and the like that might encourage vandalism.
3. Does the design provide for flexibility as new patterns or instructional modes are utilized?
4. Are space relationships such that student and faculty time can be efficiently used?
5. Do instructional activities in one area negatively affect instruction in another area?
6. Are equipment and spaces on appropriate scale for the users?
7. Are there adequate and secure storage areas close to use areas?
8. Are electrical and plumbing services available where needed?

As mentioned previously in the discussion regarding the evaluation of a new facility, the principal will be focusing on the relationship between the building and the educational programs that building is to serve. Once the process of establishing the priorities is completed with the staff and the staff to be involved in the evaluation understands the process as it applies to them, the mechanics of the evaluation, i.e., completing the forms or surveys can be dispensed with efficiently.

The communication of the results of the evaluation should follow a previously agreed-upon form and distribution schedule. As with the evaluation of a new facility, misinterpretation of the results can offset the positive gains of a careful evaluation.

Look for Alternative Uses

Most facilities are not overly endowed with storage spaces, free space, or underutilized spaces. Yet, possibilities for additional uses do exist in most buildings. Corridors present opportunities for displaying student work. Simple wooden strips can provide almost limitless tack board space. If regulations discourage the use of wood, screens of fireproof, porous tile can serve the same purpose plus add an interesting dimension to often dimensionally drab hallways. Local fire and safety regulations must be checked before changes are made.

The site can be used exclusively for recess, noontime activities, and structured physical education classes, or it can become part of nearly every class offered in the school. Science, art, history, literature, and mathematics can each become very involved in the miniature environment of a school site. Using the site as a springboard to related activities provides almost unlimited possibilities. For example, a group exploring measuring to determine area could become quickly involved in the history of surveying, the practicalities of boundaries, deeds, municipal government, and so on.

Community Uses

The use of the building by community groups is, of course, controlled by board of education policy and administrative procedures. If procedures are not clear, the principal should make every effort to clarify them and improve them where needed. The following may serve as a checklist for the principal, or preferably the services coordinator, faced with requests from community groups and as attempts are made to involve the community more through extending the use of the available facilities:

1. What written policies are available regarding the use of the school buildings?
2. Who gives final approval? What routing is specified?
3. What steps are necessary to initiate requests? What forms?
4. How are changes determined?
5. What arrangements must be made for custodial services?
6. What community services should be notified, e.g., police, security patrol, and so on? What are the appropriate procedures for this?
7. How much time should be allowed for each step and for the total request-approval process?
8. What measures should be taken with the faculty regarding the use of the building by community groups?
9. If the buildings can be scheduled by someone other than the principal, services coordinator or administrative assistant, what safeguards exist to avoid scheduling conflicts?

Given the increasing interest in continuing education, developing new skills in wiser use of time and resources and increased utilization of the school building by the community makes good economic and public relations sense. The principal's sensitivity to the interests and needs of the people surrounding the building can lead to cooperative efforts of the continuing education, recreation, and social agencies in utilizing the building more fully. While an awareness of private enterprises is essential, the creative use of the buildings in a school system might bring opportunities to people who could not otherwise have them.

Relationships and Responsibilities Regarding Custodial Staff

An important part of the organization problem is the relationship of the school principal to the custodians in the building, the director of the school plant, and/or the supervisor of custodians. Invariably, one of the contributing factors in any troubled area is a lack of a clearcut understanding of the administrative relationships of these three positions.

There need be no mystery or no man's land in this area of school operation. The relationships can be easily understood and spelled out, but mutual understanding, respect, and cooperation will still be necessary.

The principal may find him- or herself in a traditional situation in which he/she is responsible for all activities and functions carried on in the building to which he/she is assigned. Strictly interpreted, this would give the principal immediate direction and supervision over all custodial employees in the building. The question then arises: Why should someone such as the principal, who knows little or nothing about custodial work, direct it? On the other hand, if the community and the central administration hold the principal primarily or exclusively responsible for educational leadership, an assistant such as a services coordinator will be primarily responsible for seeing that the maintenance functions for the building are done satisfactorily.

Regardless of the arrangement, administrative personnel working in a school building constitute a unified administrative team established to facilitate the instructional process carried out in this school. Although they are performing many different jobs, they are all working toward one end, the education of the child.

A supervisor for custodial services, operating within this framework, may be given responsibility for and authority over the operational functions throughout the district—except direct administration of the custodian in a building. Thus, by developing schedules, the supervisor can determine what work should be done and can establish standards of how it could be done; by providing supplies and equipment, can furnish the wherewithal to do the work; by inspecting and reporting through appropriate channels, can even see that it is done the right way. In the traditional situation the principal could still be considered the immediate administrator; otherwise services coordinator or a centrally assigned supervisor would perform this function for the specific building. Further clarification of relationships may be made by spelling out some of the duties of the supervisor of the school plant operation.[1]

The principal's service coordinator's, or central office person's responsibility for the custodial services in the building includes that he/she:

1. Administratively and managerially is responsible for the custodial personnel in the building.
2. Determines in cooperation with the supervisor the personnel needed on long-term and emergency bases.
3. Confers with the custodian on work load and work schedule.
4. Checks and inspects the building, compares schedules with accomplishments, makes suggestions for improvements.
5. Directs that emergency deviation from schedules be made and out-of-routine chores be accomplished.
6. Interviews and approves custodians to be assigned to the building.
7. Recommends disciplinary action and correction.
8. Evaluates the custodian's work in line with the latter's contributions to the total objectives of the school. (This function would, in most instances, be the responsibility of the principal.)

The principal may wish to explore with central administration the possibilities of contracting for certain custodial services. Not only are there the advantages of not providing fringe benefits, hiring–firing problems, and training programs for special needs, but it often is easier to enforce performance standards.

With acceptance of the responsibility of administrator, the principal or coordinator becomes responsible for the custodian's welfare and also for general performance on the job. The custodian cannot be left to him- or herself, and the work cannot be considered beneath the dignity of the principal's concern. Above all the custodian must be accepted as part of the team assembled to render an important service to education.

Energy Conservation Considered

All slogans aside, schools simply can no longer afford to ignore energy conservation. Given tax limitations, it is probably unlikely that additional

---

[1] For additional detail regarding job expectations, supervisory responsibilities, or formulae for determining personnel needs, see Basil Castaldi, *Educational Facilities: Planning, Remodeling and Management* (Boston: Allyn and Bacon, 1977); or James Gland and Carl Wildey, *Custodial Management Practices in the Public Schools* (Chicago: The Association of School Business Officials, 1975).

revenues will be generated for supporting energy-wasting practices and facilities; therefore, the dollars will come out of some other budget line. S. Hansen of the American Association of School Administrators estimated that nearly one-half billion educational dollars can be saved by conservation efforts.[2] One report indicates that adding roof and window insulation, a night thermostat setback, and replacing incandescent lighting with flourescent lighting resulted in a fuel saving of 33 per cent and about 30 per cent in electricity use.[3] Some initial energy audits have shown schools how to reduce energy costs by as much as 50 per cent. Without doubt, many buildings have been "overbuilt" in the areas of heating systems, ventilation, lighting, and the like. It is possible that with creative scheduling, it might not be necessary to have all the building at the same temperature at the same time, or ventilated the same. It may be that annual school calendars may need to be built with "super cold" days or "super hot" days in mind as well as "snow" days. Eberhard (A.I.A.) suggests that "we seem a bit like the fat person who is looking for a pill to lose weight, without ever thinking that one could get along fine by just eating a bit less."[4]

The principal is not only involved in saving dollars, but has an opportunity to exercise some real leadership with students and the community resulting in benefits for all.

Barrier-free Design

If schools are to provide opportunities for all to achieve in the least restrictive environment possible for the individual, administrators must develop a sensitivity to the facility's barriers to the physically disabled. Nugent notes at least five groups that must be considered: "manual wheelchair users, powered wheelchair users, ambulatory handicapped, the blind, and the deaf."[5]

Too often the physical aspects of initial access and movement are all that are considered. That is, are there ramps available, or are the doors wide enough? While these things are essential, the principal should be assisting the total school in viewing barrier-freeness more broadly. For instance, once inside the classroom or general instructional space, is the student limited in access to certain types of instruction? Are the materials in a personalized learning center accessible? Can the student go to and use the library?

[2] The School Administrator, Arlington, Va.: AASA, Vol. 35, No. 8, Sept., 1978, p. 15. See also The Economy of Energy Conservation in Educational Facilities (New York: Educational Facilities Laboratories, 1978), for specific recommendations regarding economies in practice and in instruction.
[3] Education U.S.A., Vol. 21, No. 21 (January, 1979), p. 164.
[4] Education U.S.A., Vol. 21, No. 9 (October 30, 1978), p. 72.
[5] Tim Nugent, Education, U.S.A., Vol. 20, No. 33 (April, 1978), p. 253.

Would it be possible that the school might be minimally adequate for the handicapped student, but would practically preclude a handicapped adult from working in the building, or effectively deter a handicapped parent from visiting the school? If the school is used by adults for continuing education, cultural, and/or recreation activities, are only able-bodied persons privileged to participate?

The student or teacher with the seemingly inevitable broken leg, sprained ankle, or other accident-related temporary disability will benefit from the barrier-free building and site. But there are other emergency situations to be considered. If rapid evacuation of the building is necessary or quick movement to shelter areas, not only is barrier-freeness essential, but a carefully designed, well-rehearsed plan for the movement of disabled students and staff is critical.

There are many frustrations and even dangers inherent in the disabled trying to use many of the facilities the nondisabled use almost effortlessly.

Meanwhile, reader, settle into a wheelchair for a short trip. Now try to get a drink at the usual water fountain found in schools.

Little things mean much. Examples not occurring to the nondisabled might include the height of fire alarms, height of telephones, the problem of a grill-like covering in a floor or walkway, or the width of doors. The reader is referred to the available sources footnoted below for further detail.[6, 7]

Remodeling or Modernizing

Most buildings will be approaching remodeling or modernization between thirty and fifty years old for several reasons, not the least of which is the cost of maintenance, which has begun to catch the attention of whoever is watching the expenditures ledger. Several formulae are available to determine the wisdom of remodeling or modernizing. Castaldi discusses these and then suggests seven questions, the answers to which must be "yes" or serious questions could be raised about the expenditure of funds for modernization.[8]

1. Is the school building under consideration needed in its present location for at least 75 per cent of its remaining useful life after modernization?

[6] The following were noted in the April, 1978 issue of *Education, U.S.A.*, noted before: *Resource Guide to Literature on Barrier-Free Environments* (ATBCB, HEW, 330 Independence Ave. SW, Washington, D.C. 20201, 223pp., no charge); *Accessibility Modifications* (North Carolina Dept. of Insurance, Engineering Division, PO Box 26387, Raleigh, N.C. 27611, 63pp., $2 prepaid); and *Places and Spaces* (Council for Exceptional Children, 1920 Association Dr., Reston, Va. 22091, 56pp.; $3.50 prepaid).

[7] Department of Housing and Urban Development, *Access to the Environment*, Volumes 1–3 (Washington, D.C.: H.U.D., 1976).

[8] Castaldi, op. cit., pp. 336–339.

2. Is it impractical to distribute the pupil load of the school considered for modernization among nearly adequate schools?
3. Does the structure lend itself to improvement, alteration, remodeling, and expansion?
4. Does the modernized building fit into a well-conceived long-range plan?
5. Can the site of the school considered for modernization be expanded to meet minimum standards for the ultimate enrollment envisioned on the site?
6. In accordance with either the Castaldi Generalized Formula or the Boles Formula, is the annual cost of capital outlay for modernization less than it would be for a replacement building?
7. Has a blue-ribbon committee concluded that educational obsolescence of a given building can be substantially eliminated through the process of modernization?

It is obvious that the principal plays a key role in either bringing to the attention of the central administration or planning with them the solutions to providing facilities that really facilitate educational programs. It is also obvious that *need* must be stated in terms of programmatic documentation rather *than in a series* of inconvenience complaints.

Planning a New Facility

Planning a new facility affords almost unlimited opportunities for the principal to show leadership ability. The planning process should not be considered a chore or an added burden. Few situations provide greater chances for in-depth involvement with faculty and parents focusing on issues so central to what education is all about. The planning of a facility, or a major renovation of a facility, demands the clarification of the goals and objectives of a school and the identification of the means whereby those objectives are to be reached.

All parts of the education community should be interacting with each other on a common problem. The board of education, the community at large, the central administration, the building administrator, teachers, parents, pupils, and university specialists should be involved. Indeed, it is the duty of the principal to see that he/she and the staff are involved. Although complete development of the planning process is not within the scope of this chapter, the principal should be conversant with it and ever ready to influence it. Therefore, a brief description of the process follows.

The Planning Process

Planning a building does not begin with the idea that a new building is needed. The professional staff of the school system must consider continuous planning an integral responsibility of the school itself. Planning must be planned for. There are, then, two phases to planning a facility: (1) systemwide, long-range, continuous planning and evaluation, and (2) the specific planning for a specific facility.

Long-range Planning

The principal and staff need to be part of long-range planning as much as part of planning for a specific facility with which they are to be working. The principal would be involved in:

1. Continuous appraisal of existing facilities in regard to educational adequacy.
2. Continuous appraisal of population shifts in the attendance area and the enrollment implications of those shifts.
3. Awareness of new housing planned within the attendance area boundaries.
4. Awareness of changes in land usage within the attendance area boundaries.
5. Maintenance of meaningful communications with the attendance area citizens.

Much has been written about the long-range planning for school facilities. The selected readings at the end of this book will be of help to the principal who wishes to pursue the matter in depth.

Planning a Specific Facility

The principal is involved in at least five planning steps, namely, educational planning; schematic design; equipping; orienting staff, students, and communty; and continuous evaluation.

Educational Planning. The expression of the planned educational program for a specific facility should be written in the form of educational specifications.

> Educational specifications or program requirements are the means by which the educator describes the educational activities and spaces which need to be incorporated in a proposed new or renovated facility. They are written statements that serve as a vehicle of communication between the educator.

Contrary to popular belief, the architect does not and should not develop the educational specifications. This is the responsibility of the professional staff of the school. The educator, with knowledge of environmental factors important to teachers and learning, and knowledge of those human inputs important to the total process, is the person who must develop the educational specifications. The principal must insist upon being involved and that teachers are also involved. In discussing the planning of a building, Drake and Sheathelm suggested that "the insistence of the profession upon meaningful, in-depth involvement . . . is a step toward the maturity of the profession" [9] Not to be involved is to be remiss.

Yet, the principal must be alert to certain pitfalls of being involved and in involving the faculty. Where teachers are asked to assist in the preparation of educational specifications, they are too often left to work completely on their own on the requirements for grades or subjects of their own particular interest. They dream great dreams, develop exciting ideas, and then when they submit their report it is tossed out as unrealistic. This is both disheartening and unfair. Prior to their involvement the principal must see that the faculty are properly oriented to their tasks. This may be as simple as checking to see that the person responsible for the overall planning has made provision for this. If this is left to the principal, it might be helpful to prepare the faculty somewhat as follows.

1. Provide information regarding the overall charge to the building planners.
2. Provide information regarding the procedures for review and approval to minimize misunderstandings.
3. State the realistic limitations in terms of time, space, and financial considerations.
4. Provide helpful readings to stimulate ideas and to make their thinking more precise.[10]

Contents of Educational Specifications. The Council for Educational Facility Planners stated what must not be excluded from the educational specifications:

> they must, first of all, describe the learning activities that will occur. In addition, they must describe, thoroughly and concisely, the number, grouping, and nature of the people involved; the spatial relations of the facilities and site; the interrelationships of instructional programs with each other and with non-instructional activities; the major items of furniture and equipment to be used; and any special environmental provisions that would improve conditions for the learning situation as well as staff efficiency.[11]

The goals and objectives of the school are not static, and will not remain the same tomorrow as they are today. There is an increasing rate of change to the point where our society has been described as being turbulent. Therefore, the planning group is being asked to plan a structure that will be with the community for the next forty, fifty, or even seventy or more years. What will be the goals, objectives, and means of reaching those

[9] T. L. Drake and H. H. Sheathelm, "Plan Now for 2000 A.D.," *The Teachers Voice,* 47, No. 10 (February 2, 1970), p. 2.

[10] For some suggestions regarding readings see the selected readings at the end of the book. In addition, there are several other organizations that publish stimulating materials, such as the American Association of School Administrators, The Educational Facilities Laboratory (New York), and several leading architectural firms.

[11] Council of Educational Facility Planners, *Guide for Planning Educational Facilities* (Columbus, Ohio: The Council, 1969), p. 47.

objectives in A.D. 2050? Will the core of the school be a media production center with several studios for recording and for live programs? Will there need to be several computer terminal rooms and carrels? Should not all interior space be easily changed? Will there be such a thing as "classes" in terms of a fixed number of students with a teacher assigned to a single space for a year? The principal must not be trapped into planning a facility to serve today's children using today's methods only. He/she must help to plan for turbulence, for the unknown and the unforeseeable. With such a perspective clearly set, the program anticipated for the next few years can be described.

Space Relationships. Too often there is a tendency for the educator to attempt the architect's job of making specific drawings. Rather than drawing details, or even specific shapes, it is best to express space relationships between clusters of activity and within clusters of activity by using circle-like designations with some sort of means to identify the hierarchy of necessity for the relationships.[12]

Occasionally, the relationships between certain indoor-based activities and the outdoors, or the site, are overlooked. The ones usually thought of first are the physical education–sports activities. However, there are many other activities that should be considered when planning the site and relationships between the indoor and outdoor areas. Elementary school through high school science should be incorporating the outdoors. The outdoors holds a wealth of material for the mathematics class and the social studies class. In short, the site itself should be considered as learning space and planned accordingly. It should not be considered merely a place to play ball and line up pupils during fire drills or bomb scares.

Orientation to the New Facility. The following points may serve as guidelines and idea stimulators for the principal helping to plan the orientation:

1. Faculty members should know all the physical features of the building.
2. Faculty members should be able to explain *programmatically why* their particular area was designed as it was.
3. The faculty should be aware of the *true* economies in the building, such as energy conservation, time/space usage, low-maintenance materials, low-cost conversion to multiple uses, and so on. While some initial costs may have been greater as a result of some of these items, the long-range expenditures will be less.
4. Students should be made an integral part of the orientation process. The fact that students will be the taxpayers of tomorrow is no small

[12] For examples of ways to express these space relationships, see Basil Castaldi, op. cit., pp. 303–312.

consideration. In addition, the orientation process provides students with the opportunities to develop leadership among their peers, work with adults from the community and staff, and strengthen student organization ties with the total educational system.

5. The community components (e.g., scouts, study groups, clubs, community recreation, library users) who will be using the building should be made aware of the facilities available, how to schedule them, expectations of the school administration, and the rationale for each of the aforementioned.

6. The community in general should be made aware of the use of the building, its costs, and how it will help achieve the community's purposes. Faculty, staff, students and, where possible, parents should be involved in the community orientation process.

Evaluating the New Facility. The evaluation of a new facility is a necessary part of the total planning process. Such evaluative feedback to both the central administrative offices and to the architect via those offices should be accepted as routine responsibility. The principal's role will mainly focus upon the program adequacy of the new facility. The Council for Educational Facility Planners cites the following requirements underlying the evaluation process: [13]

1. The evaluation plan must lead to continued self-evaluation on the part of planners and other educational leaders.
2. Evaluation must encompass and promote the valued objectives of education and culture. It must consistently and honestly assess the relationship between community needs and educational facilities to meet these needs.
3. Evaluation plans must be developed in a manner which will produce information appropriate for a continued drive toward educational excellence.
4. Evaluation must provide continuing feedback into the larger questions of policy and the relationship of policy to the techniques of planning.
5. Evaluation must facilitate effective planning.

Various evaluation forms may be found in the literature; however, it will be desirable for the principal and staff to tailor the evaluation to their own programs. This process would center mostly upon clearly stating the program objectives and their implications for the learning environment and upon the scoring procedures, or weights, applied to specific features of the environment. For example, if a high-priority program objective is to increase the interpersonal communication skills of the students, the scoring weight assigned to provision for individual study carrels might be quite different from that which a faculty might assign to the same facilities serving a program with developing individual research skills as an objective.

[13] Council of Educational Facilities Planners, op. cit., p. 193.

Evaluation of a facility is sensitive. The principal must work with the staff and the central administration in such a way that misinformation or misinterpretations are minimized.

For Further Thought

1. "Form follows function" is an oft-quoted sentence used in connection with solutions to architectural problems. Does this phrase apply to designing a school that proposes to educate in and for an everchanging society, while the "functions" for tomorrow are unknown? Discuss.
2. Examine some schools built in the 1930s, 1950s, and 1970s. What features in these buildings reflect changes in educational practice?
3. Discuss how "opening up" an environment might cause greater restrictiveness.
4. What steps might be taken to avoid the practice of using certain spaces in certain ways from jelling into an unbendable tradition?
5. Tour a school building built in the fifty's in a wheelchair.

Part V

Conclusion

Chapter 20 Summary, Recommendations, and Conclusions

The world of the principal today is drastically different from the world of the principal when we went to elementary or secondary school. The principal of this decade deals with unfamiliar problems of tension and conflict. The social revolution that has overtaken all our communities to varying degrees has affected curriculum, school organization, discipline, student behavior, community relations, and the very nature of the teaching-learning process itself. Thus, the old ground rules that fashioned our American schools into such similar and unquestioned molds are now largely obsolete—an obsolescence that has left the principal in too many cases without an acceptable mode of administrative behavior.

In this final chapter we have attempted to review some of the important points, issues, and patterns we have proposed in this book that give direction to the administrative behavior of the principal now and into the twenty-first century. In addition, the conclusion highlights what we believe to be the greatest challenges facing our schools today.

The Myth of the Infallibility of Public Schools

One of the major problems facing the principal is that over the years a myth had developed about the infallibility of the public schools. The role of the school in regard to the building of America is no myth. However, our world of today is much different from that of early America. As our population grew and society became more complicated, fraught with tangled problems of urban migration, breakdown of the family, crime, race relations, poverty, drugs, and unemployment—people turned confidently to education to "fix it." Educators naively responded with pleas for more resources and more time with the children as a means to solve society's problems. But, just more of the same was too simple an answer. We deluded ourselves by assuming that there was a basic value system that would be an adequate base for our teaching. We assumed that all cultures, colors, and creeds just sitting together in classrooms would impart to all an understanding and respect for each other and give each the ability and the desire to become contributing, productive citizens.

The myth was that schools could do anything and anything they did was right. This is just not true! It may be more accurate to say that more responsibility has been thrust upon our schools than they should have accepted; more results have been expected than they could possibly have produced; and in too many cases, schools have assumed more than they should. An approach to dispelling this myth is to admit that the schools have been essentially maintainers and reinforcers of existing systems, and they really were not geared up to build a new social order on their own.

There is no necessity for educators, and particularly the school principal, to believe that they alone should lead the way to the good life for all of society. This viewed objectively is a most arrogant point of view. On the other hand, in the face of the great problems facing our society there is a necessity for the educator to say to the people about the schools, "We are one of the great and important social institutions of our nation. Let's work in partnership to identify important goals of our society and then let's work hand in hand in solving them."

Working in partnership does not mean being responsive only to the dominants in the power structure. There is no question but dominants and subdominants are people of power. The school must learn to do business with both. One thing is certain, it is the principal who comes in closest contact with the subdominants because their impact is usually more localized around smaller community segments. In most cases he/she may receive the brunt of direct action from this group. At the same time the principal is in a key position to show that the school wishes to and can be responsive if the decision-making apparatus is such that key decisions may be made in the local area.

Student Rights in the School Social System

The schools have been described as reflections of our democratic society where individual worth and rights are paramount and where children learn to be sensitive, productive citizens. Yet, when one reviews the litigation regarding the governing of children in school the conclusion is that rather than serving as models of a democratic institution with great reverence for individuals' rights, schools are too often restrictive and repressive.

Stranger yet, schools generally lag behind the courts and general legislation in their administration of justice and upholding the rights of the individual. It can be easily documented that schools in many cases have been inclined to suppress individual's rights and to be quite arbitrary in the suppression of unpopular and minority viewpoints. While few will openly embrace the old-fashioned philosophy of spare the rod and spoil the child, a great deal of suppression of a student's rights takes place under the guise of proper order and operation of the school. Too many school authorities assume that the discipline of the school will break down unless children recognize that the teacher is master whose rule is absolute. Uniformity rather than individuality is the major order of the day in too many schools.

As one reviews the textbooks in curriculum, supervision, and administration of elementary and secondary schools one observes a serious concern for teaching of citizenship and providing prototype adult experiences that show how our democracy works. This well-meaning approach to the education of children is an example of some of the artificiality that pervades our educational system. We do need to use make-believe situations, examples, and case studies to liven up and put more meaning in teaching, but it should be clearly understood the student community is not a make-believe situation. It is a real live situation with all the ingredients to make it a bona fide democratic community. Students are not make-believe citizens; they are actual citizens who are not only part of the school community but the community at large. The child is often called the "invisible citizen" because between the parent and the school, both of whom supposedly are acting in the best interests of the child, his/her rights as a citizen are seldom considered.

This brings us to a very sensitively balanced mode of operation for the school and raises issues in regard to administration–student, teacher–student, adult–student relationships. Immediately, one can hear the usual questions raised, "Who's in control here, anyway—me or the students?" "Are you going to let the students run the school?" "What are principals and teachers for if they can't tell students how to behave, what to do, and what not to do?"

To allow children to participate fully in their own school government threatens a very basic value system going back to the Middle Ages—a "divine right" that adults had over the young, the schoolmaster had over students. "Children should be seen and not heard." "Children shall obey the will of the master." "Teacher knows best." "The parent knows best." That school administrators and teachers must have absolute control over students or they will lose control altogether is a perpetuation of a longstanding myth.

Educators too often restrict their consideration of the school to the formal organization that they themselves set up. In any given student body the incidents of daily interaction between students can number in the tens of thousands; yet, teachers and administrators are inclined to count these interactions as inconsequential unless they themselves are involved in the interaction. Actually, the social climate of the classroom, the school, and the general community has an important influence on student behavior and student achievement.

The authors are not suggesting that students govern themselves totally. Rather, there should be well-established policies in every school system that provide guidelines for students to participate in their school social system; that there be a student Bill of Rights that clearly establishes basic rights of all students; that there be established system-wide a clear and simple, nonthreatening process for review and appeal of decisions handed down by a teacher or a principal; and that each individual school in the school system have some form of selfgovernment that operates within the limits of the district's policies and student bill of rights. This government should provide for realistic student input on decisions relating to the entire school. Some form of government in each individual school should operate according to a constitution developed by and for the members of that particular school's social system, composed of students, faculty, administration, and nonteaching personnel. If schools are to remain responsive and close to the people, if citizens and students are to remain advocates instead of adversaries of the schools, then adversary situations must be eliminated. The rule by man, whether teacher or administrator, must be replaced by a government by law and those who are in the school social system must have a meaningful input into the development of that law.

We Need Flexible Individualized Programs

Observing the universal patterns throughout the country, it might be concluded that there are indisputable laws of learning and unimpeachable, noncontroversial teaching principles that force our schools to be so characteristically similar. Such is not the case; in fact, in many instances what is known about learning is inconsistent with patterns that have become so popular. The conclusion emerges that custom, tradition, and managerial simplicity have had more impact on schools than anything else. In a sense a structure has emerged throughout the nation, reinforced by accrediting bodies and federal, state, and local educational systems. Throughout the United States boys and girls are installed into school systems that are highly structured and similarly organized. They are programmed into some variation of a college preparatory, general studies, or vocational curriculum. If they cannot adapt to that system and rebel through overt or covert behavior, a special program may be provided for them. While a limited number of school systems do provide these options, it is clear that before a child becomes eligible for most of these special programs or before some type of alternative school is provided, it requires a declaration of failure, an unusual problem, or a special handicap. The present pattern of showing national concern and establishing makeshift programs after people become failures is unfortunate.

The truth may hurt but—we do not teach as well as we know how or establish school environments that provide the best kinds of learning situations. We still teach the textbook and subject matter to classes and groups instead of teaching children. We still operate schools as if all teachers are the same and all children learn the same things at the same rate in the same way. We still teach as if the school is the only place children can learn, and that they can learn only from adults.

In other words, the thinking educator knows that there are many areas of needed improvement in our schools. Now the time is such that we no longer can make excuses, for we have a social environment conducive to change and our future demands it.

The recent establishment of alternative schools represents a protest against the rigid organizational and curricular inflexibility of the traditional public school. In turn this encouraged established schools to experiment with a myriad of plans to overcome inflexibility. These plans have various labels such as middle school, alternative school, open education, integrated day, or dual progress. Tools to effect such plans include modular scheduling, interage grouping, minicourse curriculum, team teaching, use of paraprofessionals, and so on. The means for providing for individual interests and needs are not lacking. Alternatives are available to break away from the patterns reinforced by custom, tradition, and managerial simplicity. Focusing upon the individual human being's own needs and potential contributions forces us to seek organizations that are flexible instead of rigid, that can change and thereby strengthen themselves rather than break under the stress of pressure from the outside to meet important needs.

Despite some of the recent clamor by certain ultraliberals we do not need alternatives to schools as much as we need alternative forms of schooling within the present educational community.

It is time for school systems to incorporate diversity, flexibility, and a variety of options and learning places in the school and in the community so that each pupil can find learning strategies that suit him/her best and can move forward with success in terms of his/her own talents and interests.

A Change in the Static Role of the Teacher

Educational planners appear to be completely locked into one direction, for when considering the question, "What type of education is best for the learner?" the traditional teaching pattern based on the 1:25 ratio dominates their thinking. They really are asking, "What type of education is best for the learner based upon the system of a teacher with a set number of children in the classroom?" The only way one can break away from this static, structured pattern is by concentrating on the learner, learning needs, and optimum learning styles. To do this one should forget teacher–pupil ratio and the teacher's role in front of a classroom and consider the teacher strictly as a professional who, working with other teachers, resource people, and auxiliary personnel, plans and utilizes *time, space,* and *materials* so that each student can learn at his/her optimum.

Conceptualizing the educational process in this manner one may very well end up with the traditional teacher in the traditional classroom; however, this learning situation probably will be one of many alternative learning situations for the student. Contrary to many opinions, such an approach does not "downgrade" the teacher. Rather, it places him/her in a more respected professional role. It recognizes that learning is a function of the learner and that the teachers are the professionals who engineer and set the tone of the entire learning process by:

1. Setting the goals of the institution.
2. Diagnosing the learning needs and style of each student.
3. Prescribing programs and various types of teaching–learning situations.
4. Arranging for and implementing the prescription.
5. Evaluating results.

Following this approach the collective teachers' judgments are utilized in regard to the way people learn and then personnel and material resources are appropriately deployed to meet the unique needs of the learner.

Most school systems of any size have all or most of the resources to carry out these five basic tasks; however, few have organized them into functioning operational units that continuously follow the student through the total pattern. At the same time teachers themselves agree that the diagnosis–prescription approach is the most intelligent way toward creating a productive and satisfying learning situation for the student, but operationally they appear to be afraid to move too far from the safety of their special kingdom, the classroom.

It appears that a new concept of the school instructional staff will need to be accepted before much of significance can be done to create improvement in the learning process. It will need to be a concept that focuses on instructional teams of two, three, or five professionals and paraprofessionals working together to create the best learning environment possible.

Research has repeatedly indicated that it isn't the system, the organization, the facilities, or the finances that are the key to improvement of the learning of a child. Rather, the key is the relationship between teacher and learner. It follows then that a school will be successful as far as the student is concerned if learning style and learning needs can be diagnosed and a teaching–learning environment established according to needs and style. It will be successful if the school principal can locate the best professionals and paraprofessionals possible and then create a type of dynamic organization and environment where their talents and developing skills can be used to best advantage.

Teamwork for Discipline

The need for greater teamwork brings to the front a major concern. Parents, teachers, and administrators all agree that the perceived lack of discipline, orderliness, and respect is one of the major problems of our school today. There are many underlying reasons for the existence of this problem but one big reason is that teachers, having gained more power and independence through their unions and collective bargaining, have increasingly declined to assist in the maintenance of order outside their own classroom. Claiming they are educators and not policemen, strangely enough teachers are withdrawing themselves from an arena that is a prime ingredient for educating—order. The best examples of "exemplary, well-managed" schools are those with a good "climate" where, instead of remaining glued to their classroom, or to the chairs behind their desks, teachers see themselves as part of a total team responsible for keeping the school orderly, friendly, and open. The evidence is mounting that a good school climate can prevail only when teachers team with administrators in establishing procedures so that discipline pervades the entire school environment.[1] When teachers do not share responsibility for maintaining a positive climate it does not take students long to recognize this and they react accordingly. Administrators cannot hope to be completely responsible for order outside the classroom. From sheer numbers alone this is impossible. Nor does it seem particularly appropriate to rely solely upon "hired guns." Yet, if students have free reign outside the classroom negative behavior will impact on the classroom itself. The problem becomes circular: General school tone affects the general classroom tone. Irresponsible behavior builds on itself and soon the condition prevails that creates, according to the Gallup Poll, the number one problem of the school.

Teachers need not be policemen but professionally they are the most important part of the teaching–learning team. Learning in some form, negative or positive, takes place in every school activity—in class or out. Responsible behavior is an important part of that learning process. Thus, each teacher, no matter what he/she teaches, must be considered a member of a professional team that has accepted collective leadership for developing and maintaining a conducive learning climate for all school activities. More often than not, just the presence of a mature adult in the hall, lunchroom, or lavatory, or on the recreation field, not as guards but as mentors exchanging pleasantries and showing interest and concern, will

---

[1] We are speaking of discipline only in the positive sense. See Ch. 16.

steer student behavior in a positive direction. Accepting this concept, teachers could make their adult presence known as models to students wherever they may be in the school. At the same time they could help plan activities in class and out of class, both of an experiential and cognitive nature that encourages responsible individual and group behavior.

Can the Principal Be Part of the Administrative Team and Maintain Collegial Relationship with the Faculty?

An issue that confronts many school principals today when there is such a strong management–labor division between teachers and administration is, "Can the principal be part of the total administration team and yet maintain the collegial relationship necessary for educational leadership at the building level?" This question particularly plagues the principal during collective negotiations. It forces him/her at this time to reevaluate his/her role because during this period battle lines are so sharply drawn that one is almost in the position of either being "for'em or agin'em."

Some principals believe that affiliating themselves too closely with the central administration is incompatible with the collegial type of leadership they would like to exert in their school. They are particularly concerned about creating an unsurmountable barrier between themselves and the teachers. On the other hand the majority of principals are afraid they will lose their authority role in administration if they are not considered part of the central administration. It is clear that this issue has generated insecurity in the principals. In addition, negotiations have underlined this issue because some people predict that negotiations will make the administrative role of the principal expendable. Not much can be gained by taking the approach that it is the principal with the central administration against the teachers, or the principal with the teachers against the central administration. The principal can represent both the teachers and the administration and maintain respect and collegial relationship with both. Much has been made of the point that the principal cannot serve two masters. The "therefore" deduction follows that the principal either must be with the teachers or with the central administration. This assumption or deduction is false. If the principalship is to be considered a position of educational leadership, as most principals verbally profess, it should be obvious that the principal leader must serve both administrators and teachers. The principal represents the teachers in dealing with the administration and aggressively verbalizes their point of view. At the same time, to the teachers he/she is most knowledgeable about the problems and operations of the entire school system as enunciated by the central administration and has the duty of interpreting the policies and viewpoint of the central administration to the teachers. A major part of the principal's job is to see that policies, rules, and regulations are followed. On the other hand, it is his/her right and responsibility to work with teachers in getting unworkable or repressive regulations changed. This is not incompatible with good administrative operation. It is the way of democratic administration. To assume that the principal cannot be part of administration and still be responsible and responsive and actually a collegial part of the faculty is an obsolete principle of management that must be discarded in school administration. The longer this viewpoint is held the more teachers will bypass the principal and move toward negotiating instructional policies and procedures at the bargaining table. If this is done we will soon reach the point where the educational profession will conflict with the public and in such a conflict the profession can lose much more than it will gain.

School Organization Sensitive to Changing Society

While the organizational structure of our school districts in the United States today may have some inherent and sacred values because of long and established use, they certainly cannot be retained on the basis that they are a modern adaptation to present-day society.

There is no national or state requirement that school organization be the same; but they are all very much the same—all being essentially pyramidal-type structures with the local elementary, middle, and secondary school unit having little influence in the maze of administrative and organizational lines established by central administration.

This organization is becoming too impersonal and unresponsive and too often leaves the local parents with the feeling that they can have little or no impact on the school that their child attends. Rather than being advocates of the schools, the parents become adversaries who criticize and take a negative approach to the school practices they know so little about.

The principal of the local elementary, middle, or secondary school is found with little influence in this burgeoning bureaucracy. As titular head of the school building unit he/she is the person who, with the teachers, is the closest communications link with parents and citizens in the school attendance area. At the same time the office is the closest communicating link to the superintendent's office or the central administration. Despite this, in too many cases organizational structure and operational procedures make him/her a school building manager who is responsible for maintaining the day-by-day routine but little else, bypassed by local pressure groups when they attempt to influence school activities or policy, and not included by teachers when they decide on issues for negotiations. The principal is not significantly involved by the central administration in the development of major policy decisions and operational procedures that significantly affect the operation of the school. Because there are so few opportunities for the principal and the teachers and students in the building to make important independent decisions that affect their own welfare either instructionally or otherwise, it has become almost impossible for the local school principal to be an influential leader or change agent in the school.

Of course, local schools have attempted to overcome some locked-in organizational and operational structures through special devices such as parent–teacher associations, local parent and attendance area advisory committees, parent task forces, teachers' committees. As the years have worn on, it has become obvious that such groups have less and less influence on significant matters. As their recommendations have been lost in the inactivity of the central bureaucracy, they have become less enthusiastic and effective, in many cases dying a slow and agonizing death.

Rather than trying to adapt students, teachers, and parents to the organization that exists, perhaps more significantly the organizational structure of the schools needs to be radically changed in order to adapt to society. The schools belong to the people. They require public support if they are to continue. To maintain the supportive parent–citizens advocate role (as contrasted to the adversary role), organizational structures must be developed that keep the parent–citizen in close communication with the school and allow the individual school to have greater autonomy and self-determination that they may be more responsive to students as well as to faculty and citizen concerns and needs.

The Community and a Responsive School

The rapid growth and complexity of communities with accompanying growth and complexity of school districts in the twentieth century make it impossible for schools to remain as close and responsive as they were in the eighteenth and nineteenth centuries. The feeling of actually belonging, participating, being a copartner with the school is disappearing. The intimate community spirit is becoming lost in the megalopolis and in the organization of the sprawling rural–suburban consolidated district. Many people are inclined to resent the growth, centralization, and reorganization that have taken place in schools and propose to go back to the "good old days" of the small neighborhood district. This is regressive thinking and can never really happen. The increase in population alone prohibits this as a possibility.

Democratic competence is not an inheritance that is simply passed on *in toto* from one generation to another. There are adaptations and adjustments that must be made by each succeeding generation for a democracy by its very nature is dynamic, changing day by day, week by week, month by month. Thus, the procedures and processes of democracy to be effective must be adapted to an ever-changing future. To teach democratic competence to each succeeding generation and to help them to adapt to change are among the major objectives of American education. The public schools and the community itself form the real laboratories where lessons appropriate to the present and future can be developed.

Regardless of the degree of efficiency of the central administration, a dynamic democratic organization cannot be maintained without active and intelligent participation at levels where results can be observed. A dynamic participating democracy requires that each citizen see that his/her ideas, wishes, and efforts have impact on public agencies and institutions of that unit. At the same time that unit should have strength enough to have impact on larger units and so on up to the central government.

The nucleus of people at this basic participating unit naturally should be determined by some type of community relatedness; however, a community whose boundaries are determined by the legal units of a megalopolis, or a sprawling school district, is just too large to maintain an intimate participating spirit. The complicated organizational structure of a typical school district and its relationship with regional, state, and federal educational agencies tend to create a bureaucracy that is difficult for the layman and sometimes even the average educator to understand.

An organizational change needs to be made in school government so that each school within a school district may establish a closer liaison with parents and citizen groups in the local attendance areas. School districts should be reorganized internally so that each school within the district has a maximum of self-determination, and parents and citizens within the attendance area have a reasonable impact upon the decision-making process. Only through such radical legal change in school district structure can true local citizen advocacy and partnership be maintained.

The Leadership Conundrum

The major function of the principal, whether elementary, junior, middle, or secondary, becomes a riddle of considerable proportion if one allows him- or herself to be analytical. When reading the literature, attending state and national meetings, and discussing the position with present incumbents, one senses that the principal is being torn apart on the one hand by an intense interest and desire to concentrate on improving instruction and learning, and on the other hand by responsibility to "keep school" through the proper administration and management of people and things as expected by the central administration. This appears to be an eternal struggle with always the instructional leadership role being reluctantly set aside because of the immediacy and press of everyday administrative duties. Presently, the principal is primarily an administrator and manager. The instructional leadership talk is often lip-service to create greater self-respect. To be fair, there are an overwhelming number of factors that prevent the principal from spending time on instructional leadership as noted in Chapters 2 and 8.

The reality of the situation is that the central administration and boards of education reward and reinforce the well-managed, efficiently operated school. While they will not deny that instructional leadership is important, they become concerned and fearful when individual schools deviate from normal routine instructional procedures. The dynamic interchange of ideas among faculty and with the community in experimental programs too often spells controversy and risk-taking to the central administration. When one does see real instructional leadership performed in a school it is the result of (1) a spirited, creative faculty, (2) a courageous and supportive principal, (3) a forward-looking superintendent, or (4) a dynamic community.

This story is such a common one and it is so uncommon to discover any principal who believes he/she is really satisfying the instructional leadership role, that it becomes obvious that the whole area warrants very serious review. What is needed now is an honest national appraisal of the principal's role and an honest answer by parents, board members, teachers, superintendents, and principals themselves to the question, "Do we really want the principal to be primarily an instruction leader or do we expect him/her to be primarily manager of people and things?" If the latter, who then is responsible for improving instruction?

Management by Exception

The authors are firm advocates of organizational and operational patterns that relieve the principal of much of the direct responsibility for management detail, thereby forcing his/her major responsibility to be instructional and educational leadership. We realize no executive can completely abdicate responsibility for housekeeping details but operational and staffing patterns can be established that relieve him/her of much of the daily concern for this detail without necessarily extra cost to the system. Beyond this, much can be accomplished by the willingness and ability of the principal to properly delegate responsibility. In addition, there needs to be a strong conviction on the part of central administration that this delegation is necessary and appropriate. Thus, central administration will not make the principal feel guilty about delegation nor will they require the principal to attend every meeting in relation to business management activities, to sign every paper, or to personally brief the staff on every new housekeeping development. We believe as a principle the principal's management technique in business matters should be "management by exception"; that is, routine matters would be handled by subordinates and only special and exceptional matters are referred to the principal.

Conclusion

The opening pages of this book reiterated the controversial question raised by George S. Counts in 1932: "Dare the Schools Build a New Social Order?" Counts asserted that schools not only *dare* but they *must*, and urged teachers to lead the way to the good life. Experience has shown that schools are not able to, nor is society willing to have them lead the way by themselves but certainly society needs to be pressed for a decision as to what the goals of a good life really are so that the schools may give the children a vision of the possibilities that lie ahead. Principals, teachers, and educators in general can accept leadership in urging society to identify these goals but they need to be as specific and explicit as possible in their identifications so there will be no real difficulty in incorporating them into a total school curriculum.

A special effort must be made to avoid fragmentation into discrete subject-matter areas. The school curriculum too often has been a jousting area where various scholarly groups try to gain dominance over each other. We can no longer afford the luxury of a struggle of the disciplines over the school curriculum. This fragmentation has been wasteful and has hampered efforts to view man, nature, and society as a whole, which is so necessary if we are to avoid "future shock."

Adlai Stevenson is given credit for these most apropos words about our world:

> We travel together, passengers on a little spaceship, dependent on its vulnerable reserves of air and soil, all committed for our safety to its security and peace, preserved from annihilation only by the care, the work and I will say the love we give our fragile craft. We cannot maintain it half fortunate, half miserable, half confident, half despairing, half slave to the ancient enemies of man, half free in liberation of resources undreamed of until this day. No craft, no crew can travel safely with such vast contradictions. On their resolution depends the survival of us all.[2]

Looking at our present state of affairs, there is no doubt that our scientific and technologic attainments have far outdistanced our ability to control them humanely and environmentally. This situation could bring to our world an unparalleled catastrophe.

Futurists glibly talk of supermetro areas, satellite cities, and underwater cultures. They assert that the major source of food will come from farming the ocean or from ersatz sources of chemical and fiber. They describe in awe supersonic transports capable of carrying two thousand people, of "hovercrafts" replacing automobiles, and underground gravity transportation

[2] American Association of Colleges of Teacher Education, *What Kind of Environment Will Our Children Have?* Proceedings of AACTE/OAS Conference. (Washington, D.C.: The Association, 1971), pp. 8–9.

systems. In medicine, predictions include the extension of life for years
and years, organ transplants of all types, and arms and legs regenerated by
chemical and electronic stimulation of the body. They predict fetuses being
grown outside of the mother's body according to specifications. In drugs they
tell of pills available that can control behavior, extend the memory, or
expand intelligence. The world of tomorrow will be, according to the
futurist, a fabulous place of leisure, steel, concrete, computers, robots, and
electronic gadgetry.

As we are caught up in the sweep of these possibilities, to our minds comes
the image of a man-made Garden of Eden—sans snake—where we float,
fly, and ride around in artistic, architecturally imposing malls and man-made
parks popping pills for sustenance, rejuvenation, and revelation. All the
while automated industries are grinding out every possible gadget to relieve
us of the necessity of doing anything physical for ourselves.

Schools have been blithely reinforcing this image. As Counts proposed,
teachers are giving our children a vision of Utopia—of the possibilities
that lie ahead but the vision is (as so many other teachings of our schools)
of the means and not the end. Unfortunately the end will come too soon
unless our society and our schools take a drastic turnabout. What is
happening to man and what is happening to our environment in this ever-
lasting emphasis on materialism should give us pause.

People have looked with curiosity, disdain, and some pity at religious
fanatics who have predicted that the world would come to an end on a
particular day. As the day came and went with no holocaust, people
would laugh and forget until someone else made a similar dire prediction.
Now a few experts are predicting the end of our human race based upon
misuse of people and our environment—some have struck close to the
living generation, indicating we may possibly have only fifty years left. Again
our society looks askance at these predictions, disbelieving that anything
like this could happen to our present world. Yet, there is mounting evidence for these predictions.

One of the most startling of the scientific studies in this area was conducted by the D. H. Meadows research team at Massachusetts Institute
of Technology.[3] The team identified the five major variables of our world
environment, namely, population, pollution, resources, food per capita, and
industrial output per capita. They then programmed these into a computer
model of our ecosystem to show how each variable and any combination
of variables, would affect the equilibrium of our world system in the years
ahead through the twenty-first century. The first computer run programmed
no changes and was based upon the assumption that the variables would
sustain their rate of growth and development as presently predicted. By

[3] D. H. Meadows, K. L. Meadows, J. Randers, and W. W. Behrens, *The Limits of Growth: A Report for the Club of Rome's Project on the Predicament of Mankind* (New York: Universe Books, 1972).

2017 the system became completely overloaded and collapsed. Then followed other computer runs with variations of all types such as increasing resources and food supply, establishing various pollution controls, varying and even limiting population and industrial growth. In all of the piecemeal runs the system collapsed and our world was thrown into peril. The computer was unable to predict that a stabilized world was theoretically possible until there was established the drastic measure of zero population growth, zero industrial growth along with rigorous policies of resource recycling, massive pollution control, methods to restore eroded and infertile soil, and increased lifetime for all forms of capital. Even more scary, the computer indicated that we must take decisive action of control by the year 2000 or we arrive at a point of no return in our flight toward catastrophe.[4]

The Meadows et al. study created a great deal of controversy. H. S. D. Cole et al., in their book *Models of Doom*, were sharply critical of the particulars of computer simulation used by Meadows and colleagues. Yet, in a second and later *Club of Rome* report by Mesarovic and Pestel essentially similar conclusions on impending limits to material growth were reached despite the use of different computer modeling techniques.[5, 6] William Ophuls, in his book *Ecology and Politics of Scarcity*, reinforces the general validity of the Meadows, Mesarovic, and Pestel assumptions.[7]

In studying the research it is difficult to grasp the full extent of the problem because a restriction on the variables and enforcement as to their use to allow for world equilibrium must be worldwide in scope. This is not just something the American public can shunt off to the public schools, then carry on business as usual; it isn't even something that a totally committed society in the United States can handle. It is a worldwide problem. Thus, although the evidence for these predictions is compelling, society has no sure means at hand to turn the direction of our technology to escape this destiny. Yes, man has the technical know-how to correct but not the social know-how necessary to alert and mobilize the world to save itself.

The ideological environment is changing also—in intensity if not in new ideas. The impact of the occult could be considered a symptom of an emotional need, a reality search, or even of the disappointment with material things really to satisfy. The progress of art may be a commentary on a search for reality, for universals. Gauguin's painting entitled *What, Whence, Whither?* may express this, much as Picasso's abstractions strive

---

[4] For an excellent analysis of what the future holds for us ecologically and politically from one point of view, read William Ophuls, *Ecology and Politics of Scarcity* (San Francisco: W. H. Freeman and Company, 1977).

[5] H. S. D. Cole et al., *Models of Doom: A Critique of the Limits to Growth* (New York: Universe, 1973).

[6] Mihajlo Mesarovic and Edward Pestel, *Mankind at the Turning Point* (New York: New American Library, 1976).

[7] Ibid., p. 17.

for some universal, apart from forms as we see them. Advertisements to the general public emphasize a self-centeredness, the idea that we each owe "it" to ourselves. At the same time, a number of religious groups are springing up and rapidly gaining large followings of people who appear to want to be told what to do. The mass suicides in Jonesville, Guyana, in late 1978 made it startlingly clear how leaders can mesmerize willing followers.

Some have gained support on the basis of the premise that there is no value to which we need to subscribe except to confine our own expressions so as to not harm another person. On the surface this appears to be a relatively harmless, self-centered approach—but is actually one that could create an aimless, fragmented society.

What impact are these things having on the curriculum? Are we truly in an age of fragmentation? Materials, texts, whole curricula have been written on very specific value systems and/or theological bases. Struggles have occurred between "the state" and individuals and groups of individuals who insist upon separate schooling without double costs. Will the schools as we now have them become competitors in the marketplace of values and ideas, or possibly even worse, be forced to look as if each were made in the federal education foundry from the same mold?

In a world of rapidly diminishing nonrenewable resources, are morals relevant? [8] Is the teaching of morality something to be left to someone else? Indeed, is it proper at all to say what is moral or immoral? Or, is such a question as the last one an evasion of the responsibility to search one's own mind to determine for oneself what morality is or should be? If the principal and teachers are to help improve the quality of life for each person in the school, can they do so without clarifying what values are and what they believe? We think not! We believe a principal must go beyond the maintenance of an organization, beyond even leadership in techniques and organization of instruction to face the question of who he/she is and even why he/she is. Then, and possibly only then, can he/she aid other persons in answering similar questions about themselves, and only then will they be able to grasp reality and begin to shape it, adapt to it, and be able to tell which of the two actions is appropriate.

Perhaps an impending catastrophe will force society and the schools to adopt a most compelling goal in order to save itself. Must we continuously be forced to conserve our resources? This goal would be the development of social know-how, understanding a dedication that would unite the world community in its determination to come to grips with problems brought into our culture by the excesses of man.

The authors by no means wish to be prophets of doom and gloom in regard to the future of our world. As life-long educators we are optimistic

---

[8] R. Freeman Butts, D. H. Peckinpaugh, and H. Kirschenbaum, *The School's Role as Moral Authority* (Washington, D.C.: ASCD, 1977).

about people being able to educate and adapt themselves to crisis. Clearly, however, we must recognize that we are *now* in a period of cultural, ideological, and ecological crisis. The time is *now* for society to solve worldwide problems in regard to uncontrolled physical growth as well as uncontrolled use and misuse of our fellowman.

This is the real challenge to the leadership in our schools.

For Further Thought

1. How have the ideas of acquiring wealth, materialism, success as measured by money, equating bigness with progress, and so on, influenced the development of education?
2. Is cooperation natural to humans or is competition based upon the law of the survival of the fittest the motivating force?
3. How does the statewide understanding of a problem affect local solutions to a problem? Illustrate.
4. What do you think are the educational implications of (a) a declining birth rate; (b) oversupply of teachers; (c) changing age composition of the population; (d) pollution; (e) internal migration of the population?
5. What are the principal areas of misunderstanding, misinformation, and distortion about public education? What are some effective means of clarification?
6. Analyze and discuss the following statement: "Uniformity rather than individuality is the major order of the day in too many schools."
7. Debate the issue: "Dare the principal take the lead in building a new social order?"
8. What are some important goals of our society? Can the class identify and agree on at least two? What is the school's responsibility in helping achieve these goals?
9. Reviewing the writings of futurists relative to society and our environment, it becomes obvious many of our problems are worldwide in scope. Is worldwide education in order? Are worldwide regulations necessary? What does this mean to the school principal?

Selected Readings

Chapter 1

Association for Supervision and Curriculum Development, *Freedom, Bureaucracy and Schooling*. Washington, D.C.: The Association, 1971.

Butts, R. Freeman, *American Public Education: From Revolution to Reform*. New York: Holt, Rinehart, and Winston, 1978.

Butts, R. Freeman, Donald H. Peckenpaugh and Howard Kirschenbaum, *The School's Role as Moral Authority*. Washington: Association for Supervision and Curriculum Development, 1977.

Coles, Robert, *Children of Crisis*, Vols. 1–5. Boston: Little, Brown, 1978.

Commager, Henry Steele, *The People and Their Schools*. Bloomington, Ind.: Phi Delta Kappan, 1976 (Fastback).

Cornish, Edward, *The Study of the Future*. Washington, D.C.: The World Future Society, 1977.

de Lone, Richard H., and the Carnegie Council on Children, *Small Futures: Inequality, Children and the Failure of Liberal Reform*. New York: Harcourt, Brace, Jovanovich, 1979.

Dustan, Maryjane, and Pike, Dyan, *Star Sight: Visions of the Future*. Englewood Cliffs, N.J.: Prentice-Hall, 1977.

Edwards, Newton, and Richey, Herman G., *The School in the American Social Order*, Second Edition. Boston: Houghton Mifflin, 1963.

Frymier, Jack R., *A School for Tomorrow*. Berkeley, Calif.: McCutchan Publishing Corp., 1973.

Gardner, John W., *Morale*. New York: Norton, 1978.

Keniston, Kenneth, and the Carnegie Council on Children, *All Our Children: The American Family Under Pressure*. New York: Harcourt Brace Jovanovich, 1978.

Kroll, Arthur M., Ed., *Issues in American Education*. New York: Oxford University Press, 1970.

Laszlo, Ervin, et al., *Goals for Mankind*. New York: E. P. Dutton, 1977.

Packard, Vance, *The People Shapers*. Boston: Little, Brown, 1977.

Schumacher, E. F., *A Guide for the Perplexed*. New York: Harper and Row, 1977.

Shane, Harold G., "Looking to the Future: Reassessment of Educational Issues of the 1970's," *Phi Delta Kappan*, 54, No. 5 (January 1973).

Toffler, Alvin, *Future Shock*. New York: Bantam Books, 1970.

Chapter 2

Barnard, Chester I., *Functions of the Executive*. Cambridge, Mass.: Harvard University Press, 1938.

Cronin, Joseph M., and Horoșchak, Peter M., *Innovative Strategies in Field Experiences for Preparing Administrators*. Columbus, Ohio: University Council for Educational Administration, 1973.

Culbertson, Jack A., Henson, Curtis, and Morrison, Ruel (Eds.), *Performance Objectives for School Principals*. Berkeley, Calif.: McCutchans, 1974.

Culbertson, Jack, et al., *Performance Criteria for Principals: Concepts and Instruments*. Columbus, Ohio: Charles Jones Publishing Co., 1973.

Cunningham, Luvern, Hack, Walter G., and Nystrand, Raphael O., *Educational Administration, The Developing Decades*. Berkeley, Calif.: McCutchans, 1977.

Department of Elementary School Principals, *Selected Articles for Elementary School Principals*. Washington, D.C.: D.E.S.P., N.E.A., 1968.

Erickson, Donald A. (Ed.), *Educational Organization and Administration*. Berkeley, Calif.: McCutchans, 1977.

Hoy, Wayne K., and Miskel, Cecil G., *Educational Administration, Theory, Research and Practice*. New York: Random House, 1978.

Katz, Robert L., "Skills of an Effective Administrator," *Harvard Business Review*, 33, No. 1 (January–February 1955).

Leu, Donald J., and Rudman, Herbert C., Eds., *Preparation Programs for School Administrators*. East Lansing, Mich.: Michigan State University, 1963.

Miller, James G., *Living Systems*. New York: McGraw-Hill, 1978.

National Association of Secondary School Principals, *Job Description for Principals and Assistant Principals*. Reston, Va.: The Association, 1976.

National Association of Secondary School Principals, *NASSP Bulletin* (March 1972).

National Association of Secondary School Principals, *The Senior High School Principalship, The National Survey*. Reston, Va.: The Association, 1978.

Rubin, Louis J., *Frontiers in School Leadership*. Chicago: Rand McNally & Company, 1970.

Silver, Paula, Spuck, Dennis W., et al., *Preparation Programs in Educational Administration*. The Ohio State University, 1978.

Study Commission on Undergraduate Education and Education of Teachers, *Teacher Education in the United States: The Responsibility Gap*. Lincoln, Nebraska: University of Nebraska Press, 1976.

Chapter 3

Bassett, T. Robert, *Education for the Individual*. New York: Harper and Row Publishers, 1978.

Breckenridge, Eileen, "Improving School Climate," *Phi Delta Kappan* (December 1976).

Center for Research and Education in American Liberties, *Civic Education for the Seventies: An Alternative to Repression and Revolution*. New York: Teachers College, Columbia University, 1970.

Frymier, Jack R., *Fostering Educational Change*. Columbus, Ohio: C. E. Merrill Publishing Co., 1969.

Gorton, Richard A., *Conflict, Controversy and Crisis in School Administration and Supervision*. Dubuque, Iowa: W. C. Brown Co., 1972.

Hansen, Kenneth H., *Beyond the School. What Else Educates*. Washington, D.C.: The Council of Chief State School Officers, 1978.

Kaplan, Michael H., and Warden, John W., *Community Education Perspectives*. Midland, Mich.: Pendell Publishing Co., 1978.

Lightfoot, Alfred, *Urban Education in Social Perspective*. Chicago: Rand McNally Publishing Company, 1978.

National School Public Relations Association *Alternative Schools*. Arlington, Va.: The Association, 1977.

Postman, Neil, and Weingartner, Charles, *Teaching as a Subversive Activity*. New York: Dell Publishing Co., Inc., 1971.

Rich, John Martin, *Innovation in Education*. Boston: Allyn and Bacon, Inc., 1978.

Sarason, Seymour B., *The Culture of the School and the Problem of Change*. Boston: Allyn and Bacon, 1971.

Sarason, Seymour B., *The Psychological Sense of Community*. San Francisco: Jossey-Bass Publishers, 1974.

Sarason, Seymour B., Carroll, Charles, Maton, Kenneth, Cohen, Saul, and Lorentz, Elizabeth, *Human Services and Resource Networks*. San Francisco: Jossey-Bass Publishers, 1977.

Saxe, Richard W., *School–Community Interaction*. Berkeley, California: McCutchans Publishing Corp., 1975.

Seay, Maurice F., *Community Education: A Developing Concept*. Midland, Mich.: Pendall Publishing Co., 1974.

Warren, Roland F., *The Community in America*. Chicago: Rand McNally & Co., 1972.

Chapter 4

Barnard, Chester I., *The Functions of the Executive*. Cambridge: Harvard University Press, 1938.

Cunningham, LuVern, L., Hack, Walter G., and Nystrand Raphael O., *Educational Administration: The Developing Decades*. Berkeley, Calif.: McCutchans, 1977.

Dunn, Rita, and Dunn, Kenneth J., *Administrators' Guide for New Programs for Faculty, Management and Evaluation*. West Nyack, N.Y.: Parker, 1977.

Follett, Mary Parker, *Dynamic Administration: The Collected Papers of Mary Parker Follett*, Henry C. Metcalf, and Lyndall F. Urwick (Eds.). New York: Harper, 1941.

Halpin, Andrew W., *Theory and Research in Administration*. New York: MacMillan, 1966.

Hoy, Wayne K., and Miskel, Cecil G., *Educational Administration: Theory, Research and Practice*. New York: Random House, 1978.

Meyer, Marshall W., *Theory of Organization Structure*. Indianapolis: Bobbs-Merrill, 1977.

Moehlman, Arthur B., *School Administration, Its Development, Principles and Function*. Boston: Houghton Mifflin, 1951.

Monahan, William G., *Theoretical Dimensions of Educational Administration*. New York: MacMillan Publishing Company, 1975.

Mort, Paul R., and Ross, Donald H., *Principles of School Administration*. New York: McGraw-Hill, 1957.

National Conference of Professors of Educational Administration, *Administrative Behavior on Education*. The Conference, 1957.

Owens, Robert G., *Organizational Behavior in Schools*. Englewood Cliffs, N.J.: Prentice-Hall, 1970.

Chapter 5

Bennis, Warren G., *Changing Organizations*. New York: McGraw-Hill Book Co., 1966.

Benveneste, Guy B., *Bureaucracy*. San Francisco, Calif.: Boyd and Fraser, 1977.

Blake, Robert, and Mouton, Jane, *The Managerial Grid*. Houston: The Gulf Publishing Co., 1964.

Caplow, Theodore, *Principles of Organization*. New York: Harcourt Brace Jovanovich, Inc., 1964.

Drachler, H. Peter, and Welpert, Bernard, "Conceptual Dimensions and Boundaries of Participation in Organizations," *Administrative Science Quarterly*, March 1978.

Evan, William, *Organization Theory: Structures, Systems and Environment.* New York: Wiley-Interscience, 1976, 305 pp.

Galbraith, Jay, *Organization Design.* Reading, Mass.: Addison-Wesley, 1977.

Lawler, Edward E., and Rhode, John Grant, *Information and Control in Organizations.* Pacific Palisades, Calif.: Goodyear, 1976.

Likert, Rensis, *The Human Organization: Its Management and Value.* New York: McGraw-Hill Book Co., 1967.

McGregor, Douglas M., *The Human Side of Enterprise.* New York: McGraw-Hill Book Co., 1960.

McNeil, Kenneth, "Understanding Organization Power: Building in the Weberian Legacy," *Administrative Science Quarterly,* March 1978, pp. 64–90.

Meyer, John W., and Rowan, Brian, "Institutional Organizations: Formal Structure as Myth and Ceremony," *American Journal of Sociology,* 83, 1977, pp. 340–363.

Meyer, Marshall W., *Theory of Organization Structure.* Indianapolis, Ind.: Bobbs-Merrill, 1977.

Newman, William H., *Administrative Action.* Englewood Cliffs, N.J.: Prentice-Hall, Inc., 1953.

Pfeffer, Jeffrey, and Salancik, Gerald R., *The External Control of Organizations.* New York: Harper and Row, 1978.

Roe, William H., *School Business Management.* New York: McGraw-Hill Book Co., 1961.

Sergiovanni, Thomas J., and Starratt, Robert J., *Emerging Patterns of Supervision: Human Perspectives.* New York: McGraw-Hill Book Co., 1971.

Warren, Roland L., *Social Change and Human Purpose: Toward Understanding and Action.* Chicago, Ill.: Rand McNally, 1977.

Zaltman, Gerald, and Duncan, Robert, *Strategies for Planned Change.* New York: Wiley, 1977.

Chapter 6

Briner, C., and Sroufe, G. E., "Organization for Education in 1985," in *Educational Futurism 1985.* Berkeley, Calif.: McCutchan Publishing Corp., 1971.

DuBrin, A. J., *Fundamentals of Organizational Behavior.* Elmsford, N.Y.: Pergamon Press, 1974.

Erickson, Donald A., *Educational Organization and Administration.* Berkeley, Calif.: McCutchan, 1977.

Ewing, David W., *The Human Side of Planning: Tool or Tyrant?* New York: The Macmillan Co., 1969.

Fiedler, F. E., and Cheners, M. M., *Leadership and Effective Management.* Glenview, Ill.: Scott Foresman, 1974.

Handy, H. W., and Russain, K. M., *Network Analysis for Educational Management*. Englewood Cliffs, N.J.: Prentice-Hall, Inc., 1969.

Havighurst, Robert J., "Educational Leadership for the Seventies," *Phi Delta Kappan*, 53, No. 7 (March 1972).

Hendrix, W. H., *Contingency Approaches to Leadership*. Lackland AFB, Texas: Air Force Human Resources Laboratory, 1976 (ERIC Document No. ED 130013).

Knowles, Henry P., and Saxberg, Borje O., *Personality and Leadership Behavior*. Reading, Mass.: Addison-Wesley, 1971.

Likert, Rensis, *New Patterns of Management*. New York: McGraw-Hill Book Co., 1961.

Luthans, F. *Organizational Behavior*. New York: McGraw-Hill, 1977.

Owens, Robert G., *Organizational Behavior in Schools*. Englewood Cliffs, N.J.: Prentice-Hall, Inc., 1970.

Ramseyer, J. A., "A Concept of Educational Leadership," in *Leadership for Improving Institutions*. Washington, D.C.: Association for Supervision and Curriculum Development, 1960.

Saunders, Robt. L., Phillips, Ray C., and Johnson, Harold T., *A Theory of Educational Leadership*. Columbus, Ohio: Charles E. Merrill, 1966.

Shaw, M. E. *Group Dynamics: The Psychology of Group Behavior*. New York: McGraw-Hill, 1971.

Stodgill, R. M. *Handbook of Leadership*. New York: The Free Press, 1974.

Van Dusseldorp, Ralph A., Richardson, Duane, and Foley, Walter J., *Educational Decision Making Through Operational Research*. Boston: Allyn and Bacon, Inc., 1971.

Vroom, V. H., "Leadership," in M. D. Dunnette (Ed.), *Handbook of Industrial and Organizational Psychology*. Chicago: Rand McNally, 1976.

Vroom, V. H., and Yetton, P. W., *Leadership and Decision-Making*. Pittsburgh: University of Pittsburgh Press, 1973.

Chapter 7

Center for Law and Education, *Student Rights Litigation Packet*. Cambridge, Mass.: Center for Law and Education, 1972.

Center for Law and Education, *Inequality in Education* (a series of legal reviews on educational issues). Cambridge, Mass.: Harvard Center for Law and Education, Oct. 1969 to Dec. 1979.

Delon, Floyd G., *Administrators and the Courts*. Arlington, Va.: Educational Research Service, 1977.

Drury, Robert L., and Ray, Kenneth C., *Principles of School Law With Cases*. New York: Appleton-Century-Crofts, 1965.

Garber, Lee O., *Yearbook of School Law*. Danville, Ill.: Interstate Printers and Publishers, Inc., (published annually).

404

SELECTED READINGS

Gauerke, Warren E., *School Law*. New York: The Center for Applied Research, Inc., 1965.

Gee, Gordon E. and Sperry, David J., *Education Law and the Public Schools*. Boston: Allyn and Bacon, 1978.

Kern, Alexander, Corns, Ray, and McCann, Walter, *Public School Law, Cases and Material—Supplement*. St. Paul, Minnesota: West Publishing Co., 1973.

Ladd, Edward T., "Regulating Student Behavior Without Ending Up in Court," *Phi Delta Kappan*, 54, No. 5 (January 1973).

National Education Association Research Division, *A Pupil's Day in Court*. Washington, D.C.: National Education Association (updated yearly).

Reutters, E. Edmund, and Hamilton, Robert R., Jr., *The Law of Public Education*. Mineola, N.Y.: Foundation Press, 1970.

Stern, Ralph D., Ed., *The School Principal and the Law*. San Diego, Calif.: National Organization on Legal Problems of Education, 1978.

Tilles, Roger B., *The Principal and the Law*. Ann Arbor, Mich.: Michigan Association of Secondary School Principals, 1975.

Vacca, Richard S., "The Principal's Responsibility in Relation to Court Decisions Involving Public Education," *The High School Journal*, 53 (Feb. 1970), pp. 323–332.

Chapter 8

Blake, Robert R., and Mouton, Jane S., *The New Managerial Grid*. Houston: Gulf Publishing Company, 1978.

Krasnow, B., "What Kind of Principal Do Teachers Want," *Phi Delta Kappan*, October, 1978.

National Association of Elementary School Principals, "The Principalship: 1978 Update," *The National Elementary Principal*, March, 1978.

Trump, J. Lloyd, *A School for Everyone*. Reston, Va.: National Association of Secondary School Principals, 1977.

Chapter 9

Baldridge, Victor, and Deal, Terrance E. Eds., *Managing Change in Educational Organizations*. Berkeley, Calif.: McCutchans, 1975.

Borg, Walter, *Ability Grouping in the Public Schools*, Second Edition. Madison, Wisc.: Dunbar Educational Research Service, 1966.

Butts, R. Freeman, *Public Education in the United States from Revolution to Reform*. New York: Holt, Rinehart, Winston, 1978.

Chamberlin, Leslie J., *Team Teaching: Organization and Administration*. Columbus, Ohio: Charles E. Merrill Publishing Co., 1969.

Coombs, Arthur M., Madgic, Robert F., Oakford, Robert V., Sato, Toshio, and Talbert, Ray L., *Variable Modular Scheduling: Effective Use of School Time, Plant and Personnel.* New York: Benziger Brothers, Inc., 1971.

Dunn, Rita, and Dunn, Kenneth J., *Administrators' Guide for New Programs for Faculty Management and Evaluation.* West Nyack, N.Y.: Parker, 1977.

Estes, Nolan, and Waldrip, Donald, Eds., *Magnet Schools: Legal and Practical Implications.* New York: New Century Education Corporation, 1978.

Gard, Robert R., "A Realistic Look at the Flexible Schedule," *The Clearing House* (March 1970).

Glatthorn, Allan, *Alternatives in Education: Schools and Programs.* New York: Dodd, Mead, 1975.

Graubard, Allen, *Free the Children: Radical Reform and the Free School Movement.* New York: Pantheon Books, Inc., 1972.

Heathers, Glen, *Organizing Schools Through the Dual Progress Plan.* Danville, Ill.: The Interstate Printers and Publishers, Inc., 1967.

Hicks, Warren B., and Tillin, Alma, *Developing Multi-Media Libraries.* New York: R. R. Bowker Co., 1970.

Lightfoot, Alfred, *Urban Education in Social Perspective.* Chicago: Rand McNally, 1978.

National Alternative Schools Program, *National Directory of Public Alternative Schools.* Amherst, Mass.: University of Massachusetts, 1978.

National Association of Secondary School Principals, "A Decade of Alternative Schools and What of the Future?" *The Curriculum Report.* Reston, Va.: The Association, October, 1978.

National School Boards Association, *Research Report: Alternative Schools.* Evanston, Ill.: NSBA, 1976.

National School Public Relations Association, *Alternative Schools: Why, What, Where, and How Much.* Arlington, Va.: The Association, 1977.

Phi Delta Kappa, "Special Issue: Alternative Schools," *Phi Delta Kappan,* **54,** No. 7 (March 1973).

Richmond, Mossie J., Jr. *Issues in Year-round Education.* North Quincy, Mass.: Christopher Publishing, 1977.

White, William D., "Year-Round Education for K-12 Districts," *Phi Delta Kappan,* **54,** No. 5, January 1973.

Chapter 10

American Association of Colleges for Teacher Education, *Educational Personnel for Urban Schools: What Differentiated Staffing Can Do.* Washington: The Association, 1972.

Baldridge, J. Victor, and Deal, Terrance E., *Managing Change in Educational Organizations.* Berkeley, Calif.: McCutchans, 1975.

Bassett, T. Robert, *Education for the Individual.* New York: Harper and Row, 1978.

Bloom, Benjamin S., *Human Characteristics and School Learning.* New York: McGraw-Hill, 1976.

Cogan, Morris, *Clinical Supervision.* Boston: Houghton Mifflin, 1973.

Dempsey, Richard A., and Smith, Rodney, P., Jr., *Differentiated Staffing.* Englewood Cliffs, N.J.: Prentice-Hall, Inc., 1972.

Georgiades, William, *How Good is Your School?* Reston Va.: National Association of Secondary School Principals, 1978.

Lightfoot, Alfred, *Urban Education in Social Perspective.* Chicago: Rand-McNally, 1978.

Lucas, Christopher, Ed., *Challenge and Choice in Contemporary Education.* New York: MacMillan, 1976.

Meacham, M. L., and Wiesen, A. E., *Changing Classroom Behavior: A Manual for Precision Teaching.* Scranton, Pa.: International Textbook Company, 1971.

Norris, William C., "Via Technology to a New Era in Education," *Phi Delta Kappan,* February 1977.

Olivero, James L., and Buffie, Edward G., Eds., *Educational Manpower: From Aides to Differential Staff Patterns, Bold New Venture.* Bloomington, Ind.: Indiana University Press, 1970.

Rich, John Martin, *Innovations in Education.* Boston: Allyn and Bacon, Inc., 1978.

Rose, Robert E., "Elementary Teaming, Learning Improvement or Administrative Ploy," *Peabody Journal of Education.* April, 1978, pp. 265–270.

Talmage, Harriet, Ed., *Systems of Individualized Instruction.* Berkeley, Calif.: McCutchans, 1975.

Trump, J. Lloyd, and Georgiades, William, *How to Change Your School.* Reston, Va.: National Association of Secondary School Principals, 1978.

Trump, J. Lloyd, *A School for Everyone.* Reston, Va.: National Association of Secondary School Principals, 1977.

Wittrock, Merlin C., *Learning and Instruction.* Berkeley, Calif.: McCutchans, 1977.

Chapter 11

Clelland, Richard, *Civil Rights for the Handicapped,* Arlington, Va.: American Association of School Administrators, 1978.

Federal Register, Vol. 42, No. 86, May 4, 1977, Nondiscrimination on Basis of Handicap.

Federal Register, Vol. 42, No. 163, August 23, 1977, Education of Handicapped Children.

Kirp, David L., *Trends in Education: The Special Child Goes to Court.* The University Council for Educational Administration, Columbus, Ohio, 1976.

Meisgeier, Charles H., and King, John D., *The Process of Special Education Administration,* International Textbook Co., Scranton, Pa., 1970, 730 pp.

Meyerson, Lee, "Somatopsychology of Physical Disability," in *Psychology of Exceptional Children and Youth,* Second Edition, W. W. Cruickshank, Ed. Englewood Cliffs, N.J.: Prentice-Hall, Inc., 1963.

National School Public Relations Association, *Educating All the Handicapped,* NRSPA, Arlington, Va., 1977.

Nazzaro, Jean, *Exceptional Timetables: Historical Events Affecting the Handicapped and Gifted.* Reston, Va.: Council for Exceptional Children, 1977.

94-142 and 504: Numbers that Add up to Educational Rights for Handicapped Children—A Guide for Parents and Advocates, Children's Defense Fund, Washington, D.C.

Passow, A. Harry, *Opening Opportunities for Disadvantaged Learners.* New York: Columbia University, Teachers' College Press, 1972.

Reynolds, Maynard C., and Birch, Jack W., *Teaching Exceptional Children in All America's Schools.* Reston, Va.: The Council for Exceptional Children, 1977.

Turnbull, A. P., Strickland, B. B., and Brantly, J. C., *Developing and Implementing Individualized Education Programs.* Columbus, Ohio: C. E. Merrill, 1978.

Chapters 12 and 13

Anderson, Scarvia B., *Encyclopedia of Educational Evaluation.* San Francisco, Calif.: Jossey-Bass, Inc. Publishers, 1975.

Anderson, Scarvia B., Ed., *New Directions for Program Evaluation.* San Francisco, Calif.: Jossey-Bass, Inc., Publishers, 1978.

Bloom, Benjamin S., Hastings, Thomas J., and Madaus, George F., *Handbook on Formative and Summative Evaluation of Student Learning.* New York: McGraw-Hill Book Company, 1971.

Blount, Gail, *Teacher Evaluation: An Annotated Bibliography.* Washington: ERIC, March 1974.

Borich, Gary D., *The Appraisal of Teaching-Concepts and Progress.* Reading, Mass.: Addison-Wesley Publishing Company, 1977.

Brown, Donald J., *Appraisal Procedures in the Secondary Schools.* Englewood Cliffs, N.J.: Prentice-Hall, Inc., 1970.

Cogan, Morris L., *Clinical Supervision*. Boston: Houghton Mifflin Company, 1973.

Colorado Journal of Educational Research. Greely, Colo.: University of Northern Colorado, Vol. 17, No. 4, Summer 1978.

Dizney, Henry, *Classroom Evaluation for Teachers*. Dubuque, Iowa: William C. Brown Company, 1971.

Educational Research Service, Inc., Evaluating Teacher Performance. E.R.S., Inc.: Princeton, 1978.

Flanders, N. A., and Simon, A., "Teacher Effectiveness," *Encyclopedia of Educational Research*, 1969.

Gottmann, S. M., and Clasen, R. E., *Evaluation in Education: A Practitioner's Guide*. Itasca, Ill.: F. E. Peacock Publishers, 1972.

Karmel, Louis J., *Measurement and Evaluation in the Schools*. New York: The Macmillan Company, 1970.

Krathwohl, D. R., Bloom, Benjamin S., and Masia, B. B., Eds.,*Taxonomy of Educational Objectives: The Classification of Educational Goals, Handbook II: Affective Domain*. New York: David McKay Company, Inc., 1956, pp. 107–117.

Lyman, Howard, *Test Scores and What They Mean*, Second Edition. Englewood Cliffs, N.J.: Prentice-Hall, Inc., 1971.

McNeil, J. D., *Toward Accountable Teachers: Their Appraisal and Improvement*. New York: Holt, Rinehart and Winston, 1971.

Mosher, Ralph L., and Purpel, David E., *Supervision: The Reluctant Profession*. Boston: Houghton Mifflin Company, 1972.

Popham, W. James, *Educational Evaluation*. Englewood, N.J.: Prentice-Hall, Inc., 1975.

Rosenshine, B., "Evaluation of Classroom Instruction," *Review of Educational Research*, **40**, No. 2, April 1970.

Saadeh, I. W., "Teacher Effectiveness or Classroom Efficiency: A New Direction in the Evaluation of Teaching," *The Journal of Teacher Education 21*. No. 1, Spring 1971, pp. 73–91.

Schneider, E. Joseph, "Researcher Questions Use of Standardized Test Results," *Educational R & D Report*, Vol. 1, No. 3, St. Louis, Mo., 1978.

Sergiovanni, Thomas J., and Starratt, Robert, *Emerging Patterns of Supervision: Human Perspectives*. New York: McGraw-Hill Book Company, 1971.

Simon, Anita, and Boyer, E. Gil, *Mirrors for Behavior: Anthology of Classroom Observation Instruments*. Vol. 1, Philadelphia: Research for Better Schools, Inc., and Center for the Study of Teaching, Temple University, 1967, p. 2.

Smith, B. Othaniel, *Research in Teacher Education: A Symposium*. Englewood Cliffs, N.J.: Prentice-Hall, Inc, 1971.

Stake, Robert E., "The Countenance of Educational Evaluation," *Teachers College Record*, **68**, April 1967, pp. 523–540.

Stufflebeam, Daniel L., et al., *Educational Evaluation and Decision Making.* Bloomington, Ind.: Phi Delta Kappa, 1971.

Sutman, Francis X., et al., *Education Personnel for Bi-Lingual Settings: Present and Future.* Washington, D.C.: American Association of Colleges for Teacher Education, 1979.

Travers, Robert M. W., Ed., *Second Handbook of Research on Teaching.* Chicago: Rand McNally and Company, 1973.

Williams, Samuel L., *The Development and Implementation of a Planned Program of Classroom Observation at the Elementary School Level.* Dissertation published by ERIC, 1975.

Wittrock, M. C., and Wiley, D. E., *The Evaluation of Instruction—Issues and Problems.* New York: Holt, Rinehart and Winston, Inc., 1970.

Chapter 14

Amidon, Edmund, and Hunter, Elizabeth, *Improving Teaching.* New York: Holt, Rinehart and Winston, 1966.

Bishop, Leslie J., *Staff Development and Instructional Improvement.* Boston: Allyn and Bacon, 1978.

Blumberg, Arthur, *Supervisors and Teachers: A Private Cold War.* Berkeley, Calif.: McCutchans, 1974.

Burrell, David, "The Teacher Center: A Critical Analysis," *Educational Leadership,* March 1976.

Carkhuff, Robert R., et al. *The Skills of Teaching.* Amherst, Mass.: Human Resource Development Press, 1976.

Cogan, Morris, *Clinical Supervision.* Boston: Houghton Mifflin, 1972.

Edelfelt, Roy A., and Johnson, Margo, *Rethinking Inservice Education.* Washington: National Education Association, 1975.

Gaff, Jerry G., *Toward Faculty Renewal.* San Francisco: Jossey-Bass, 1975.

Grambs, Jean D., and Seifeldt, Carol, "The Graying of America's Teachers," *Phi Delta Kappan,* December 1977, p. 260.

Hoover, Kenneth H., *The Professional Teacher's Handbook.* Boston: Allyn and Bacon, 1976.

Johnston, I. J., *Teachers' Inservice Education.* Oxford, England: Pergamon Press, 1971.

Lortie, Dan C., *School Teacher: A Sociological Study.* Chicago: University of Chicago Press, 1975.

Reavis, Charles A., *Teacher Improvement Through Clinical Supervision.* (FASTBACK) Bloomington, Ind.: Phi Delta Kappa, 1978.

Rubin, Louis, *The Inservice Education of Teachers.* Boston: Allyn and Bacon, 1978.

Tyack, David B., *The One Best System: A History of American Urban Education.* Cambridge, Mass.: Harvard University Press, 1974.

Chapter 15

Vandalism and Violence

National Institute of Education, *Violent Schools—Safe Schools*. Washington, D.C.: Department of Health, Education and Welfare, U.S. Government Printing Office, 1978.

National School Public Relations Association, *Violence and Vandalism*. Arlington, Va.: The Association, 1975.

Subcommittee to Investigate Juvenile Delinquency, "Challenge for the Third Century: Education in a Safe Environment"—Final Report on the Nature and Prevention of School Violence and Vandalism. Washington, D.C.: U.S. Government Printing Office, 1977.

Subcommittee to Investigate Juvenile Delinquency, "School Violence and Vandalism: The Nature, Extent, and Cost of Violence and Vandalism in our Nation's Schools," and "School Violence and Vandalism: Models and Strategies for Change." Washington, D.C.: U.S. Government Printing Office, 1977.

Sexism

Boundy, Kathleen B., "Elementary Sex Bias and Discrimination in Vocational Education" *Inequality in Education*. Cambridge: Harvard University Center for Law and Education, July 1977.

Center for Law and Education, "Sex Discrimination" *Inequality in Education*. Cambridge: Harvard University Center for Law and Education, October 1974.

Frazier, Nancy, and Dalker, Myra, *Sexism in School and Society*. New York: Harper and Row, 1973.

National Project on Women in Education, *Taking Sexism Out of Education*. H.E.W. Publication NO (O.E.) 77-01017, Washington, D.C.: U.S. Government Printing Office, 1978.

Pottker, Janice, and Fishel, Andrew, Ed., *Sex Bias in the Schools*. Cranbury, N.J.: Fairleigh Dickenson University Press, 1977.

Women's Educational Equity Communications Network, Bibliographies of all types on women and womens' rights may be obtained from the WEECN Central Office 1855 Folsom St., San Francisco, California 94103.

Child Abuse

Cohen, S. J., and Sussman, A. "The Incidence of Child Abuse in the United States," *Child Welfare*, Vol. 54, No. 6, June, 1975.

DeFrancis, Vincent, "American Humane Association publishes highlights

of a National Study of Child Neglect and Abuse Reporting for 1975,"
Child Abuse and Neglect Reports, June 1977.

Fraser, Brian G., *The Educator and Child Abuse.* Chicago, Ill.: The
National Committee for the Prevention of Child Abuse, 1977.

Chapter 16

Collective Bargaining

Administrator—School Board Relationships: An Annotated Bibliography.
Arlington, Va.: Educational Research Service (1815 North Fort Myers
Drive), 1974.

Cresswell, Anthony M., and Murphy, Michael J., *Education and Collective
Bargaining.* Berkeley, Calif.: McCutchans, 1976.

Educational Research Service, *Collective Negotiations Agreements for
Administrators.* 1815 North Fort Myers Drive, Arlington, Va.: Educational Research Service, Inc., 1976.

National School Public Relations Association, *Communicating During Negotiations and Strikes.* Arlington, Va.: The Association, 1976.

Perry, Charles R., and Wildman, Wesley A., *The Impact of Negotiations in
Public Education: The Evidence from the Schools.* Worthington, Ohio:
Charles A. Jones Publishing Company, 1970.

Shannon, T. A., "Principals' Management Role in Collective Negotiations,
Grievances and Strikes," *Journal of Secondary Education,* **45**, (February 1970), pp. 51–56.

School Discipline

Center for Law and Education, *Inequality in Education,* "Discipline and
Student Rights." Cambridge: Harvard Center for Law and Education,
July 1975.

Goldstein, William, "Dealing with the 'Irreverent' Student," *NASSP Bulletin,* (Feb. 1977), pp. 79–83. Note: There are several other good
articles on discipline in this issue.

Krumboltz, John, and Krumboltz, Helen, *Changing Children's Behavior.*
Englewood Cliffs, N.J.: Prentice-Hall, Inc., 1972.

Long, James D., and Fry, Virginia H., *Making It Till Friday.* Princeton,
N.J.: Princeton Book Company, 1977.

National School Boards Association, *Report: Discipline in our Big City
Schools.* Washington, D.C.: Ad Hoc Committee on Discipline, Council
of Big City Boards of Education, The Association, 1977.

National School Public Relations Association, *Suspensions/Expulsions:
Schools Respond to New Laws.* Arlington, Va.: The Association, 1976.

National Association of Secondary School Principals, *NASSP Bulletin.* February 1976. The theme of this issue is school discipline. There are several good articles.

Tanner, Laurel, *Classroom Discipline for Effective Teaching and Learning*. New York: Holt, Rinehart and Winston, 1978.

Vredevoe, Lawrence E., *Discipline*. Dubuque, Iowa: Kendall/Hunt Publishing Company, 1971.

Wallen, Carl J., and Wallen, LaDonna L., *Effective Classroom Management*. Boston: Allyn and Bacon Inc., 1978.

Testing and Back to Basics

Armbruster, Frank, with Paul Bracken, *Our Children's Crippled Future*. New York: Quadrangle Books, 1977.

Educational Testing Service, *Basic Skills Assessment Around the Nation*. Princeton, N.J.: Educational Testing Service, 1979.

Mecklenburger, James, "Minimum Competency Testing: The Bad Penny Again," *Phi Delta Kappan*, June 1978, p. 697.

National School Public Relations Association, *Releasing Test Scores: Educational Assessment Programs*. Arlington, Va.: The Association, 1976.

National School Public Relations Association, *The Competency Challenge— What Schools Are Doing*. Arlington, Va.: The Association, 1978.

National Association of Secondary School Principals, *Guidelines for Improving SAT Scores*. Reston, Va.: The Association, 1978.

Neill, Shirley Boes, *The Competency Movement*. Arlington, Va.: American Association of School Administrators, 1978.

Phi Delta Kappan. The May 1978 Issue deals essentially with "Minimum Competency Testing."

Schoolgirl Pregnancy (Sex and Sex Education)

Gordon, Sol, "But Where Is Sex Education?" *Education Digest*, February 1978.

Gray, Ted W., "The Teen-age Parent: An Educational and Social Crisis," *Phi Delta Kappan*, **52**, (October 1970).

Jekel, James F., "Preventing School Age Pregnancies," *Journal of School Health*, October 1977.

National School Public Relations Association, *Schoolgirl Pregnancy: Old Problem, New Solution*. Arlington, Va.: The Association, 1972.

Planned Parenthood Federation of America, *Family Planning Perspectives: Teenage Pregnancy*. Alan Guttmacher Institute, 1978.

Chapter 17

Bragin, Jeanette, *Guiding Principles and Practices in Office Management: A Handbook for School Business Officials*, Research Bulletin No. 4.

Chicago: Research Corporation of the Association of School Business Officials, 1969.

Burns, James W., and Sorsabel, Donald K., *A Handbook for In-Service Training of Classified Employees*. Chicago: Research Corporation of the Association of School Business Officials, 1970.

General Service Administration, *Guide To Record Retention Requirements*. Washington, D.C.: U.S. Government Printing Office, 1977.

Greenhalgh, John, *Practitioners' Guide to School Business Management*. Boston: Allyn and Bacon, 1978.

Keeling, B. Lewis and Nevner, John, *Administrative Office Management*. Cincinnati, Ohio: South-Western, 1978.

Morrison, Phyllis, *The Business Office*. New York: Gregg/McGraw-Hill, 1978.

National School Public Relations Association, *Office Personnel Kit*. Arlington, Va.: The Association, 1975.

Oliverio, Mary Ellen, and Pasewark, William R., *Secretarial Office Procedures*. Cincinnati, Ohio: South-Western, 1977.

Ripnen, K. H., *Office Space Administrators*. New York: McGraw-Hill, 1974.

Shout, Howard F., *Start Supervising*. Washington: BNA Books, 1977.

Wolf, Morris P., and Aurner, Robert R., *Effective Communication in Business*. Cincinnati, Ohio: South-Western, 1974.

Chapter 18

Alioto, Robert F., and J. A. Jungherr, *Operational PPBS for Education: A Practical Approach to Effective Decision Making*. New York: Harper and Row, Publishers, 1971.

Andrew, Gary M., and Moir, Ronald E., *Information-Decision Systems in Education*. Itasca, Ill.: F. E. Peacock, 1970.

Council of State Government, *State and Local Government Purchasing*. Lexington, Ky.: The Council, 1977.

Curtis, William H., *Educational Resources Management System*. Chicago: The Research Corporation of the Association of School Business Officials, 1971.

Greenhalgh, John, *Practitioner's Guide to School Business Management*. Boston: Allyn and Bacon, 1978.

National School Public Relation Association, *Cutting Costs*. Arlington, Va.: The Association, 1977.

Roe, William H., *School Business Management*. New York: McGraw-Hill, 1962.

Rhone, David H., *Wage and Salary Administration for Classified Employees*. Chicago: Association of School Business Official, 1976.

U.S. Office of Education, *Elementary and Secondary Education Financial*

Accounting Handbook. Washington: U.S. Department of Health, Education and Welfare, 1973.

U.S. Office of Education, *Elementary and Secondary Education Property Accounting. Handbook III,* Washington: U.S. Government Printing Office, 1977.

Chapter 19

Castaldi, Basil. *Educational Facilities: Planning, Remodeling, and Management.* Boston, Allyn & Bacon, 1977.

Council for Exceptional Children, *Places and Spaces.* Reston, Va.: The Council.

Council of Educational Facility Planners, *Guide for Planning Educational Facilities.* Columbus, Ohio: The Council, 1969.

Department of Housing and Urban Development. *Access to the Environment.* Vols. 1–3. Washington: H.U.D., 1976.

Educational Facilities Laboratories. *The Economy of Energy Conservation in Educational Facilities.* New York: E. F. L., 1978.

Gland, James, and Wildey, Carl. *Custodial Management Practices in the Public Schools.* Chicago: Association of School Business Officials, 1975.

Griffin, C. W., *Systems: An Approach to School Construction.* New York: Educational Facilities Laboratories, 1971.

Laramy, John E. *Organizational Behavior in Schools Differing in Architectural Openness.* Minneapolis: Educational Research and Development Council of the Twin Cities Metropolitan Area, 1976.

Zeisel, John, *Stopping School Property Damage.* Arlington, Va.: American Association of School Administrators, 1976.

Chapter 20

Bowen, Howard R., *Investment in Learning.* San Francisco: Jossey-Bass, 1977.

Broudy, Harry S., *The Real World of the Public Schools.* New York: Harcourt Brace Jovanovich, 1972.

Brown, Lester R., *The Twenty-Ninth Day.* New York: W. W. Norton, 1978.

Brown, Neville, *The Future Global Challenge.* New York: Crane, Russak and Company, 1977.

Butts, R. Freeman, Peckenpaugh, Donald H., and Kirschenbaum, Howard, *The Schools' Role as Moral Authority.* Washington, D.C.: Association for Supervision and Curriculum Development, 1977.

Butts, R. Freeman, *American Public Education: From Resolution to Reform.* New York: Holt, Rinehart and Winston, 1978.

Cole, H. S. D., *Models of Doom: A Critique of the Limits to Growth*. New York: Universe, 1973.

Emery, Frederick E., *Futures We Are In*. Atlantic Highlands, N.J.: Humanities Press, 1977.

James, Charity, *Young Lives at Stake*. New York: The Agathon Press, 1972.

Levine, Daniel U., and Havighurst, Robert J., *The Future of Big City Schools*. Berkeley, Calif.: McCutchans, 1977.

Londberg, Louis B., *Future Without Shock*. New York: W. W. Norton and Company, 1974.

Meadows, D. H., Meadows, D. L., Landers, J., and Behrens, W. W., *The Limits of Growth* (A Report for the Club of Rome's Project on Predicament of Mankind). New York: Universe Books, 1972.

Mesarovic, Mihajlo, and Pestel, Eduard, *Mankind and the Turning Point*. New York: New American Library, 1976.

Ophuls, William, *Ecology and the Politics of Scarcity*. San Francisco: W. H. Freeman Company, 1977.

Rosen, Stephan, *Future Facts*. New York: Simon and Schuster, 1976.

Roueche, John E., with John G. Pitman, *A Modest Proposal: Students Can Learn*. San Francisco, Calif.: Jossey-Bass, 1972.

Theobald, Robert, *An Alternative Future for America's Third Century*. Chicago: The Swallow Press, 1976.

Wilsher, Peter, and Righter, Rosemary, *The Exploding Cities*. New York: Quadrangle Books, 1977.

Index